T0154046

The *Disperata*

RESEARCH IN MEDIEVAL AND EARLY MODERN CULTURE

Medieval Institute Publications is a program of
The Medieval Institute, College of Arts and Sciences

 WESTERN MICHIGAN UNIVERSITY

The *Disperata*

from Medieval Italy to Renaissance France

by
Gabriella Scarlatta

Research in Medieval and Early Modern Culture

MEDIEVAL INSTITUTE PUBLICATIONS
Western Michigan University
Kalamazoo

**Library of Congress Cataloging-in-Publication Data
are available from the Library of Congress.**

ISBN: 9781580442640
eISBN: 9781580442657

Printed and bound by CPI Group (UK) Ltd, Croydon, CR0 4YY

A Sierra, Leah e Graham

Contents

List of Illustrations

Acknowledgments

I HAVE SO MUCH TO be grateful for regarding this book, and so many people to thank for helping me in this journey. First, my dear professor and mentor, Michael Giordano, whose seminar on the French Baroque in grad school at Wayne State University incited my love for the Italian and French poets of the *disperata*. Throughout the years, Michael has encouraged me in all of my personal and professional endeavors, read my manuscript and tirelessly provided invaluable feedback.

My colleagues at The University of Michigan-Dearborn have fostered my research with their intellectual and emotional support: Stéphane Spoiden, Jackie Vansant, Carolyn Kraus, Rashmi Luthra, Liz Rohan, Pam McAuslan and Paul Hughes, and for that, I am forever indebted. I am also indebted to my dean, Marty Herschock, for his support and the time he has granted me to continue writing and revising, as well as to my chair, Troy Murphy, for his encouragement and support. The intellectual, professional and emotional community to which I am so fortunate to belong at the University of Michigan-Dearborn is a steady and warm source of humanity and friendship.

My gratitude also goes to JoAnn DellaNeva who has read parts of my manuscript and offered her expert feedback, to Gary Ferguson who encouraged me to continue to revise the manuscript, and to the erudite peer reviewer who suggested references and connections between poets and ideas. I wish to thank Melody Herr and Erika Gaffney for their helpful advice, and my editor extraordinaire, Patrick McGraw, for his attentive readings and corrections.

I also want to acknowledge the Mardigian Library staff for their help in locating rare manuscripts and books, and for their patience with the countless interlibrary loans, as well as the University of Michigan-Dearborn for the generous grants that have allowed me to conduct my research in Paris.

Of course, all of my appreciation and love go to my family—my husband, Greg Rademacher, my three children, Sierra, Leah and Graham, and my parents—whose unwavering patience, love and support have nurtured my ideas, allowed me to write, and grow as both a person and a scholar. Vi voglio tanto bene!

Introduction

La nuda terra s'ha già messo il manto
tenero e verde, e ciascun cor s'allegra
ed io pur do principio al mio gran pianto.

Il Pistoia[1]

THE POET ANTONIO CAMMELLI, known as il Pistoia (1436–1502), sent an undated letter to his patron Lodovico Sforza, known as il Moro. He included twenty-six sonnets and a long composition in *terza rima* as an offering meant to alleviate the loss of il Moro's wife, Beatrice d'Este, sister of Isabella d'Este. In the letter, il Pistoia wrote:

Invictissimo principe unico de Italia lume a tutto el mondo transparente non altrimenti che il Sole, a me pareria la verità tacere: et le fatiche perdere: se io a luce venir non facesse alquanti epigrammi in sonetti in laude et meritamente ala tua Excellentia trà quali forse alchuni n'hai veduti, pronostici sono quasi tutti o per la magior parte veri stati. Dopo li quali troverai scritta la felicissima fine di quella tua si chara anci charissima coniuncta da te amata in terra Beatrice ora nel cielo tra le caste martire locata la cui anima del tuo tempo che a viver ti resta per te priega a li piedi di Jove di continuo prostrata, si che adverso caso alcuno non temere ti bisogna: Acepta Signor mio Clementissimo con questo poco dono el core del devoto servo tuo Antonio da pistoya.[2]

Very invincible prince, the only light of Italy, to all the world you are visible and even brighter than the Sun, I would not want to silence the truth: and I would lose all effort if I did not bring to light my praises in sonnets duly deserved by your Excellency, of which you might have seen a few, which they have been almost all promised or have been all true. After them, you will find the very happy ending of your dear, rather very dear spouse Beatrice, so loved by you on earth, now in Heaven in the company of martyrs and whose soul will pray for you and for the time you have left, constantly kneeling at Jupiter's feet, so that you must not fear an adverse fate: Accept, my very merciful Lord with this small gift the heart of your devout servant Antonio da Pistoia.[3]

The purity and brightness of il Moro's beloved Beatrice to which il Pistoia implies in his letter is not reflected in his long composition. Rather, the long composition embodies the speaker's deeply personal dark mood and emotional state of inconsolable hopelessness. Il Pistoia prefaces his long composition with the words "la felicissima fine di questa tua si chara anci charissima coniunta da te amata in terra," beginning with "La nuda terra s'ha già messo il manto." These words were designed to be issued directly from il Moro's mouth as an inner, painful monologue of inconsolable despair.

This long composition enclosed with the letter and sonnets is titled "Disperata," and although it was not the first of its genre, it was certainly the most popular. In fact, it came to be known as "La disperata," as almost all manuscripts and prints of this poem call it "The disperata."[4] Not much is known about il Pistoia, but his letter, written in 1497, has been used by scholars as a benchmark of his life, as well as to pinpoint the poet's whereabouts.[5] Most importantly for our purpose, this letter greatly contributed to identifying the writer of the most famous and widespread *disperata* of the fifteenth century. The manner in which the letter is addressed, to his "very invincible prince, the only light in Italy," also epitomizes the strong but delicate bond between the poets of the *disperata* and their powerful patrons. Most *disperata* poets were court poets, forced to write, travel, and survive at the whims of their benefactors. Additionally, the letter illustrates how the poets' livelihood hinged on the political and economic welfare of the court. Their poetry greatly benefited from the power and culture of the court and from other intellectual circles directly or indirectly influenced by the court. These circumstances allowed poets to expand their horizons, knowledge, and trade, as this letter demonstrates. As I will argue throughout this study, the social, historical, and cultural context also illuminates the environment that surrounds the creation, publication, and circulation of most *disperate* throughout the period in question, the fourteenth through sixteenth centuries.

At its origins, the *disperata* genre, from the Italian *la poesia della disperata* and therefore feminine, first assumed the *capitolo*, *canzone*, or epistle form, and it was written in *terza rima*.[6] It was extensively employed by Italian poets during the fourteenth, fifteenth, and early sixteenth centuries, especially those working in the confines of the Northern Italian courts. In the Trecento, it came to be known and became popular in the *canzone* form. Later in the Quattrocento, the form of the *disperate* by Simone Serdini, known as il Saviozzo, developed from a *canzone* into a *capitolo*, with a true emphasis on a narrative rich with morose invectives in tercets. Thus, the *canzone* and *capitolo* became the *disperata*'s most recognized and appreciated forms.[7] Although, as a genre, it came to be codified for its *capitolo ternario* (in *terza rima*) form, as it progressed through the centuries, and as it moved from Italy to France, the *disperata* changed and assumed other lyric, forms, such as the *strambotto*,[8] the sonnet, and the ode, as well as other characteristics, and functions: an important point to which I will return throughout my study. In fact, since its beginning and early developments, the *disperata* genre has been classified by its original lyric forms, but also by its subject and content, the poetry of despair. Moreover, when it crossed national boundaries, it was adapted to French forms such as the *stance*, the *plainte*, and *complainte*. These adaptations in form and metric contribute to the definition of the *disperata* genre, as well as to implications concerning intepretation, imitation, circulation, and, of course, fortune. In fact, although some early modern anthologies list the *disperata* as "*capitolo*"—*capitolo* was the *disperata*'s most employed form, and like the *dipartita*, the *ritornata*, the love epistle, the elegy, or the *serenata*, it shares its appearance, length, and metric with the *capitolo ternario*—almost all single-authored *canzonieri* listed the *disperata* separately from the other genres on the front page or index.[9] This well-defined classification and distinction between the various lyric forms contained in the *canzonieri* is one of the aspects that establish it as a distinct genre.

By examining several paradigms of the genre, and by providing core characteristics that remain constant from the fourteenth to the sixteenth century in both Italy and France, I show how the genre was codified, and how it remained so active for several generations of writers in two countries. Furthermore, I illustrate how, when the *disperata* was adapted into other forms, it generated models that more closely responded to the literary culture of the time, its content and essence remained intact, thus renewing the *disperata* tradition.

The *disperata* finds its origins in the love complaint, *canzone-lamento*, and in the Ovidian erotic epistle,[10] and can also be classified as a type of *vituperium*, that is, an outburst against a person, a particular occurrence, or, more generally, against life itself.[11] It shares several similarities with the Latin elegy, and in particular with Ovid's *Heroides*, including the powerful monologues pleading and lamenting in order to move the audience, and the despondent mood of the speakers, whose cause is hopeless, as they feel mistreated, neglected, and abandoned. These words are usually the last ones they will utter as despair pushes them to suicide.[12] The *disperata* is named after its very specific content: in a crescendo of despair, the poet-persona damns and condemns the beloved or the enemy, destiny, Fortune, Love, and often himself or herself. In her groundbreaking article on the genre, Rinaldina Russell notes that its thematic structure, which is almost always faithfully followed by all of its writers, involves two fundamental elements: persecution at the hands of Love or Fortune, and the reactions of the persecuted speaker.[13] Another integral element is its conclusion, consisting of a final declaration in which the distressed poetic persona calls for a violent death. This rather rigid thematic structure is one of the genre's markers. Further elements of the *disperata* are a tragic story in which the poet-persona describes countless calamities, inhabited by the beloved, patron, or both, bursting with monsters, fierce animals, ominous birds, mythological figures, personal evils, and apocalyptic scenarios. The most unique trait of this genre is the invectives. Although the intensity of the invectives varies from author to author, they are particularly emblematic of the *disperata* mood and tone, and they are an integral component of the tradition. Hence, the *disperata* deploys a number of poetic forms, some using the *terza rima*, with these narrative elements. Its stanzas and rhymes merge harmoniously with its descriptive beginning, its development of a series of damnations and extremely dramatic circumstances, concluding in suicide or calls for a violent death.

Another peculiar characteristic of the *disperata* genre is that it assigns the reader a specific status: that of the spectator who witnesses, in horror, numerous violent scenarios described in detail by its speaker and who also endures a sequence of colorful maledictions. The readers of the *disperata* are not merely readers, but they are also engaged spectators of a drama that literally and literarily unfolds before their eyes. It is through the direct involvement of the reader that the author of the *disperata* is able to establish a more intimate and concrete interchange that captures the audience, their complete attention and compassion. Thus, the *disperata* portrays a lyric story that fits Terrence Cave's definition of *enargeia*, or ecphrasis, typical of Renaissance reading texts, casting "the reader in the role of spectator or eyewitness to a dramatic scene."[14] The *disperata* paradoxically sets the stage for an inner monologue, uttered, though, *ad alta voce*, aloud, and often shouted. It is as if this internal voice first troubles its narrator, and then it bursts out to haunt the reader. Furthermore, it faithfully embodies the personal style of its writer. In fact, a close reading of some of the *disperate* reveals the individual preferences and particular qualities that their authors intended to bestow upon their creation.

One of my objectives in later chapters is precisely to highlight these differences, their nuances and meaning, which will allow us to better appreciate the adoption of the *disperata* tradition by several generations of Italian and French poets, all the way to the late Renaissance. We will see that the organic transition from the Italian text to the French text allowed the *disperata* content to gain strength and vibrancy throughout three centuries. All of the writers considered in this study are in various ways affiliated with the Italian *disperata*, and have contributed to its intriguing development, and national and transnational circulation. Although they did not all adopt the original form and meter, they adapted its content to other lyric forms.

My study of the *disperata* begins in Medieval Italy, with poets such as il Saviozzo, Antonio Beccari da Ferrara, and Francesco di Vannozzo, and investigates its progress and change throughout the Quattrocento and Cinquecento, thus analyzing its reading and rewriting by its main inter-preters. Although some of the poets in my discussion are undoubtedly already well known, I mostly concentrate on their *disperate* because these remain, for the most part, very seldom discussed. My literary and cultural exploration concludes with the end of the French Renaissance, through-out which poets made use of the *disperata* model, including its themes, images, and *topoi*, as a remarkably fruitful source.

The Italian and French authors who wrote *disperate* had a lot in common, both socially and culturally, despite the differences in time and place. Fundamentally, they express a malaise and an existential crisis brought by harsh socio-historical circumstances. First, they endured particularly challenging times, as their lives were constantly threatened by wars, pov-erty, religious persecution, and political instabilities. Second, since most of them were court poets, they migrated from one court to another to serve various lords in diplomatic missions or military campaigns, or were exiled and expatriated for political and religious reasons. Their audiences changed as well, further defining their roles and purpose, as the court poet assumed the role of cultural mediator, carrying with him to new lands and courts his Lord or Lady's power. *L'uomo di corte*, or his French equivalent *le courtier*, was after all a figure whose responsibilities constantly evolved: at times a diplomat, the official poet, a secretary, an advisor, a confidant, a functionary, or simply a companion.

In both Italy and France, the court functioned as a space of exchange as it pressured the writer to please the patron or patroness, to constantly compete with other poets, and also to beg for official charges or monetary compensation. The principal social circumstances drawn upon in the *disperata* are exile, moral disheartenment, tyranny, social injustice, subjugation, freedom, war, the profound disconnect between the luxuries and excesses of the court, and the suffering and deprivation of the writer. The feelings expressed are of alienation, solitude, abandonment, and most of all, self-cosuming despair. Many court poets were drawn to this dramatic genre. Some of them are still considered "minor poets," as they are not well known and often are not included in the main canon, which is also why the *disperata* has been much neglected as a lyric genre by literary history. As JoAnn DellaNeva has convincingly argued in her work, minor model imitation was very successful in sixteenth-century Italian and French poetry.[15] Yet, despite the success, the genre has been less popular among modern readers and scholars, which has had the effect of scholars overlooking some of these models and their intertextual products of the Italian and French Renaissance.[16]

In the coming chapters, I will address that oversight as we follow the *disperata* genre from its origins to its developments and its transition from Italy to France, underscoring how each interpreter's unique contributions helped to spread and strengthen the genre. Chapter One, The Italian *Disperata*—Origins and Definitions, provides a definition of the *disperata* and a historical, cultural, and literary framework. It also examines its constant and variable characteristics. The *disperata* genre is instantly recognizable because of its content, on which it heavily relies. Thus, I discuss the notion of genre in relation to the *disperata* and its origins through a close reading of the work of its first interpreters, Antonio Beccari da Ferrara and il Saviozzo. I also discuss Francesco Petrarca (Petrarch, 1304–74), whose *canzone* "Quel antiquo mio dolce empio signore" is a timid example of *disperata*. During the period in question, Petrarchism often merged with the attitude, dark visions, and violent language of the *disperata*, as well as with its unique *topoi*, such as the deserted and infernal landscape.

Chapter Two, The Female-Voiced *Disperata*, starts with a discussion on *disperata* and gender. The interplay between genre and gender is crucial because at times the beloved signifies the object of desire. Genre and gender come together in the several examples of *disperata* written in a ventriloquized female voice by il Saviozzo, Antonio degli Alberti, and Domenico da Prato, where they blur gender lines and stage hopeless tableaus of betrayal and abandonment. Il Saviozzo's own introduction to his poem provides an excellent description of this genre:

Capitolo d'una fanciulla la quale fu tradita e ingannata da un suo amante, e infine morta; e fece saviamente l'autore d'esso a non ci mettere il nome d'alcuno di loro, perché fu gran signore che commise tale errore e inconveniente.[17]

A young woman's *capitolo* who was betrayed and deceived by her lover, and who then died; and its author wisely omitted their names, because it was a great Lord who committed this mistake and inconvenience.

These ventriloquized lamentations were very popular throughout the fourteenth, fifteenth, and sixteenth centuries, and exemplify accomplished models of female-voiced *disperate* because of their variety in *topoi* and emotional depth. How, then, did male writers express hopelessness in the female language of despair? How is despair gendered, and how is it performed? I argue that by dramatizing what I call "intratextuality," the writers are able to compose accomplished *disperate* voiced by both male and female personae, creating fundamental connections between the two gendered poems. This imitation thus multiplies their own texts. The transgender implications of the appropriation of the female voice of despair are echoed again in France, where, about two centuries later, Clovis Hesteau de Nuysement ventriloquizes the voice of his despairing muse, Telie. Therefore, these female- and male-voiced *disperate* maintain an intimate, gendered dialogue that provides readers with an additional stimulating insight into the sophisticated bond between the Italian and the French literary culture.

Chapter Three, The *Disperata* in the Quattrocento, closely examines practices of imitation by focusing on the *disperate* of Quattrocento poets such as il Pistoia, Panfilo Sasso, and Galeotto del Carretto. I analyze the rare Italian Manuscript 1543, housed at the Bibliothèque Richelieu in Paris, which contains six *disperate*, thus documenting the genre's transmission and fortune in France. Despite its importance, this manuscript has yet to receive the proper scholarly attention. Finally, I explore Sasso's "Disperata contro l'amore," another rarely discussed poem, and I show how, although Sasso was a gifted Petrarchist, in this text, he remarkably subverts some of Petrarch's conventions. Because this *disperata* and Manuscript 1543 only exist in fifteenth- and sixteenth-century editions, I provide most of the texts and discuss them extensively, thus bringing them to light and to the attention of a larger public interested in transnational literary developments.

I continue to trace the genre's development in the fifteenth century, especially through the work of Rosello Roselli, Felice Feliciano, Leonardo Giustiniani, Antonio Tebaldeo, Serafino Aquilano, and Benedetto Gareth. The early twentieth-century French critic Joseph Vianey, the first French critic to discuss the *disperata* and to appreciate its impact and developments in France, stressed its significance in the compilation of a *canzoniere*.[18] However, we will see that the *disperata* genre originally was often confounded with the *capitolo*, or with the eclogue or elegy, because of their analogous meter, form, and length.[19] In the Quattrocento, the *terza rima* was widely used. Due to the popularity of Dante's *Divina Commedia*, the *terza rima* was the preferred poetic meter for the translation of the Classics. Its popularity also greatly contributed to the appeal of the *disperata*, from both writers' and readers' perspectives. Thus, during the second part of the Quattrocento and at the height of court literature, the *terza rima* appeared in poetry, especially when the *capitolo ternario* and its diversified, derivative genres competed with sonnets in the most popular *canzonieri*.[20] However, as Antonia Tissoni Benvenuti has shown, the *terza rima* also easily bends and allows itself to be used in other Italian literary genres, enabling authors to be creative in its adoption.[21] Meanwhile, as court poets started to increasingly favor shorter forms such as the sonnet and *strambotto*, they primarily adopted the *disperata* content, namely its themes, *topoi*, and tone, rather than its original form. Writers introduced new variable traits, and maintained constant ones, such as the maledictions, the infernal landscape, the apocalyptic descriptions, the world upside down, and, of course, the expression of despair. Like all other genres, the *disperata* changed with history and with its readership, and in relation to other genres and their popularity. In fact, according to H. R. Jauss, genres inscribe themselves in history as they continue to transform themselves.[22]

Chapter Four, The *Disperata* in the Cinquecento, focuses on the *disperata* in the Cinquecento and discusses how three writers, Pietro Aretino, Eurialo Morani d'Ascoli, and Isabella di Morra, adopted its unique traits. While Aretino did not divert much from the genre's original form and content, Morani reshaped the model into a grand spectacle of despair, describing in great nuances each of its facets and painful consequences. Here, I illustrate how the *disperata* is constructed and reconstructed, with its content sometimes adopted in a *canzone* and other times in a long composition comprised of stanzas,[23] thus showing how the individual poet added his or her own voice to the genre, interpreting and narrating it in a unique way. Hence, by looking at Aretino's *capitolo*, Morani's *stanze*, and Morra's sonnets and *canzoni*, we can better delve into the question of how the poets adapted its content to their preferred forms.

Furthermore, I closely examine Isabella di Morra's sonnets and *canzoni*, and her unique interpretation and rewriting of the *disperata*, an important aspect of her poetry that has yet to receive scholarly attention. Her tragic existence, enforced by strict patriarchal rules, shaped a distinctive account of female despair deeply rooted in gender paradigms. As my discussion will show, she broke the barrier of genre and gender with her female-authored and female-voiced *disperate*. Hence, by looking at how gender interacts with despair, I show how Morra is one of the most genuine *disperata* interpreters.

In Chapter Five, The *Disperata* in France, we will trace how the *disperata* moved to France. First, we will examine how the Cinquecento poets Angelo di Costanzo, Luigi Tansillo, and Bernardino Rota also incorporated the *disperata* into their verses and produced love lyrics that were meant to make a strong impression on their audience. They are known in France as "the poets of the *disperata*" because of their tormented verses that express hopeless complaints about the beloved or Love itself.[24] The *disperata*'s fortune, major representations and new forms, provided inspiration to French poets, including Jacques Peletier du Mans, Joachim Du Bellay, Olivier de Magny, and François d'Amboise. Most of all, the *disperata* genre was adopted by the court poets of the last decades of the sixteenth century at the court of Henri III of Valois. Thanks to the popularity and widespread circulation of the Italian anthologies in France, many Italian poets were widely read by the French poets. The circulation of their work was vital to the survival and transmission of the *disperata*, because of the imitative practices vastly adopted by the French writers, as many scholars of Franco-Italian poetry have noted.[25] Specific examples of *disperate*, such as those of Serafino, Nocturno Napolitano, il Saviozzo, and il Carretto, and of their interpretations by Desportes, d'Aubigné, and Nuysement compellingly illustrate that the Italian model was enthusiastically adopted and creatively adapted.

This adoption is a pivotal moment as it marks the creation of the *disperata* tradition in France. Guided by Renaissance practices of imitation, and by intertextuality and history, I show how the *disperata* content was embraced and then adjusted into other genres and into different metric configurations, thus bringing about the transformation of the *disperata*. While the French poets abandoned its form and metric, they fully incorporated its content into French genres, such as stances, *plaintes*, sonnets, odes and elegies.[26]

This chapter also revisits the interplay between gender and the *disperata*, and the ways in which despair is foregrounded in gender in an important, yet rarely discussed poem, "Plainte de Telie à Eco." Here, Nuysement impersonates the voice of his imagined muse, Telie, and borrows her lament focusing specifically on the female experience of despair. Like il Saviozzo, degli Alberti, and da Prato, Nuysement's male- and female-voiced poems are in a dialogue as he, too, contended with writing the experience of women in a plausible and compelling manner. As Meredith K. Ray and other scholars have convincingly shown, the Renaissance produced an increased interest in appropriating, defining, and examining female experiences, which resulted also in the codification of women's behavior and speech.[27] Thus, my analysis focuses on how Nuysement's poetry of female despair took control over a woman's voice and its power.

Finally, Chapter Six, *Disperata* and *Désespoir*, follows in the footsteps of the work of Henri Weber, Gisèle Mathieu-Castellani, and Claude-Gilbert Dubois, who identified the *disperata* in the poetry of the French neo-Petrarchan and baroque poets.[28] In *Eros Baroque*, Mathieu-Castellani argues that to the Classical landscape—countryside, meadows, forests, rivers, and fountains—a more recent model was added, that of the Italian *disperata*, which depicts a wild decor, a sinister desert, and infernal sites, thus providing a new, exemplary landscape.[29] This chapter further focuses on how the *disperata* represents a sound model for the writers at the courts of Charles IX, Henri III, Henri IV and Louis XIII, who combined it with Petrarch's refined language and images. It also shows that, despite the differences between Italy and France, the *disperata* and the works of French poets display not only similar interests and themes, but also similar attitudes and psychology. The desolate and infernal landscape, the depiction of a world turned upside down, wild and fierce animals, Fortune's adversity and Love's cruelty, death, and despair are evoked insatiably by these writers, as these traits became prominent key elements of intertextuality. In fact, I credit the poetics of the *disperata* with the generative lyric qualities that invigorated the French texts, meshed with their authors' baroque sensibility, and provided much of the ability to move the reader.

In order to comprehend and appreciate the transformations that the *disperata* undergoes in its manifestations in France, it is necessary to investigate why and how its psychology and themes became pertinent to late sixteenth-century French poetry during the Wars of Religion. According to Jeffrey C. Alexander, "The cultural construction of collective trauma is fueled by individual experiences of pain and suffering, but it is the threat to collective rather than individual identity that defines the suffering at stake."[30] This seems an accurate description of the miseries experienced by the Renaissance poets in question, in both Italy and France, as the pervasive socio-political instability created a quotidian necessity to seek refuge in solitary and infernal places, a *topos* of which the *disperata* provided numerous and varied examples. Furthermore, the many reenactments and interpretations of the trauma in their work substantiate "collective trauma" because of the writers' deliberate sharing of their grievance and conflicts with their readers.[31] This book shows that the poetry of the *disperata* constitutes a cultural interpretation of the emotional and existential grief that the political and religious institutions of the period inflicted on their people. As the book progresses, what becomes more and more apparent are the ways in which collective trauma is written and rewritten in the poems. These, in turn, are connected to one another, as are their authors' lives, history, and culture. Therefore, the evolution of the *disperata* illustrates important transnational aspects that are embedded in the vibrant literary and cultural exchanges between France and Italy.

Here, I also investigate how many of the French poets combined some of the *disperata* elements with Petrarchism but at times, subverted its code as well. This combination and destabilization often became their primary model in which despair became a fascinating force. Taken collectively, the paradigms that I discuss chart the vital and continuous transmission of the poetics of despair. In the roughly two-hundred-year span that will be considered in this book, the poetry of despair follows the many authors' personal and individual interpretation, style, and historical and geographical circumstances, thus fundamentally expressing a malaise, and an existential crisis. To study the *disperata* is, therefore, to unravel a dramatic narrative that flourished during particularly challenging historical, social, and political periods.

The *Disperata*: A Theoretical Framework

Given the diverse manifestations of the *disperata*, I mainly draw on the theories of imitation and intertextuality, which provide a lens to view the relationship between the *disperata* and Petrarch, and between the many Italian and French poets who used the genre and its traits. Since imitation was one of the main literary practices in the Renaissance and in the countries that I examine, many authors are considered "imitators" or "emulators." The *disperata* traveled through cultural, geographical, and temporal boundaries, favoring the confines of the court and other milieus governed by its influence, where imitation elicited the expansion of its themes, *topoi*, and images. Imitation, therefore, fueled and nourished the *disperata* poetry, strengthening it and allowing it to surge and expand from the fourteenth to the sixteenth century. Furthermore, it connected these poems and their writers to one another in a cultural continuum that transcended boundaries of time, place, genre, and gender.

The practice of imitation, whether of minor models or major canonical models, was wide-spread. Several scholars have already noted that Renaissance writers felt compelled to position their own writings in the literary tradition by adhering to the conventions established by previous writers, a practice that is intrinsic and fundamental to most early modern works.[32] Whether to a higher or lesser degree of imitation, authors wrote for the most part in relation to what had been previously written. The main and most authoritative work during the period in consideration was that of Petrarch, which, according to Jean Balsamo, defines the fifteenth and sixteenth centuries.[33] When composing love verses, the *Rerum Vulgarium Fragmenta* or *Canzoniere*, with its codified language, metaphors, and distinctive images was undeniably the main model to study and emulate. As William J. Kennedy notes, for writers of the early-modern period, "To question either Petrarch's authority or the authority of subsequent interpretations and imitations is to evoke a scandal of authority in both the Middle Ages and the Renaissance."[34] However, as I will show, the poets in this book both adopted and subverted Petrarch and Petrarchism in nuanced and compelling ways, thus providing additional models that were also widely imitated.

Earlier on, humanists such as Erasmus claimed that writers must assert their independence by both multiplying and fragmenting their models, so that they would not be trapped by the prestige of a single author.[35] This task would be later facilitated by the many Petrarchists who produced countless new sources, and whose work was widely circulated and read, thanks mainly to the anthologies by Gabriel Giolito and his rivals, thereby legitimizing, strengthening, and further establishing Petrarch's tradition. Clearly, by legitimizing the canon, authors brought credibility and substance to their own writings.[36] This "transparent" imitation was important in several ways. It gave writers the opportunity to show off their erudition, to fit into a well-established and thriving tradition, and to follow the literary vogue of their times, thus pleasing and satisfying readers who also sought familiar themes and language, but narrated by new voices and talents. In fact, imitation was not meant to be concealed, on the contrary, it was supposed to be recognized by the readers and by the other writers. Therefore, imitation implies a transformation, as many of the poems here discussed will show.[37] Moreover, a comparison between the source and the new creation would likely draw attention first, to the early-modern poets' qualities in *aemulatio* and *dispositio*; second, to their aptitude and dexterity in rearranging the material; and, lastly, to their competence in contributing to the canon. Because most of the *disperata* poets were also gifted Petrarchists, they skillfully merged the two models, and were vastly imitated. However, although their work served as intertext for many important French writers such as Pierre de Ronsard, du Bellay, and Desportes, some of them were considered minor poets, and thus, have been neglected by main-stream Renaissance scholarship.[38] Imitation thus, is central to my analysis as it creates those transformations in which the differences and similarities between the intertexts are not only important, but also organic and generative.

Several critical works concentrated, and still do, on unveiling and analyzing the precise source of a poem in order to better understand it and in order to expound the imitative practices that the poem might reveal.[39] In the early modern period, the ability to recognize the poem's source led to its appreciation and fortune: a connection was established between writer and reader, and thus, the two were able to share an intertextual and cultural competence.[40] In fact, according to Mathieu-Castellani, French poetry used a double-play to inscribe the Petrarchan text so that it would be both recognizable and non-recognizable. To exhibit the model was a necessity, in order first, to place oneself in the tradition, and second, to claim a prestigious affiliation.[41] The same is true for the poetry of the *disperata*.

There are, however, various levels of imitation. During the Renaissance, translation was considered a form of imitation because it entailed the transformation of a text from one vernacular to another, Italian to French in our case, with numerous cultural and textual makeovers. Furthermore, French poets translated in order to improve their language as well as to also enrich their national linguistic patrimony.[42] The Pléiade poets in particular sought to accomplish for vernacular French what Dante, Petrarch, and Boccaccio had accomplished for vernacular Italian.[43]

By replacing Latin, French became the language of France's new great literature. This was obviously another reason why Petrarch prospered to such a great extent in France, as he was able to literally erect an *exegi monumentum* to his native language with and in his *Canzoniere*, a work entirely written in vernacular Italian that immediately became a literary sensation.

At the other end of the spectrum, there is involuntary memory, the furthest form of imitation, where the writer may not even realize she or he is imitating another writer. Michel de Montaigne provides a compelling description in his essay "De la praesumption": "Je feuillette les livres, je ne les estudie pas: ce qui m'en demeure, c'est chose que je ne reconnois plus d'estre d'autruy; c'est cela seulement dequoy mon jugement a faict son profict, les discours et les imaginations dequoy il s'est imbu; l'autheur, le lieu, les mots et autres circonstances, je les oublie incontinent."[44] Therefore, imitation implies not only a specific mode of writing, but a specific mode of reading as well. The reader is invited to a double reading, or a "mirrored" reading of the text itself, and invited to recognize the source or the intertext.[45] Dubois has labeled this "imitation différentielle," a form of imitation that inscribes a subtext within a surface text in such oblique but recognizable ways that it insists simultaneously upon sameness and difference, upon continuity and discontinuity.[46] As such, the writer imposes a comparison meant to call the reader's attention to his or her erudition and skills in "rewriting" the model.[47]

Intertextuality is fundamental to imitation and to my close reading of imitation. Julia Kristéva calls it "un mosaïque de citations" (a mosaic of citations), which surely applies to my analysis as each generation of writers manipulated the *disperata* and nuanced it with their particular taste and tone. Furthermore, each text, having absorbed another text, transforms it.[48] Thus, intertextuality is a central premise of the relationship between the *disperate* written in the fourteenth, fifteenth, and sixteenth centuries in both Italy and France as they all share specific traits.[49] As one text is bound to appear in a subsequent text, imitation and intertextuality are principles of literary and cultural authority in my discussion of the *disperata* and its tradition.

Genre and gender theories also inform my exploration of the *disperata*, in particular: how did the *disperata* attain its status as a genre, and how did it establish a tradition? Early modern scholars of genre theory in both Italy and France, such as Thomas Sebillet, Cian, Tartaro, Jauss, Mathieu-Castellani, and Javich lay out a sound foundation, which allows me to establish the *disperata*'s status and tradition as a genre. Finally, how is genre related to gender as far as both the author's sex and his or her speaker's voice are concerned? As already mentioned, intratextuality helps to clarify how a poet transferred his creative skills from the male- to the female-voiced *disperata*. Furthermore, Elisabeth D. Harvey's concept of ventriloquism, that is, a male author appropriating the female voice of his speaker, is also linked to both intertextuality and intratextuality, and therefore beneficial to my discussion of gender and the *disperata*.[50]

A note on translation and sources

All translations from Italian and French are mine. Most of the primary sources I analyze were discovered at the Bibliothèque nationale in Paris during my research visits, and to this day remain only in fifteenth- and sixteenth-century editions. These documents provide direct and compelling evidence of the *disperata* and its manifestations in France.

NOTES

[1] It is the lyric *reverdir*, celebrated by the poets of the Sicilian School and by the French *troubadours*. See Henri Weber, *La Création poétique au XVIe Siècle en France*, 292–293.

[2] Rodolfo Renier, ed. *I sonetti del Pistoia giusta l'apografo trivulziano*, 402. See also Carla Rossi, *Il Pistoia,* 60.

[3] All translations from Italian and French are mine.

[4] Pèrcopo, "Una disperata famosa," 701.

[5] Ibid., 703.

[6] A *capitolo* is an Italian form written in *terza rima* with a series of three-line stanzas. Following the rhyme pattern of ABA, BCB, CDC, etc. Its length varies. The last stanza is composed of four verses and forms the conclusion to the composition. A *canzone* is an Italian form often on the subject of love, designed at first to be sung to music. It consists of a series of stanzas, from about seven to twenty lines, with a concluding envoy. See Karl Beckson and Arthur Ganz, *Literary Terms*, 34.

[7] Rinaldina Russell, "Intenzionalità artistica della disperata," 166.

[8] The *strambotto* is a short lyric form composed of six or eight verses.

[9] See Vittorio Cian, *Le rime di Bartolomeo Cavassino*, 1:lxxxvii. In Italian literature, the *dipartita* is a long composition that mourns the poet's absence from his beloved, the *ritornata* is also a long composition that instead celebrates the poet's return to his beloved, and the *serenata* is meant to be sung at night, under the beloved's window.

[10] Cian, *Le rime di Bartolomeo Cavassino,* 1:163.

[11] On this genre, see also Achille Tartaro, *Forme poetiche del Trecento*, 55.

[12] See Ovid's *Heroides*, W. S. Anderson "*The Heroides*" in *Ovid*, 49–83, and Howard Jacobson's *Ovid's Heroides*.

[13] Russell, "Intenzionalità artistica della disperata," 166.

[14] Terence Cave, "The Mimesis of Reading in the Renaissance," 161.

[15] See JoAnn DellaNeva, *Unlikely Exemplars*, 14–15, where she discusses the common practices of minor model imitation by the poets of the French Pléiade.

[16] See for example Pèrcopo on "the disperata," "Una disperata famosa," 706.

[17] Simone Serdini da Siena, detto il Saviozzo, *Rime*, Emilio Pasquini, ed. 185. All references to il Saviozzo's poetry will be based on this edition.

[18] Joseph Vianey, *Le Pétrarquisme en France*.

[19] See *L'elegia nella tradizione poetica italiana*, Andrea Comboni and Alessandra Di Ricco, eds.

[20] Comboni and Di Ricco, 303–304.

[21] Tissoni Benvenuti, "La tradizione della terza rima e l'Ariosto," 303–304.

[22] H. R. Jauss, "Littérature médiévale et théorie des genres," 86.

[23] This trend is closely discussed by Paola Vecchi Galli, "Percorsi dell'elegia quattrocentesca in volgare," 37–79, and by Gaia Gentili, "Il capitolo in terza rima di Niccolò da Correggio: non solo elegia," 115–146, both in *L'elegia nella tradizione poetica italiana*.

[24] These poets are known as "poets of the disperata" mainly by critics such as Claude-Gilbert Dubois, Gisèle Mathieu-Castellani, and Henri Weber, as we shall see in the following chapters. See my articles, "Adopting and Adapting: The Case of the Disperata," and "The Continuity of Baroque Poetic Vision: From the Italian Disperata to the French Neo-Petrarchans."

[25] DellaNeva, *Unlikely Exemplars*, 91.

[26] Two major studies on Renaissance imitation remain valuable: Terence Cave, *The Cornucopian Text* and Thomas Greene, *The Light in Troy*.

[27] Meredith K. Ray, *Writing Gender in Women's Letter Collections*, 10.

[28] Roughly the literary period between 1570 and 1610. See the important study by Jean Rousset, *La Littérature de l'âge baroque en France*.

[29] Mathieu-Castellani, *Eros Baroque*, 27.

[30] Jeffrey C. Alexander, *Trauma: A Social Theory*, 2. I will use Alexander's definition of collective trauma throughout my study.

[31] Alexander notes that, "The lives lost and pains experienced are individual facts; shared trauma depends on collective processes of cultural interpretation." *Trauma: A Social Theory*, 3.

[32] See G. W. Pigman III, "Versions of Imitation in the Renaissance," as well as Cave, *The Cornucopian Text*, and Greene, *The Light in Troy*.

[33] Jean Balsamo, "'Du Florentin les lamentables voix,'" in *L'Italia letteraria e l'Europa*, 110. This article provides a concise history of French Petrarchism.

[34] William J. Kennedy, "Petrarchan Textuality," 151–168.

[35] Cave, *The Cornucopian Text*, xi.

[36] See for example François Rigolot, who argues that writers were forced to reproduce the inherited structural and thematic models with simple modifications, or, more precisely "ces modifications devront apparaître comme 'legères' pour être admissibles (à l'auteur comme à son public)." "Quel genre d'amour pour Louise Labé?" 304.

[37] See Pigman III, "Versions of Imitation in the Renaissance," 11–12.

[38] See DellaNeva, *Unlikely Exemplars*, 15–24.

[39] I am thinking in particular of Philippe Desportes's case. Articles such as Yves Bellenger, "Desportes imitateur de Domenico Ragnina, poète ragusain," Victor E. Graham, "Some Undiscovered Sources of Desportes," and Vianey, "Un modèle de Desportes non signalé encore: Pamphilo Sasso."

[40] Cave skillfully describes the relationship between readers and writers in the sixteenth century in "The Mimesis of Reading in the Renaissance," 151.

[41] Mathieu-Castellani, "Les Enfants de Pétrarque," 638.

[42] For a thorough discussion on translation, vernaculars, and imitation, see Balsamo, *Les Rencontres des muses*, and his article "Traduire de l'italien: Ambitions sociales et contraintes éditoriales à la fin du XVIe siècle." For the various forms of imitation from Italian to French, see also Mathieu-Castellani, "Les Enfants de Pétrarque."

[43] See Joachim Du Bellay, *La deffence et illustration de la langue françoyse* and

Grahame Castor, *Pléiade Poetics*.

[44] Michel de Montaigne, "De la Praesumption," *Essais*, 3:314. All references to Montaignes's essays will be based on this edition.

[45] See Umberto Eco, *The Role of the Reader*, 9.

[46] Dubois, "Imitation Différentielle et poétique maniériste."

[47] Riffaterre, too, argues that the text itself forces the reader to play "le jeu de l'intertextualité," that is, a game of recognition and appreciation between writer and reader. See "Un faux problème: l'érosion intertextuelle," 58.

[48] Julia Kristéva, *Semiotikè*, 146.

[49] Riffaterre argues that that intertextuality is a relationship between one text and another text, which institutes a semiotic system that is intrinsic to each poem, "Un faux problème: l'érosion intertextuelle," 52.

[50] See Harvey, *Ventriloquized Voices*.

Chapter One

The Italian *Disperata*:
Origins and Definitions

Maledetto el voler ch'accese el padre
de le mie triste membre,
a spargere 'l suo seme e 'l suo dolere.
Poi maladico el corpo de la madre,
dove se aggiunse insembre
l'anima tapinella a questa pasta

Antonio Beccari

The *Disperata* Genre and Its Definition

"*Disperata*," from the Latin *desperàre*, contains the prefix *de*, meaning moving away from, and *spès*, to hope (the verb *sperare*), and denotes the action of losing hope, lacking hope, and turning away from it. *Disperare* is also the action of losing faith in something or somebody and giving into desperation. The despairing speakers refer to themselves with the noun *disperato* (masculine) or *disperata* (feminine), terms that I will use as well throughout my discussion to indicate the male and female poetic persona. Furthermore, both function as an adjective as well to signify a person in the depths of despair, filled with hopelessness, and lacking the will or desire to hope. Therefore, the *disperata* (because of the Italian feminine form of *poesia*) is a lyric composition that expresses despair, hopelessness, and a lack of will, or desire to hope. It is the name of the poetics of despair that encompasses and expresses all of the above etymological meanings.

Few scholars have provided a definition of *disperata*, and fewer yet have actually studied it closely.[1] Before analyzing the *disperata* itself, it is necessary to review the notion of genre, a fluid concept that has been approached inconsistently during the Renaissance.[2] Genre theory became a field of study during the sixteenth century.[3] In an important article, H. R. Jauss traces the origins of genres from the Classical period through the Middle Ages.[4] He convincingly shows that genre theory developed according to literature's social and practical function, and that the definition of genre changed according to its particular time in history and literary culture.[5] Hence, by looking at several paradigms of the *disperata* genre, and by providing core characteristics that remain constant from the fourteenth to the sixteenth centuries, in both Italy and France, this study investigates how this poetry became functional for several generations of writers throughout this period.

Because genres alter with history and with their readership, and in relation to other genres, their success and popularity, a phenomenon that Jauss calls the historiography of a genre,[6] the *disperata* genre as well changed its lyric form and introduced new elements and images. However, its content remained fundamentally recognizable and predictable, albeit with some modifications. The *disperata* closely intersects with the historical, cultural and social backdrop in which it flourished, and it benefited from the transnational aspects of these developments. In fact, each text fits in and adds fundamentals to the tradition despite its formal changes. Thus, the *disperata* is a genre in which its subject and dominant features guaranteed its continuity from the Middle Ages to the late Renaissance, and from Italy to France, while its variations allowed it to better fit in the literary cultures it served.

As has been stated before, what sets the *disperata* apart is the strong reliance on its content. While other lyric forms, such as the *capitolo* or the sonnet for example, are not directly dependent on their content or subject matter, but rather only delineate and shape their space with their meter and fixed number of lines or stanzas, the *disperata* is a genre that is very much reliant on its content, and exists because of it.[7] In fact, without its specific despair narrative, the *disperata* would cease to exist. When the genre first developed, the *terza rima* was also an important intrinsic element, because then, it was the most popular meter of literary court production in Italy, further linking the *disperata* to the *capitolo ternario*.[8] If at the beginning the *disperata* assumed the *capitolo* and the *canzone* forms, with a series of stanzas in *terza rima*, as it evolved, it also morphed into both shorter and longer forms. As I examine each paradigm, I call attention not only to its core traits, but also to its variables, in order to illustrate how these are connected to, and entwined with, the historical and cultural contexts, and how they collectively establish a continuum during the period in review, from the end of the Middle Ages to the late Renaissance. Thus, the *disperata* is a genre that relies heavily on its themes, *topoi*, and tone, rather than on a specific form and metric.

During the Trecento and the Quattrocento, some of the authors labeled their *disperate capitolo* or *canzone*, because of the series of stanzas in *terza rima*. Although its content sets the *disperata* apart from the *capitolo ternario*, its form anchored itself to the latter's tradition, thus presenting a challenge over the centuries to readers and scholars in identifying it as a separate genre.[9] Though these circumstances have led some scholars to mis-identify some *disperata* poetry or to compare it to a type of "elegiac" com-position, I argue that a close examination of its themes and internal struc-ture—persecution at the hands of Love or Fortune, the persecuted speak-er's reaction, and a final declaration for a violent death—demonstrates that this poetry sets itself apart and constitutes its own genre fully dedicated to the poetics of despair.[10] A testimony to its popularity and legitimacy as a distinct genre is that, at the beginning of the Cinquecento, it generated a new genre, the *contro-disperata*, where, in order to counter the tirades of despair and calls for death, its author expresses hope and praises life.[11] Thus, as in the history of most genres, the *disperata* too organically grew into a new genre known for its direct response to damnations and curses.[12]

The few scholars who have studied the *disperata* agree about its definition. Francesco Saverio Quadrio provides an accurate and succinct designation: the Italian *disperata*, he claims, is characterized by strong feel-ings of anger and disdain, expressed by long tirades. Tracing the *disperata* back to the Classics, he explains that the Greeks called it *Erinni*, and that the Romans called it *Dire*. Quadrio also notes that *disperata* is the noun that the writers of vernacular Italian used for this type of poetry full of invectives.[13] Furthermore, he compares the *disperata* to some of Horace's, Catullus's, and Ovid's poems, as well as to some compositions by the Greek writers Alceo and Callimachus, since all of these Classical poets wrote vituperations against different people.[14] Quadrio lists some of its writ-ers, including il Saviozzo, Felice Feliciano, Jacopo Filippo di Pellenegra, Tebaldeo, and Serafino, and notes that almost all of the fifteenth and six-teenth century *canzonieri* contain this type of composition of despair.[15]

In a second important and authoritative study of the genre's history, Vittorio Cian shares Quadrio's opinion and provides a useful and more exhaustive definition of the *disperata*. He notes that the *disperata* is gen-erally formed by a sequence of maledictions and invectives composed by a hopeless poet, most often because of a romantic betrayal.[16] Russell also concurs that the maledictions are an essential part of both the genre and its place in history, and she notes that they are not only the primary trait of the *disperata*, but also what distinguishes it from other similar genres, like the love complaint.[17] As we shall see, the invectives are one of the constant elements of the genre, varying against whom or what they are uttered.

According to Cian, the first *disperata* in Italian literature is Cecco Angiolieri's sonnet "Sio fossi fuoco, arderei lo mondo."[18] This is also one of the earliest examples of the genre's ability to conform to various lyric forms. Francesco Flamini also mentions Angiolieri's sonnet, but he mostly associates the *disperata* to a type of *vituperi*, that is, invectives against all women, Fortune, and Love.[19] He notes that the *disperata* is precisely a sort of invective in which the poet damns himself and those close to him, including the beloved.[20] Thus, all critics agree that damnations and vituperations are an intrinsic trait of the *disperata*, one that allows us to define it, and furthermore, they agree its lyric form is not fixed as it changed over the years. While it is indeed a poem that usually comprises invectives, the *disperata* is also shaped by several other constant elements—and by few variable ones. For example, in the case of Isabella di Morra, her invectives are directed at Fortune, solitude, and uneducated people, because of her particularly unfortunate life plagued with abandonment and desolation, and devoid of romantic love. Furthermore, in contrast to the violent declarations of the male-authored *disperate*, hers peacefully rebel against patriarchal subjugation (Chapter Two). What is particularly remarkable about the *disperata* is that it always comprises a colorful inventory of resentful and bitter curses not only against those and that which the speaker hates the most, but often against the people and things he or she holds the most dear, and actually pursues. In fact, the curses might also be against an unreachable or lost object of desire, and against unrequited love spurring contradictory feelings of love and hate. More than anything else, the *disperata* speakers damn their life, rather than merely vent their bad mood, because they are irrevocably lost to despair, a state from which there is no return.

More recently, Vittorio Rossi defined the *disperata* as a long list of outbursts and lamentations: "'disperate,' bizzarri componimenti—canzoni o capitoli quanto alla metrica," in which the poet vents his bad mood and anguish with blasphemies, and by wishing the worst disasters on the entire universe.[21] This statement is exemplary of the difficulty readers of the *disperata* genre have because Rossi's comments add to the confusion surrounding it while understating the degree of despair. By calling it a "composition" whose metric mimics the *canzone* or *capitolo*, Rossi is here only considering its original forms in the Trecento and early-Quattrocento. Furthermore, the *disperata* does not only serve the purpose of "venting one's bad mood," rather, it contains a microcosm of narrative that ensues from, and deals with, wretched feelings of self-consuming despair, which is another constant trait of the genre. Despair is celebrated as an overbearing feeling that is both felt and expressed by the isolated *disperato* and *disperata* stemming from deeply personal reasons. It encompasses an existential anguish in which the dejected speaker sees no way out and no solution, and is overcome with both sorrow and hopelessness. Furthermore, each *disperata* conveys a unique intensity of despair, according to its speaker's mood.

The close reading of these texts points to one crucial conclusion that unites them all: there is no future to be had in the *disperata*. Death becomes the poet-persona's ultimate aspiration: wishing the worst and calling for an atrocious death, including being devoured by the devil or by ravenous beasts, or often conspiring a violent suicide. Each *disperata* is, therefore, the very last the speaker writes, and serves as a suicide note and confession. Since, through realistic images and language, the moment of birth is emphatically damned and also remarkably depicted as the moment of death, death itself becomes the object of desire, as it is seen as the beginning of the end of suffering. Death, thus, is another constant component of the *disperata* throughout the centuries, and in both Italy and France. It was, after all, historically present in the genre's continuum, as both countries were ravaged by wars, whether political, religious, or both. Moreover, the desire to die a violent death is directly interrelated to the speakers' living conditions and experiences, and thus, it is ingeniously embedded in their verses.

As mentioned, the *disperata* is also often a suicide poem. In the contemplation of their own despair, the *disperata* speakers isolate themselves from the rest of the world and its happenings: they cannot partake of the joys, love, and of all that there is to enjoy in life. The expression "only I" in both Italian and French recurs in many *disperate* expressing precisely this conscious parting from the world and other human beings. Since suicide or calls for death are almost always present in the *disperata*, the speaker goes against Catholic theology and, later, other Christian denominations, as suicide is a sin equaled to murder. Dante, for example, places suicides driven by despair in *Inferno*'s Canto XIII of his *Divina Commedia*.[22] Furthermore, despair is considered a sin by some Catholic theologians, including Thomas Aquinas, who, in his *Summa Theologica*, dedicates to it four articles, and notes that if we despair, we turn away from the hope of receiving God's glory, and thus, we turn away from our personal salvation found in God's love.[23] Aquinas believes that "despair consists in a man ceasing to hope for a share of God's goodness."[24] Therefore, despair is dangerous because it denotes a loss of hope that would otherwise bring us back from evil, in order to pursue good. Moreover, together with the sins of suicide and despair, the *disperata* speakers at times express a wish to descend into hell, dead or alive, where they feel they belong and in order to meet their punishment.

The *disperata* is also a confession, a narrative in which the desperate speakers find themselves at the very end of their capacity to withstand the many tragedies that life has been dealing them since birth. It is the locus of private outbursts of angst and frustration, not only aimed at external elements, but at oneself as well, often culminating in a death wish. Taken collectively over centuries, it offers a window into history—and what drives us into despair. It also articulates a profound existential crisis, from its beginning in the Trecento to its end at the culmination of the French Renaissance. As a genre, it is fashioned to elevate and intensify the hopelessness and violence of the poets' personal and historical circumstances, of their inability to reach the object of desire and to fully live a respectful and gratified life.

As previously mentioned, though, some misperception arises from the fact that several *disperate* in fifteenth-century *canzonieri* were listed as *capitoli*, therefore disguised as another poetic form. Examples include Sasso's "Era la stella sotto la qual nacque," Nicolò da Correggio's "Furia infernal dal lito ormai mi scoglia," and Tebaldeo's "Già con suavi e mansueti carmi", true *disperate*, yet catalogued as *capitoli*, as Antonia Tissoni Benvenuti points out.[25] Nonetheless, early modern readers were familiar with the *disperata* and its original *capitolo*-like form. Therefore, throughout this study, I argue that the *disperata* constitutes a distinctive genre not only because of its origins and its cultural and literary history throughout the Renaissance, but also because many title pages and indexes catalogue the form separately from *capitoli, canzoni,* and elegies, thus making a net distinction among the various *capitoli ternari,* and clearly classifying each and every genre. For example, in the early-modern editions of Serafino's and Tebaldeo's work their *disperate* are listed distinctly and separately from their *capitoli* (Figure 1).[26]

As I have already stated, the definition and tradition of the *disperata* are inextricably linked: as a genre it appears to have been particularly popular throughout the fourteenth, fifteenth and beginning of the sixteenth centuries in Italy, with poets employing both the *capitolo ternario* form and the content, or, at times, the content alone adapted to other lyric forms, which led to some confusion regarding its genre status during the Renaissance. Quadrio and Cian both point out that many fifteenth- and sixteenth-century *canzonieri* written by court poets include *disperate*,

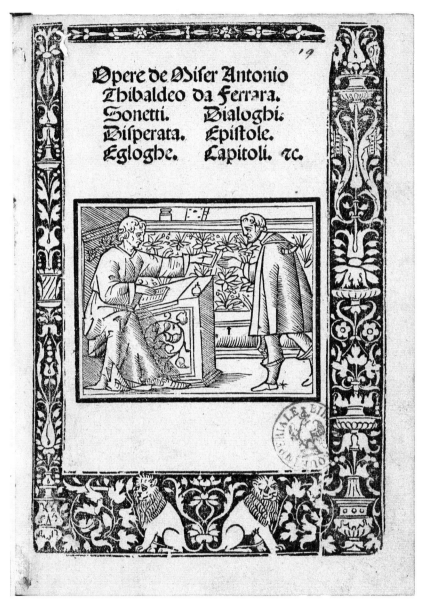

Figure 1. Opere del Miser Antonio Tibaldeo da Ferrara.
Sonetti. Dialoghi. Disperata. Epistole. Egloghe. Capitoli.
(By permission of Bibliothèque nationale de France.)

although they are at times listed as *capitoli*, *canzoni*, or even *epistole in terza rima*. Some Italian scholars such as Vecchi Galli, Gentili, and Comboni consider the first examples of *disperate* written in the *capitolo ternario* form a sub-genre of the elegy, because the elegy is a form of lament that belongs to the tradition of court poetry, and because there are overlapping traits in the elegy and these *disperate*, as both are long forms written in *terza rima*.[27] Furthermore, both elegy and *disperata* stage speakers whose voice is at center stage. Indeed, the "I," "io," and "je," constitute the poet's primary concern in most of the texts here examined. However, despite the many similarities between the Latin and Italian elegy, and the structural elements shared by all *capitoli ternari*, the *disperata* differs from the Italian *canzone*, elegy, and *capitolo* because of its content and the unique combination and concentration of its traits.

Vittorio Rossi describes several *strambotti* written by the fifteenth-century poet Andrea Michieli, known as Strazzòla (ca. 1450–ca. 1510) as "true" *disperate*, thus remarking on the change in form and metric from the long *capitolo* to a short octave.[28] Abandoned by his family and friends, Strazzòla composed verses that indeed echo the more famous *disperate*.[29] In the following example, the speaker is so unhappy that he actually envies the "desperate" man because, just like him, he has no hope or fortune left in this world:

> che invidia porto a ciascun *disperato*; [emphasis mine]
> speranza mi agomenta e si me dice:
> 'Strazzola non sperar che sei spacciato

> (Because I envy every *disperato*,/hope argues with me and tells me,/ Strazzola do not hope because you are done).

This example is precisely one in which the *disperata* content was adapted to a shorter form. The first verse undoubtedly makes reference to the *disperata* genre itself and to its speaker, the "disperato," that is somebody who is thus allowed to freely express his despair and is to be envied because of his role in the literary tradition and the ability it provides to freely express despair in a poem.

All of the *disperata* poets considered in this study produced a plethora of lyric forms, excelling in few particular ones, while mainly responding to their cultural and literary context. Very few of these poets are known for their *disperate*, and as we will see case by case, their *disperate*, in fact, represent a small percentage of their verses. These texts, however, contribute to their conspicuous lyric ability to use a variety of Renaissance forms, thus favorably impressing their patrons and readers, and filling their prized *canzonieri*. Furthermore, the *disperata* is deftly connected to their other works and provides precious autobiographical content, characterized by a concrete preoccupation with daily life's necessities, such as surviving destitution, war, solitude, and political and religious trauma— issues that severely marginalized the poets despite their intellectual aspirations and literary talent.

Whereas in Italy the *disperata* in the more popular *capitolo ternario* form disappeared after the 1530s, its content remained a strong and vital intertext, especially in the work of court poets, who eagerly adopted it and its unique manner of narrating despair. Therefore, one of my main arguments is that the *disperata* tradition can be traced not only in the more traditional form, but also in the other forms that compellingly defy metric, gender, borders, and language. Eventually, Pietro Bembo (1470–1547) and his literary pro-Petrarchan reforms put an end to the genre's adoption in Italy,[30] but in France its intertextual connections resurfaced and spread to other lyric forms, strengthening its bonds and meaning and providing poets an additional stimulating and generative intertextual model.

However, despite its early popularity, today the *disperata* is almost forgotten. With the exception of the few literary critics cited in this study, it has yet to be given due scholarly attention and has not yet been credited with contributing to some of the poems written by both well-known and less-known authors throughout the Italian and French Renaissance. Jauss notes that "L'historicité d'un genre littéraire se manifeste dans le processus de création de la structure, ses variations, son élargissement et les rectifications qui lui sont apportées; ce processus peut évoluer jusqu'à l'épuisement du genre ou à son éviction par un genre nouveau."[31] This is an accurate depiction of the *disperata* as well since its structure, variations, and developments included new forms. It therefore continued in its constant and variable elements that were at times expanded on, and at other times narrowed. One of the primary reasons for remaining popular and relevant throughout the early-modern period for both writers and readers is that it was adopted by popular Italian writers, including Serafino, Tebaldeo, Sasso, and Tansillo, who were four of the most imitated poets in France.

The *Disperata* and Its Characteristics

As Daniel Javitch suggests, by inferring from a representative sampling of prior models, a genre's thematic and formal properties provide both a retrospective and a historical deliberation.[32] Therefore, I discuss the *disperata*'s variable as well as constant traits in order to provide a more inclusive and precise definition; how its *topoi* remained a relevant source for several generations of poets, and how it was imitated from the beginning in the Trecento to the end of the Renaissance in both Italy and France.[33]

As a cultural reading, through the Italian *disperata* the court poet can be viewed as a victim of misunderstandings, peregrinations, and moral disheartenment.[34] The genre was overtly attuned to the general sociopolitical and cultural realities of its time, including the wars and conflicts between the various city-states and kingdoms during the fourteenth century.[35] These conflicts continued well into the next two centuries in Italy,[36] although between different factions, while in France it was mostly the Wars of Religion that shaped literary history.[37] In fact, for both countries these were times of transition, marked by the many shifts in power in the Italian political scene and by the bloody civil wars that plagued France in the last decades of the sixteenth century. These historical aspects blend in unison with the image crafted by the speaker's autobiographical and introspective experience, creating a realistic picture in both mindset and its linguistic expression that is then colored in its entirety by dark views and feelings and by an intense pessimism.

Readers of the *disperata* are often called to witness, feel, and experience what Cave calls *enargeia*, or ecphrasis. *Enargeia* is a rhetorical term for a visually powerful and dramatic description that recreates something or someone.[38] Indeed the text often demands its reader to witness and experience firsthand the poet's despair, his many disillusions and tragic experiences encompassing all aspects of his life. Thus, the reader, be it the poet's patron or an anachronistic and unattached reader such as ourselves, is always cast as a witness. We are persuaded and called to feel for the speaker, to believe him or her, because no one has ever suffered this much and been wronged so many times. The intended effect on the reader is emotional; and death plays a more crucial role than Love.

As has already been stated, most *disperata* speakers subvert Christian teachings and beliefs, because they wish not only for their death, as suicide is a major sin in itself, but also for everlasting hell, contrary to the true devotee who instead longs for Paradise. The *contro-disperata,* as already stated, is prompted by this heretical trait to counter the maledictions with multiple benedictions and praises for the Virgin Mary, as its speaker worships life.[39] Thus, the *disperata* is striking in its contrast with other genres that filled the Renaissance collections and the single-authored *canzonieri*, in particular love and mystical lyrics. However, as already noted, poets who wrote *disperate* in the *capitolo* form also authored love lyrics and employed other canonical genres, including the sonnet, thus creatively partaking in the many poetic intersections of Renaissance forms.

There are, however, some variations in the texts that I examine. At times, despair caused by Love is pushed to the limit, though at other times, Love is not mentioned at all. Society in general, usually the court, patrons and rivals, as well as the whole macrocosm and all of its elements, which are often enumerated in tedious lists, conspire against the poet-persona in order to destroy him or her. Furthermore, many *disperate* portray a world turned upside down, in which things, places, and people and their relationships are overthrown in precisely opposite scenarios. Cataclysms and apocalyptic visions become a common recurrence. Everything is destabilized and perfectly at odds with the narrator's plaint, who passionately calls and wishes for these catastrophes, as in the following verses by il Pistoia:

> Vorrei veder il foco su la sabbia, ...
> E che Eolo lasciasse tutti i venti,
> sì che cadesse a terra ogni edifficio;
> e, invece de gli uccei, volar serpenti.

(I would like to see fire on the sand,/ ... /And Aeolus release all the winds,/So that all buildings fall down;/and, instead of birds, snakes fly.)[40] (vv. 55–60, 244).

The *disperata* takes place in and chooses as its favorite site a desolate and desert-like natural environment plunged in the most forsaken wilderness, far away from society and from the beaten path. Often, it is a hellish landscape inspired by Dante's *Inferno*. Here, the poetic persona is not cut off from the natural world; rather, he seeks a way to reunite with nature. It is here that his violent streak is free to flow and to nurture his furious temperament and narrative. However, the speaker is not completely alone: monsters, and savage and cruel animals, such as lions, snakes, tigers, bears, and ominous birds become his companions. At times they are thirsty for the poetic persona's blood and life, and at others they symbolize his miserable soul or imminent death.[41]

There are numerous invocations of nature and of its power and beneficial effects. Nature offers a space in which to retire, a backdrop in which to mourn and despair, and also a witness to it all. Ernst Robert Curtius has already shown how the invocation of nature as a poetic *topos*, which originally had a religious significance, "serves the heroic emotion of tragic situations," as it adds gravitas to the hero-persona's voice.[42] In the *disperata*, nature and the speaker's voice become a chorus, as in the following verses by il Saviozzo:

> E vo' che la pietà per me si dorma,
> per monti alpestri e per diserte piaggi
> vo' seguitar de' faüni la torma;
> orsi, tigri, leon crudi e selvaggi
> vo' in compagnia, e per abitazione
> caverne e antri e pruini e folti faggi.

(I go so that pity is far away from me,/through mountains and through deserted beaches/I go and follow the troop of animals;/ cruel and wild bears, tigers, and lions/in their company, and for abode,/I go to caverns and grottoes and thorn bushes and dense beech trees.) (vv. 52–57, 219).

Nature and its portrayals will gradually darken and become more hopeless as my analysis moves from the Italian *disperata* to the poetry of despair of the French neo-Petrarchans at the end of the Renaissance. Often, an enumeration of natural elements—earth, sky, stones, rocks, grass, valleys, mountains, grottoes, and animals—is used to demonstrate the gravity and all-encompassing despair of the circumstances.

Finally, the rhetoric used in the texts, as we will discuss further, is also particularly unvarying, including verbs of want, wish, and desire; repetitions and anaphors; the conditional, future, imperative, and subjunctive verb modes; and the colorful language of the many maledictions, such as "Maledetto sia" and "Maudit soit!" Indeed, the poet-persona becomes the *porte-parole* for all *disperati* who share the same wretched condition of hopelessness, and which sets him or her apart from the rest of the world.

Petrarchism and *Disperata*

A brief analysis of the humanist, writer, and philosopher Francesco Petrarca (Petrarch) and of his love poetry becomes necessary and fruitful at this juncture, as Petrarchism and *disperata* intersect and often commingle in the poetry discussed throughout this study. As a set of linguistic codes, rules, and themes, Petrarchism began in Italy as soon as Petrarch's *Rime Sparse* started to circulate in 1359.[43] His *canzoniere*, titled *Rerum vulgarium fragmenta*, is a collection of 366 sonnets, *sestine*, *canzoni*, ballads, and madrigals that form a biography in which the poet's love for the beautiful Laura, the *infinita bellezza*, constitutes the main inspiration and the essence of his lyrical work. Petrarch's models for his collection were Virgil's *Eclogues*, Horace's *Odes*, Propertius's and Ovid's elegies, as well as Dante's *Vita nova*. Beginning with the first sight of Laura in the Church of Santa Chiara in Avignon, the magical moment of the *innamoramento* where Love shot its first arrow and found him "tutto disarmato" (39), Petrarch guides us through the journey of the rest of his life: his first meeting with Laura; his struggles with the temptations of desire and of glory; the painful encounter with her death and her memory; and finally, the recognition that earthly aspirations are vain, a theme already announced in the very first poem, "che quanto piace al mondo è breve sogno" (37). Even after Laura's death, she continues to inspire Petrarch's verses with her unparalleled beauty and with the invincible and eternal love she inspired. With the exception of two poems, and starting with sonnet 267, the poet will only write about the joys and the torments that this great love causes him, as demonstrated in his poem "Quel antiquo mio dolce empio signore."

Petrarch's writing becomes the testimony of his suffering: in fact, the *Canzoniere* is a monument to its author, whose passion and pain are inseparable from his love. This forces him to reflect and write about his status as a "martyr of love"; thus, his analysis of the psychology of Love turns out to be more important to him than his love for Laura. The lover-persona becomes a master of self-examination and self-discovery, bestowing on the *Canzoniere* its particular character. This is an innovative approach, and it constitutes Petrarch's main contribution to fourteenth, fifteenth, and sixteenth-century poetry.[44] His literary production bears a profound introspective analysis, in which feelings and *stati d'animo* are examined, explored and confessed, and reproduced on the page so that the speaker and reader can experience and relive them. Of central importance is the poetic persona's inability to satisfy desire, which itself is torn between humanism and religion. As Charles Trinkaus explains, Petrarch embodies the tradition of "double-consciousness," because he is caught between Christianity of late medieval culture and paganism of the classical world.[45] This tension creates a profound melancholy that often lies between hope and despair. Such a conflict becomes more and more complex, and it unfolds before the reader's eyes, but it is never resolved or mastered. Thus, Petrarch's love for Laura is never consummated poetically in the *Canzoniere*. This is another fundamental element of the lyric system of Petrarchism: the lady's unattainability and the lover-persona's physical and emotional frustration, which also haunts the poets of the *disperata*.

Petrarch's language, figures of speech, psychological attitudes, themes, *topoi*, images, and physical sensations form a code that many poets after him will embrace, emulate, and mold, resulting in a true *imitatio-dispositio* practice that, as Balsamo eloquently explains, became the only way to formulate love in a dignified way, and the whole sixteenth-century love experience referred back to Petrarch's code.[46] Indeed, I would argue that Petrarch taught early-modern European poets to properly and poetically talk about Love, and even to narrate one's love story and pangs. Thus, from the Petrarchan poets of the fourteenth and fifteenth centuries, to the neo-Petrarchan poets of the sixteenth century, in both Italy and France, this approach would continue to be elaborated, developed, at times improved, personalized, adopted, and adapted, hence nurturing European Petrarchism.[47] Accordingly, imitation and intertextuality provide a framework that allowed Petrarchism not only to expand but also to engage with themes and images from the *disperata*, while maintaining and developing Petrarch's refined and codified language, his metaphors, and some of his attitudes.

Leonard. W. Forster notes that Petrarchism is "the second great international system of conventional love, between the chivalric love of the middle ages and the romantic love of the eighteenth and nineteenth centuries."[48] "System" is indeed a key word in the understanding and appreciation of how and why the work of Petrarch and his disciples had such an immense impact on future writers. Klaus W. Hempfer also uses this term (sistema petrarchistico), which he describes as a system generated and formed by the work of the Italian poet that consists of a set of linguistic, rhetorical, and psychological elements that contributed to erect this major lyric tradition. As Hempfer convincingly argues, poets who imitated Petrarch were themselves well aware of the existence of such a system.[49] When it comes to language, Balsamo also views Petrarchism as a system that allowed writers and readers to understand and express love, and that was readily adopted by poets who provided new variations throughout the sixteenth century.[50]

The ever-expanding moment of suffering becomes the crucial moment of Petrarch's *poesis*, so much so that it often eclipses that of the *innamoramento*, and this aspect becomes a crucial *topos* in most *disperate*.[51]

In suffering lies pleasure and, more importantly, the astonishing creative source of self-discovery. Petrarch's melancholy or *accidia* was mostly bitter-sweet, painful but still pleasing, which is a trait that not only became a trademark of his poetry, but also contributed to his success and provided much inspiration to his emulators. Even though Laura is unattainable— her unattainability is obviously the main source of Petrarch's melancholy and the motivation for his writings—the lover-persona fully accepts and endures this rejection and consequences. However, the *disperata* poets not only expand on this point, for moments of pleasure are rare in their narrative, but also make room for more suffering, bitterness, and invectives. Furthermore, they capitalize on Love's cruelty and adversity, turning it into the target of their most fierce outbursts and maledictions.

Some poems in Petrarch's *Canzoniere* are directly engaged in an intertextual dialogue with few of the *disperata*'s main *topoi* and attitudes. In particular, according to Flamini, the *canzone* "Quell'antiquo mio dolce empio signore" can be considered a prototype of *disperata* because of the ways in which Love is treated.[52] The poem is divided in two parts.[53] In verses 1 to 75, the lover-persona speaks about and attacks Love, while in verses 76 to 157, he crafts a rebuke by Love, who defends itself and accuses the narrator of complaining about life and Love. In addition, the poetic persona pleads with it, his cruel master, and in a powerful simile he compares himself to a man who fears death and asks for justice: "quasi uom che teme morte et ragion chiede" (v. 8, 561). An association between the *disperata*'s and Petrarch's speakers can indeed be drawn in the first part of the *canzone*: they both demand and seek justice, as their condition as passionate men and lovers is perceived as a constant injury. Petrarch further explains his sorrow, "'l mio infelice stato" (v. 21, 561) and ends the first stanza in a powerful verse full of despair: "e 'n odio ebbi la vita." (And I hated life). (v. 15, 561) Like the *disperata* lover, Petrarch's persona also hates his life, and crafts his plaint around this primary theme.

The second stanza continues in a buildup of sorrow and despair: the lover-persona's life is plunged in a disarray of fire and pain, and Love transports him from a restful state of peace to a restless state of war: "e' mi tolse di pace et pose in guerra." (v. 30, 561) War is the backdrop for many of the *disperate* in both literal and figurative terms, because, as we shall see throughout the texts examined, most Italian and French *disperata* poets were engaged in or witnessed firsthand horrific scenes of war. Just like war, Love is inhumane, cold, and devious. Among other things, it forces the speaker to lose hope, to question himself, to despair, and to long for death.

Furthermore, here too we encounter depictions of the poet's life before and after he was afflicted by Love.

Petrarch prolongs his grievance in the third stanza, where he directly accuses Love of making him love God less, "questi m'à fatto men amar Dio" (v. 31, 563). This is indeed a serious accusation in a century characterized by its deep devotion, an accusation that also marks strong intertextual connections with many of the *disperata* complaints where the speaker too questions his faith in God. Death becomes the object of desire; a mirage pined for over and over so that it may terminate the speaker's misery. The accusing tone continues and intensifies in the following verses:

> Così in tutto mi spoglia
> di libertà questo crudel ch'i'accuso,
> ch'amaro viver m'à vòlto in dolce uso.

(Thus, it strips me of/all liberty the cruel one that I accuse,/and turned bitter living into a sweet habit.) (vv. 43–45, 563).

The admonishments and complaints that Petrarch so skillfully weaves in this song indisputably constitute another main connection between his and the *disperata* poetry, as Love is directly accused rather than Laura herself. In fact, the beloved's name is rarely mentioned in the *disperata*; rather, Love is the target of much blame and invectives. Furthermore, it is in the fourth stanza that one of the *disperata*'s main *topoi* comes alive, its distinctive setting of desert and solitary places, often inhabited by wild and fierce animals, rapacious thieves, harsh peoples and their customs. Here, Love banishes the lover-persona:

> Cercar m'à fatto deserti paesi,
> fiere et ladri rapaci, ispidi dumi,
> dure genti et costumi,
> et ogni error che pellegrini intrica;
> monti valli paludi et mari et fiumi,
> mille lacciuoli in ogni parte tesi,
> e 'l verno in strani mesi
> con pericol presente et con fatica.

(He forced me to seek out deserted places/wild beasts and rapacious thieves, and harsh dunes,/hard peoples and customs,/and all mistakes that travelers combat;/through mountains, valleys, marshes, and seas and rivers,/a thousand snares everywhere,/and winter comes in strange months/and with present dangers and hard labor.) (vv. 46–53, 563).

This stanza demonstrates a strong intertextuality with the *disperata*'s geography, language, and descriptions: Love's miseries force the lover-persona to seek out and portray this bleakly inhuman surrounding. Furthermore, the unusual and eerie image created by the verse: "e 'l verno in strani mesi" unambiguously brings to mind many of the most recognizable common places of the *disperate* written from the fourteenth to the sixteenth century, in which the speakers suggest the unusual, the extraordinary, and the strange in a very negative sense, as well as the cruel world they are forced to inhabit and face every day. In this setting, the universe is turned upside down, and winter occurs in the summer.

Melancholy undoubtedly remains one of the main characteristics of Petrarch's *canzoniere* expressed in antitheses, as Forster notes: "The fundamental note of his poetry is therefore melancholy and resignation. [...] He designates this state of affairs by a characteristic antithetical paradox. He speaks of '*dolenti voluptas*.'"[54] Love's cruelty and its unrequited nature become the target of venomous vituperations, but never quite as violent as in the *disperata*, where the speaker rebels against Love and does not accept its cruelty and rebukes. In fact, Love is personified as a bitter enemy, without compassion, and filled with vengeance for the lover-persona. For the most part, the *disperata* mood, attitude, and the previously discussed characteristics meet and blend with Petrarch's refined language, clichés, metaphors, and rhetorical settings in a variety of dark and conflicting images. Therefore, I suggest that in the *disperata* we encounter a fundamentally altered Petrarchan system, one infused with rebellion and violence, as well as a penchant for darker thoughts. This will be particularly true in French poetry at the end of the Renaissance when the neo-Petrarchan poets borrowed language from the Italian master and his disciples, and they combined it with the *disperata*, thus acclimatizing this double inheritance in the poetry of the Wars of Religion. Hence, the two literary traditions mingled and spread throughout the prestigious Italian and French courts.

In both Petrarchism and the *disperata*, the speaker is by definition a rejected lover, and the inaccessibility of the beloved is the *sine qua non* condition of both systems. However, in the *disperata*, the poetic persona is also plagued by other trials, such as misfortune, poverty, the perils of patronage, abandonment, and a world torn by war.[55] These aspects combine and conspire to render a truly miserable and hopeless existence. Thus, while both *poesis* indeed are in a meaningful intertextual dialogue—most *disperata* poets are Petrarchist poets after all—in the *disperata* genre, unrequited desire is exaggerated, becoming larger than life, and is projected onto other dark topics with renewed violence. In fact, while hope is never truly abandoned by Petrarch, in the poetry of the *disperata* the poet not only abandons hope but quickly damns even the dare to hope because despair always prevails. Therefore, the desire to find equilibrium, harmony, and peace always fades, and the reader is faced with a narrative in which *all* hope to ever find them vanishes, slowly and painfully, forever.

Finally, as I will show, unlike Petrarch's persona, the *disperata* poets do not graciously accept their beloveds' refusal; rather, they emphasize with great masochism the moments of deep sorrow and despair. In their verses, Love takes on a secondary role, as pain becomes their muse and their force. While Petrarch never fails to express the lacerations that haunt him,[56] since, as Aldo Scaglione explains, in the Petrarcho-Platonic assumption "satisfying the desire would be morally and psychologically injurious to both,"[57] in the *disperata* narrative these lacerations become true inspiration and ethos. Indeed, the *disperata* speakers are also frustrated, conflicted, and their own desires, whether inspired by a lover or by other preoccupations, are doomed to remain forever unfulfilled.

The success, translation, and imitation of Petrarch's works created a European phenomenon to which the great majority of Renaissance love poetry is connected. Throughout the early modern period, Petrarchism and the *disperata* intermingled in the poetry of some of the court poets as we shall see in the following chapters. Clearly, a few of Petrarch's poems skirt some of the *disperata* themes.[58] Undoubtedly, the *disperata* thrived and flourished within the realm of Petrarchism. The horrors of war, poverty, misfortune, and unrequited love came together and fused with Petrarch's refined and codified language in order to please the court and fulfill its socio-cultural scope of entertainment production. However, when despair overpowers the speaker's microcosm, and Love and the world no longer make sense, the poetry of the *disperata* subverts Petrarchism in captivating ways, hence uncovering the inventive side of imitation. Indeed, as *emulatio* and *dispositio* are both part of the process of rewriting the model, by subverting the very model, the *disperata* poet directly destabilizes and challenges it with alternative renditions that better fit the cultural and historical backdrop of the text and its readers as some of the poems that follow amply demonstrate.

The *Disperata* and Its Origins

Antonio Beccari da Ferrara's Cosmic Despair

The first known *disperata* belongs to Maestro Antonio Beccari, born in 1315 in Ferrara.[59] Russell and other critics agree that his *disperata* "Le stelle universali e i ciel rotanti" is the first in the Italian tradition,[60] and thus, Beccari is unanimously considered the "architect" of the *disperata* genre. Beccari wrote *disperate* in the *canzone* form that express an existential crisis, extensively listing his own personal miseries culminating in a distressed death wish. As already stated, the highly autobiographical aspect of the *disperata* remains one of its distinct and powerful traits, at least throughout the fourteenth and beginning of the fifteenth century. Though Beccari wrote three *disperate*, "Diviso sia per l'universo pace," "Amor con più sospir conven ch'io canti," and "Le stelle universali e i ciel rotanti," it was this latter that set the genre and became one of its best and accomplished exemplars.[61] Throughout the ninety-six verses, the poetic persona uses eighteen maledictions with variations such as "maledetto" and "maledire" (damned and to damn). The composition also develops several important traits of the genre, which can be found in other *disperate* of the Trecento, Quattrocento, and Cinquecento.[62]

According to Natalino Sapegno, Beccari's entire *canzoniere* is an important text that documents fourteenth-century court culture.[63] In fact, the *disperata* is mainly centered around court life, and as such, it ought to be considered not only a form of literary expression, but also a socio-cultural document. It is very often a poem in which the court poet voices his most personal confessions and chronicles his anxieties in the context of his times and circumstances.[64] Therefore, "Le stelle universali e i ciel rotanti" is undoubtedly a literary and cultural document establishing the genre and its characteristics, as well as inaugurating its popularity.[65] Moreover, Beccari shares fundamental characteristics with other interpreters of the *disperata* genre: he was poor, a slave to his vice or vices (in Beccari's case, dice games); he was compelled to seek favors at his patron's court; he had to serve various men in power, sometimes at the expense of his own creative nature; he was forced to move from one city to another, and thus lead a nomadic life, and all in order to survive.[66] In sum, Beccari's work articulates many of the socio-economical adversities and the very few successes encountered by the majority of the writers of this period. As Sapegno remarks, Dante, Petrarch, and Boccaccio's greatness contrasts with the other so-called "minor writers,"[67] who also composed *disperate* and had to vie for readers' and patrons' attention. For some of them, this trend would continue well into the fifteenth and the sixteenth centuries, but also into the present, when names such as Beccari remain unknown to the majority of scholars and readers of Italian literature.

In Beccari's *disperate* in particular, the reader finds an intense voice that sets the genre's persuasive tone that would then draw other writers to adopt it. Because of its powerful and macrocosmic beginning, in which the whole universe is called to witness the desperate speaker's misery, "Le stelle universali e i ciel rotanti" lyrically unfolds a personal tragedy that quickly and efficiently moves to engulf different elements and people that affect his existence. From an idyllic macrocosm, the narrator moves inward to his own tormented microcosm, where all is doomed, damned, and cursed. Thus, the poem opens with a catastrophic malediction of universal dimensions:

> Le stelle universali e i ciel rotanti,
> le loro 'nfusïone,
> l'eterno moto e tutta la sua forza,
> e propriamente quelle impressïone,
> i abiti e i sembianti ,
> che da lor prese mia natural scorza
> e l'alimento che mai non se ammorza,
> l'aere, l'acqua e la terra
> che 'n mia forma se serra,
> sian maladetti e tutto lor podere.

(The universal stars and the revolving skies,/their influence,/the eternal movement and all of its strength,/and their true characteristics,/the inclinations and appearances/that my body took from them/and the fire that never goes out,/the air, the water, and the earth/which blend in me,/they be damned with all their power.) (vv. 1–10,127).

The inventory of natural elements, which include the all-encompassing air, water, and earth, constitutes the first unrestrained damnation that is literally projected at the reader: "That the whole universe and its elements, and all of their power be damned!" Moreover, the poem is in the *canzone* form, and its first stanza sets a tragic tone that is rhythmically felt throughout the entire composition thanks also to its rhyme. This tone and rhythm will become the standard in all subsequent *disperate* that use the *capitolo* and *canzone* forms. In fact, Beccari's *disperata* contains all of the genre's *topoi*, such as maledictions, a search for solitary places, the presence of terrifying wild beasts, a codified language, infernal landscapes, and finally, a hopeless call for death and suicide wish. In addition, the speaker's mood is anxious, distressed, and violent from the first to the last verse.

The maledictions are first directed towards the precise year of his birth and the very beginning of life:

> Mille e trecento quindici ov'io nacqui,
> tempo crudele e rio,
> nemico de vertù, sia maladetto

(One thousand three hundred and fifteen when I was born,/a cruel and wicked time,/enemy of virtue, that it be damned) (vv. 34–37, 128).

The poetic persona also damns his father and mother for having conceived him:

> Maledetto el voler ch'accese el padre
> de le mie triste membre,
> a spargere 'l suo seme e 'l suo dolere.
> Poi maladico el corpo de la madre,
> dove se aggiunse insembre.

(Damned be the will that turned my father on/for my sad limbs,/ to spread his seed and his pain./Then I damn my mother's body,/ where they came together.) (vv. 11–15, 127).

Both parents are seen as condemning their own son to a miserable life from the very moment of his conception, which is transformed from loving and passionate, to sinful and catastrophic. His father's desire and his mother's fertile body become the locus of much hatred. The nourishment he received when very young is also damned because it allowed him to survive and to grow:

> Maladette le fasse e 'l nudrimento,
> che cominciâr per tempo
> a darme la cason de questa rima!

(Damned be the swaddling cloth and nutrients/that started/to give me the reason for these rhymes!) (vv. 21–23, 127).

It was then that his wretched life began, prompting the writer to compose his poem of despair, "this miserable rhyme." His misfortunes—"la mia bassa fortuna"—are many and are also damned: his intellect (v. 41,

128); his studies (vv. 45–46, 128); and his vice of playing dice, which has the power to determine his fortune and whether he is sad or happy.[68] The desperate speaker then blames his poverty:

> Maladette le terre e l'ampio mondo
> ch'i' ho tanto cercato,
> povero e disviato,
> senza trovar già mai don de fortuna.

(Damned be the lands and vast world/that I searched for so long/ poor and wihtout a destination,/without ever finding any luck.) (vv. 58–61, 128).

Indeed, poverty and misery are an essential *topos* of the *disperata*, yoked together by the historical circumstances of the poet. As has already been stated, most poets of the *disperata* were forced to write on command, to please and appease a patron, and to attract new benefactors in order to secure their livelihood, something that Beccari directly addresses in the following verses:

> Maladetti i servigi ricevuti,
> maladetto el servire
> ch'io feci altrui o con borsa o con bocca!

(Damned be the services received,/damned be the services/that I did to others with money or words!) (vv. 69–71, 129).

Though poets might lament their financial dependence, it could be far worse to be without a patron. After Beccari's patron, Giovanni degli Ordelaffi from Forlì, died, he was left unprotected, poorer, and without hope of a stable financial future. Therefore, he invokes death to come quickly and end his desperate life:

> Maladetta la morte che non scocca
> l'ultimo stral de sua possente cocca
> fra mia indurata mente,
> disperata e dolente,
> priva d'ogni speranza e de conforto,
> po ch'egli è morto el Segnor che me dava
> frutto, speranza e norma
> de la mia vita ria giogner al porto!

(Damned be death that does not come/the last arrow of its bow/in my harden mind,/desperate and sorrowful,/and devoid of all hope and comfort,/because he died, the Lord who gave me/assistance, hope and norm/for my wretched life to get to safety!) (vv. 74–81, 129).

These verses in particular are significant because they refer directly to the unpredictable condition of dependence on an influential, political figure who was expected to protect and economically support the writer, a condition shared by many poets in this study. What transpires is a constant state of uncertainty as to whether he has a home, a dependable occupation, and a reliable future. His "desperate and sorrowful mind, devoid of hope and comfort," is a condition that recurs often in the poetry of despair and is well expounded in a prominent point of the poem. It is also one of the variable elements that characterize the *disperata* in both Italy and France, because the court poet is often preoccupied with maintaining his good favor with his patron. The instability of both the period and people in power prevents him from feeling safe and threatens his already volatile life.

Finally, this poem of desperation concludes with a death wish, already mentioned in the suggestive verse: "Maladetta la morte che non scocca," thus damning death itself because it is not coming soon enough to carry the speaker away. To call for his own end, or even more dramatically, to end his own life, is again an intrinsic element of most *disperate*, as death literally and figuratively takes the narrator out of his misery due to his destitution and despair.

Beccari ends his poem with another fundamental *topos* of the genre: the speaker personifies his rhymes, here a desperate one, and addresses it directly to urge it to herald his despair:

> Tua disperata rima e tristo verso,
> canzon nova de pianto,
> i' la confermo, e sì te benedico:
> e s'tu trovassi alcun che se dia vanto
> in pene esser sommerso,
> disperato de ben, lasso e mendico,
> fammeli amico, se amistà pò essere
> tra 'nfortunati e rei;
> ...
> ch'assai son presso a privarme de l'essere.

(Your desperate rhyme and sad verse,/tearful new song,/I endorse you and thus bless you:/and if you find somebody that boasts/ about his many sorrows,/desperate, tired and begging,/make him my friend/if friendschip can exist/among wretched and unfortunate souls/ ... /as I am very hard-pressed to end my life.) (vv. 86–96, 129).

This last verse states the speaker's suicidal intent and the reasons that press him to take his own life. This central aspect will become particularly relevant in the compositions of il Saviozzo and in many other poems discussed throughout this book. Furthermore, the speaker turns to his reader in order to find a listener, a witness who is as unfortunate as himself, and therefore can relate to his despair. He is also looking for compassion and companionship in his misery, but at the same time, he seriously doubts whether friendship could even exist among miserable souls such as his. Possibilities and impossibilities are thus equally considered and quickly discarded, but death is earnestly solicited to end both. This personal cry for a collectivity of desperate souls reaches beyond Beccari's pages all the way to the next *disperata* writer and the next, who also struggle to be part of this same community. It is this call for solidarity that renders this poetry even more transmittable, as it is not only a matter of imitation and of genre dissemination, but it is also a legacy which seeks to unite other writers in the same precarious condition and who would rather die than continue to endure such unpredictability and hopelessness.

Aside from the numerous maledictions, the most striking verses in "Le stelle universali e i ciel rotanti" are those written as a reflection on Beccari's own profession, a frustrating curse against what Tartaro calls "una realtà socio-culturale che fa dello scrittore un impiegato":[69]

> Maledetti i servigi ricevuti,
> maledetto el servire
> ch'io feci altrui o con borsa o con bocca!
> (vv. 69–71, 129).

His profession as writer and his intellect render him a meager employee whose life depends on the whims of his powerful patrons. In addition to the self-reflection above, the convincing labeling "Tua disperata rima, e tristo verso,/canzon nova de pianto" contribute to the definition of *disperata* as a new type of composition, characterized by sad and tearful verses. A new "desperate, tearful song"—such is Beccari's definition of his *disperata*, a conscious labeling of the form (*canzon*) and content (*pianto*) that will prove to be a model for others to follow.

Each of Beccari's stanzas concludes with a mythological or biblical reference to a tragic character, serving as a reminder of the speaker's erudite education, and cultural and intellectual background, as a way to fit into the literary vogue of the day. Indeed, these reflections situate the *disperata* as a genre that is fundamentally humanistic because of its autobiographical and psychological content, its erudition and display of classical themes, and, of course, its composition in Italian vernacular, rather than Latin. The narrator evokes, revitalizes, and skillfully adapts Classical references to fit his personal predicaments. These will inhabit other *disperate* as well, including those written by the French poets.

Sapegno notes that the realism and introspective lyricism of this poetry constitute a response to the socio-economic and cultural events that characterized Italy in the fourteenth century.[70] Beccari experienced the financial difficulties of many *disperata* poets, traveling from Ferrara to Bologna, to Venice and then to Padua, and finally to Ravenna in order to find work. The reality of exile, marginalization, and lack of authority undoubtedly clashed with the poet's superior humanist knowledge and intellect, and with the consciousness of his role as a depositary of the cultural and literary patrimony of his region and of his art, which he felt responsible to disperse among his benefactors and audience. Therefore, the fourteenth-, fifteenth-, and sixteenth-century *disperate* altogether stage the chasm between the reality of the humiliated artist, who was forced to beg, and his mission as "prophet of the world." These texts exemplify their authors' experience as victim of Destiny and Fortune, or lack thereof. The same isolation and malaise are also encountered in Isabella di Morra's *canzoni* and sonnets, as well as in some of the French writers at the end of the Renaissance.

Simone Serdini, Known as Il Saviozzo's Existential Despair

Considered by many to be the most skilled writer of *disperate*, Simone Serdini was born in Siena in 1360. Known as il Saviozzo, he is acclaimed for his three widely circulated *disperate*, "Cerbero invoco e il suo latrare," "Le 'nfastidite labra in ch'io già pose," and "Corpi celesti e tutte l'altre stelle."[71] He is also known for his *disperate femminili*, which I will discuss in the following chapter. Here, I examine and trace the genre's themes throughout each of these three *disperate* in order to show how il Saviozzo cultivated the genre and how he creatively elaborated on motifs and images with nuanced language. Furthermore, he was able to express more than any other writer the existential crisis that became an intrinsic characteristic of the genre. His *canzoniere* is one of the most extensive and comprehensive fourteenth-century collections, because its poetry encompasses many and varied topics and genres. Although there have been questions of attribution, Emilio Pasquini, il Saviozzo's modern editor, has convincingly

¶ Cerbero in uoco compoſto per Simone Sardini Seneſe uocato Sauiozo.

¶ El contrario di Cerbero che comincia Certo Ieſu intendo di chiamare.

¶ La diſperata compoſta da Antonio de Tibaldi Ferrareſe.

Erbero iuoco el ſuo crudo latrar
che liſio mio igegno a ſe racoglia
& facci mie ſcuri uerſi mughiar
Acio chi moſtri la infinita doglia
quale ognora ſento il ben chi ho pduto
che acio penſando triemo come foglia
Veggiomi in tāto ſterminin uenuto
che al miſero Atheon inuidia porto
& come dido la uita rifiuto
Hor mhaueſſi il furor di Gioue morto
quel giorno chi rimaſi ne la rete

damor crudel che mi fa ſi grā torto
O dardi di Vulcano hor ui mouete
uenitemi a cauar dellaberinto
che di ueder Plutone ho molta ſete
Ome chio ſon ſi laſſo ſtanco & uinčto
per ſeguitar amore falſo & crudele
che alleſſer micidial di me ſon pinto
Fra glialtri inamorati un ſi fidele
uno non e quale io ſempre a Venere
che mi promiſſe dolze hor mi da fele
Hor fuſſi ſtato lhora el giorno cenere

a

Figure 2. Cerbero invoco composto per Simone Serdini Senese vocato Saviozo/
El contrario di Cerbero Che comincia Certo Jesu intendo di chiamare/
La disperata composta da Antonio de Tibaldi Ferrarese.
(By permission of the Bibliothèque nationale de France.)

proven his authorship.[72] His popularity, the fact that he was much anthologized, read, circulated, and imitated, explains in part the many attributions of his poems to other writers.[73]

In literary history, il Saviozzo's name is almost always associated with the *disperata* genre. His "Cerbero invoco e 'l suo crudo latrare" has been printed numerous times with another *disperata* written by a more popular and fortunate poet, Antonio Tebaldeo (see Chapter Three). A beautiful exemplar found in the National Library in Paris is titled *Cerbero invoco composto per Simone Serdini Senese vocato Saviozo/El contrario di Cerbero Che comincia Certo Jesu intendo di chiamare/La disperata composta da Antonio de Tibaldi Ferrarese* (Réserve Yd. 617, ca. 1510–13).[74] In addition, Dennis Rhodes lists ten more editions of this *disperata*, all dated between ca. 1495 and ca. 1513; thus, several of these are considered *incunabula*, and are accompanied by beautiful, detailed reproductions of their first pages (Figure 2).[75] Il Saviozzo's three texts mark a crucial moment in the history of the *disperata* because they represent the genre's transformation from a *canzone*-like form, as seen with Beccari and mostly throughout the Trecento,[76] to the *capitolo*-like form in *terza rima*, characterized by a narrative list of elements that would be fully adopted by later generations of poets.[77]

Il Saviozzo mostly wrote love poetry, but he also wrote political and religious verses that were directly addressed to powerful figures including Pope Innocent VII.[78] He wrote on command and traveled from court to court, spending most of his life in various towns in Tuscany.[79] As with many of his fellow poets, he was hired to write, but after finding his way into several disputes with his employers as well as with other powerful men, he was unable to lead a successful and relatively peaceful life.[80] Fortune is, therefore, a central theme in his poetry, a key figure that the poet-persona repeatedly and vociferously blames for his unhappiness and adversities.[81]

Il Saviozzo's three *disperate*, all in the *capitolo* form, are long compositions pervaded by the main, traditional traits of the genre. However, il Saviozzo personalizes and enriches the genre with the darkest despair and other *topoi*, which are new elements that will thereafter become inherent characteristics of the *disperata*. Moreover, these *disperate* are suicide poems: because despair is no longer bearable, the text becomes a suicide note in which the *disperato* communicates his final wishes, and the stark realization that death has become his only last hope and desire. However, he longs not for a quick death, but one filled with drawn out and tortured moments.

The first *disperata* that I discuss is "Cerbero invoco e 'l suo crudo latrare," which contains one hundred and forty-five intense verses full of hopeless images and misery, marked by an austere confessional tone. From the first to the last line, readers are absorbed in the ominous curses that pervade the text. Furthermore, the lover-persona blames Love for all of his anguish, and he fills his last days with the memory of the names of the miserable mythological lovers who, like him, have been doomed, deceived, and abandoned. However, among all of these unfortunate lovers, the speaker himself is by far the most harmed by Cupid, and he is worse off than if he were dead:

> Non fe' d'alcun Cupido tanto strazio
> Quant'egli ha fatto della vita mia,
> Che son peggio che morto e non è sazio.

(Cupid didn't torture anybody else/As much as he tortured my life,/As I am worse than dead, and he is still not satisfied.) (vv. 46–48, 219).

As mentioned, another characteristic of the genre is the lover's search for solitary and forsaken places in which to freely voice his sorrow. Il Saviozzo makes the most of this *topos* by nuancing it with personal and intimate reflections. The quest for exile is obsessively repeated by the verb "vò," "I go." Only cruel animals accompany the poetic persona:

> Ma poi che piace al ciel che così sia,
> abitar vo' fra boschi e mutar forma,
> menando vita indomita e restìa.
> E vo' che la pietà per me si dorma,
> per monti alpestri e per diserte piaggi
> vo' seguitar de' faüni la torma;
> orsi, tigri, leon crudi e selvaggi
> vo' in compagnia, e per abitazione
> caverne e antri e pruni e folti faggi.

(Since this pleases the sky,/I go to inhabit the woods and change my appearance,/leading an indomitable and restless life./I go so that pity is far away from me,/through mountains and through deserted beaches/I go and follow the troop of animals;/cruel and wild bears, tigers, and lions/in their company, and for abode,/I go to caverns and grottoes and thorn bushes and dense beech trees.) (vv. 49–57, 219).

The search for solitary places, abandoned forests, grottoes, and the wilderness goes hand in hand with fierce animals, another one of the main characteristics of the *disperata*, which welcome the hopeless poet-persona and become witnesses of his despair.[82] Lions, falcons, wild birds, tigers, bears, and snakes inhabit this infernal landscape, surrounded by macabre settings that mirror the narrator's frame of mind and add an element of eeriness to the *disperato*'s sense of space. Rather than with fellow humans, he would rather be alone with wild beasts, oppressed by the constant threat of being devoured by them. This is still a better prospect than the hell he is enduring on Earth.

The poetic persona often blames Love for much of history, mythology, and his own world's misfortunes:

> E voi, giovan gentil, che incominciate
> a seguitar le vestigie d'Amore
> che già tante camicie ha 'nsanguinate,
> prendete esempio al mio grave dolore

(And you, kind youth, who start/to follow Love's traces/who has already stained of blood so many,/let my grave sorrow serve as an example). (vv. 73–76, 220).

This *disperata* is particularly rich with invectives against Love, as in verses 82 to 102, "Amore fe' fratricida esser Medea" (Love made Medea commit a fratricide) (v. 82, 220), "Amor fe' convertir Damne in alloro" (Love changed Daphne into laurel) (v. 85, 220), "Amor crudel con la sua voglia innorma" (Cruel Love with its enormous desire) (v. 91, 220), and "Amor protervo, ingrato e traditore" (Arrogant Love, ungrateful and treacherous) (v. 94, 220), because Love, and not the beloved, becomes the target of the poet-persona's many outbursts. Moreover, in a stern warning, the reader is advised not to fall under its cruel spell:

> E per mille ragioni il ver discerno:
> Chi prende questo Amor falso a seguire,
> Uccide il corpo e l'alma va all'inferno

(And for a thousand reasons I tell the truth:/Who follows this false Love,/Kills the body and the soul goes to Hell) (vv. 112–114, 221).

In order to learn more about Love's deceptions, the reader is encouraged to read Ovid, who has already denounced Love:

> Io non potrei con mille lingue dire
> quel c'ha già fatto Amor con falsi inganni,
> ma legga Ovidio chi ne vuol sentire
> (vv. 114–116, 221).

Thus, the one hundred and forty-two verse *disperata* continues to fiercely condemn Love and Fortune, and then ends with a desperate final death wish:

> Preso ho partito e disposto il core
> morir contento e non mi doler d'altro,
> purché pace mi renda il mio signore,
> se non è in questo mondo, almen nell'altro.

> (I have made my decision and ordered my heart/I die happy and nothing else hurts,/as long as my master grants me peace,/if not in this world, in the next.) (vv. 139–142, 222).

The "I" of the speaker is omnipresent in the first-person verbs and in the repetition of the pronouns "mine" and "me." It is mostly through these personal markers that the poet-persona asserts himself, invades the space of his composition, and gets in the readers' face to exert his power of persuasion. While a series of mythological characters infiltrate the text, a close reading reveals that these are all reflections of the poet-persona's subjective "I," as they are metaphors for the speaker himself. Their sad, timeless adventures are used to mirror his many misfortunes, which have themselves become myth in the poetry of the *disperata*, and, therefore, not to be forgotten. Since Love is being blamed for much of history's, mythology's, and his own misfortunes, he shall join the company of mythological lovers that greatly suffered. "Cerbero invoco e il suo latrare" is a particularly compelling *disperata* precisely because of the speaker's vicious curses against Love launched by the anaphora "Amor" from verse 82 to verse 102: "Amore fe' fratricida esser Medea," "Amor fe' convertir Damne in alloro," "Amor crudel con la sua voglia innorma," "Amor protervo, ingrato e traditore." Love becomes the target of the speaker's many outbursts. In a repetition of maledictions, he blames Love and forewarns those who long to fall under its cruel spell. Death should be much preferred to this state of hopelessness, waiting for Love to be kind:

> Or m'avesse il furor di Giove morto
> quel giorno ch'i' rimasi nella rete
> d'Amor crudel, che mi fa tanto torto!

(I wish Jupiter had struck and killed me/that day when I was caught in the net/of cruel Love, who wrongs me so!) (vv. 10–12, 218).

The poem ends with an inner reflection on the world which feels eerily real, and it is clearly centered on the poetic persona's feelings and the ways in which he perceives his reality.

> Dolenti versi miei, vo'vi pregare
> ch'andiate a ciascheduno innamorato,
> piangendo, il mio dolore a raccontare.
> Direte loro il mio misero stato
> e qual fu la cagion ch'Amor mi prese
> col laccio che m'ha il cor tanto serrato.

(Oh my sorrowful verses, I beg you/go to each lover/crying, divulging my pain./Tell them of my miserable state/and the reason Love took me/with its lasso which tightens my heart so.) (vv. 127–132, 221–222).

Il Saviozzo's second *disperata*, "Le 'nfastidite labbra in ch'io già pose" is his most famous. Here, the speaker powerfully captures the reader's attention with his ferocious and vivid images, beginning with the very first verse, "Le 'nfastidite labbra in ch'io già pose" (68). The poem opens with a contemplation of his art of composing verses, first in the past, when his lips sang Love rhymes, and then now in the present, when they instead ought to lament his misfortunes. This personal reflection is encountered in other *disperate* as well, such as, for example, in Nocturno Napolitano's poem, where bitter thoughts abound on the speaker's life before his misfortunes began, and at present, when all hope and prospect for a better life are gone (Chapter Five).

Rather than addressing the Muses, here il Saviozzo destabilizes the lyric tradition by addressing the infernal Furies. This is yet another fundamental element that distinguishes the *disperata* from other genres.[83] Furthermore, the first verses are a tragic call for death because life is not worth living:

> O Furïe infernali,
> …
> voi m'aiutate, e poi ch'alla partita
> de l'alma trista mia (d)el corpo infetto
> sarà da voi accolta e seppellita.
> …
> venga per me con Cerbaro e Anteo!

(Oh infernal Furies,/ ... /help me and then, when my sad soul/leaves my infected body/it will be welcomed and buried by you./ ... / Come for me with Cerberus and Antaeus!) (vv. 7–16, 69).

The poem then exhausts all other *topoi* of its genre and builds in a crescendo of maledictions, starting with the first days of the narrator's life, as in Beccari's poem above, which prompts the very first curse. In crude and realistic terms, the speaker asserts that his mother's vulva should have been closed so that he could have died at birth:

> O vulva adulterata, orrida e vana,
> perché non ti serrasti sul dolore,
> sì che con teco insieme io fusse morto?
> (vv. 23–25, 69).

But having been born, he asks, why could he not have been born crooked or without limbs so that his heart could be fed to dogs? (vv. 26–28, 69). After all, his life should have not continued beyond his first breaths. Il Saviozzo is obsessed with his birth as the beginning of his wretched life, but in a very subversive way. Instead of venerating both and valuing his days, he focuses on the idea that if his conception hadn't happened, he would have not known such suffering.

The *disperata*'s maledictions go hand in hand with desire, often in the emphatic form of the conditional "vorrei," "I wish," because contradictory emotions and wishes are both typical elements of the genre, as are expressions such as "I should want" and "I wish," especially when they are positioned and repeated as anaphora, tercet after tercet. Il Saviozzo's wishes are rooted in the speaker's desire to assert his will, "vorrei" or "vorria," and are used frequently in order to emphasize his wants and demands, but also actions, as in the following example:

> Vorrei, poi ch'io men veggio esser di fora,
> con quanti mai ne piobber fitto al centro
> e chi più 'l cielo adora
> fusse con meco rüinato dentro!

(I wish, since I see myself be out of sorts/and with all that comes straight down/and those who adore the sky/would be ruined inside with me!) (vv. 92–96, 71–72).

Moreover, they craft a role for the reader as witness to the poetic persona's many misfortunes and dramas. We are called to watch and to listen as his desires are one by one defeated despite his mighty will.

It should be noted that this *disperata*, "Le 'nfastidite labbra in chi'io già pose" features two captions. The first reads, "Since Simon was kicked out of Siena, he composed this written malediction," and the second reads, "*Canzone* by Simone di ser Dino da Siena, chancellor of the Count of Urbino, written while in prison, and then with a knife he miserably killed himself. Moral *canzone* in which he damns everything."[84] The first caption describes his poem as simply a "written malediction," as it indeed contains an abundance of curses, while the second names it a *canzone*, twice, as other writers do when referring to their *disperata*, such as, for example, Beccari's "canzon nova di pianto."

Together with other conventional *topoi* of the genre, this *disperata* is particularly rich in suggestive images of cannibalism, starting with the very first verse, as lips and mouth symbolize an entrance to the inner self of the writer; his mother's vulva, which, if kept closed, would have killed him; the dog meant to devour the speaker's heart; his own wish to devour his sad father; and dreams of being devoured by a wild beast. Once in hell, Satan will certainly devour him, and then the Centaur will do the same. Hence, the verb "devour" and its derivatives reappear throughout the text and become a central thematic metaphor: the desire to completely disappear in somebody or something else's body, flesh and soul consumed and gone forever. Il Saviozzo capitalizes also on the *topos* of the descent into hell, from which he weaves these images of cannibalism. Hell and all its creatures swallow the speaker, together with all prospects to ever come back to earth. And this is clearly what he desires the most.

This disturbed vision continues as well in il Saviozzo's third *disperata*, "Corpi celesti e tutte l'altre stelle," a popular text that, according to Martines, expresses the poet's experience of a reality thoroughly lived: "The poem's rush of cruel maledictions is calculated to offend by turning all established values upside down; but its real work is to keep Serdini focused, to hold him together in the midst of his furious reality, as he strives to transmute horror."[85] As has been stated before, depictions of an overturned world and its values are a well-established *topos* of the *disperata*, and one intended to better depict the speaker's "furious reality." Furthermore, many of this poem's verses are fashioned from a ready collection of maledictions—melancholic relics from a happier past that are forced to look toward a completely doomed future. In reality, however, there is no future to be had because the speaker's full being is consumed by a fundamental burden: the profound belief that he is at the end of the world as he knows it. Because of the calls for his own death, this *disperata* as well becomes a suicide poem, a bequest from a desperate man who no longer sees redemption in his future and is determined to write his final words.

"Le 'nfastidite labbra inch'io già pose" depicts a macabre and realistic description of hell and of its inhabitants, providing suggestive images and language that will inspire other poems of despair. Dark caverns, grottoes, and crypts, as well as hell's entrance are again the *disperato*'s favorite setting. Here is where he longs to be the most, and hell becomes a comfortable setting. Thus, the descent into Avernus embodies the ultimate wish:

> Or fusse tosto almen che l'impudico
> corpo si separasse fra' mortali
> e l'anima ch'io dico
> portassin poi le Furïe infernali!

(I wish at least that the indecent/body separate itself from the mortals/and that the soul that I name/be carried away by the infernal Furies!) (vv. 61–64, 70–71).

The descent becomes the speaker's wish because it is an easier endeavor than his current life's tribulations. In hell, at least the devil is ready to welcome him:

> Quivi Satàn, coi dispietati artigli
> m'accogliarà fra tanti incliti viri,
> da poi che 'l corpo fia pasto di fera;

(Here, Satan, with his fierce claws/will welcome me among the many prone creatures,/so that my body may be fed to the beasts;) (vv. 65–67, 71).

There, he will be in the company of other miserable souls and of infernal monsters, where he will be slowly devoured by beasts and the Centaurs. This scenario is better than his current life, which he wishes to end as soon as possible. Hence, the poem also deals with life before and after death, but, contrary to Christian teachings, the speaker wishes to be in Hell rather than Paradise. After a thorough comparison of his miserable existence on Earth and in hell, the poet-persona determines that nothing can come close to his current life. Thus, after contemplating the most horrific scenarios, he unequivocally chooses to be devoured by monsters, as he will be finally liberated from his current earthly pangs.

Few scholars have commented at length about il Saviozzo's violent death in prison, which took place after the writing of his last *disperata*, "Le 'nfastidite labbra in ch'io già pose," around 1419–20.[86] Although the threat of suicide and the wish for a violent death is a *topos* of all *disperate*, il Saviozzo seems to have been the only writer to have actually fulfilled his wish to die by supposedly violently stabbing himself to death.[87] As in other *disperate*, il Saviozzo's ends with the speaker addressing his own poem, which also will be better off lodged in horrible places with similarly desperate souls, because this is where they both belong:

> Canzon, tu cercarai Cariddi e Silla
>
> ...
> poi te ne va fra le maligne stelle.
> Con le più disperate e tapinelle
> anime parlarai

(Song, you will find Charybdis and Scylla/ ... /then you will go among the malignant stars./With the most desperate and miserable/souls you will talk) (vv. 97–104, 72).

The poem and its author are better off dead than alive. In another reversal of the literary tradition, the "canzon" is doomed to travel and be known among the dead, and not among us readers. The fatal promise, "do tell them that soon I'll be among them" (vv. 97–106, 72), recurs in other *disperate*, such as, for example, in Morra's *canzoni* (Chapter Two).

Finally, the last *disperata* I examine by il Saviozzo, "Corpi celesti e tutte l'altre stelle," abounds with maledictions that spare nothing and nobody. Although it is a much shorter poem with only eighty-one verses, it repeats a devastating series of damnations that start with "Let them be damned" and few variations seventeen times. As in Beccari's *disperata*, it begins with the contemplation of the macrocosm:

> Corpi celesti e tutte l'altre stelle,
> sette pianeti, tutti i cieli e'segni
> sian maledetti

(Heavenly bodies and all other stars,/seven planets, and all heavens and signs/be damned) (vv. 1–3, 215).

The speaker then moves on to curse the whole human species, Fortune, poetry, science, the seven virtues, trees, fruits, herbs, and rocks. Since all hope is gone, he wishes to see his heart totally consumed: "poi che speranza contra me succede,/veder summerger tutto il mio cor bramo" (vv. 29–30, 216). He then curses his parents, the day he was born, and everything else: "ogni cosa in tutto maladico" (v. 65, 217). However, what distinguishes this poem is the way in which il Saviozzo creatively weaves his maledictions with an elaborate image of the world turned upside down *topos*, thus giving the whole *disperata* a tone and atmosphere of final, infernal doom:

> Sommerga il cielo, si che tenebrosa
> la luce torni e sia perpetüale,
> e in molestar giamai non trovi posa!
> Fame con guerra e morbo sia mortale,
> e, ch'egli è paradiso, caggia al fondo
> sì che si spenga per fiamma eternale;
> E Satanàs resurga, quel furbondo,
> su l'alte sedie e segnoreggi il tutto,
> poi che cotanto d'ogni ben son mondo!

(That the sky be submerged, so that a dark/light may return and be perpetual,/and that it may never stop to torment!/That hunger with war and an epidemic be mortal,/and, if it is paradise, that it may fall down,/so that it turns off as an eternal flame;/and that Satan may resurrect, that despicable one,/on the high seat, and that he may rule everything,/since I am deprived of all that is good!) (vv. 16–24, 215).

This haunting vision overturns the regular order of things: light gives way to darkness, hunger and war take over, Paradise is exhausted, and Satan rules the world as the new normalcy.

Il Saviozzo's three compositions are accomplished models of *disperata*, featuring the repetition of a rich variety of maledictions and the combination of the genre's core elements, such as fierce animals, mythological characters, desolate places, and tropes, which combine in order to inspire future writers including Serafino, Tebaldeo, Sasso, and Morra. Furthermore, the use of the *terza rima* reaches a pinnacle in his poetry, as il Saviozzo demonstrates his skills and agility with this meter. He not only adopted the genre, but he also built on it, developing and increasing its notoriety, as shown by the many editions of "Cerbero invoco" in both Italy and France, thus solidifying its images, language, and narrative structure. His deeply personal narrative had a vast and profound impact throughout the Quattrocento, and his name came to be closely associated with the *disperata* genre.[88] Moreover, il Saviozzo's dramatic demise contributed to his renown and fueled the eccentric legend that would endure in the following centuries.[89] He is undoubtedly accountable for solidifying the *disperata* genre and its expansions in Southern Italy, and mainly at the Naples court, where it was readily adopted by poets such as Cariteo, Morra, and

Nocturno, as we will see in the following chapters.[90] He also authored *disperate femminili*, written in the voice of a young woman, that testify even more to his dexterity and popularity in this genre as will be discussed in Chapter Two.

The Fourteenth-Century *Disperata*

Beccari and il Saviozzo are undoubtedly the two main interpreters of the *disperata*. However, the Trecento offers additional significant examples of *disperate* starting with those by Giannozzo Sacchetti (ca. 1340–79), who used this genre to express his misery, employing particularly numerous and fervent invectives against Fortune. Despite the fact that Sacchetti was an ambassador at the court of Milan and was part of the literary circles in Northern Italy, he struggled economically and politically throughout his life, ending with a tragic death sentence in Florence. Rooted in specific biographical tragedies, Sacchetti's verses are sparse but demonstrate a keen literary intensity and passion.[91]

> Poich'io son giunto in parte che'l dolore
> tanto m'aggrava e sì forte m'afferra
> che m'abbatte per terra
> si com'uom da Fortuna vinto e stanco,
> aprirò il petto mio con quel valore
> che debolezza chiave lo disserra,
> narrando l'aspra guerra
> ch'alla mia barca Fortuna fa anco

(Since I have come in part to be/so afflicted by sorrow and so tightly held/that this pushes me down/as a man won and exhausted by Fortune,/I will open up my chest with that valor/that weakness locks up with a key,/and I will tell of the harsh war/that Fortune wages against my ship) (vv. 1–8, 148).[92]

The first image is one of deep pain that pushes the speaker to literally "open up" about it and figuratively open up his chest, "aprirò il petto." He also speaks of his intention to narrate his harsh reality, again, in order to make his despair well known to his readers. As with other *disperate*, Fortune is a key oppositional figure that sparks many outbursts, vituperations, and condemnations. Although Sacchetti's images are not as violent as those found in other *disperate*, the poet-persona fully develops some of the genre's constant themes, such as hopelessness, "già fuor d'ogni speranze e di soccorso" (v. 12, 149), and a call for his own death, "fa' ch'i morto diventi" (v. 63, 150). Death always elicits vivid praises and desires, because, as the *disperata*'s final request, it symbolizes the antidote to all earthly misery. Although a pathetic and gloomy tone lingers in Sacchetti's text, his verses, referred to by their author as "canzon," never reach violent excesses and tirades as in other compositions, and conclude with a sober acceptance of life's tribulations and man's inability to influence, let alone control, his own destiny:

> Canzon, tu vedi ben com'io rimango
> padrone afflitto della trista nave;
> però non ti sia grave
> d'andarne tosto dove più ti cale:
> dì che contro a Fortuna nessun vale.

(Song, you can well see how I remain/the afflicted captain of my sad ship;/but it is not hard/for you to go where you wish:/and do tell that no one has any worth against Fortune.) (vv. 87–91, 151).

Francesco di Vannozzo (ca. 1340–ca. 1390) is also a writer who skillfully adopted the *disperata* genre. Like other fellow poets, he traveled from court to court in Northern Italy and France in order to follow possible writing and diplomatic assignments.[93] Considered by critics to be the most important and rich in court lyric of Northern Italy during the Trecento, his *canzoniere* presents a wide variety of poetic genres that intersect with his *disperate*.[94] In fact, Vannozzo's poetry is greatly characterized by auto-biographical content and by a concrete preoccupation with daily life's necessities and vices, such as gambling, drinking, and surviving destitution—issues that severely marginalized the poet despite his intellectual and literary aspirations and gifts.[95] Vannozzo's many roles and varied professional experiences, such as writer, singer, *giullare* (lute and harp player) also characterize his poetry.

His work, *Rime di Francesco di Vannozzo*, remains to this day a cultural and literary document that provides a valuable insight into the role he played as a prolific and popular intellectual who worked in and around various courts.[96] The Italian scholar Ezio Levi describes at length Vannozzo's misery, poverty, and the squalor of his life, cleverly expressed in his verses:[97]

> e son da tutti abbandonato.
>
> ...
>
> il mio Signor mi stenta

poi giunge povertade a 'sti dispetti
che mi fa voglia de gettarmi en Brenta.

(I am abandoned by all./ ... /my Lord makes me struggle/then comes poverty in addition to these spites/which makes me want to throw myself in the Brenta.)[98]

The state of his living conditions is expressed in realistic images, as with the way the poet-persona is forced to sleep on stones, beaten by the wind. Furthermore, he laments how everyone abandoned him, including his patron, "il mio Signore," to which poverty adds its torture. Driven to suicide by throwing himself in the river, the poet-persona fits the profile of the *disperata* writer: poor, destitute, and forced to rely on a patron in order to survive. To end his misery, he eventually seeks his own death.

Levi has established a compelling link between Vannozzo and the French troubadour Eustache Deschamps (ca. 1340-ca. 1404), arguing that the two poets had similar characters and creativity, as well as historical circumstances, as both lived in a world dominated by the tyranny of the court. On one hand, they both witnessed grandiose balls and festivities, and on the other, they lived in deep squalor and poverty and were often threatened by war and hunger.[99] Furthermore, Vannozzo had traveled to the court of Avignon and was very familiar with French poetry of the time.[100] His *disperate* can be compared to Deschamps's verses in which the speaker also damns the time of his birth, "l'heure que je fu nez," and looks forward to his death: "à la mort humbleument je me presente/pour les tourmens dont je suis fortunez."[101] Levi quotes Deschamps's "Ballade de la vie dolente" as an example of the intertextualities shared by the two poets:

Je hais mes jours et ma vie dolente,
Et si maudis l'heure que je fus né,
Et à la mort humblement je me présente
Pour les tourments dont je suis fortuné.
Je hais ma conception
Et si maudis la constellation
Où Fortune me fit naître premier,
Quand je me vois de tous maulx parsonnier.
Car pauvreté chaque jour me tourmente:
Par son fait suis haï et diffamé.

(I hate my days and my sorrowful life,/and thus, I damn the day I was born,/and I humbly present myself to Death/for all the torments of which I am fortunate./I hate the day of my conception/Thus, I

damn the constellation/Where Fortune first gave me life,/When I
see myself afflicted by all these evils./Because poverty torments me
everyday:/And because of it, I am hated and slandered.)[102]

Several of the poem's *topoi* appear in a list that deeply exemplifies the texts
by Beccari and il Saviozzo examined above. Deschamps hates his painful
life; he damns the moment of his conception, of his birth, and the whole
cosmos ("la constellation"); he calls for his own death because of his misfortunes; and he denounces the poverty that makes other people hate and
vilify him. These are the constant elements that characterize the *disperata*
and that establish a first intertextuality with the Italian and French poets
in this study.[103]

Both Vannozzo and Deschamps carefully compile their many misfortunes in a long list where Fortune, Love, and poverty are resentfully and
vociferously blamed. Furthermore, they curse other courtiers, patrons, and
known political figures of the similar social milieus in which they both
lived.[104] Therefore, the use of maledictions and vituperations directed at
court princes, and denunciating them as the culprit for the speaker's misfortunes, also echo the many *disperate* discussed in this book. Thus, it is
important to note that, already in the fourteenth century, Vannozzo's verses
seem to establish a strong connection between French and Italian court
poetry, a relationship to which I shall return in the following chapters.

The unique nature and influential power of court life in both countries represent one of the most significant transnational aspects of this
poetry because it contributed enormously to the fortune of the *disperata*
intertext in French poetry two centuries later—as a continuum and persuasive power of the genre.[105] Deschamps describes not only his many
personal plights, but also France's darkest moments of the Hundred Years
War, descriptions that the poetry of despair in both Italy and France renders familiar in a great variety of paradigms. Vannozzo, on the other hand,
embodies the stereotype of the court poet, as he traveled, begged, and
wrote in order to please his patrons and to survive. During the fourteenth
century, the Scaligeri's court in Verona, the Carraresi's in Padua, and especially the Visconti's in Milan, greatly flourished and expanded their cultural and political influence on the entire Po Valley region.[106] As Tartaro
so eloquently calls it, the courtly "ethical-intellectual conscience" is personified by the professional court poet, whose tasks are not well-defined,
but nonetheless include several secretarial, ambassadorial, and entertaining duties stipulated by his Lord or patron.[107] This trend will continue
throughout the fifteenth and sixteenth centuries, and will develop into a

more sophisticated persona: the court humanist poet who is trapped in a socio-cultural reality that, as Tartaro describes, "fa dello scrittore un impiegato," that is makes an employee out of the writer.[108]

In conclusion, this chapter has shown the main characteristics of the genre from the beginning, how they were adopted and at times changed by each interpreter. This *poesis* generated not only a new literary tradition, but also a cultural phenomenon embraced by other Renaissance poets. Hence, my study suggests that the *disperata* embodied and carried on a rich literary culture that was embraced by the thriving courts and literary circles in Italy and France. In the latter, it is mainly through the Italian Petrarchist poets that the *disperata* tradition developed, because they were greatly anthologized, and thus more vastly read and imitated.[109] However, other less known poets wrote *disperate* that were also quickly and widely spread, as we will see in the following chapter.

NOTES

[1] Essays by Russell, Stephen Murphy, Jean-Jacques Marchand, Carla Rossi, and myself will be referenced in this study.

[2] See Paul Zumthor, "Perspectives Générales," 7.

[3] In Italy, it was developed by three influential writers: G.B. Giraldi Cinthio, Gian Giorgio Trissino, and Torquato Tasso; in France, the sixteenth century was characterized by manuals on "art poétiques", such as those by Jacques Fabri, Jacques Peletier du Mans, Thomas Sebillet, and Joachim du Bellay. See Daniel Javitch, "Self-justifying Norms in the Genre Theories of Italian Renaissance Poets," François Leclercle, "Théoriciens Français et italiens: une 'politique' des genres," Ellen Ginsberg, "Genre Theory in the French Renaissance," and Gerard Gros and Marie-Madeleine Fragonard, *Les Formes poétiques du Moyen Age à la Renaissance*, 95–98.

[4] Jauss, "Littérature médiévale et théorie des genres," 79–101.

[5] Ibid., 81.

[6] Ibid., 95.

[7] For the "space" of the poem, see Jean Jaffré, who convincingly shows that the poem is surrounded by large, white margins, and the verses seem to trace it. *Le vers et le poème*, 30.

[8] Tissoni Benvenuti for example, considers the *disperata* a *capitolo ternario*, "La tradizione della terza rima e l'Ariosto", 304–306. This also follows Dante's *Divina Commedia*'s rhyme scheme with a long series of tercets that end with a single, final line as a concluding verse.

[9] See Chapter Three, in which I discuss this phenomenon at length. Since genres such as the *capitolo* or elegy were more popular, some writers and editors would index the *disperata* under them. This is also the case of some French Medieval genres, such as the *chanson de toile*, the *reverdie*, and, the *aube*. See Zumthor, "Perspectives générales," 9.

[10] See for example Jean-Jacques Marchand, "Le disperate di Antonio Tebaldeo," 163.

[11] See Giovan Mario Crescinbeni, *Dell'Istoria della volgar poesia* who mentions an anonymous *contro-disperata* found in *Fioretto di cose nove di diversi Autori*, 204.

[12] See for example Pèrcopo who mentions the most popular *contro-disperata*, "Lauda contro la 'Nuda terra', dita Disperata" in "Una disperata famosa," 702, and Cian, who discusses few manuscripts that contain *contro-disperate*. In *Le rime di Bartolomeo Cavassino*, ccxxxii–ccxxxv. However, the *contro-disperata* never reached the popularity of its counter genre.

[13] Francesco Saverio Quadrio, *Della storia, e della ragione d'ogni poesia*, 2:567.

[14] Quadrio offers several anecdotes, for example from Horace, who calls these poems "Preghiere Tiestee" because Tieste damned his brother Atreo who murdered Tieste's son, and served him to his father as a meal. Quadrio thus, calls *disperata* those pomes filled with curses. *Della storia, e della ragione*, 567–568.

[15] Ibid., 568. See also Crescinbeni, *Dell'Istoria della volgar poesia*, 69–70, 204–5, and 449.

[16] Cian, *Le rime di Bartolomeo Cavassico*, LXXXVIII.

[17] Russell, "Intenzionalità artistica della disperata," 168.

[18] Cian, LXXXVIII. Other critics as well find in this poem the same grotesque maledictions. See for example Vittorio Dornetti, *Aspetti e figure della poesia minore trecentista*, 126. However, although Angiolieri's is also a poem of deep personal angst, its content does not encompass the macrocosmic hopelessness that we find in the *disperata*.

[19] Francesco Flamini, *La lirica toscana del Rinascimento*, 531–532.

[20] Ibid., 532.

[21] Vittorio Rossi, *Il Quattrocento*, 372.

[22] Dante Alighieri, *The Divine Comedy*.

[23] See Joseph Delany, "Despair" in *The Catholic Encyclopedia*, Vol. 4 (New York: Robert Appleton Company, 1908). (29 Dec. 2015), http://www.newadvent.org/cathen/04755a.htm. Kierkegaard offers an interesting philosophical approach to despair in his *The Sickness onto Death*.

[24] Aquinas, *The Summa Theologica*, http://www.sacred-texts.com/chr/aquinas/summa/sum275.htm

[25] Ibid., 306.

[26] Russell groups *disperate* with *canzoni*, *capitoli* and sonnets written against Fortune, and against the narrator's socio-economical hardships and malaise, arguing that this particular content had a specific socio-cultural function, because, fundamentally, "the *disperata* is an expression of profound rage and autobiographical conditions." 166. However, her article on the *disperata* is part of a book that studies priceseley medieval genres as its title clearly indicates: *Generi poetici medievali: modelli e funzioni*.

[27] See *L'elegia nella tradizione poetica italiana*, and in particular, Vecchi Galli's contribution, "Percorsi dell'elegia quattrocentesca in volgare," 54–55, and Gentili, "Il capitolo in terza rima," 118. They both cite Antonio da Ferrara's *disperata* "Le stelle universali e i ciel rotanti" as an influential intertext for other compositions written in *terza rima*. On the *disperata* and the elegy, see also Marchand, "Le disperate di Antonio Tebaldeo," who argues that fundamentally, the *disperata* is an elegiac text, 163. I will also discuss the relationship between genres in a later chapter, as in France as well we see the same phenomenon. However, the *terza rima* will slowly disappear due to Bembo's popularity, and his predilection for shorter lyric forms, and for Petrarch and his style. See Vecchi Galli, "La poesia cortigiana tra XV e XVI secolo," 125.

[28] Vittorio Rossi, "Il canzoniere edito di Andrea Michieli detto Squarzòla o Strazzòla," 17.

[29] Ibid., 17.

[30] Tissoni-Benvenuti notes that Bembo in the 1530 edition of his *rime* excluded all *capitoli*, except for one, and instead favored the sonnet. "La tradizione della terza rima e l'Ariosto," 305.

[31] "A literary genre's historicity can manifest itself in the creation process of its structure, its variations, its expansion and in the changes that it undergoes; this process can evolve until the extinction of the genre or until it is eradicated by a new genre." Jauss, "Littérature médiévale et théorie des genres," 86.

[32] Javitch, "Self-justifying Norms in the Genre Theories," 196.

[33] See Floyd Gray who notes, "Since a *topos* is a fragment of discourse which is constantly rewritten, its repetition in successive texts causes a replacement or displacement of its meaning, making a cultural reading theoretically problematic." *Gender, Rhetoric, and Print Culture*, 165.

[34] Tartaro, *Forme poetiche*, 153.

[35] See Natalino Sapegno, *Poeti minori del Trecento*, viii.

[36] For a concise history of Renaissance Italy, see J.H. Plumb, *The Italian Renaissance*.

[37] For a concise history of Renaissance France, see Robin Gibbs, *Early Modern France*, Emmanuel Le Roy Ladurie, *L'Etat royal. De Louis XI à Henri IV*, and Mark Greengrass, *Governing Passions. Peace and Reform in the French Kingdom, 1576–1585*.

[38] Cave also explains that in humanistic rhetoric, *enargeia* is "a powerful but local device: the momentary illusion that it creates is harnessed, in theory at least, to a persuasive or epideictic function." "The Mimesis of Reading in the Renaissance," 161.

[39] Pèrcopo provides Antonio Salvazo's poem of 1512 titled "Canzone contra 'La nuda terra' per le proprie rime fata per Antonio Salvazo," as an example. This poem is a direct rebuke to il Pistoia's *disperata* beginning with its first verses, "Se la nuda tera ora muta 'l manto/verdigiante ognor, e più s'alegra,/per primavera e mi da l'altro canto." "Una disperata famosa," 705–706, and 717–718. See also Russell, "Intenzionalità artistica della disperata," 173–174.

[40] For the *topos* of "the world upside down," see Ernst Robert Curtius, *European Literature and the Latin Middle Ages*, 94–98.

[41] See Massimo Malinverni, "Note per un bestiario lirico tra Quattro e Cinquecento," 7–31.

[42] Curtius, *European Literature and the Latin Middle Ages*, 94.

[43] *Petrarch's Lyric Poems*. Robert M. Durling, ed. and trans. All references to Petrarch's poetry will be based on this edition.

[44] See the most recent *Petrarch: A Critical Guide to the Complete Works*, Victoria Kirkham and Armando Maggi, eds.

[45] Robert Trinkaus, *The Poet as Philosopher*, 27.

[46] Balsamo, "'Du florentin les lamentables voix,'" 118.

[47] A phenomenon described by Ernest Hatch Wilkins as "the writing of lyric verse under the direct or indirect influence of Petrarch in a period beginning in his lifetime and ending about 1600." In *Studies in the Life and Works of Petrarch*, 281. See in particular his chapter "A General Survey of Renaissance Petrarchism," 280–299.

[48] Forster, *The Icy Fire*, 2.

[49] Klaus W. Hempfer, "Per una definizione del Petrarchismo," 30.

[50] Balsamo, *Les Rencontres des muses*, 230.

[51] In this study, I focus on the *poesis* of Petrarch and his emulators that most intersect with *disperata* themes, images, and language. Many excellent studies have been published on Petrarch and his imitators. See *Petrarch: A Critical Guide to the Complete Works*' exhaustive bibliography.

[52] Flamini, *La lirica toscana*, 460.

[53] *Petrarch's Lyric Poems*, 561–569.

[54] Forster, *The Icy Fire*, 3–4.

[55] See Lauro Martines, "Love and Hate in Renaissance Patronage: Italy," 5–31, and "Ritual Language in Renaissance Italy," 59–76.

[56] Giuseppe Mazzotta, *The Worlds of Petrarch*, 28.

[57] Aldo Scaglione, "Cinquecento Mannerism and the Uses of Petrarch," 129–130.

[58] As do Dante's *Rime petrose*, "stony rhymes," where the poet portrays a cold and harsh woman, hard as a stone, because of her cruel indifference towards the lover-persona. See Dante Alighieri, *Rime*, in *Le opere di Dante Alighieri*, 561. See also www.danteonline.it

[59] For Beccari's biographical information, see the modern edition of his poetry, *Le Rime di Maestro Antonio da Ferrara*. All references to Beccari's poetry will be based on this edition.

[60] Russell, "Intenzionalità artistica della disperata," 164. Bellucci argues that Beccari might be the inventor of the genre, *Rime*, xxx.

[61] See Sabine Verhulst, "Fortuna, gioco e disperazione, in Antonio Beccari da Ferrara," 594.

[62] Raoul Blomme sees Beccari's poetry as possessing its very own inventiveness, particularly in this *disperata*. Blomme, however, never calls this text a "disperata," but he refers to it as "la sua più nota canzone disperata," whereby the word *disperata* is used as an adjective to qualify the *canzone*. In "'Le stelle universali e i ciel rotanti' di Maestro Antonio da Ferrara," 12.

[63] Sapegno, *Poeti minori del Trecento*, 125. At the end of this important volume, the author does not list the *disperate* in the "Indice dei capoversi," rather he identifies them as *canzoni*. Under Antonio da Ferrara's *disperata*, the critic notes "Canzone 'disperata'. È probabilmente uno degli esempi più antichi di questo 'genere', che ottenne grande fortuna nella seconda metà del Trecento e poi nel secolo seguente." 126.

[64] For an additional study on Trecento court poetry, see Dornetti, *Aspetti e figure*, 125.

[65] See Verhulst, "Fortuna, gioco e disperazione," 586.

[66] An adjective that is often associated in the Trecento and Quattrocento with the *disperata* poets is "stravagante" as if to describe a somewhat queer, extravagant, eccentric, bizarre, and certainly unconventional man of letters. See for example

Sapegno, *Poeti minori del Trecento*, 125, and Carla Rossi, *Il Pistoia, spirito bizzarro del Quattrocento*.

[67] Ibid., vii.

[68] "sia maladetto e 'l tempo vagabondo,/poich'i' son fatto tanto pusillanimo,/ ch'una pizzola volta/de dadi me pò far tristo e giocondo." (vv. 54–57, 128) Verhulst notes that the central theme of the narrator's desperation in Beccari's poetry stems from two topics: Fortune and game. In "Fortuna, gioco e disperazione," 585.

[69] Tartaro, *Forme poetiche del Trecento*, 145.

[70] Sapegno, *Poeti minori*, viii.

[71] See Flamini, *La lirica toscana*, 174, Pèrcopo, "Una disperata famosa," 706, and Guglielmo Volpi, "La vita e le rime di Simone Serdini, detto il Saviozzo," 45. This *disperata* has also been attributed to Beccari. The modern edition of Serdini's *Rime* by Giuseppe Pasquini lists all prints and manuscripts of his poetry, and indicates the various and many attributions that help to shed some light on the transmission of the poem and of the genre.

[72] See Volpi, "La vita e le rime di Simone Serdini detto il Saviozzo," who already pointed out the critics who wrote or commented on Serdini's poems, and who, according to him, published misleading information about his life and work, 1–2.

[73] See Martines, *Strong Words*, 114, and Pasquini, "Saviozzo, Simone Serdini detto il," 317–323.

[74] This is the *disperata* by il Pistoia, thus here mistakenly attributed to Tebaldeo. The poem "El contrario di Cerbero" is a *contro-disperata*.

[75] Rhodes, "Le antiche edizioni a stampa," 253–66.

[76] When discussing the *disperata*, several scholars refer to it as a *canzone*, while others refer to it as a *capitolo*. However, it is important to point out that those who refer to it as a "disperata" argue that it is indeed a genre on its own standing, with its particular content and merit. As mentioned, some *canzonieri* list *disperate* separately, others list them under *capitoli* or *canzoni*.

[77] Russell, "Intenzionalità artistica della disperata," 166.

[78] Martines provides a compelling analysis of the main themes in il Saviozzo's work: political, religious, and love poetry, as well as his treatment of "Dame Fortune" and its various personifications. According to Martines, Saviozzo's drama of unrequited love is particularly telling: "But whatever the nature of his loves –hence the mystery- Saviozzo's way was for deep involvement, in contrast to other Renaissance poets, for whom love, as voiced in verse, was more often and more nearly the striking of a social stance and a self- definition ... His about-face against love, therefore, could be vehement enough to carry him toward the desolation of his suicide poems." *Strong Words*, 128.

[79] Martines notes that il Saviozzo traveled in various capacities, but mostly as a *condottiero* to rulers, thus, Martines's conclusion that he "lived with (and from) some of the worst of men." *Strong Words*, 129–30. This itinerant life, lack of a fam-

ily and of a stable home, very lonely conditions, dubious friendships, and harsh lords would explain in part the gruesome outlook on life found in his poetry.

[80] For a detailed account of il Saviozzo's life, see Volpi, "La vita e le rime di Simone Serdini," and Martines, *Strong Words*, 113–136.

[81] See for example Canzone VI, where its two captions accuse Fortune of his misery, the first, "Canzon sesta, ove non osando incolpare cui forse credo, al mio martire, incolpo Fortuna" (Sixth song, where I accuse Fortune of my martyrdom, rather than accusing the person I think I should), and the second, "Canzon morale del detto Simone, dove si lamenta della Fortuna" (Moral song by the so called Simone, where he complains about Fortune). Serdini, *Rime*, 17.

[82] See Malinverni, "Note per un bestiario lirico," 8–31.

[83] See Curtius, who notes that addressing the Muses is one of the main constants in the early western literary tradition. *European Literature and the Latin Middle Ages*, 228.

[84] First caption, "Essendo Simon per parte distaccato da Siena, fece l'infrascritta maleditione." The second caption, "Canzon di Simone di ser Dino da Siena, cancelliero del conte d'Urbino, la qual composta essendo in presone, con uno coltello miseramente si uccise. Canzon morale dove maladice tutte le cose." Ibid., 68.

[85] Martines, *Strong Words*, 133.

[86] Volpi, "La vita e le rime di Simone Serdini," 17, and Martines, *Strong Words*, 113.

[87] However, Volpi only sees in these lines the same threat found in most *disperate*, and wonders how these claims were never made for other *disperate*'s authors. He then argues that the *disperata* is a suicide poem and that the call for death is a literary *topos*. Due to the lack of documents, il Saviozzo's cause of death cannot be verified.

[88] See for example Dormetti, "Aspetti," 127.

[89] See for example Flamini: "il Serdini ha coltivato meglio di tutti questo genere di poesia; probabilmente, come fu osservato, perché rispondeva a sentimenti da lui provati davvero." *La lirica toscana*, 533.

[90] See Pasquini, "Il Saviozzo e la poesia cortigiana nel Quattrocento," 322. Pasquini convincingly traces il Saviozzo's intertextuality from Siena to the courts of Northern and Southern Italy.

[91] Sapegno, *Poeti minori del Trecento*, 147.

[92] Ibid., 148. All references to Sacchetti's poetry will be based on this edition. This very violent image of the narrator's chest being opened up by adversity, whether is misfortune or a cruel lady, will be found also in d'Aubigné's and Nuysement's poetry, discussed in the following chapters. See also my "*Le Printemps* and the Poetics of Dissection," in *European Studies Journal*.

[93] Sapegno, *Poeti minori del Trecento*, 191, and Ezio Levi, *Francesco di Vannozzo*, 307. This study closely analyzes Vannozzo's and Deschamps's lyrics, and compellingly points out the many parallels between the two writers. For a modern

edition of Vannozzo's poetry, see *Le Rime di Francesco di Vannozzo* and Roberta Manetti, "Per una nuova edizione delle rime di Francesco di Vannozzo, 403–417. See also Tartaro, *Forme poetiche del Trencento*, 148–156.

[94] See Sapegno, *Poeti minori del Trecento*, 191.

[95] See Francesco di Vannozzo (Vannozii, Vannocci, de Vanotio, de Vannocchio), Gabriella Milan, ed. *Dizionario Biografico degli Italiani*, Vol. 50 (1998) in http://www.treccani.it/enciclopedia/francesco-di-vannozzo_%28Dizionario-Biografico%29/.

[96] *Rime di Francesco di Vannozzo tratte da un codice inedito del secolo XIV*.

[97] Ibid., 305. Vannozzo's *canzoniere* contains 5 *canzoni*, 4 *frottole*, 4 *ballate*, 2 *madrigali*, and 153 sonnets. In the sonnets, Levi identifies many of the *disperata*'s themes and attitudes, xvi.

[98] Cited by Levi, *Francesco di Vannozzo*, 305.

[99] Ibid., 307, and Manetti, "Per una nuova edizione," 403–17.

[100] Ibid., 292.

[101] Ibid., 305. See *Oeuvres Complètes de Eustache Deschamps*.

[102] Levi, *Francesco di Vannozzo*, 306.

[103] In another ballad, Deschamps damns his patrons: "Princes, gens plus mauvaiz ne vy/De ceulz qui ne m'ont pas en grace./Pour ce leur offre et ce leur di:/ Maudiz soiez de par Eustace." Here, the poet describes the injuries and brutalities he suffered at the hand of the court. In *Eustache Deschamps et son temps*, 201–202.

[104] France's role in the development of Medieval literature was crucial, thanks to its geographical centrality between the Roman Empire and the Germanic territories, as well as to its humanistic enterprises, and to its schools of Provençal poetry. See Luigi Rango, "Prospettive di Letteratura Europea," 1056.

[105] Stephen G. Nichols explains that Deschamps stands in his time as "a lively observer of his tumultuous century, a century afflicted by war, climatic changes, the plague, and economic downturns." In *Eustache Deschamps*, viii.

[106] See also Malinverni, "La lirica volgare padana tra Boiardo e Ariosto". For additional examples of fourteenth-century texts, see also Giuseppe Corsi, *Rimatori del Trecento*.

[107] See Tartaro, *Forme poetiche del Trecento*, 128.

[108] Ibid., 128.

[109] The Giolito anthologies became the main vehicle through which Petrarchism disseminated. See DellaNeva, *Unlikely Exemplars*, Diana Robin, *Publishing Women*, Angela Nuovo and Christian Coppens, *I Giolito e la stampa del XVI secolo*, Balsamo, *Les Rencontres des muses*, Louise George Clubb and William G. Clubb, "Building a Lyric Canon: Gabriel Giolito and the Rival Anthologists," Bodo L. O. Richter, "Printers and Poets: Notes on Giolito and the Petrarchists," Vianey, *Le Pétrarquisme en France*, and Salvatore Bongi, ed. *Annali di Gabriel Giolito de' Ferrari da Trino di Monferrato*.

Chapter Two

The Female-Voiced *Disperata*

In questi luoghi oscuri,
Non voglio ch'el tuo canto mai si tempre,
Ma che tu piangi, piangi, sempre, sempre.

Felice Feliciano

Intersections of Genre and Gender

In this chapter, I explore the intersections of genre and gender and the appropriation of the female voice in the *disperata femminile*. We will examine despair, which is central to the *disperata* genre, and how it is articulated in female and male voices, including the strategies used to create these voices. We will seek to answer how a female voice fits within the genre and whether the male authors can authentically express female despair. As *disperata* and Petrarchism intersect, so does genre intersect with gender. This chapter investigates the interplay between the *disperata* genre and gender; how the beloved is portrayed; how Love itself becomes more important than the beloved, and, most of all, how female despair is appropriated, voiced, and represented by a male author. Furthermore, since many *disperate* were written or were part of collections for women patrons, including Galeotto del Carretto's and Antonio Tebaldeo's work, gender is deeply inscribed in the genre and an integral component of the socio-economic issues intrinsic to the court. Female patrons, including Isabella d'Este and Elisabetta Gonzaga, entertained deep friendships and correspondence with many of the poets studied in this book.[1]

As has been stated before, the beloved depicted in the *disperata* is not painstakingly described in all of her splendor, unlike Petrarch's Laura, for example, nor do the effects of her physical beauty cause the poet-persona either much admiration or harm. If Petrarch praises Laura and her beauty in countless poems of his *Canzoniere*, "Donna, per me vostra bellezza in rima" (XX, vv. 2, 55), as he literally scatters her loveliness in his verses— her beautiful eyes, ruby smile, and golden hair—the *disperato*, on the other hand, does not praise his beloved and her body, nor does he overtly admire her beauty. In fact, instead of praises, she incites damnations, and instead of her beauty, it is her cruelty that is exposed. She is blamed, cursed, and chastised for the speaker's misery and hopelessness. For example, Rosello Roselli depicts a sadistic woman who destroyed him: "costei che m'ha distrutto" (v. 102, p 29); d'Aubigné a cruel one: "Plus cruelle que tout ce que puis nommer" (v. 98, 15), and Théophile de Viau blames the lady for his death: "elle a des choleres/Qui me poussent au monument." (vv. 17–18, 30).[2] Remarkably, feminine physicality is almost always absent in the *disperata* genre. Furthermore, while the beloved is an object of desire, she is not an object of contemplation; therefore, readers are often left to imagine what she looks like, and soon, they realize that the poem is really not about the beloved. Rather, it is about the despair and suffering she causes, and thus, the poem is poet-centered and focuses deeply on the writer's or the speaker's wretched state. Hence, a detailed, blazon-like description of the beloved would take the readers' attention away from the poets' main concern, which is instead their true stories of hopelessness. The poetic persona has to remain the focal point throughout his tales of despair.

While Love is certainly an important presence in Petrarch's poetry, as seen in the previous chapter, its manifestation is strictly related to Laura and the descriptions of her beauty. In the *disperata*, on the other hand, Love is the main culprit of much misery. For example, in Panfilo Sasso's "Disperata contro Amore," (Disperata against Love) which became an authoritative intertext for many other *disperate*, Love is cursed and blamed for all of the speaker's inner turmoil. Its presence on the page represents rejection and suffering. Thus, the poet feels even more marginalized. Moreover, self-love and unfulfilled love provide ample opportunities for introspective analysis, in which suffering replaces the beloved who only hovers at its periphery. The poet directs the narrative and the reader onto himself, rather than onto the "other," who, in turn, embodies only an excuse, because the poem is already about a time and space of complete rejection and solitude.

Remarkably, in their other lyric work, the poets of the *disperata* almost always adopted Petrarch's highly conventional system, as in this sonnet by Sasso, where the beloved is described and admired in detail. She is immediately identified as a woman and as the object of desire and devotion: "Chi vuol conoscere veramente quella/La gual devotamente in terra adoro." (Who wants to meet the one/Whom on earth I devotely adore.)[3] The poetic persona then focuses on her physical attributes, clearly inscribing this sonnet in the Petrarchan tradition:

Immagini più fila d'un fin oro:
Questa è la chioma sua candida e bella.
L'un occhio e l'altro son la prima stella
E la quarta che adorna il sommo coro;
La mano e 'l petto un bel pezzo d'avoro,
L'aspetto di colomba e tortorella.
Le labbra rose, e le dolci parole
Un canto ben soave e misurato,
Il riso un prato adorno di viole.

(Imagine more strings than fine gold:/This is her light and beautiful hair./One eye and the other are the first star/And the fourth that adorns the high choir;/Her hand and chest a beautiful piece of ivory,/The appearance of a kind dove./Her ruby lips, and sweet words/A pleasing and dignified song,/Her laugh a meadow adorned with violets.)

This sonnet is entirely concerned with the blazon-like description of the lady's body, part by part, and based on the awareness between male sonneteer and reader of the immense pleasure he receives in admiring and depicting such beauty, as stated in the last tercet:

Il resto tutto insieme avrai formato
Immaginando in mezzo al cielo il sole
La notte, quando è piú chiaro e stellato.

(You can put together the rest/By imagining the sun in the middle of the sky/At night, when it is brighter and starry) (vv. 9–12).

Here, I seek to show the difference between Sasso's *disperata* and his other lyric work, in order to highlight how they relate and often contrast.

Another significant deviation from the lyric tradition that deals with gender is that in the *disperata*, the poetic persona refuses to accept the beloved's rebuffs. Instead of acceptance, there is rebellion and violence expressed in both attitude and language. Indeed, when it is obvious that the beloved can no longer be dissuaded to accept the speaker's advances, *le désespoir amoureux* pervades the page, and death replaces Love as the object of desire. Furthermore, desire and passion drive to madness, to *l'amour furieux*, as no other lover has ever suffered as much as the speaker. The rhetoric is harsher, and anger is more palpable. Thus, Love is a negative force, which sets the speaker apart from the rest of the world, and makes him unique in his despair. Despair always prevails over Love, resulting in dark thoughts of suicide. Thus, Eros and Thanatos, the personification of death, are intertwined in the poetry of the *disperata*, where the moment of the *innamoramento* is often represented as the beginning of the end.

The female-voiced *disperate* (the *disperate femminili*), which I will discuss shortly, are written *by* men and mostly *for* women, so genre and gender intersect once more. In these texts, writers attempt to re-gender the *disperata* and appropriate the female speech, thus demonstrating an interest and maybe curiosity about female desire and despair. Furthermore, some of these poems, including those by il Saviozzo, Domenico da Prato, and Antonio degli Alberti, stage overtly erotic and detailed descriptions of the male body, its beauty, its strength, and its power to seduce and lead the young woman to perdition. She lusts after the beloved, who, unlike Laura, is attainable. Thus, same-sex desire is an important trans-gender facet of the female-voiced *disperata*, as the male author fully describes the male object of desire, while foregoes any depiction of the young woman whose voice he ventriloquizes. Rather, he focuses in particular on her perceived inappropriate passion. As Elizabeth D. Harvey suggests, "For a male author to assume the feminine voice is thus necessarily to confront in complex ways the 'issue' of female sexuality, since the source of feminine verbal facility was thought to be coexistive with her erotic nature."[4] Undoubtedly, the ventriloquized *disperate* show that their authors assumed the protagonists' voices in order to also appropriate their desire, thereby staging a young woman who was not respectable, and who succumbed to physical temptations. Indeed, the female voice in general portrays herself as too weak, easy to be seduced, and, therefore, easily abandoned by the man and consequently afflicted by despair. Moreover, as early as the presentation of the female protagonist to the readers, the poet establishes a deep connection between his authorship and his authority over her speech and body. Thus, a close link is established between her speech, and its unguarded expression, and early modern gendered expectations of female silence and chastity. Indeed, for the most part, the young women staged in the female-voiced *disperata* are not quiet, nor chaste, as we will shortly see.

Intersectionalities of the female voice, male voice, and imitation also emerge in what I call "intratextuality," that is intertextuality between the male- and female-voiced texts authored by the same poets, including il Saviozzo, da Prato, and degli Alberti, and later on by Nuysement, who were skilled writers of *disperate*. They successfully established their authority in the genre and also showed their dexterity in switching the speaker's voice and gender within the same genre. However, since gender, like genre, is a cultural construct, I establish the difference between the representation of female and male despair, and the gendered ways in which the two voices are articulated. For the most part, unlike in the male-voiced *disperata*, despair is not only a result, but also a severe punishment for the young woman in the female-voiced texts. Thus, despair is constructed as directly related to female desire, and as its dire consequence.

Finally, the interplay of genre and gender will be examined again in Morra's poems, the only *disperate* written by a woman author during this period. Beyond the rarity of a female voice in the genre, I seek also to demonstrate how this voice clearly articulates issues of gender and hopelessness that are unique from the voice of male authors. Indeed, hers is an authentic voice that erupts from the confines of a barren and desolate space, including the landscape surrounding her family castle where she was forced to live in complete obscurity. What is different, then, between Morra's poems and the female-voiced *disperate* ventriloquized by male authors? For one, she speaks for herself, and she expresses the depths of despair, her desires, and aspirations with a clearly articulated and assertive voice. Furthermore, conventional romantic desire is absent all together, but it is replaced by a passionate longing for paternal, social, and intellectual recognition.[5]

Appropriating Women's Despair

The *disperate femminili* are poems in which male authors appropriate, or to use Harvey's language, ventriloquize a young woman's voice, as well as their despair.[6] These female-voiced poems share several characteristics with the traditional *disperata*, but some of the main principles are different, including gender assumptions and the narrative structure. In these poems, the authorial voice appropriates the female voice and manipulates it in order to express a woman's despair. For example, the poet both controls her voice, and her actions as his authorial agency seizes the power to manipulate both in order to create his own version of her desire and despair.

Unlike the male-authored poetry, Morra, a woman, is the protagonist of her own narrative and in full control of her own representations. In the male-authored poems, on the other hand, the male author manipulates the female voice and her despair. In order to establish authenticity in narrating female despair, the male poet ventriloquizes the female voice to create a sense of truthfulness and authenticity to the despair of the *disperata*.

The female-voiced *disperata* became extremely popular in the second half of the Quattrocento, starting a tradition that, according to Flamini, was a real school of "lamenti femminili."[7] Undoubtedly, these texts continue the tradition of the Latin elegy, in particular Ovid's *Heroides*. They were written by poets who were already well versed in the genre, which provided them an opportunity to assert their (male) "voice" of reason in matters of female domain and romance. Thus, male authors can, here too, have their say and exercise their power of speech over women's silence. Certainly, by taking over her voice the author reaffirms his authority over his creation and over her narrative. This exercise of the male author's power of speech is also an example of male thought and reason triumphing over female irrationality and emotions: if left loose, the young woman will lose herself. Therefore, the male voice seeks to balance out the woman's behavior, so to speak, as the following examples show.

The socio-cultural construction of gender plays a significant role in the composition and reading stages of the female-voiced *disperate*. According to Russell, the authors change their female-voiced *disperate* in order to better adapt to the woman's social condition.[8] We will see this adaptation and the socio-cultural construction of gender in the five *disperate* I examine: Il Saviozzo's "O specchio di Narciso, o Ganimede" (Oh Narcissus's mirror, oh Ganymede), and "O magnanime donne, in cui biltade" (Oh magnanimous women, on whom his beauty); degli Alberti's "Donne leggiadre, cui d'Amor la spera" (Graceful women, who hope in Love); and da Prato's "Poi che nel tristo fin convien ch'io scopra" (Since in the sad ending I must discover) and "Già con lo estivo tempo ambo i Gemelli" (Already with summertime, both Twins).[9] These compositions exemplify accomplished models of the female-voiced *disperata* genre because of their diversity in the constant and variable *topoi*, and emotional depth. As Harvey has shown, the male's appropriation of the female voice is itself a form of intertextuality, because "an intertextual allusion opens a text to other voices and echoes of other texts, just as ventriloquism multiplies authorial voices, interrogating the idea that a single authorial presence speaks or controls an utterance."[10] In these poems especially, the male author imitates, and thus multiplies, his own texts in order to ventriloquize the female voice, imposing his presence and control over the young girl's words to make her narration of despair more authentic and credible. Furthermore, especially with il Saviozzo, fundamental connections exist between the two different gendered poems: those written by men about a male persona, and those written by men about a female persona, as in this case. Therefore, inter- and intratextuality are at play in these texts, as their approaches to and treatment of the genre are transposed from the male poet-persona to the woman's voice in their female-voiced texts.[11] These poems contain what Silvia Longhi calls a "voce femminile finta," a false female voice as well as a "scrittura per interposta persona," that is, a writing spoken through a third party or intermediary.[12]

Several Italian critics, including Longhi and Giuseppe Rosati, have compared the female-voiced *disperate* to the elegy.[13] They have made this comparison as both genres stage a female speaker who laments the misery of the human condition and the hardships caused by Fortune and Love. Both genres also issue from the court lyric tradition and were written in *terza rima* or in quatrains. As has been stated, Ovid's *Heroides*, fifteen epistolary poems spoken by Roman and Greek heroines lamenting their lovers' neglect and abandonment, is a powerful intertext that was particularly popular in the Renaissance and also influenced the Italian elegy. According to Rosati, Ovid first humanizes his heroines by exploring their feminine psyches; second, uses a feminine language to better express the woman's lament; and finally, skillfully represents the woman's unfortunate condition.[14] The female-voiced *disperata* employs similar approaches. A second important text in this literary tradition is Giovanni Boccaccio's *Elegia di Madonna Fiammetta*, in which the female protagonist tells the story of her unrequited love for Panfilo. This is the first Italian prose text explicitly titled "Elegia."[15] The female-voiced *disperata* is thus situated at this juncture and shares much of the tradition with the elegiac genre.

Furthermore, although the elegy is in epistolary form, the two genres also bear other similar structural and thematic traits, including the monologue, Love's excesses, Fortune's spitefulness, the woman's wanderings in the forest, the desolate landscape, the woman as an example for other women, as well as the presence of mythological lovers named as exemplum, and finally, the protagonist's epitaph.[16] The female-voiced *disperate* had a direct influence on the elegy, and in fact Vecchi Galli refers to il Saviozzo's work, in particular to the two female-voiced *disperate* that I examine shortly, as one of the main models for the elegy.[17] One of the two, "O magnanime donne, in cui beltate," which is a long poem of 706 verses, is particularly credited with inspiring the Italian elegy throughout the Quattrocento.

In examining these poems, several questions emerge repeatedly: how does a woman's voice fit in the *disperata* genre, one known for its violent tirades, and with conventions usually associated with masculine lyrics and language? Do the feelings connected to despair change when a woman is perceived to feel them and express them? And finally, are il Saviozzo, degli

Alberti, and da Prato able to speak effectively of female despair once they have borrowed the woman's voice? Or did they, as Volpi suggests, merely take the woman's lament and lend their deftness and agility in composing *disperate* because it was a popular subject, and therefore, it would bring popularity to its authors?[18]

Il Saviozzo's *Fanciulle Abbandonate*

Il Saviozzo's caption of "O specchio di Narciso, o Ganimede" presents the subject matter in a revealing way: "This chapter relates how a young woman fell in love with a pilgrim lad; and since he was free of Love's chains, he did not want to see her. Hence, she lamented, calling to her side four of the most beautiful young men that ever existed, and thus she despairs."[19] It is immediately obvious to the reader that the speaker has crafted a distance from the protagonist of the unfortunate tale through the third-person pronouns "he" and "she," rather than the first-person narrator "I," like in il Saviozzo's other *disperate* seen in the previous chapter. This technique is typical of his introductions to ventriloquisms: even if the story itself is narrated in the first-person persona, the poet stresses her despair as if it was somebody else's, and thus distances himself from the female voice. This device is essential to our discussion of the borrowed voice, as it detaches the male author from the protagonist and her speech, thereby creating some distance between him and her.

The 191-verse poem states at the onset that the young woman is dying because of love and describes her in positive terms:

> Io son fanciulla, come ogni om sì vede,
> nobile e vaga, benché innamorata,
> e sono abbandonata
> dal più bel volto che mai fusse in terra

> (I am a young maid, as every man can see,/noble and vague, although in love,/and I have been abandoned/by the most beautiful face that was ever on earth) (vv. 5–8, 91).

The poem immediately stresses male beauty and the young man's god-like appearances (vv. 13–32, 91–92), which become an important aspect of the love story, since they immediately captured her heart and now consume her soul, "quell'amoroso strale/che mi consuma" (vv. 51–52, 92). Indeed, these poems are remarkable in that the young male lover's beauty is described in greater detail than that of the young woman, a practice found more frequently in male poems praising a lady, especially in court culture. Indeed, in both the male- and female-voiced *disperate* references to female beauty are almost nonexistent, while here, all three poets portray the attractiveness and physical perfection of the male lover in order to focus on female desire.[20] As the female voice depicts the beloved's god-like body, it keenly evokes her desire, and at times even lust:

> Gli occhi ciascun par stella tramontana
> e le polite guance escon del sole
>
> ...
>
> Denti di perle e 'l naso profilato
> e la candida gola isnella e schietta:
> e tanto ben s'assetta
> fra le possenti spalle il fiero petto;
> nella cintura sua isvelto e stretto,
> le respondenti braccia a quella mano,
> che non par corpo umano
> a chi ben mira tutta sua persona

(His eyes seem like a northerly star/and the shiny cheeks come from the sun/.../Teeth like pearls and a well-outlined nose/and a candid throat, slender and true:/and he carries himself well/between his strong shoulders there is his proud chest;/in his belt he is lean and tight,/the arms go well with his hands,/so much so that it does not look like a human body/when you look well at his appearance) (vv. 17–28, 91).

These physical details are very reminiscent of Petrarch's and his followers' blazon-like descriptions of the beautiful beloved. Here though, the masculine body and its beauty are stressed in order to show, once again, the young girl's helplessness in front of the man and his physicality. Moreover, in the female-voiced *disperata*, the *innamoramento*, also a crucial moment of the Petrarchan system, signals the particular instant at which time the young woman loses herself and is no longer in control of her body. This is also a crucial moment because it further empowers the poet's authority over her speech.

As the poem continues, passion and desire hold their grip on the young woman, driving her to madness, "O trista me, già diventata pazza" (v. 53, 93). Insanity then sends her wandering with self-pity in the forest, deprecating her body:

> girò demente furïosa errando,
> piangendo e disprezzando
> queste misere carni ov'io so' involta! (vv. 54–56, 93).

Here, Love is, again, *l'amour furieux* that exiles the lover in the canonical landscape of the *disperata*, "fuggirò fra le spine,/fra folti rovi in grotta o in caverna" (I will run through thorns,/among thick bushes in a grotto or cavern) (vv. 63–65, 93). It is only toward the end of the poem that the reader learns that the young man betrayed her, which is why she plans to kill herself. Here, she accuses her beloved, and she begins referring to him as a traitor, "E questo traditor che mi ci mena" (v. 161, 98). Death appears as a solution that will put an end to her grief, as it did for all other unfortunate lovers, "quante son l'altre tapinelle gionte,/a quel fine mortal che mi ci chiama" (vv. 105–106, 95), but like other *disperate* personae, no other lover has ever suffered as much as her, "Io avrò maggior fama/di crudeltà che mai portasse alcuna;" (I will be more famous/ for having endured more cruelty than anybody else;) (vv. 106–107, 95). She repeats this motif often throughout the poem, since her unique sufferings as an abandoned and tormented woman set her apart even from the most wronged lovers in literary history: "peró che sotto il ciel qui della luna/Amor non punse mai cor di donzella,/quanto mai tapinella" (vv. 109–111, 95). As a final gesture, she decides to throw herself into a volcano because being burned alive is less painful than the current misery and feelings of despair.[21] This scorching hell will become her final destination, and her suicide will ultimately please Love, "Quivi mi gittarò, come a Amor piace" (v. 145, 97). Therefore, she too chooses to take her own life and commit a sin against her religious beliefs.

The monologue stages despair and the *disperata topoi* in several ways. Despair sets in early in the narration, shortly after the description of the young woman and her beloved, and the moment of the *innamoramento*, and it never lets its grip:

> Lassa, tapina me, che son sola io
> a sostener questo amoroso foco,
> nel quale a poco a poco,
> pure sperando, mi consumo e ardo!

(Tired, miserable me, I am alone/to sustain this passionate fire,/in which, little by little/while hoping, I consume myself and burn!) (vv. 37–40, 92).

Her martyrdom is such that it keeps her awake at night and crying during the day, and it must be told. Before jumping to her death, she wants to proclaim her misery once again, but she also wants everyone to learn from her foolishness. Her final wish is for the young man to witness first-hand her cruel end:

Oimè, ch'io moro, lassa, e tu nol sai,
ma ben vorrei che tu fussi presente
veder la fiamma ardente
dov'io mi gitto, qui nel monte o presso!
Oimè, oimè, che Cerbaro è già presso,
le Furie e gli altri spirti tapinelli
presa m'han pei capelli:
oimè, ch'io ardo e vommene in inferno!
Qui fia il mio pianto e 'l mio dolore eterno,
dove né Dio né 'l ciel mi può aitare,
ma solo tu me ne potrai cavare!

(Alas, I die, exhausted, and you don't know it,/but I would like for
you to be present/to see the ardent flames/in which I throw myself,
in this mountain and near it!/Alas, alas, Cerberus is approaching,/
the Furies and the other miserable spirits/grabbed me by my hair:/
Alas I burn and go to hell!/Here, may my tears and pain be eternal,/
where neither God nor Heaven can help me,/but only you can pull
me out!) (vv. 181–191, 99).

The final lines describe a painful death witnessed by Cerberus and the
Furies, and the persistence of her sorrows that continue to be voiced even
after her death. Since only the young man can deliver her from so much
pain, she is condemned to an afterlife of eternal despair, an ending found
in il Saviozzo's other *disperate* as well, including those voiced by a male
persona.

Il Saviozzo's ability to produce female-voiced *disperate* can also be
observed in the following text, whose caption is a lot more descriptive and
promptly presents the three important moments of the narration. Here
too, the speaker, "its author," identifies himself as separate from the protagonist: "A young woman's *capitolo* who was betrayed and deceived by
her lover, and who then died; and its author wisely omitted their names,
because it was a great Lord who committed this mistake and inconvenience."[22] Nelia Saxby suggests that this story, also known as "The story of a
young abandoned girl" ("Storia di una fanciulla abbandonata") (Figure 3),
seems to be linked to real events with a real young woman and young man,
because the author signals his reluctance to name the two.[23] This detail
would, of course, make the story more likely, "verosimile," and thus, a lot
more interesting and tragic to the reader. As the caption indicates, the
three important moments of betrayal—the *innamoramento*, deception,
and death—are narrated in 705 verses that meticulously depict the young

woman's tragic story, her beloved's role, the place and time of their first meeting, their escape, their coupling, perceived and portrayed as a sin, his abandonment, her despair, and finally her death. This is one of il Saviozzo's longest *disperate*. The young woman's despair is dissected and described moment by moment, in excruciating details that allow the poetic persona and the reader to understand how a woman can easily fall in a state of abandonment and hopelessness. Therefore, while in the male-voiced *disperata* despair is presented as a consequence of life itself and its misfortunes, here, it is staged as a direct aftermath of the young woman's weakness, almost a punishment, hence also revealing that women's predisposition to sin is a gendered construct central to the female-voiced *disperata* genre.

The poem debuts with a stern warning to all women about the temptations of Love:

> O magnanime donne, in cui biltate
> posto ha sua forma, e voi, superni dei,
> udite i dolor mei,
> dell'impia morte e aspra crudeltate!

(Oh magnanimous women, on whom his beauty/put its mark, and you, heavenly gods,/hear my pain,/in impious death and harsh cruelty!) (vv. 1–4, 185).

They must not only listen carefully, but they must also learn from the young woman's mistake, "Prendete essemplo e prendavi pietate/leggiadre giovinette, al mio cordoglio" (vv. 5–6, 185). Hence, the speaker broadens the didactic scope of the female-voiced *disperata* from the very beginning, teaching women how to behave and warning them not to fall into Love's spell. The first part of the composition is dedicated to the description of the two young protagonists: while she is very young and naïve, he is very handsome and his speech is irresistible:

> il mento piccinino e 'l fiero petto,
> la bianca man che a Bacco saria bella,
> i modi e la favela
> arieno inamorato un cor di pietra

(his small chin and proud chest,/a white hand that would please Bacchus,/his manners and words/would have enamored even a heart made of stone) (vv. 85–88, 188).

Once again, while his physical attraction is emphasized, her gullibility is paraded throughout the text underscoring and building on gender assumptions that penalize and undermine the female speaker.

Il Saviozzo ventriloquizes the young woman throughout the long narrative, even when it is the young lad who speaks in order to impart more credibility to the woman's side of the story and to her voice, as well as more depth to her love despair. It also gives the poet a chance to display his own ability to articulate a woman's despair and its complexity. The more trustworthy and authentic the female voice is, the more is its author and his ability to represent her in writing. In the poem, as different moments of the day are also painstakingly described with mythological references and erudition, the monologues at times become dialogues, first between the woman and Love, and then, between the two lovers.

> E poi diceva, 'O dispiatato Amore,
> che m'hai condotto a questo ministerio,
> perché 'l suo desiderio col mio non fai in un punto felice?

(And then she would say, 'Oh ruthless Love,/who brought me to this moment,/why will you not join his desire to mine in happiness?') (vv. 109–111, 189).

He sees her already in a state of anguish and perdition, stunned by despair, "già come disperata" (vv. 139, 190), and thus, immediately takes advantage of her, and pretends to have compassion of her:

> Le pene tue mi dan maggior martìre,
> gentil madonna, assai che 'l mio dolore
> (rispose il mio signore)

(Your pangs cause me great suffering,/kind madonna, as much as my own pain – answered my Lord) (vv. 181–183, 192).

While her distress and passion start growing, so does his grip and power of persuasion over her.

The young woman continues to describe the lovers' travails and agony. Desire becomes more and more manifest:

> e stavàn come Tantal che vuol bere
> e non ne può avere,
> ben che abbia assai dell'acqua intorno al viso

(and I was like Tantalus who wants to drink/but cannot,/even if there is plenty of water around) (vv. 190–192, 192).

The young man finally finds a solution: hoping to convince her to follow him, he describes his family's impressive credentials and good lineage,

> e di stirpe gentil son procreato,
> e sono più onorato
> che uom che viva in tutto mio paese (vv. 201–203, 193),

and then proposes to escape together, promising a "happily ever after" life, "facciàn dunque partenza,/che insieme viveren sempre felici!" (vv. 206–208, 193).

She agrees to follow him, but she asks him to promise that he will marry her once they arrive to his village. To sound more convincing, he swears he will make her his wife or he will be struck by great destruction. Apocalyptic calamities foreshadow the tragic ending, as we have seen in other *disperate*:

> Io priego il ciel che ciaschedun mio nervo
> sia fulminato simile a' Giganti,
> e gli dei tutti quanti
> mi sien contrarii e tutto il mondo in guerra;
> chiudasi l'aere e aprasi la terra
> ad inghiottirmi sensa alcun riparo,
> ...
> s'io non ti sposo ancor per mia mogliere

> (I pray the heaven that each of my nerves/be struck by lightening like the Giants/and all the gods/be against me, and the whole world at war/the air shut down and the earth open up/and swallow me without any help,/ ... /if I don't marry you and make you my wife) (vv. 233–245, 194).

Moreover, the world will turn upside down and he himself will lose his life not only if he fails to marry her, but also if he does not treat her like a "madonna." These words and descriptions convince her to flee with him that very night, "Questo parlar produsse tanto effetto" (v. 249, 194). His speech, therefore, is successful in persuading the protagonist, and maybe even the reader, of his good intentions. However, shortly after, omens begin to warn her of the impending tragedy, and when they reach the secluded forest, he takes advantage of their isolation—and of her. Here, the tone of the narration suddenly shifts: he is no longer the beautiful lad, but instead he becomes "il traditore," "the traitor" (v. 360, 198), and she can no longer keep him at bay: "Poi ch'io non potti più stare alla dura,/per minor male al suo voler m'adusse" (vv. 369–370, 198).

This is the midpoint of the story, and it is here that the narration changes and assumes the tragic nuances of the *disperata*, because, immedi-

ately after stealing and enjoying her virginity, he abandons her to the wild
beasts in the doom of the deserted woods:

> Preso che 'l traditore ebbe sollazzo
> e di mia fanciullezza il fior rapito,
> tra sé prese partito
> lassarmi tra le fiere in quel diserto (vv. 373–376, 199).

Therefore, in contrast to the male-voiced *disperate* where the speakers seek
out desolate settings populated by wild beasts in which to despair, here, the
young women are abandoned to it, as if discarded and left alone in ominous and forsaken places. This gender difference is significant as it underscores the woman's powerlessness once again, as she is unable to choose
her own settings, while the *disperato* is free to select the site in which to
let his hopelessness flow. As in the *Heroides*, the woman is abandoned to a
powerless state of affairs and feels herself ruined.

In a touching moment of intimacy, the speaker then addresses the
readers directly, so as to solicit their compassion and participation in her
misery:

> Io t'ho il principio e 'l mezzo discoperto,
> lettor, perché bel fin la crudeltade
> ti commuova a pietate
> e a maledir l'impetüosa mano

> (I have told you the beginning and the middle of the story,/reader,
> so that its cruel end/might move you to pity/and to damn his
> impetuous hand) (vv. 377–380, 199).

She also damns the young man. We are once again witnesses of a tragic
scene to which we cannot remain indifferent and are asked to partake in
cursing the impostor. Her plea is clearly a compelling attempt to manipulate the reader to feel her despair.

The maledictions are pronounced throughout the poem, not only
against the traitor, but also against Fortune and Love, "E lacrimando a'
pie' del muro spesso/malediceva i fati e la fortuna" (vv. 129–130, 190),
"Mentr'io andavo Amor maledicendo" (v. 141, 190), as well as against the
Furies of hell, "o furia dell'abisso" (v. 382, 199). After the young woman
is abandoned and left alone in the middle of the dark, cold forest to be
devoured by the wild beasts, she feels discarded and afraid. She then starts
to wander randomly, imagining fierce animals that threaten her life:

> ma ad ora ad ora mi par sentire i denti
> di tigri e di serpenti,

> di idre, di lion, di lupo e d'orso
>> (vv. 442–444, 202).

As all *disperati*, she feels she is the only one in such tragic predicaments:

> Ahi, lassa me, che mai sì grave invito
> contra d'Amor non ebbe donna alcuna
> né che sotto la luna
> fusser le carni sue tanto straziate!

> (Alas poor me, because not ever such grave invitation/against Love
> has caused any other woman /under the moon/to have her flesh so
> painfully torn apart!) (vv. 461–464, 202).

And although she recollects all of the unhappy female lovers, such as Dido, Philomena, Medeas, she realizes that she is however the unhappiest of them all, "Ma io, she son tra le dolente donne/la più infelice" (vv. 501–502, 204).

Surprisingly, the traitor finally returns, and he demands that she go back home and leave him alone. She, again, turns directly to the reader to solicit some pity, "Pensa fra te, lettor, come 'l mio core,/udendo tal parlar, diventò ghiaccio" (Think my reader, how my heart/in hearing these words, turned into ice) (vv. 541–542, 205). Then, with a final damnation against his life, she asks him to kill her with his own sword. Her invectives continue for several more verses, arousing the wild animals to come and devour him, and to rejoice with her over his well-deserved death, while she, on the other hand, will find the compassion of all of the souls who have suffered for love. However, without hesitation, he readily complies and kills her with his sword (vv. 693–695, 211). Because of her death, she cannot continue the story and thus has to end:

> Seguir non posso la dolente istoria
> ...
> infin ch'io caddi morta alla foresta
>> (vv. 697–701, 211–212).

However, as she's dying, her voice continues on for four more verses, where we learn that he fled immediately after killing her, and that the wild beasts devoured her dying body, thus making the isolated forest her final resting place: first because of her perdition, a symbolic end in itself, and then because of her death. This is the most tragic of the five *disperate* I examine in this section.

Figure 3. Cerbero Invoco. El qual narra, come una
Fanciulla abbandonata dal Suo innamorato si lamenta, e contra
le bellezze di lui, e poi per disperata si buttò in Mongibello.
(By permission of the Biblioteca Universitaria Alessandrina Roma.)

Il Saviozzo's two *disperate* present a ventriloquized female speaker whose voice is appropriated by a male author who was well versed in the genre, in its main *topoi*, and narration of despair. In both poems, the progression of events centers on the feelings of despair due to unrequited love, to treason and abandonment. Indeed, even when the speaker dreams about the beloved and his beauties, there is the onset of deep despair as a foreshadowing of the tragic events that will follow. Moreover, both female protagonists contend with issues of sexuality: the first stages a desire disguised in the fervor of love that consumes her, "quell'amoroso strale/che mi consuma" (vv. 51–52, 92); and the second describes a desire that is at first appeased in their escaping together, but then, it quickly degrades as soon as their union is physically consumed. Il Saviozzo capitalizes on this moment: because of the sex act, the young woman is abandoned, and despair ensues. Thus, by assuming the young women's voices, he confronted their desire and sexuality. Moreover, despite this different outcome, their sexual consummation culminates with a punishment, as both are betrayed and then abandoned, and thus, chastised for their illicit passion and for giving into it. The second woman is even violated twice for her desire, first sexually, and second lethally. However, both have limited control over their own situation: while both women wish to be with their lovers, ultimately, both suffer the same fate of abandonment. Furthermore, while both female speakers amply warn their female audience against Love's attacks, traps and miseries, they also seem to mainly urge women to behave, and to not give in their desires and temptations. Ultimately, the poet seems to assign the final responsibility to the two women themselves for having desired, abandoned their families to follow a young man, and transgressed society's conventions, unlike the male-voiced *disperate* where Love, not the man, is assigned responsibility.

Although less violent, the female-voiced *disperata* delivers a stern moral message to its readers, which is imparted directly and thus more efficiently through the voice of the female speaker.[24] As each poem demonstrates, il Saviozzo does not choose the usual forceful language and raw images that characterize his male-voiced *disperate* (see Chapter One).[25] Rather, these ventriloquized poems are more moderate, and while still employing the genre's major *topoi*—including Fortune's and Love's adversarial roles, their persecutions, the nature and landscape in which the young *disperata* wanders, frequent allusions to other iconic, doomed lovers, despair, and finally death—the author also strives to impart a lesson. Therefore, with the gender shift in the poetic persona, the didactic purpose becomes an intrinsic component of the female-voiced *disperata*, as women were expected to behave and were punished by sorrow and even death if they did not. This is also stressed in the distance created between the author and his ventriloquized voice: first in the captions, where he announces his own recounting of a young woman's despair, and second, when he shows no compassion for her and instead harshly judges her actions.

Antonio degli Alberti's Female Despair as "Exemplum"

Similarly, Antonio degli Alberti (1363–1415)[26] distanced himself from his female protagonist from the very start, and his warning carries the overtones of a lesson that he, the male author, wishes to impart to all women. For example, he addressed his female-voiced *disperata*, "Donne leggiadre, cui d'Amor la spera," to the "Graceful ladies awaiting Love". Here too, the poet uses a woman's voice to speak in the first person in order to harness her experience and misery for other women's benefit, as stated in the very first verses:

> Donne leggiadre, cui d'Amor la spera
>
> ...
>
> volgete gli occhi alla mia gran misèra
> che sarà essempio all'altre giovinette
> di farle più corrette
> che non fu' io

(Graceful ladies awaiting Love/ ... /turn your eyes to my great misery/that it may be an example to other young maids/to make them better behaved/than I was) (vv. 1–8, 234).

Thus, the poem's didactic purpose is established and announced from the very beginning with clear words, in order to "better correct the female audience." Furthermore, the young woman is also seeking the compassion of her own gender, "Forse che moverovvi/i cori a compassion del mio martire" (vv. 12–13, 234). In other words, she feels compelled to tell her story not only because it might serve as example to other young women and to deter them from sinning, but also because these women are susceptible to persuasion by verse and, thus, likely to sympathize with the speaker.

From the onset, the poem assumes a tragic tone: we learn that she has already decided to die, "Chiamerò Morte con acerbo strido" (v. 16, 234), and, like Dido, she too is mourning her state of abandonment.[27]

What follows is the description of the young man's physical beauty, which she accuses of greatly rousing her desire and of making her fall in love with him:

> la cui magnificenza e atto pio
> mi mise un tal disio
> nel cor ch'ancor nel duol mi dà diporto
>
> (vv. 23–25, 234).

The moment of the *innamoramento* is also evoked and shown as the dramatic result of her desire at the onset of despair: "e non credo che mai/ tale amor fusse fra Leandro ed Ero/qual fra noi era, ond'io mi dispero" (vv. 32–34, 235).

Despair is portrayed throughout the poem as a deep-rooted and somber feeling that causes the woman to wander around the world in search of her beloved. It also convinces her that suicide is the only solution to her misery as was the case for other hopeless ladies:

> Veggio che, disperata
> come Biblide già, per gran dolore
> andrò tapina in atto vagabondo
> e con disdegno al mondo
> starò vivendo; ma con la mia mano
> penso far qual Bellisa per Tristano.

> (I see that, in despair/and just like Byblis, because of my great grief,/I will wander miserably/and with disdain for the world/I will live; but with my hand/I think I will do like Bellicies for Tristan.) (vv. 46–51, 235–236).

Her prayers, tears, and grief are not enough to convince her beloved to stay with her, so he ends up abandoning her with only her unquenched desire and deep despair. As already stated, the *Heroides* are an intertext that is present in the female-voiced *disperata* as they too stage a woman who was abandoned by her lover. Here, the woman compares her waiting for the return of the young man to that of other heroines who, like her, had been abandoned by their lovers, as Penelope in Ovid's "Heroides I," "t'aspetterò con fè più che non fe'/il caro sposo suo Penelopé" (vv. 84–85, 237), and concludes her poem with a final attempt at getting him back.

Although the tone is somber, the young female persona charges her own rhymes to find her beloved, to tell him of her sorrows so as to move him to pity and to bring him back:

Canzon, vestita a bruno, or lagrimosa
n'andrai da quel signore che m'ha in balìa

...

gli narra sì che a pietate il mova

...

fallo tornar volenteroso,
ché insino allor non aro mai riposo

(Song, dressed in black, tearful/you will go to that lord who enchained me/ ... /speak to him so that piety might move him/ ... /convince him to come back willingly,/as I will not be able to rest until he does) (vv. 103–110, 238).

Despite the tragic tones and nuanced depths of despair revealed by some of its images, this poem remains non-violent and never stages the fierce behaviors encountered in the *disperate* written and spoken by male authors. However, degli Alberti succeeds, I believe, in ventriloquizing despair, and in touching his readers through unrequited love, unquenched desire, and the feeling of abandonment that his speaker deftly articulates. Moreover, despite the didactic purpose of the poem, the author does not attempt to distance himself from his creation and lets the borrowed voice flow with despair, a theme that recurs at regular intervals, including the following: "or mi dispero" (v. 84, 235); "E fammi disperar" (v. 85, 235); "con dubbioso sperare" (v. 41, 235); and the protagonist referring to herself as "disperata" (v. 46, 235). Degli Alberti's appropriation and expression of female despair indeed upstages female desire and its punitive consequences. Despair is represented as an inner state of hopelessness, rather than as a consequence of a lascivious female behavior, and thus, it succeeds in narrowing the distance between the male narrator and the borrowed voice of the young woman.

Domenico da Prato's "Eulogia"

In contrast with the poems of il Saviozzo and degli Alberti, the female-voiced *disperate* by Domenico da Prato (ca. 1370–ca. 1432)[28] showcase the pleasures of desire, in addition to its pain and consequences. His compositions articulate greater nuances of the complex relationship between genre and gender, and, though they can be similarly didactic in their warnings against the dangers of men and Love, they can also be more sympathetic toward their female protagonists. Da Prato was a prolific writer of this genre,[29] so here I will focus on two of his poems, "Poi che nel tristo fin convien ch'io scopra" (Since I must sadly discover in the end) and "Già con lo estivo tempo ambo i Gemelli." (Already with summertime both Twins). The first caption clearly states the nature of the poem, "Moral *canzone* written by Ser Domenico done in the place of a young noble woman, who was abandoned by her husband and deceived by her lover, finding herself chained up miserably in prison by her family, she thus shares her sorrow."[30] Although the caption is descriptive, the narration remains vague about what happened and in what order, except for her falling in love, sharing some moments with her beloved, and then being abandoned by him, which resulted in her suicide. The poem encompasses all of the genre's *topoi*, and as in the *disperata* by degli Alberti, the woman's voice announces from the very beginning her death wish. However, before she dies, she wants her grief to be heard and to caution other women so that they learn from her tragic experience:

> Ma prima che fuggita
> dal corpo affranto sia la dannata alma
> udite il pianto e 'l suon d'ogni mia palma
> (vv. 9–11, 531).

Moreover, together with the unquenched desire caused by her beloved's absence, the recollection of the pleasures found in his arms are also vividly evoked. In fact, the more she reminisces and tells her readers about it, the more her desire and inner turmoil double:

> E voi che amate – riterrete a mente,
> Lassa, ché mi sovien quand'io solea
> nelle braccia serrate,
> ch'or son legate – tener strettamente
> il mio amante ed ei me sì dolcemente
> co i piacevoli motti e le parole!
> Omè, ché più mi dole
> questo desio, che con duol duolo accoppia,
> e più pensando, più pena raddoppia.

(And you who love – keep in mind./Miserable, I remember when I was/in his arms,/that now are tied – holding tightly/my lover and he me, so sweetly/with pleasing remarks and words!/Alas, that this desire hurts/and that when grieving, grief multiplies,/and, the more I think, the more grief doubles!) (vv. 36–44, 532).

The speaker addresses her audience to alert them of her imminent end, "Correndo, a morte vonne,/e con voi donne – non parlo più omai"

(vv. 61–62, 532), so that they may forewarn other women about her tragedy, "e voi poi l'altre ne farete accorte" (v. 66, 532). In a chain reaction
meant to warn as many female readers as possible, this poem seeks to create a community of women who are well-educated about Love's dangers.
This community is urged to ponder this message in order to avoid the
depths of despair that the speaker is experiencing. For her, however, it is
too late, and soon hopelessness invades her soul and drives her to a violent
suicide. She claims that death will gratify Love and her lover, and thus, she
will stab herself:

> Selvagge fiere, omè, pietà prenda!
> Ogni cosa creata pianga meco!
> Ecco che già mi reco
> l'armata mano al disperato core,
> per far contento lo mio amante e Amore

(Wild beasts, alas, take pity on me!/Every creature cry with me!/
Now I carry/my armed hand to my desperate heart,/to please my
lover and Love) (vv. 73–77, 533).

However, before her death, she damns her beloved for causing so much
grief with his low deceits. He too will be punished by Love and by Jupiter.[31]
These stanzas are similar to those found in the male-voiced poems, particularly in the violent damnations and the presence of wild animals. Finally,
she turns to her own poem and charges it once again to disseminate her
lamenting story, "quivi pietosi dite i miei lamenti" (v. 95, 533), and find
her lover in order to show him the site of her burial place as a last attempt
to move him and bring him back.

The text, with its didactic undertones, focuses in particular on
warning other women against Love's passion and deceptions, and against
men in general. Indeed, in the female-voiced *disperate*, not only they are
portrayed as unattainable and indifferent traitors, but they are also never
to be trusted. Furthermore, the poetic persona feels an obligation to narrate the distressing events that led her to her tragic end, again stressing a
didactic intention: the more women are warned against Love's traps, the
better off and free they will be. This theme recurs also in da Prato's other
disperata, which stages a young female speaker. The caption reads "Poem
by Ser Domenico about a young woman in her room, who herself laments
about Love because her beloved does not notice her love."[32] Here, unlike
in the other texts discussed, da Prato identifies himself as the narrator,
Ser Domenico, who recounts the story of the young woman crying in her

room. In fact, he witnesses first-hand her lamentations and often intervenes in relating his side of the story to the reader, thus, the two voices
often crisscross and weave a long account, nuanced with tragic events and
emotions. This approach to narration undoubtedly provides more authenticity to the voice of the young woman, because, while painting in the garden, Ser Domenico states that he is directly repeating what he hears, the
young woman lamenting her love's sorrow and despair.

The *disperata* is set in the spring, with descriptions of nature:

> Li fauni fra le selve fan ritorno;
> ogni letizia cresce
> a tutti li animal che sono in terra

(The fauna returns to the woods;/every amusement grows/for all
animals that are on earth) (vv. 12–14, 544).[33]

Her name is symbolically Eulogia, which originates from the Greek and
means blessed or benediction, and carries a religious meaning: Eulogia is
a blessing. Furthermore, the young girl is at first presented as *anti-disper-
ata*, the opposite of a desperate lover, since she supposedly is blessed and
blesses those around her. However, the name itself does not counter all
the maledictions that she will utter throughout the poem. Furthermore,
the term *eulogia*, eulogy, is also a literary genre mourning the death of an
individual, and this meaning better fits the poem's character, as her voice
laments her misfortunes, suicidal wishes, and state of near-death. Da Prato
undoubtedly meant to play with the name of his female creation—being
blessed is after all the opposite of being suicidal—as well as to identify her
to the reader with a real name in order to make his story more credible.

To stage a more credible and original tale of female despair, the poet
is hidden in the garden and listens carefully. As he becomes more and
more captivated by the tale, he decides to stay put in a distinctly voyeuris-
tic position. Suddenly, he hears the young woman's pleads for death:

> un scuro
> e grave strido attonito mi volse
> verso le finestre:
> seguendo un altro, io m'accostai più al muro,
> perché di quella camera si sciolse;
> e con parole alpestre
> in voce mesta udì chiamare: 'O Morte!'

(a dark/and grave cry directed me astonished/toward the win-
dows:/following another cry, I got closer to the wall,/because it

originated from that room;/and with harsh words/in a desperate
voice I heard her call: 'Oh Death!') (vv. 78–84, 545).

Eulogia then speaks of her grief and solitude, and of the physical and emotional torture caused by her lover's absence. We do not learn why he is
absent, or if she was purposely abandoned. The narration is more focused
on her reaction to her miserable solitude, rather than on the events that
led to it. She also talks of the ardent desire that sets her apart from the
other girls as the one who suffers the most,

> Lassa, ch'io son tra l'altre unica e sola
>
> ...
>
> quando ho, gli occhi fermi
> nell'atti vaghi e accorti,
> del mio signore un ardente desio

(Exhausted, I am among the others the only and lonesome one/ ... /
in having, with my eyes closed/and with vague and wary actions,/a
burning desire for my lord) (vv. 92–98, 545–546).

Ser Domenico is completely mesmerized by Eulogia's weeping and continues to listen carefully, but also cautiously, as somebody might see him hiding. Their voices continue to alternate, moving the narration forward. She
describes the physical beauties of her lover in blazon-style, which increases
both her desire and despair,

> Tapina me!
>
> ...
>
> Meco piangete, o insensibil sassi
> (vv. 123–127, 546).

In erotic terms, she imagines his naked body and each of its parts:

> Ma poi ti vorrei gnudo,
> sì ch'io vedessi scoperto ogni membro.
> La tua candida gola, ch'io rimembro,
> in furia annoderei con le mie braccia,
> i belli occhi baciando

(But then I want you naked,/so that I can see all of your body./Your
candid throat, which I remember,/in wrath I would tie with my
arms,/while kissing your beautiful eyes) (vv. 138–142, 546–547),

and continues to fantasize about him while her desire intensifies feverishly. She sees herself in his arms kissing him and being kissed by him:

la mia bocca la tua bacerebbe

...

stretta nelle tue braccia dilicate,
gustando il dolce pome,
fin che l'ultimo gioco incominciasse.

(my mouth would kiss yours/ ... /held tight in your delicate arms,/
tasting your sweet Adam's apple/until the last game would begin."
(vv. 148–154, 547).

This scene is described in vivid details by the dramatic voice of the young woman: while unbeknownst to her, the voyeur-poet hears the most intimate details of her yearnings and secret fantasies, which he then faithfully reports to his readers.

These moments of imagined pleasure, though, are closely followed by moments of despair, as Eulogia comes back to her current state of physical frustration and emotional loss. Furthermore, the invectives against Fortune and against her miserable condition recur throughout the poem: "Ahi, ria fortuna, quanto mi fai torto!" (v. 175, 547). Eulogia cries inconsolably, until the poet hears her talk about death, "Ecco, io sono morta" (v. 188, 548). However, her wet nurse intervenes, tries to console her, and begs her to eat something. She urges her to take interest in her own life again, thus leaving the poet and reader with some hope of recovery. Henceforth, Eulogia's voice is completely silenced by the poet's reflections on the events he witnessed and the laments he heard. He speaks of his compassion for the young woman and formulates his own invectives against Love and its many deceptions. Although for a short time it seems like he wanted to intervene and console her, he soon decides to leave, concluding that he was deeply touched by Eulogia's "sweet" lament. His pity for her wins him over, generating feelings that he still carries with him,

Così quel giorno fui
dal dolce lamentar per pietà vinto,
sì che nel core il porto ancor dipinto

(Thus, that day I was/moved to pity by that sweet lament,/so much so that I still carry it in my heart) (vv. 271–273, 549).

Indeed, the poet-persona is clearly moved by the girl's misery, and throughout the narration he displays an interest in not only her, but also in her physical and emotional wellbeing. This is a clever manipulation by the poet: if he is so moved and touched by Eulogia's despair, so should his audience be. As the self-identified author, Ser Domenico is fully invested in his own composition and in his ventriloquism of Eulogia's speech.

The poet-voyeur listens very carefully, emerging here and there to better eavesdrop. Even when he thinks she is dead, he awaits anxiously for any word she might still utter, making her voice significantly more prominent than her body. After all, from the beginning to the end of the story, the poet only hears her voice—he never sees Eulogia. Nor does she see him, a detail that strengthens his claim of telling a true story, albeit unauthorized by its protagonist. However, her words come to him in a way that still allows him to ventriloquize them for his readers, intertwining them with his own reflections on the tragedy and on Love, and judgments on her illicit desire. Throughout the narration, it is Eulogia's voice that holds his attention, and it is the interlacing of her voice and his that consequently holds ours. This literary device bestows on the poem more authenticity and intimacy, which also renders it more interesting and compelling for the women and readers to whom it is addressed.

Furthermore, although da Prato ventriloquizes her voice, it is his own voice that indisputably carries more authority because he is in a dialogue with the reader, directly reporting what he hears and sees. He is an intermediary between her despair and the readers who long to learn about it, rather than dialoguing with the young woman, whose voice was borrowed. Indeed, his voice has more agency and authority than the female voice. Therefore, this poem is slightly different from the other female-voiced *disperate* discussed above, because da Prato directly combines his own speech and reflections with those ventriloquized by an abandoned and hopeless woman. Moreover, because of his continuous dialogue with the reader, his detachment with the female voice is intentionally proclaimed in the caption. Although fully engrossed by Eulogia's grief, as the narrator of a particularly tragic event, Ser Domenico's complete authority over her voice is assumed and assented. In fact, in both poems, da Prato identifies himself as their writer (vv. 531, 543).

In their *disperate*, il Saviozzo, degli Alberti, and da Prato use similar approaches to both genre and gender, ventriloquizing the voices of young women, producing intratextual meaning, and imparting both lessons and judgments. In male-voiced *disperate*, the speakers despair at having their love unrequited. In contrast, in their female-voiced *disperate*, their speakers are portrayed as lustful, victimized by the lovers who abandoned them, and guilty of seeking their own perdition for having loved and desired. Their own realization that they are lost in their sin is hauntingly voiced out loud, at times even shouted. Moreover, the poems weave prayers, maledictions, and threats together in order to depict a daunting reality in which the young women are marginalized, chained up, and exiled within the family walls or in a secluded forest as shameful punishment for their illicit infatuations or physical encounters with their lovers. As mentioned, in these portrayals and plots there is a transparent detachment between the male author and his female creation, as their voices do not fuse, and instead remain distinct at all times,[34] with the exception of degli Alberti's poem, where a vague authorial compassion seems to transpire.

There is a striking intertextuality between il Saviozzo's and da Prato's female-voiced *disperate*. First, both hint at homosexual love on behalf of the authors, especially in the portrayals of the beauty of the object of desire, the young man. They both use the very same mythological allusions to ill-fated and handsome lovers, including Ganymede, Polydorus, Hippolytus, Narcissus, and Leander.[35] Il Saviozzo employs this *topos* in both of his texts: the first starting, "O specchio di Narciso, o Ganimede,/o Ippolito mio, o Polidoro" (vv. 1–2, 90), and the second in even more suggestive verses,

> Qual Ganimede, omè, qual Polidoro,
> qual Ipolito bello, qual Narciso
> non rimarria conquiso
> di biltà da costui ch'ogni altro eccede?

(Which Ganymede, alas, which Polydorus,/which handsome Hippolytus, and Narcissus/would not be conquered/by such beauty that exceeds everybody else's?) (vv. 73–76, 188),

as if to suggest an inability to resist this man's perfect beauty. Here, same-sex attraction is clearly stated in a rhetorical question: which of the four legendarily handsome young men would not be conquered by the beauty of the young woman's beloved? In his second *disperata*, da Prato composes a very similar verse,

> Qual Ganimede mai, qual Polidoro
> qual Absalon, qual Patroclo o Parisse ...
> per cui io more,
> unico idol mio crudel Narcisse
>   (vv. 113–116, 546).

Interestingly, the male beloved's beauty is meticulously and erotically described, while the female protagonist's physical appearance is not, as has already been noted. Second, here in particular, the relationship between Narcissus and Echo is subtly suggested and persists throughout the long poem. Eulogia plans to wither and die of starvation, just like the nymph Echo, who in the third book of Ovid's *Metamorphoses* wasted away because of her unrequited love for Narcissus, until only her voice alone remained.[36] When Eulogia's wet nurse comes to her room, alerted by the young woman's wearying voice, she finds her much altered and emaciated, and asks what is happening to her: "Lassa! che fia?/Oimè, Eulogia, che hai?" (vv. 191–192, 558). Eulogia responds that she is probably wasting away because she hasn't eaten in a while,

> Forse ch'io venni meno
> -disse Eulogia- perché ier digiunai,
> ed esta mane ancor poco mangiai
> (vv. 222–223, 548).

Although Echo is not mentioned, it is clear that the nymph is here embodied by Eulogia, who pines after her Narcissus and disappears because of starvation to the point where only her voice is heard. This voice is audibly and symbolically present in the long *disperata*, an important aspect to which I will come back to in my discussion about Nuysement's "Plainte de Telie a Echo." In fact, when staging female despair, da Prato and Nuysement rewrite Echo as a symbol of female despair in similar ways through the ventriloquized voices of the young suffering women. Thus, Echo as a symbolic figure of female despair establishes a direct intertextuality between their two female-voiced *disperate*, thereby strengthening the continuity between the classical tradition, and the Italian and French female-voiced *disperata*, almost a century later.

Both desire and despair are deeply gendered, because il Saviozzo, degli Alberti and da Prato depict the two passions as being interrelated. In female-voiced *disperate*, despair is portrayed as a punishment, both physical and emotional, as a result, mainly, of having desired and, at times, having acted on that desire. On the other hand, the male-voiced and male-authored *disperate* articulate unrequited love and unquenched desire, which cause despair not as a punishment, but as a corollary consequence. Thus, although the desire and despair expressed by men are not inherently different from desire and despair expressed by the ventriloquized women, the consequences, on the other hand, are inherently different and decidedly gendered. The female voice is, in fact, judged and even punished in these poems, which also serve as a moral lesson to an audience specifically distinguished, or at least envisioned, as female. Moreover, all three poets have demonstrated their creative skills and aptitude in intratextuality, thus composing both gender-specific *disperate*. They have also proven a human and literary curiosity in women's despair and in how it could be imagined and expressed in their own texts. As Ray has suggested in her discussion of women's letter books in Renaissance Italy, "This deep curiosity about a wholly female world also reflects an element of literary voyeurism, an out-sider's reimagining rather than a genuine investigation of female epistolar-ity."[37] Returning to Volpi's question of whether these poets merely took a popular topic and added it to a popular genre, it does, indeed, appear that rather than investigating female despair, these writers merely described it and used it for the genre's sake, thus remaining mere observers rather than accomplices.

Finally, by telling the sad stories of these young women, they con-tributed compelling variations to the *disperata* genre as accomplished poets, but also, as "voyeurs" and interpreters of female despair. Ultimately, they used their talents to fit women's speech in a familiar and popular genre, albeit a less violent and furious version, as mere outsiders, and as onlookers and witnesses to a tragedy to which they remained for the most part detached. Since they positioned themselves as external judges, look-ing from a pedestal into the tragic narratives, they remained separate from the protagonist. Thus, although their deftness and agility in composing *disperate* certainly allowed them to create accomplished specimen of the genre, I argue that, because of their role and authority, they were not able to speak effectively of female despair, feelings of abandonment, betrayal, grief, and death. Ultimately, although literary competence is present, gen-der authority is lacking.

NOTES

[1] See Sheryl E. Reiss and David G. Wilkins, eds. *Beyond Isabella: Secular Women Patrons of Art in Renaissance Italy*, and Alessandro Luzio and Rodolfo Renier, *Mantova e Urbino: Isabella d'Este e Elisabetta Gonzaga*.

[2] Rosello Roselli, *Il Canzoniere Riccardiano*, d'Aubigné, *Le Printemps Stances et Odes*, and Théophile, *Œuvres Poétiques*, I. All references to Roselli's, d'Aubigné's, and Théophile's poetry will be based on these editions.

[3] Sasso, in Alessandro Tortoreto, *Lirici cortigiani del Quattrocento*, 388.

[4] Harvey, "Ventriloquizing Sappho: Ovid, Donne, and the Erotics of the Fem-inine Voice," 130.

[5] Janet Levarie Smarr argues that some women poets, including Morra, Vit-

toria Colonna, and Marguerite de Navarre sought to replace desire for a man with an "irreproachable male object of desire", in Morra's case, her father. "Substituting for Laura," 9.

[6] Harvey, *Ventriloquized Voices*.

[7] Flamini, *La lirica toscana del Rinascimento*, 455. See also Harvey who notes that the complaint as a genre, voiced by the seduced and abadoned woman, is "the paradigmatic ventriloquized text." This genre also greatly flourished during the English Renaissance. *Ventriloquized Voices*, 140.

[8] Russell, "Intenzionalità artistica della disperata," 175.

[9] Several other examples are provided by Russell, 175–181.

[10] Harvey compellingly shows that "ventriloquism and intertextuality overlap, for, in both cases, a putatively single and bounded utterance is destabilized by questions of origin, authorship, and ownership." *Ventriloquized Voices*, 10.

[11] On this type of transposition, see Kristéva, *Revolution in Poetic Language*, 59–60.

[12] Silvia Longhi, "Lettere a Ippolito e a Teseo. La voce femminile nell'elegia," 389–390.

[13] Longhi, "Lettere a Ippolito e a Teseo," 394, and Rosati, "Epistola elegiaca e lamento femminile," 34–35, and "L'elegia al femminile: le *Heroides* di Ovidio," 29: 71–94.

[14] Rosati, "Epistola elegiaca e lamento femminile," 34–35.

[15] Stefano Carrai, "Appunti sulla preistoria dell'elegia volgare," 13.

[16] Some of the *disperata* poets, such as Tebaldeo and Serafino also wrote elegies.

[17] Vecchi Galli, "Percorsi dell'elegia quattrocentesca in volgare," 54–56. Vecchi Galli convincingly argues that the personification of Love, Death and Fortune is something that the elegy borrows from the *disperata*, 55.

[18] Volpi, "La vita e le rime di Simone Serdini," 38. According to Volpi, this is the most popular poem written by il Saviozzo, 43.

[19] "In questo capitolo si contiene come una giovane s'inamorò d'un pellegrino garzone; e perché esso da' lacci d'Amore in tutto sciolto era, non la volea vedere. Ella si lamenta, chiamando in suo favore quattro i più bei gioveni che fûr mai, e poi si dispera in questa forma." 90. The four most beautiful young men are Narcissus, Ganymede, Hyppolitus, and Polydorus.

[20] For a discussion on descriptions of male physical beauty in Renaissance poetry, see Gary Ferguson, *Queer (Re)Readings in the French Renaissance*, 156–160.

[21] This image is very similar to the ones found in Feliciano's and d'Aubigné's poems discussed in chapters Three and Five.

[22] "Capitolo d'una fanciulla la quale fu tradita e ingannata da 'n suo amante, e infine morta; e fece saviamente l'autore d'esso a non ci mettere il nome d'alcuno di loro, perché fu gran signore che commise tale errore e inconveniente." Serdini, *Rime*, 185.

[23] Nelia Saxby, "Strutture narrative nella 'Storia di una fanciulla tradita' di Simone Serdini," 108.

[24] Russell has already pointed out that desperation and persecution are expressed in seduction and abandonment, while the male cursing and destructive violence are not present.

[25] Martines, however, notes that: "The darkness and anguish of love also appear, even more movingly, in his narrative of 'a girl betrayed and deceived by her lover.' Here he seems able to project his own rue and despondency into the figure of the wretched girl, thus intensifying the poem's impact." *Strong Words*, 129.

[26] See Sapegno, *Poeti minori del Trecento*, 231–238. All references to Alberti's poem will be based on this edition. See also Flamini, *La lirica toscana del Rinascimento*, 389–392, and 452, and *Enciclopedia Treccani*, http://www.treccani.it/enciclopedia/antonio-degli-alberti_%28Enciclopedia-Italiana%29/

[27] See Ovid's "Heroides VII."

[28] See Antonio Lanza, *Polemiche e berte letterarie nella Firenze del primo Quattrocento*, 66–76, his *Lirici toscani del Quattrocento*, 549–584, and Flamini, *La lirica toscana*, 289–290. See also *Enciclopedia Treccani*, http://www.treccani.it/enciclopedia/domenico-da-prato_%28Dizionario-Biografico%29/ All references to da Prato's poems will be based on Lanza's edition in *Lirici toscani*.

[29] Flamini, *La lirica toscana del Rinascimento*, 455. Flamini provides a brief analysis of other poems as well, from il Saviozzo's to "Le Stanze della Ruffianella di Siena," to da Prato, 450–467. He too sees Ovid's *Heroides* and *Metamorphoses* as source texts for these compositions.

[30] "Canzon morale del detto ser Domenico fatta ad istanzia d'una nobile iuvene, la quale abbandonata dal marito e da l'amante ingannata, veggendosi da i parenti legata miseramente in prigione, in cotal forma si conduole." 531.

[31] "E tu, per cui tante lacrime verso,/lieto delli mie affanni,/.../no passerai molti anni,/ché in crudi danni – Amor porratti al fondo./Muova Iunon quell'ira a te, secondo/che al teban sangue, e Iove e i fati e i cieli!/Piovan li vulcan teli/sopra di te!" vv. 78–87, 533.

[32] "Rimolatino del detto ser Domenico come una vaga fantina in una sua camera seco stessa si conduole d'amore e perché l'amato non s'accorge del suo amore." 543.

[33] These verses closely echo il Pistoia's *disperata*'s famous beginning, "La nuda terra s'ha già messo il manto" (Chapter Three).

[34] Here is where these female-voiced *disperate* differ from Ovid's *Heroides*, as he is completely absent from the epistles' narration.

[35] On the myth of Ganymede, see James M. Saslow, *Ganymede in the Renaissance*, 155–160, and Joseph Cady, "Renaissance Awareness and Language of Heterosexuality," 143–158.

[36] Ovid, *Metamorphoses*, 83–84. All references to Echo and Narcissus will be based on this edition.

[37] Ray, *Writing Gender in Women's Letter Collections*, 214.

Chapter Three

The *Disperata* in the Quattrocento

Quanto qui legi scritto,
Ti manda quell'afflitto – e sventurato,
Che vive desperato – in vita obscura,
Lontan da tua figura – & di sua vita.

Il Cariteo

Quattrocento Poets as Models for the *Disperata* Genre

To understand how the *disperata* genre developed in later centuries and
spread throughout Italy and into France, we need to understand the role
imitation plays. In addition, by examining the early models of the genre––
their background, the courts, their *topoi*––we can see the influence they
had on later poets. Imitation was one of the main literary practices in the
Renaissance in both Italy and France. Its application allowed the adoption
and transformation of the *disperata*, thus further implementing the genre
and allowing it to organically surge and expand from the fourteenth to the
sixteenth century. Imitation is, therefore, crucial to the transmission of the
genre. As seen in the previous chapter, the *disperata* genre closely intersects
with gender and with imitation, as the intertextual and intratextual relations from text to text are crucial to the literary culture of the Medieval
and Renaissance periods. The *disperata* writers of the Quattrocento,
working mostly at court, established and popularized it throughout Italy.
Although Dante, Petrarch, and Boccaccio dominated the poetry of the
previous century, other poets as well were able to pursue their own literary conventions, following the Petrarchan model but also drawing inspiration from sources particular to their geographical region.[1] For the most
part, three *disperata* writers influence this century: in the North, Serafino
de' Ciminelli, known as l'Aquilano, and Antonio Tebaldeo; and in the
South, Benedetto Gareth, known as il Cariteo. Indeed, all three writers
saw their poems circulated in manuscript form, printed in several editions,
anthologized, read, and often put to music. The many editions of Serafino,
Tebaldeo, and Cariteo, and their reputation in both Italy and France, tes-

tify to their fame.[2] Their *disperate* spread the genre throughout the entire century, North and South of the peninsula, and on to the work of the next wave of *disperata* poets in the sixteenth century, hence securing its continuity and recognition.

In recent years, court poetry has attracted more attention, particularly from Italian scholars,[3] finally bringing further consideration and appreciation to other authors whose work is vital to my discussion. These authors include Antonio Cammelli, known as il Pistoia, Panfilo Sasso, Galeotto del Carretto, Rosello Roselli, Felice Feliciano, and Leonardo Giustiniani. They were important figures in constructing and directing real poetic tastes and reading trends, as they not only traveled throughout the courts of Northern Italy due to the social and intellectual nature of their commitments, but they also influenced literary culture all over the peninsula.[4] Literary scholars have recently historicized the lyric production of these Northern courts, the so-called "corti padane" of the "Quattrocento lombardo," by closely reexamining their political and cultural surroundings and corollaries.[5] This effort has convincingly established a direct link between this lyric, that of the Sicilian School, and of the literature of *langue d'oc* and *d'oïl*. As previously discussed, several scholars have called attention to the intertextualities between a few French authors, including Deschamps and Rutebeuf, and *disperate*'s authors.[6] The reception of French texts, especially in the Northern Italian courts and in Provençal language, is well documented in the many translations and adaptations of medieval and early-Renaissance writings.[7]

There are several common threads to these Italian poets' biographies, including their extensive travels, their relations to important noble families, very often the same influential ones, such as the Estes and the Gonzagas, their roles at court, their connections with each other, and the fortune and influence that they secured through their diplomatic and literary endeavors. However, the similarities are not all positive. Each poet also experienced great trauma in times of war and economic uncertainty, life under political pressure, and exile, all of which recur in their verses. Historical events adversely impacted these authors' lives, as political unrest affected and often upended their livelihood: Italy was ravaged by relentless wars for a hundred years, from 1350 to 1450, and in 1494, King Charles VIII descended upon Italy, starting the first Italian War. Struggles intensified until 1527, the year of the Sack of Rome, when the French kings fought against the Habsburg emperors for the dominion of Italy. The city-states of Northern Italy were deeply involved in these wars, and deeply distressed by them. As John Harold Plumb notes: "Politics became a murderous game in which death in bed came only to the skillful or the lucky. The savagery used by men in pursuit of power was due to the nature of society and the prizes that it offered."[8] Furthermore, a weakened Italy was still trying to recover from the great bubonic plague of the previous century, and tyranny flourished in such conditions.[9] The role of the court intellectual was tightly entwined with that of the soldier, as many poets also fought alongside their patron, as we shall soon see.[10] Thus, they were haunted by an ever-present sense of death and danger, which found uninhibited expression in their *disperate*. These historical circumstances haunted the lives of the French *disperata* authors as well: when the genre spread to France, it thus found a similarly devastated culture.

The court lyric of the Quattrocento, the so-called "lirica cortigiana," has often prompted negative critical judgments as frivolous, ornamented, precious, superficial, easy, and pervaded with witticisms.[11] Giuseppe Manacorda's judgment is characteristic of this type of critique. In referring to Carretto, Manacorda notes that he "poetasse alla maniera dei rimatori cortigiani del restante d'Italia" as if all Italian court poets "poeticized" in the same manner.[12] Despite few regional and personal variations, court lyric often includes the following traits: a linguistic code, mostly inspired by Petrarch's *Canzoniere*; a particularly refined style; dedicatory verses that praise capricious or benevolent lords, kings, or patronesses; themes and images focusing on Love, the beloved, her body and her body parts; and suffering mostly related to Love's pangs. Thus, court lyric displays fairly unified and consistent language and themes.[13] The poets within this tradition were not only poets working at the court, with an audience of mainly court members, but they were also courtiers themselves who participated in most court activities and politics. They favored genres such as the sonnet, the *strambotto*, the eclogue, the *capitolo*, and of course, the *disperata*, and demonstrated dexterity with the *terza rima*. Furthermore, they published successful *canzonieri*.[14]

There is a close relationship between court poetry and the *disperata*. Poets used this genre because of its suggestive content, but also because they wanted to display and prove their literary skills. The Quattrocento and early-Cinquecento *canzonieri* featured the same variety of genres, so court poets used the *disperata* as an additional proof of their creative skills to be appended to their already prolific catalogue.[15] As Vecchi Galli notes, "la maniera cortigiana fu assunta come linguaggio comune di poesia" (the courtly manner was assumed as a common poetic language),[16] and indeed, the courtly manner became itself the common lyric language. Writers hence subordinated their language, manner and style to court culture, whose poetry became part of the fabric of late fourteenth-, fifteenth- and sixteenth-century tradition, and greatly influenced its many unrivaled manifestations.[17] Furthermore, the court milieu in both Italy and France was instrumental in producing, consuming, and spreading lyric creations, including *disperate*, to other literary circles, salons, and academies.[18] This discussion will continue in later chapters because in the imitation of the *disperata* by the French poets we encounter variations and interpretations that demonstrate the range and depth of court culture, as well as its impact.[19]

Italian court poetry was met with admiration in both Italy and France, which is also why the *disperata* genre became known and valued. In France, the *disperate* of il Pistoia, il Saviozzo, Sasso, Carretto, Tebaldeo and Serafino were well known. The Bibliothèque nationale in Paris houses several original Italian *disperate* that undoubtedly offered French poets a variety of imitative sources, from the Italian Trecento, Quattrocento, and Cinquecento. Although these are original *disperate*, their authorship is not always sound. One example stands out as an archetype of *disperata* and its circulation as an instance of its transmission from Italy to France. Réserve Yd 617 is a remarkable book, in *quarto*, titled *Cerbero invoco, composto per Simone Sardini ["sic"], ... vocato Saviozo. El Contrario di Cerbero che comincia: "Certo Jesu intendo di chiamare." La Disperata, composta da Antonio de Tebaldi* (See Figure 2, p. 26). A library note however, explains that the *disperata* here attributed to Tebaldeo is different than the one which appears under the same title in other books, also by Tebaldeo.[20] Moreover, this *disperata* is also titled "La disperata III" in Serafino's *canzoniere*. Indeed, this *disperata* wrongly attributed to both Tebaldeo and Serafino is "The disperata" by il Pistoia, which I have briefly discussed in the Introduction and which I will analyze in more details later in this chapter.[21] Unfortunately, it is impossible to trace an accurate genesis for this thin volume, but it is interesting to note that it does contain the best-known *disperata*, written by il Pistoia, albeit falsely attributed, as well as Serdini's famous *disperata* "Cerbero invoco," and finally a *contro-disperata* that proves the popularity of this genre, as this is a response against the *disperata*. Thus, it is easy to see how the genre, although it was not always transmitted in straightforward ways, had an important place in the fifteenth-century and sixteenth-century book market. Indeed, the *disperata* was a genre that attained importance, a reputation and even admiration, as various editions and manuscripts acquired by French bibliophiles and libraries attest.

Il Pistoia's *disperata* also appears in the Appendix of Weber's 1960 critical edition to d'Aubigné's *Le Printemps*, yet again misattributed to Serafino dall'Aquila as "Disparata Terza."[22] Thus, up to the twentieth century, Serafino and Tebaldeo were erroneously known in France as the authors of this widely circulated composition.[23] "La disperata" can also be found in another rare volume housed at the Bibliothèque nationale, titled *La disperata. Sventurato Pelegrino. Littera damore. Sonetti* (Yd 621) (Figure 4). Atlhough the composition is anonymous, the library catalogue attributes it to Serafino Ciminelli, but again, the text is il Pistoia's *disperata*, with only slight variations in some verses, such as the following variations in the very first stanza:

> La nuda terra sa Gia misso il manto
> tenero verde e ogni cor sallegra
> e io pur ora do principio al mio pianto

(The naked earth has already put on its/tender and green cloak, and every heart rejoices/and now I start my weeping)

However, its last stanza is drastically different:

> In abisso alloco piu profondo
> fra disperati mi retroverrai
> parlor di questo cieco e falso mondo.[24]

(In the deepest abyss/among the *disperati* you will find me/talking about this blind and false world.)

This misattribution is particularly significant in France, as poets and scholars alike thought that this poem was authored by Serafino because it is included in many editions of his *canzoniere*.[25] However, this *disperata* belongs undoubtedly to il Pistoia, as Pèrcopo and Carla Rossi demonstrate. They also provide its few variances, noting as well the aforementioned two volumes now housed at the Bibliothèque nationale in Paris.[26] Thus, since the same text appears with several disparities in small volumes, its attribution has been often debated and misattributed, generating literary assumptions and confusions that have affected the genre's reception and scholarship. Most importantly, it has affected the history of imitation of this particular text, as well as the subsequent intertexts, something that I intend to ratify.

Figure 4. La disperata. Sventurato Pelegrino. Littera damore. Sonetti.
(By permission of the Bibliothèque nationale de France.)

Antonio Cammelli, Known as Il Pistoia and "La Disperata"

As discussed in the Introduction, the author of the famous "La disperata" is Antonio Cammelli, known as il Pistoia (1436–1502), who was an
important intellectual figure in Northern Italian court society. Il Pistoia's
text is fundamental because it served as a rich source for future *disperate*:
its *topoi* and attitudes developed into a strong model and starting point
for other writers to read, appreciate, and eventually imitate. As Carla
Rossi notes, il Pistoia was acclaimed during his lifetime and venerated
during the Cinquecento, a personality in whose company were poets such
as Serafino, Antonio Alamanni, and Galeotto del Carretto.[27] Il Pistoia
was also in direct contact with Tebaldeo and Sasso at the main courts of
Novellara, Correggio, Mantova, and Ferrara, until his death in 1502, perpetuating the tradition of the migrant intellectual and *literato*, whose fate
was strictly dependent on his pen.[28]

Scholars agree that il Pistoia's famous *disperata* is the concluding
poem of his *canzoniere*. Carla Rossi discusses it at length in an article,
but does not include it in her monograph on the writer.[29] Spoken on
behalf of Lodovico Sforza to lament the loss of his young wife Beatrice
d'Este, who died of childbirth in 1497, it is a depository of the main
and constant *topoi* of the genre, such as the integral role of nature and
its relationship with the poet; the presence of numerous wild and fiery
animals; the many outbursts and damnations; the speaker's repetitive
references to, and calls for death; mythological and literary figures and
allusions; a fraught search for solitary and dark places; sadism and masochism; persuasive pleas to the reader to witness and believe his emotional
and physical distress, and finally, the crucial moments of hopelessness
and dark despair. A continuous intertextuality is thus established with
other *disperate*, but also with the lyric tradition of court poetry, in which
Petrarchism and Classical poetry intimately mesh.[30] The combination of
these elements makes this *disperata* a well-accomplished model for others to follow.

Il Pistoia's long poem starts with the image of winter changing to
an idyllic spring, which traditionally represents a time to rejoice, to fall in
love, and a new beginning in the speaker's life and nature:

> La nuda terra s'ha già messo il manto
> tenero e verde, e ciascun cor s'allegra
> ed io pur do principio al mio gran pianto
> (vv. 1–3, 243).[31]

For him, though, spring is a time of sorrow and tears, and his pain unleashes an expression of the battered self. As spring begins and all other creatures celebrate, he alone initiates his sorrow.[32] The conflict between the detached "I" and his joyful and unfazed surroundings continues in the following verses:

> Gli arbori piglian frondi, io veste negra,
> gli animal rinova la sua spoglia,
> la mia, squarciata ognhor, men si fa integra

(The trees bear their leaves, I wear dark clothes,/the animals renew their fur,/mine, all ragged, is less unspoiled) (vv. 4–6, 243).

And while nature rejoices and the sun brightens the universe, the desperate persona prefers the seduction of darkness: "Io vo cercando tenebre profonde" (v. 12, 243).

The first twenty-five verses of the poem emphasize the difference between the suffering speaker and the rest of nature and the world, which rejoice in their happiness. He alone is left by himself to suffer, at war, under the ground, and most of all, free to pursue death: "io ad ogni passo più la morte invoco" (v. 21, 243). Besides, when he suffers, cries and yells, the world is indifferent to his pain, and to the many dreadful calamities that only affect the poet-persona thus preventing him from enjoying his existence: "e grido e piango, e tutto il mondo tace" (v. 105, 246).

Ten verses begin with the anaphora "the others" (Gli altri), as to indicate, and even heighten, the distance between the persecuted speaker and the rest of the world, which instead remains at peace. Through descriptions of the others' happiness, he is better able to convince the reader of his many tragedies:

> Gli altri scaldansi al sole, io adiaccio al foco,
> Gli altri braman vivento esser felici,
>
> ...
>
> Gli altri cercan compagni, gli altri amici,
> ed io d'alcun trovar mi doglio e lagno,
> bramando quei che mi sono più nemici.
>
> ...
>
> Gli altri veder vorian ciascun contento:
> ed io ogn'uom morir d'ira e di rabbia,
> e in caos ritornar ogni elemento.

(The others warm up in the sun, and I freeze by the fire,/The others wish to live happily,/ ... /The others look for a companion, some others for friends,/and I complain and lament with everybody,/ wishing for my enemies./ ... /The others would like to see everybody happy:/and I want to see every man dying of anger and rage,/and every element be in chaos.) (vv. 19–54, 243–244).

Like all other *disperate*, the poem alludes to and ultimately calls upon death. The word death, "morte", drums at irregular intervals, but all along the 196 verses it remains the only faithful companion of the *disperato*. Indeed, it is the variety and intensity of death's appearance that is the most striking in this poem, as it slowly penetrates all other dimensions of the narration. Remarkably though, what sets this *disperata* apart is that it is not about death. Rather, it is about a darkest hopelessness that not even death can appease, because the speaker is imagining an afterlife that is steeped in damnation. In fact, despite the many calls for death—"or Morte vien, ch'io non ti temo," (death please come as I do not fear you) (v. 180, 248)—despite suicide and violent fatalities, such as an invocation to Cerberus to open his mouth and swallow him:

> Apri, Cerbero, omai a questo passo
> tutt'e tre bocche e giù vivo m'ingolla,
> ché volentier nel tuo gran ventre passo!
> (vv. 181–183, 248),

the poet-persona is condemned to confront eternity in despair. This suggestive narrative functions as a mirror into which readers can see themselves, so as to experience death as fully and as many times as possible. Just like before, readers are urged to witness the spectacle of the speaker's death, this time by a very inventive and powerful verse, as if he was walking death himself: "Chi non sa che sia morte, in me si specchi!"—"If you do not know death, just look at me!" (v. 30, 243). All hope and promises are gone: "io piango mie speranze al tutto rotte" (v. 33, 243). In a dark, masochistic mode, the speaker wishes for his suffering not only to continue, but also to intensify. His death, as the final verses proclaim, will be an example to the rest of the world: "Mia morte a tutto il mondo sia palese,/ché un solo essempio schiva molti danni." (vv. 195–196, 248) Indeed, in the last ten lines, the lover-persona aspires to serve as an exemplum for other lovers as the *disperato* who suffered first and most, and whose tragic adventure and end should spare other lovers from the same tragic experience.

As in the previous century's *disperate*, this composition also demands the witness' undivided attention, and the whole world becomes the speaker's stage where to enact and re-enact his death, over and over.

Often, he demonstrates with concrete examples his despair in order to persuade his audience, and with a decisive verse—"Questo è quel mal che m'ha posto l'assedio," "This is the evil that besieged me" (v. 139, 247)— he summons up all of the evils that wrecked his life and that left him no choice but to despair. This compelling image will resonate in other texts, thus strengthening the tradition.

The ninth stanza begins with another common *topos* of the genre, the enumeration of wild animals:[33] "Guffi, cornici sonanmi alle orecchi," (v. 28, 243) and,

> Tigri, leöni, e voi, fiere silvestre
> vaghe di sangue uman, presto venite
> a sbranar queste membra mie terrestre!
> (vv. 172–174, 248).

The animals summoned by the narrator are wild and blood-thirsty; some of them belong to the imaginary and fantastic world, as they do not inhabit Italy. Tigers and lions in particular add an exotic flavor to the poem, while night owls, birds and snakes belong to the Italian lyric tradition and symbolize ominous premonitions. However, in the *disperate* they become entrenched in the persona's curses and add to his angst, while at the same time deepening the general disconsolate tone. Furthermore, they are also portrayed in an unnatural way, as verse 60 demonstrates, in which snakes, rather than birds, fly, undoubtedly to depict a world turned upside down by the *disperata* imaginary: "e, invece degli uccei, volar serpenti" (v. 60, 245).[34] Mostly, they foreshadow the speaker's bitter and violent end in the tight grasp of wild beasts' teeth, such as in wolves' mouths: "il corpo lasso/ a' lupi" (vv. 179–180, 248). Although these animals are summoned to hasten death and, at times, the end of the entire world, they are also witnesses and accomplices to the poet-persona's hopelessness. They are, thus, simultaneously signifiers and enablers of his death, and they embody a premonition of his own death wish throughout the text:

> Che ogni augurio a me fusse mortifero,
> tutti in me coniurati li animali,
> ed ogni cibo mio fusse pestifero
> (vv. 88–90, 245).

As previously mentioned, nature as well becomes a witness and an accomplice (vv. 4–6, 243). Like all other *disperate*, here too nature is personified and serves as consoler with an active role. In fact, from the very beginning of his *disperata*, il Pistoia positions nature as a juxtaposition and as a personal oxymoron: nature and animals rejoice, while he, alone, cries. Despair splits the speaker from the rest of the world. Nature's colors are vibrant and cheerful, while his are mostly black, and while the sun enlightens the earth, he is plunged in darkness and buried alive: "Il sol più luce e più rende splendore;/a me par notte ed esser giù sotterra" (vv. 14–15, 243).

The speaker dwells in isolated places, drenched in darkness; grottoes and solitary forests symbolizing nature at its best for the desperate lover, as for il Pistoia's: "io vo cercando tenebre profonde" (v. 12, 243). They paint a world turned upside down, in which the poetic-persona calls for a complete chaos to overwhelm the universe: "e in caos ritornar ogni elemento" (v. 54, 244), and for the world to be overturned so that everything may lose its order, sense and meaning:

> non si vedesse più sera o mattina,
> ma oscurità di nebbia e fumo nero;
> il sol nascesse là, dove declina.

(that we might not see evening nor morning,/but an obscurity of fog and black smoke;/the sun would rise where it sets.) (vv. 67–69, 245).

Three rhetorical questions underscore the nonsensical situation faced by the poetic persona:

> Come può mai parlar un che sia morto,
> come pò mai veder un che non vede?
> come a un ch'ha ragion, mai se fa torto?

(How can the dead ever speak/how can the blind ever see?/how can someone who is right, ever be wronged?) (vv. 112–114, 246).

This type of interrogations becomes a motif in the *disperata* and in its future adaptations, and rather than an answer, they are meant to elicit the reader's attention and allegiance.[35] The oxymoronic language and attitude, though perfectly adhering to the genre's general stance that the world does not make sense, seamlessly function with the speaker's frame of mind. In fact, verses 55 to 76 (244–245) present a series of absurd situations that he wishes to see as total emotional turmoil and physical cataclysm ("Vorrei veder", v. 55, 244).

Just like Antonio Beccari, il Pistoia projects a sadistic viewpoint onto the world premised by the anaphora "vorrei," one of the genre's integral rhetorical elements:

Vorrei veder il foco su la sabbia,
fulgurar poi dove abitan le genti,
stridi, pianti, lamenti, aprir de labbia;
E che Eolo lasciasse tutti i venti,
sì che cadesse a terra ogni ediffico;
e, invece degli uccei, volar serpenti.

(I wish to see the sand on fire,/lightening strike where people live,/
screaming, crying, lamentations uttered by mouths;/And Aeolus
let all winds,/so that every building on earth falls;/and, instead of
birds, snakes would fly.) (vv. 55–60, 244).

Cerberus, Lucifer, and all infernal furies are summoned to devour the
battered body (v. 66, 245). They inhabit this long composition and ani-
mate its infernal landscape. Furthermore, the speaker recalls the sad lives
and deaths of many mythological figures such as Sisyphus, Meleager,
Erysichthon, and Acteon, and is gravely determined to bring to life all of
the unfortunate lovers that belong to the lyric tradition, from Antiquity to
his present. His intention is to add his own voice to this tradition, thereby
guaranteeing the genre's continuity and survival.

The lyricism often intensifies throughout il Pistoia's poem, as in the
following verses, where both the world and Love are blamed for their blatant indifference toward the lover-persona:

O mondo cieco, o mondo falso e vario,
o Amor senza pieta, o Amor fallace,
a me sì aspro, a me tanto contrario!

(Oh blind world, oh false and varied world,/oh Love without pity,
oh misleading Love,/so harsh and hostile toward me!) (vv. 100–
102, 246).

Finally, in his conclusion, he addresses his beloved in a strong plea, again
with the use of an imperative anaphora, "Hear!" "Odi." Here he is able to
systematically summarize his many tribulations, pain and its reasons, and
his desperate resolution to shun life:

O anima gentil che mi tormenta,
odi il mio pianto! odi il dolore amaro!
odi un che per tua causa si lamenta!
odi collui che non vede il sol chiaro!
odi collui che la vita rifiuta!
odi collui cui il morir gli è caro!

(Oh gentle soul that torments me,/hear my crying! hear my bitter sorrow!/hear the one who laments in your house!/hear the one who cannot see the bright sun!/hear the one who refuses life!/hear the one who wishes to die!) (vv. 163–168, 248).

Il Pistoia's *disperata* is undoubtedly rich in images and attitudes that will recur in other Quattrocento texts, as in the following text by Panfilo Sasso, and that will further establish some of the genre's *topoi*.

Panfilo Sasso's "Disperata contro l'amore"

Panfilo Sasso (ca. 1447–1527) was a renowned and respected poet of the Italian Renaissance, who entertained friendships with many other famous poets, such as Serafino and Cassandra Fedele.[36] In his poetry, in addition to building on the *topoi* of the genre, Sasso both imitates and subverts Petrarch, and his poetry will become an intertext for the French poets. Sasso's poetry appears in another text in the Bibliothèque nationale in Paris, alongside il Pistoia's *disperata*. The title of the work, *Novelle et lamenti et poesie d'amore italiani* (Réserve Yd 608–620), reflects its content: a collection of poems, *novelle*, and various laments against the pangs of Love, in which the *disperata* genre fits well.[37] It comprises "Cerbero invoco" by il Saviozzo; a *contro-disperata* titled "El contrario di Cerbero che comincia Certo Jesu intendo di chiamare," which remains anonymous; and "La disperata composta da Antonio Tebaldi Ferrarese," which is indeed il Pistoia's *disperata*, discussed above, and thus here again falsely attributed to Tebaldeo. The small volume ends with the "Disperata del Clarissimo Poeta Miser Pamphilo Sasso," titled "Disperata contro l'amore" (1503).[38]

Sasso's poetry can certainly be classified under the rubric of "lirica cortigiana," and thus, has been often studied and judged in these terms and together with Serafino's and Tebaldeo's poetry, a triumvirate of notorious court writers of Northern Italy. However, despite his significant renown and productivity during his time period, nowadays Sasso's work is not often read, nor studied. His collection includes 537 poems, comprising 406 sonnets, 39 *capitoli*, 5 eclogues, and 87 *strambotti*.[39] Two other *disperate* are listed as *capitoli*: "Poi ch'ogni arbor si spoglia e già la terra" and "Era la stella sotto la qual nacque", two blatant examples of how the *disperata* was listed as a *capitolo*.

In an analysis of Sasso's poetry and impact on the literary tradition, Malinverni claims that Sasso is a true "virtuoso del più tipico registro 'dis-

perato' tartoquattrocentesco," that is a "virtuoso of the most typical reg-
ister of 'despair' of the late fifteenth century" because many of his poems
carry indeed an attitude, approach, and language of despair.[40] However,
it is his sonnets that have spurred the most critical interest, and not his
disperata, probably because they better responded to his readers' thirst for
light and graceful verses steeped in the Petrarchan tradition, as exempli-
fied by the sonnet discussed in the previous chapter.[41] Though these *disperate* have gone largely unnoticed, Sasso's biography also mirrors that of
other *disperata* authors. Girolamo Tiraboschi notes that he enjoyed much
fame during his life; he traveled often for political reasons especially from
Modena to Mantova, and from Verona to Brescia.[42] In 1523, Sasso was
accused of heresy, an event that adversely impacted his life, but that aligns
him with other poets of the Italian and French Renaissance, who also were
persecuted for sympathizing with the Reformation, or, as in the case of
some French poets, for being Protestant.[43] These biographical events—
constant travel between courts and adaptation to new lords' expectations,
and accusations or investigations of heresy—defined the lives of *disperata*
authors in both Italy and France.[44]

Sasso's "Disperata contro l'amore" is a rich text encompassing most
of the *disperata topoi*, as well as images and themes common to other
Petrarchan poets of the period. However, since it concentrates on maledictions "against Love," it does not encompass other topics found for
example in il Pistoia's or in Beccari's texts. It is interesting to note that
Sasso specifies the content of his *disperata* in the title: "Disperata against
love" thus characterizing it from the outset as a complaint about Love,
which also warrants its place in the collection *Novelle et lamenti et poesie d'amore italiani*. Indeed, the poem is a long lament against both Love
and its unfair treatment of the poetic persona, populated by lovers from
the literary tradition who have been wronged and have suffered greatly
because of their unrequited passion. Its very beginning shares significant
intertextualities with il Pistoia's *disperata*, such as the naked earth, and its
animated address to nature:

> Poi chogni arbor si spoglia: & gia la terra
> De fiori: & ver de herbette e fatta nuda
> E l'aria sapparecchia a farne guerra

(Since every tree undresses: and the earth already/is stripped of
flowers and grass/And the air gets ready for war) (vv. 1–3).[45]

The damnations and vituperation are numerous. First, the lover-persona damns
the moment of the *innamoramento*, an invective that is repeated several times:

> Ahi crudo amor: sia maladetto l'arco
> Col qual me desti la mortal ferita
> E me pligliasti come cervo al varco
>
> (vv. 82–84),

and: "Ahi crudo amor sia maladeta lhora" (v. 97), and: "Ah crudo amor sia maladetto el giorno" (v. 112). Indeed, the anaphora "Ahi crudo amor," "Alas cruel love," appears nine times in the text, and the anaphora "Amor amar sia maladetto," "Love, damned be to love," appears five times. In the *disperata* genre, Love and maledictions go hand in hand, and they are strictly and lyrically conjoined as to better represent and illustrate the miseries of love. Thus, its injustices, its ruses, and the harshness the lover-*disperato* has to endure are blamed throughout:

> Sanguinoso Tyran: tu dai la forma
> Del viver sencia regula a la gente
> E como bestia gubernarse in torma

(Bloody Tyrant: you know how to give life to people/and make them live without rules/Like animals live in throng) (vv. 267–269).

Love makes a beast out of a man and is portrayed as an infamy that afflicts and threatens human life: "Tu sei la infamia della vita nostra" (v. 231). As already noted, the beloved is barely mentioned and is not the object of damnations, as in many other *disperate*. On the contrary, Sasso's poem is a very focused and organized composition: the lover-persona considers Love, "crudo amor," responsible for all of his misfortunes and pangs and for delivering him to the beautiful lady who immediately won him over with her sweet smile,

> Ahi crudo amor tu m'hai purtroppo offeso
> A darme tanta doglia: e tanta pena
> Essendo in le tue man ligato e preso

(Alas, cruel love, you have offended me so/You give me so much pain: and so much sorrow/As I lie caught and constrained in your hands) (vv. 279–281).[46]

What is particularly striking about Sasso's *disperata* is his complete and unequivocal accusations against Love, which is described as bitter, proud, without piety nor mercy, and the main reason for man's ruin:

> Amor amar: amor fiero e sleale

> Amor sencia pieta: sencia mercede
> Amor cagion d'ogni ruina e male

(Bitter Love: proud and disloyal love/Love without pity: without mercy/Love, you are the reason for all ruin and evil) (vv. 324–326).

Other *topoi* of the genre emerge as well. For example, the narrator wishes for the world to be turned upside down, "Voria che andaste la terra sotosopra" (v. 126). Three anaphors debut with "Voria," in order to express catastrophic wishes and scenarios, while vividly describing images that depict a world whose order and values are in complete turmoil:

> Tu non riguardi lo amico: el parente
> El figliol fai congiongere con la matre
> Tanto gli accende de furor la mente
> La sorella al fratel: la figlia al patre

(You don't look at the friend: or at the parent/The son you join with the mother/For you set his mind afire/The sister with the brother: the daughter with the father) (vv. 270–273).

The association of bizarre and incestuous relationships—mother and son, sister and brother, and daughter and father—is meant to not only shock the reader, but also to gather these unthinkable scenarios in order to better represent the poet-lover's despair. The *disperata* flaunts a nonsensical and apocalyptic world order, without reasonable laws to govern humanity and nature. This sense of chaos continues throughout the poem. As it reaches macrocosmic proportions, Mars and Saturn will be conjoined (vv. 144–145) and assume additional negative connotations. While the vituperations abound throughout the poem, they form twelve verses in particular that start with the familiar "Sia maladetto" (vv. 297–308) damning the narrator's birth ("del nacer mio" v. 298). Furthermore, the lover-persona describes his "infectious" relationship with God and adversarial to other men in predominantly resentful words, as if to illustrate a disconnected life: "Che la infelice mia persona naque/A gli uomini nimica: infecta a dio" (That my unhappy person be born/an enemy to all men: infectious to God) (vv. 301–302). The maledictions also encompass the various forms of nourishment he received since birth and that condemned him to a life of great pangs and tortures, a *topos* widely exploited in the *disperata*. In retrospect, the speaker wishes for death at the very offset of his life, and lives throughout longing for death, a paradox that will also appear in the verses of the French poets. Likewise, terrible monsters, nocturnal birds and wild animals threaten a world in which order and peace are lost forever: "Vol gli uccelli: che stridon la notte/La nottula: la loccho: el guffo vanno" (vv. 13–14) and, "Venga el leon nemeo: l'harpia: e l'ydra/ El porco etholo: el maratonio Tauro" (vv. 107–108).

The landscape is infernal, rugged, yet fully welcoming for the *disperato* and his sorrow, "Piangendo per spelonche: rupe, e grotte" (v. 15). However, because Love and its tribulations are the main culprit and antagonist of the text, there are not as many descriptions of nature as in other *disperate*. The lover-persona ends his tragic lament with a warning, "Voglio finir la vita con lamento"—"I want to end my life with a lament" (v. 334). Because those who follow the cruel tyrant will undoubtedly die in a state of despair, he wishes to write this warning with his own blood on the cold marble as his epitaph (v. 339) and ends with a final admonition against Love:

> Colui che siegue el tyran crudo amore
> El cor con le sue man si straccia e parte.
> E disperato al fin per doglia more.

> (The one who follows love, the cruel tyrant/Tears his heart out with his own hands, and leaves./And in the end, he dies *disperato* because of grief.) (vv. 340–342).

Thus, the text concludes with death by despair, one that the speaker has longed and wished for throughout the poem, and that he inflicts upon himself. Though this ending is common among *disperate*, the poem is also a repository of traditional and Petrarchan elements, as for example "mio primo giovenil error" (the first mistake of my youth) (v. 3, 37) and the damning of the month, day, and hour of the fateful *innamoramento*. The poem is, therefore, a good example of the interplay between Petrarchism and *disperata*. However, there is an important difference: while Petrarch's lover-persona "blesses" these fatal moments, the *disperato* damns them. Petrarch writes:

> Benedetto sia 'l giorno e 'l mese et l'anno
> E la stagione e 'l tempo et l'ora e 'l punto
> E 'l paese e 'l loco ov'io fui giunto
> Da' duo begli occhi che legato m'ànno
> Et benedetto il primo dolce affanno

> (Blessed be the day and the month and the year/And the season and the time and the hour, and the moment/And the town and the place

where I was struck/By the two beautiful eyes that bound me/And blessed be the first sweet grief) (vv. 1–5, 139).

While Sasso writes:

> Ahi crudo amor sia maladetta lhora
> Chel parlare scoltai vano: e fallace
> Che a ciascun fai: che prima sinamora
>
> ...
>
> Ahi crudo amor sia maladetto el mese
> Che me condusse in obscur precipitio
> E fu cagion de le mie prime offese

(Alas cruel love, damned be the hour/When I listened in vain: and the way you deceive/everybody who first falls in love/ ... /Alas cruel love, damned be the month/That brought me to this dark downfall/ And was the reason for my first offences) (vv. 97–131).

Remarkably, in his *disperata*, Sasso subverts Petrarchism with his persona's attitude and response to the cold and cruel beloved. Thus, in the case of the *disperata*, we must consider not only the genre's place in the canon and literary culture, but also as responding and even rejecting this very canon and culture. Indeed, the genre is inserted within the canon, namely fifteenth-century Petrarchism, alongside more popular genres, such as sonnets and *sestinas*, for example, but it also infringes on this canon by destabilizing some of its principles. In this case, Love is viciously cursed, and the beloved and the moment of the *innamoramento* are not remembered fondly and sung as by Petrarch and his emulators. Frederic Jameson argues that genre criticism involves "that series of concrete historical situations within which the individual works were realized, and which thus stands as something like a parallel sequence to the purely formal one."[47] In the case of the *disperata*, not only do key images from Petrarch's *Canzoniere* acquire intensity and become more obsessive and vigorous, as for example verse 114, "Vinto a un dolce riso: e guardo adorno," they are also completely turned around, as benedictions develop into maledictions in which the word "maledico" and its variants are repeated *ad nauseam*.

Though many critics consider Sasso a strict imitator of Petrarch, Serafino and Tebaldeo, his *disperata* demonstrates an original approach to the genre, with its firm focus on a destructive interpretation and portrayal of Love, its manifestations and effects.[48] Sasso is an essential contributor to the court culture and literary production of the last decades of the Quattrocento and beginning of the Cinquecento: his *disperata* was printed alongside his sonnets, *capitoli*, eclogues, and *strambotti*, which were thoroughly popular during his life and well into the sixteenth century,[49] becoming an undeniably strong intertext for the French poets.[50]

Galeotto del Carretto and the Italian Manuscript 1543 (MF 13315)

Galeotto del Carretto's *disperate* are found in an important manuscript currently housed at the Bibliothèque nationale de France,[51] a document that is both valuable and telling of the history and fortune of the genre, as it contains six *disperate*, two written by Galeotto del Carretto, one by Gianpietro da Pietrasanta (Zampetro de l'Eremita), and three by Tebaldeo.[52] The manuscript is particularly central to my discussion because it brings together these *disperate* with a wide-range of popular genres and writers from the Italian Quattrocento.[53] In 1885, Rodolfo Renier used this manuscript to publish ten poems that he believed to be the most relevant and characteristic of Carretto's style, but did not include his *disperata*, supposedly because of its length.[54] However, one of the *disperate*, "Canzone disparata facta per il preducto" (Desperate song written by yours truly), was later included in an 1888 collection of Carretto's *rime*, as a testimonial, I believe, to the significance of the genre in the early-modern literary culture.[55]

Carretto (ca. 1455–1530) was a poet tightly connected with the courts of Casale, Milan, and Mantova, where he befriended Serafino and Tebaldeo. He often fought alongside his lord, the Marquis of Monferrato, and was a devout supporter of Isabella d'Este, the Marchioness of Mantova, and wife of Francesco Gonzaga. They exchanged a rich correspondence, which remains a precious historical and cultural document of the Italian Renaissance.[56] "Canzone disparata facta per il preducto" is a *disperata* that comprises the traditional *topoi* of the genre. Its beginning is an ode to the natural elements, again enunciated by an assertive voice:

> Esci fuor voce, e con tua tromba spacha
> La terra el fuocho, l'aria l'acqua e sassi
> E' con lamente alati altre lire attaccha

(Come out voice, and with your sound (trumpet) shutter/The earth, the fire, the air, the water and the stones/And with your winged laments attack the other lyres) (vv. 1–3, 42).[57]

This strong first verse will be a source of similar verses by other Italian and French poets, because the strength and volume of the voice match the power and intensity of the speaker's despair. It calls for the readers' attention and for everyone to pause and listen to the speaker's hopelessness. Crying out loud, "con ululati e lacrimosi pianti" (v. 5), the poet-persona visits hell and Earth in order to profess his unhappiness and martyrdom, "E per piu dire il mio martir diffuso," (v. 13, 42) and his permanent slavery to Love, "Amor m'à posto una catena al collo/Con dissolubil nodi" (vv. 25–26, 43).

As in most *disperate*, the anaphora "vorrei" dominates a good part of the poem, always expressing a wish to see the world turned upside down and dominated by an unnatural order: "Veder vorrei cangiar questo ori-zonte/In altra nube, et tucto in sangue el mare" (I would like to see the horizon change/Into another cloud, and the sea into blood) (vv. 43–44, 43). Religion as well is overturned, as the speaker wishes for the Antichrist to descend and profess deceit, and despite this profane wish, the world would still follow him with honor as if he were the legitimate savior:

> Venga antichristo in forma d'hermito
> Predichi el falso, con parlar fervente
> Et sia dal mondo con onore seguito

(Come antichrist disguised as a hermit/Preach falsehood, with fervent words/And may he be followed by the world with honor) (vv. 52–54, 44).

This element is unique to Carretto's *disperata*, and it increases not only its doom, but also a strong sense of religious defiance to the entire narrative as it stages an Antichrist in direct conflict with Church theology, an aspect that also reverberates in the *disperati*'s desire to commit suicide. Moreover, the poem as a whole adds to the catalogue of the genre's impious maledic-tions. The speaker wishes on himself the worst calamities that entangle the Earth, thunder, the animals, body parts, and a destructive deluge ending with the coveted apocalyptic end, where Megaera will destroy the universe and an immense deluge will swallow the world (vv. 73–82, 44–45).[58]

Carretto's final wish is for his life to be instantly truncated by a death sickle:

> Poi venga quella inexorabil che ange
> Ogni mortale, et con la falce aduncha,
> Senza rispecto, taglia, miete et frange.
> Et faccia in tucto la mia vita troncha
> (vv. 85–88, 45).

In this original metaphor, the sickle comes down on the speaker, as it does on the harvest ("miete"), snapping off a life from its earthly shell; a life that was already dead. In fact, the *disperato* often reminds the reader of the thin line that exists between life and death, the latter being the only desire that can be fully attained. Finally, the poet-persona announces that he shall serve as example of despair for all other spirits who have suffered because of Love: "et sono a tutti exempio" (v. 145, 47), once again rewriting a fairly common attitude shared by many other *disperati* united by hopelessness.

Carretto wrote another *disperata* that can be found in the same manuscript (pages 124 to 126), which remains to this day unpublished and fairly unknown. Indeed, it is not mentioned in Renier's study, nor by any other critic.[59] Titled "Disperata" and dated 1497, the poem starts with a similar image of the trumpet, this time marking the hour of judgment:

> La tromba suona io son verso al giudizio
> Morte ministra alla sua frusta monta
> Ove di sangue human fa sacrifizio
> Veggio la fiamma de mio fuoco avanza

(The trumpet plays as it is judgment day for me/The minister of death flings its whip/Which sacrifices human blood/And I see the flame of my fire advancing (vv. 1–4, 124).[60]

All natural elements are involved in the speaker's emotional turmoil, "Fiore: ramo: cadere: troncho: herba e foglia" (v. 15, 124), as well as a series of vile cataclysms (vv. 28–30, 125). Moreover, the maledictions grow in ferocity, as the poem draws to an end. The final verses call for more evil to engulf the world and all of its living beings, and for the speaker's life to go back to his first days in the cradle, where it should have been annihilated at its very beginning.

Although the Parisian document contains other texts in various genres that bear Carretto's name for a total of 132 verses,[61] some of his poems still remain of uncertain attribution.[62] However, his two *disperate* advance and renovate the genre's tradition. By drawing from and bringing together lyric models and regional experiences mainly through familiarity and exchanges with other court poets, Carretto became an important figure in the courtly culture of his times,[63] fostered by what Vecchi Galli calls "the connecting fabric and reciprocal influences among the court culture poets".[64] Although his *canzoniere* has not been entirely recovered at this time, literary critics agree that his lyric production was vast and varied.[65]

The Development and Progression
of the *Disperata* in the Quattrocento

The Italian poems canonized in the French libraries mark a period of significant literary production. Indeed, critics of the Quattrocento have often commented on the frequency and number of publications, even if they have also lamented the lack of diversity in the lyric collections' content and substance. Furthermore, as Vecchi Galli has demonstrated, the linguistic, metric, syntactic, and thematic levels of these publications offered a wide variety of genres, including *disperate* composed in the *capitolo* form.[66] Many more *disperate* were written, read, adopted, and imitated during this period, and several *canzonieri* and collections of *rime* featured *disperate* in their indexes.[67] The genre remained popular for several reasons. First, the length of the composition allowed the poet to fully evoke in detail the pangs of the martyr of love, a role thoroughly entrenched in the canon. Second, the *disperata* blended stylistically—the *terza rima* and lyrically—themes, images, and metaphors, with Dante's and Petrarch's eminent, well-established *poesis*. Third, it revisited and expanded Dante's "Inferno" in a landscape that is both chilling and familiar. Finally, it employed Petrarch's refined language and code, which appealed greatly to a court audience, thirsty for new, yet recognizable material. In short, the *disperata* allowed authors to both draw on the canon and locate themselves within it, in slightly altered ways; for as we have seen, although the *disperata* took inspiration from Petrarch's *Rime*, it departed significantly from that source's constraint and moderation. Thus, a real tradition of the *disperata* was established, whereby each text became a model for subsequent writers. However, as already seen, one of the central features of the genre is its propensity to subvert the Petrarchan tradition in unique ways. The French poets at the end of the Renaissance would continue this tradition of simultaneously invoking and subverting Petrarch.

The imitation of the *disperata* is also closely linked to the success of the *terza rima*, the meter chosen by writers for their *capitoli ternari*, whether of moral or amorous matter, and in a variety of genres, including the *disperata*, *dipartita*, elegy, epistle, and eclogue. The use of the *disperata* became a way for poets to distinguish themselves and display their literary dexterity. Although some critics have equated the *disperata* to a tedious list of lamentations, it in fact challenged its writer to retell a story of profound hopelessness using the same parameters and elements, but in rather different ways.[68] As in many imitations, variations and derivations occurred, thereby crafting more accomplished poems. By the mid-Quattrocento more and more *disperate* were written and more *canzonieri* and single-authored volumes included them.[69] Furthermore, its content was also adjusted to fit shorter forms, such as sonnets, *sestine*, *barzellette*, and *strambotti*.

In the Quattrocento, *disperata* poets were, therefore, responding both to the canon, including Petrarch and Dante, and to their contemporaries. As already mentioned, the imitation network was remarkably diverse, yet close-knit, and it mostly clustered around the court poets, including Beccari, il Saviozzo, Sasso, Tebaldeo, Serafino, il Correggio, and Cariteo. This is a cultural-literary aspect that greatly contributed to the intertextual development of the *diperata*, not only in textual terms, but also in geographical ones. The *disperata* is the product of Medieval and especially Renaissance imitation culture, in which the tradition dictates that the writer pays not only attention but also tribute to what had been previously written, and also to what was being contemporaneously written, as with all other literary and artistic forms. Thus, by legitimizing the tradition, one directly legitimized one's own writings. As Rigolot eloquently explains, writers were forced to reproduce the traditional thematic and structural models and were allowed to only add slight modifications, which will have to appear minimal to both the writer and the public, because "une déviation minime peut entraîner d'importantes subversions qui affectent les principes mêmes de l'idéalisation, tels qu'ils étaient jugés acceptables par les lecteurs de la poésie courtoise et pétrarquisante."[70] The *disperata* falls well within the above stated imitation principle: its followers had to somewhat strictly adhere to the genre's conventions in order not to deviate or "betray" it. The *disperata* is a well-codified genre, with a well-defined structure,[71] thus leaving little room for its writers to deviate from this tradition and its codes. In order to better illustrate this principle, I will discuss three Quattrocento poets and their *disperate*: Rosello Roselli (1399–1451), Felice Feliciano (1433–79), and Leornardo Giustiniani (1388–1446). They adopted and adapted the genre following mainly Beccari, il Pistoia, and il Saviozzo.

Rosello Roselli, Felice Feliciano, and Leonardo Giustiniani

Rosello Roselli's writing serves as a prototype of *canzoniere* that appears to be inscribed within the Petrarchan tradition, but in truth subverts it. Just like for Carretto's work, his *disperata* was only recently included by Giovanni Biancardi in a compendium of unpublished *rime*.[72] As his editor observes, Roselli's verses praise the beloved and narrate the poet's attempts to win her over, but soon, the compliments turn to invectives and desperation. Love and Madonna are both damned for his immeasurable sufferings.[73] Not surprisingly, the darkest moments in Roselli's *canzoniere* are contained in his *disperata*, which, together with twelve other gloomy poems (nine sonnets, two ballads, and one *sestina*), break the thematic and lyrical flow of the collection. The *disperata* starts with an ode to an idyllic and barren landscape:

> Fiere selvaggie e inabitati boschi,
> Crudel fortuna, aspro e rio destino,
> Spirito Pellegrino
> Che volesti nel cielo equarti a Dio;
> Anime disperate, e tu divino
> Cerbaro crudo, lochi negri e foschi,
> E voi, serpenti toschi,
> Movetivi oggi mai al mio disio!

> (Wild beasts and deserted woods,/Cruel fortune, harsh and adverse destiny,/Wandering spirit/Who wanted to be equal to God in Heaven;/Desperate souls, and you divine,/Cruel Cerberus, dark and sinister sites,/And you, poisonous snakes,/Move today to assuage my desire!) (vv. 1–8, 26).

Roselli deploys all of the *topoi* that characterize the *disperata*: from the beginning and throughout the text, the poet-persona addresses himself to the "wild beasts" and to the "deserted forests." Rather than evoking the Muses, the *disperata* subverts the Classical and Renaissance traditions and instead calls upon the infernal furies to assist the speaker. Stifled by immeasurable love pangs he sets himself apart from other people, "son solo io"—it's only me. Throughout the poem in fact, Love remains the main culprit: it wraps the speaker's neck with a golden chain, which causes him to weep and to die, "la qual mi fu cagion ch'io piango e moro" (v. 36, 27). No other lover has suffered as much as him; and with precise biographical elements such as the lengths of his martyrdom, "Son visso in tanta doglia gia sette anni" (v. 55, 27), the lover-persona describes a life of betrayals, deception, and an emotional death that forces him to seek a physical death, which he is unable to find: "cerco morte e non posso morire" (v. 62, 27).

His maledictions begin with verse 70, and closely rebuke Petrarch's benedictions of sonnet sixty-one.[74] Thus, for each of Petrarch's benedictions, Roselli retorts with a malediction:

Sia maledetto l'anno,
El mese, el giorno e l'ora ch'io fui preso,
Ché più non posso sostener tal peso!

(Damned be the year,/The month, the day and the hour when I was
captured,/Since I can no longer endure such burden!) (vv. 70–72, 28).

Although Roselli is considered a faithful Petrarchist,[75] his *disperata* clearly
engages the Petrarchan tradition by blatantly subverting it. In fact, like
Sasso, he challenges it primarily in the attitude and response of the lover
toward his beloved. Moreover, Roselli replicates the vituperations in one
of his sonnets as well, an example of how the *disperata* content, in particular the maledictions and their essence permeate other forms as well, sonnets in particular.[76] With Roselli, though, they are restricted to damning
Love and its pangs, and the beloved, "madonna," for the many tears and
unrequited desire he has wasted in vain. (v. 36).

The *disperata* continues with a despondent narration and incessant
calls for death:

Per certo amante al mondo amante non visse
con tanta fé suggetto a sua madonna
quanto io a costei, che la mia morte brama

(For sure, no other lover was ever seen/so devoted to his madonna
with so much faith/than myself to the one who covets my death)
(vv. 45–47, 27).

The poet-persona begs the infernal furies to end his days and to rescue him
from his miserable existence. Furthermore, he depicts a cruel and sadistic woman who enjoys watching his agony. Finally, he addresses his own
poem, identified as "my crying," and urges it to fly and reach all creatures
in hell, so that they are aware of his martyrdom:

Sì che, si vòli aitarmi
E far che 'l mio gran pianto non sia etterno,
Commover tí convien tutto l'inferno.
(vv. 134–136, 29).

Roselli was part of a group of engaged humanists whose close interactions
and literary and cultural exchanges at the courts in Northern Italy contributed to the spread and flourishing of the *disperata* genre.[77] Another
of these humanists was the Veronese Felice Feliciano, a Renaissance man
who fulfilled many roles as a *literato*, an antique dealer, a writer, and a

collector of vulgar poetry. He wrote numerous poems in various forms, including sonnets, *capitoli ternari*, *canzoni*, and *seventesi*, as well as a rich epistolary collection, and an anthology that includes poems by il Saviozzo, Dante, Cino da Pistoia, and Petrarch.[78] Feliciano traveled often, mainly between the courts of Verona and Venice.[79] Like other poets, he struggled to find and keep protectors and, consequently, suffered both existential and economic hardship.[80] His *disperata* is fairly long, with 300 verses, and it is unique because it starts strongly with gripping opening verses, unlike other *disperate* that start with descriptions of a serene nature, and whose fury builds with each verse:

> L'horrido canto, anzi tristizia e pena,
> Dolori, affanni, stento e gran martyre
> Mi fa come fantasma gir' errando
> La mia dolente e sfortunata vita.

(Horrid song, sadness and sorrow,/Pain, grief, struggles and great martyrdom/Make me wander like a ghost/In my anguished and unfortunate life.) (vv. 1–4, 183).[81]

The speaker continues with very strong language and boldly announces the poem's conclusion in the very first stanza: "che non si trovi fine al mio tormento" (v. 14, 183), as he wants his readers to know at once that the *disperato*'s anguish never ends. Russell argues that Feliciano's verses represent the *disperato*'s extreme attempt to express his estrangement from the world, an alienation encountered in many other *disperate* as well.[82] Although this kind of isolation and persecution is also present in other Renaissance genres, in the *disperata* it becomes a customary indicator of extreme suffering and hopelessness, which empowers the speaker to be different in his torment. Thus, the speaker feels entitled to distinguish himself from other martyrs of love as the most persecuted and exasperated of all:

> Non credo che nel mondo mai si trove,
> Né trovarassi ancor chi più mi aguagli
> De inopia, de miseria e povertade

(I don't believe that in the world/One can ever find somebody who equals me/In destitution, misery and poverty) (vv. 31–33, 184).

Further emphasizing his existential marginality as poet, as man, and as *disperato*, the world, in turn, also isolates him:

> E la vita è di speranza priva:
> Cieschuno pur mi schiva,
> Né so donde deriva
> Ch'ogni persona sempre me dischaza,
> E par ch'el cielo, el mondo me minaza.

(Life is deprived of hope:/Everybody avoids me,/I don't know why/
Everybody always moves away from me,/And it seems that the sky,
and the world threaten me.) (vv. 56–60, 185)

Although Feliciano's *disperata* comprises all of the genre's *topoi*, he retells
these *topoi* by focusing in particular on the theme of isolation and on specific biographical facts:[83] referring to his parents, he reproaches them the
fact that they named him "Felice," "happy," an oxymoronic name; a proph-
ecy that seems to condemn the speaker to eternal punishment since birth:

> Il nome tuo serà Felice,
> Contrario e falso e colmo di menzogna;
> ... E per che con più doglia ti confondi,
> Starai tra dui nimici in questo loco,
> Né amico troverai che ti nascondi,
> Consumando tua vita al tristo ioco
> Con più dolore e guai e con tormento
> Si chome siecha foglia cadde al vento.

(Your name will be Felice,/The opposite and false and filled with
shame;/.../And because you will be engrossed in more sorrow,/You
will be with two enemies right here,/You will not find a friend to
hide you,/Wasting your life with this sad game/With more sorrow
and troubles and torment/Just like a dry leaf that fell in the wind.)
(vv. 135–142, 187).

Destined to seclusion and to desperation, without any friends, "vivendo
disperato," he has to endure both physical and spiritual tortures, that are
gruesomely described: his chest is torn apart by pliers, "le tenaglie afogate
a mezo il pecto" (v. 167, 188), and his bones are slowly dismembered, "e
qui mi smembra l'osse a poco a poco" (v. 172, 188). This language and these
images evoke the Baroque, and so do the fascination with the divulged
body and its violent and masochistic treatment and portrayal. Together
with mental torture, these motifs are meant to persuade the reader of the
disperato's worst enduring and suffering, and they will reemerge about a
century later in the poetry of some of the French neo-Petrarchan poets,
such as d'Aubigné, Nuysement, and Béroalde.

Like in other *disperate*, death is obsessively summoned, begged and lured, again and again, so that the lover-persona may quickly end his excruciating struggles on earth: "e ognuno ritrovi diverso martyro/pur ch'io non vivi più sopra la terra" (vv. 202–203, 189). Death is also the object of desire and therefore, it could not come too soon. However, the poem's one hundred more verses will be devoted to a detailed description of his anguish, adorned by countless mythological and biblical figures, all mustered in order to alleviate the poetic persona's love pangs (vv. 241–264, 190–191), and to convince the readers of the urgency of a long awaited death.

Despite the intensity of this *disperata*, and unlike endless maledictions of other *disperate*, Feliciano will pronounce only two maledictions: one to Love and its poison, "ch'io maledico, Amor, el tuo veneno," (v. 233, 190), and one to his own poem: "Maledecta canzon da Dio e da Santi," (v. 271, 191). However, in its last part we find a fervent concentration of fire, ominous natural disasters, and the privileged *disperata* deserted sites: "negli averni ombrosi campi" (v. 281, 191), and "nelle caverne e tumbe cuppe" (v. 288, 191). Here, Feliciano's song of despair may never quieten down:

> In questi luoghi oscuri,
> Non voglio ch'el tuo canto mai si tempre,
> Ma che tu piangi, piangi, sempre, sempre.

> (In these dark places,/I don't want your singing to soften,/But you must cry, cry, forever and ever.) (vv. 298–300, 192).

Just like its author, the *disperata* is condemned to never-ending suffering and weeping. Noticeably, the strong conclusion captures one of the genre's main *topoi*: in a secluded and dark space, seldom identified as no more than "luoghi," or "lieux" for the French writers, the song of despair need not to fade, but rather, it has to continue, strong and magnified, forever and ever, in order to be heard, its lessons to be learned.

Feliciano's poem develops the conventional *topoi* not only by emphasizing suffering, but also by focusing on solitude and friendship, or lack thereof. Petrarch's and Dante's models converge, but so do the *disperate* written by il Saviozzo and Beccari, which were well known by Feliciano as he had already included them in his anthologies.[84] Furthermore, Feliciano was a "madman enthusiast" of the *disperata*, as Giulia Giannella points out.[85] In his poetry, Petrarch's discrete lamentations and complaints become blatantly emphasized, and attitudes of despair are repetitively stressed, thus earnestly merging the Petrarchan and the *disperata* traditions.

To conclude, I will briefly examine Leonardo Giustiniani, an accomplished poet and politician in Venice, whose text demonstrates the progression of the genre in the Quattrocento. His *disperata*, is categorized as a *capitolo* by Berthold Wiese, editor of *Poesie edite et inedite di Leonardo Giustiniani*.[86] Wiese edited this poem only up to verse 121, and Ernesto Lamma included the remaining verses in his article "Intorno ad alcune rime di Leonardo Giustiniani";[87] thus, readers can easily access the entire text. Cian notes that this is indeed a "true and authentic" *disperata*, as the poem contains the majority of the genre's *topoi*.[88] Titled "Io vedo ben, che 'l bon servire è vano," it mostly complains about Love and damns its malign nature:

> Ben posso sempre biastemare amore
> e starme sempre lacrimoso e afflicto,
> poyche ho perduto un si lizadro fiore.

(I can always curse love thoroughly/and remain teary and afflicted forever,/because I lost such a precious flower.) (vv. 7–9, 385).

Giustiniani does not deviate much from the *disperata* structure and themes, but rather, he methodically utilizes its main *topoi* and adopts its desperate attitude to gain sympathy for his *disperata*. Giustiniani describes the speaker's physical condition as such that he is forced to walk with his head down, "Sempre andrò con la testa clinata" (v. 79, 387). His battered body is gruesomely portrayed in realistic images of dismembered body parts, blood and bulging veins, "Le membre e 'l sangue schipa da ogni vena" (v. 105, 389). However, the *topos* employed the most by Giustiniani is by far the assorted damnations. First, the lover-persona curses the entire universe, then Fortune:

> Io maledisco ogni celeste lume
> E ciel e sol e le stelle e la luna,
> La terra e 'l mare e l'acqua d'ogni fume,
> Io maledico la crudele fortuna,
> Io maledico la spietata sorte,
> Che non me occise essendo puto in cuna
> Io maledico mia fera sorte

(I damn every celestial light/And the sky and the sun and the stars and the moon,/The earth the sea the water and every river,/I damn cruel fortune,/I damn my ruthless fate,/That did not kill me in the cradle/I damn my cruel fate) (vv. 115–121, 389).

The maledictions continue and greatly intensify against his harsh fate, the day he was born, his tears, words, including all of the verses he wrote, "le rime tante e le mie canzonette" (vv. 124–132, 375), as well as his own body, "Sian tutte le mie membre maledecte" (v. 133, 375). He then tries to get his audience to feel sorry for him:

> Piangeti, genti, et cum voi piangha anchora
> le pietre et saxi et piangha ogni animale
> la mortal doglia o 'l fuoco che m'achora

(Cry, people, and with you/the stones the rocks and every animal cry/and the deadly sorrow and fire that begrudges me) (vv. 148–150, 375).

With a final call for death, Giustiniani's *disperata* concludes with another conventional *topos*: the heralding of his despair and imminent death, strengthened by a series of imperatives, "I want you to know" and "be certain":

> Voglio che sapi et che sij certa assai
> che sola cruda morte serà quella
> che potrà poner fine a li miei guai

(I want you to know and be certain/that only death will be able/to put an end to my troubles) (vv. 157–159, 375).

This kind of unique and disturbing rhetoric will reemerge in later *disperate* and in French poems.

Although Roselli, Feliciano, and Giustiniani remain relatively unknown to scholars and readers of the Italian Renaissance, I seek to show that they skillfully interpreted the genre, thus providing noteworthy variations that make each of their poems unique in linguistic and thematic developments. Concurrently, these poets were also responding to the canons of Petrarchism and court culture and to contemporary trends, such as, for example, the vogue of the *capitolo ternario* and the necessity to prove one's creative skills in a variety of lyric genres. Hence, the popularity of the *disperata* developed and expanded considerably in both production and reception. Furthermore, if in the late Quattrocento traditional poetic genres and themes continued to evolve, at the same time, so did various poetic experiments that have yet to secure comprehensive scholarly attention, as some of the poems discussed in this chapter confirm. Thus, alongside the imitation of the Petrarchan sonnet and the Italian *strambotto*, the *disperata* as well continued to be adopted as a viable and generative model.

Antonio Tebaldeo, Serafino de' Ciminelli, Known as L'Aquilano, and Benedetto Gareth, Known as Cariteo

The names of Tebaldeo (1463–1537), Serafino (1466–1500), and Cariteo (ca. 1450–1514) are well known to literary and cultural critics of the Italian and French Renaissance. Many studies have shown the considerable similarities in style, language, and themes in their poetry, as well as the varied intertextualities with the French poets discussed in this book.[89] Their influence and popularity were considerable, so much so that at one point they were imitated even more than Petrarch himself. Vianey, among others, has thoroughly documented the fruitful intertextuality between these poets and Clément Marot, Lemaire de Belges, Sainct-Gelays, the poets of the Pléiade, including Du Bellay and Ronsard, the School of Lyon, especially Maurice Scève, and the neo-Petrarchans, including Desportes, d'Aubigné, and Nuysement.[90] Giovanni Parenti convincingly argues that it was the Pléiade who first introduced Cariteo to the history of European Petrarchism.[91] According to DellaNeva, on the other hand, it was Marot and Scève who had principally adopted lyrics from Serafino, Tebaldeo, and Cariteo, while the Pléiade and the neo-Petrarchans mostly used the Giolito anthologies.[92] Indeed, the French writers read and imitated poems found in the anthologies and did not always read the Italian single-authored volumes.[93]

The *disperata* genre spread from the poetry of the Quattrocento poets, including Tebaldeo, Serafino, and Cariteo, and expanded again in the poetry of the Cinquecento, such as the broadly anthologized sonnets and stanzas by di Costanzo, Rota, and Tansillo. However, very few scholars have discussed the *disperate* authored by Tebaldeo, Serafino, and Cariteo, let alone in relation to the French poets, apart from d'Aubigné, as discussed in Chapter Five. Rather, critics focused their attention on their sonnets and *strambotti* and concentrated mainly on their use of the Petrarchan code, including its *précieux* language, metaphors, and *concetti*.[94]

As mentioned, the great majority of the *disperata* poets were part of the literary circles of the Northern and Southern courts that had ties with Isabella d'Este Gonzaga.[95] Their prolific production and network were dependent on the court as a socio-cultural framework that stipulated a common thread, themes, and fairly similar style. The connections and friendships, as well as animosities, between the court poets created a court network that enabled the *disperata* to continue to flourish and thrive from the North to the South of Italy. The confines of the court in particular, such as those of the Sforzas in Milan, the Gonzagas in Mantua, the Estes in Ferrara and Modena, and the Aragons in Naples, were reputable *cénacles* in which ideas, personalities, and words periodically collided. Moreover, these came to be literary and cultural centers of great influence within both Italian and French court society.[96]

Serafino, Tebaldeo, and Cariteo and their works met substantial success at these courts because of their talent in creating verses that pleased and awed patrons and courtiers alike. The connections between Serafino and Tebaldeo in particular strengthened the court culture to which the *disperata* meaningfully contributed.[97] The two poets shared similar existential and literary experiences because they frequented the very same courts and circles.[98] These poets are fundamental in themselves, but together with their literary community, including poets such as Cariteo, Carretto, Sasso, Sannazzaro, Gaspare Visconti, Antonio Fileremo Fregoso, Nicolò da Correggio, and many others, they developed and defined the lyric tradition from the Quattrocento to the mid-Cinquecento, and at the courts and *cénacles* in France through the late Renaissance.[99]

Antonio Tebaldeo

Tebaldeo is a major representative of court poetry in Northern Italy.[100] A native of Ferrara, he began his career as Isabella d'Este's tutor, and later became Lucrezia Borgia's secretary and a favorite of Pope Leone.[101] He was a regular presence at the courts of Ferrara, Modena, Siena, and Rome, and was thus a poet-functionary gifted with sophisticated intellectual and diplomatic skills. Today, he remains a key figure of his time, whose work allows modern critics to better understand and contextualize court poetry, especially the production concentrated around what Antonio Rossi calls the influential union Tebaldeo-Serafino.[102] Persuasive links can also be made between Tebaldeo and Antonio Beccari da Ferrara, particularly in their *disperate*, as they clearly demonstrate their close connections and interdependence with the Este-Gonzaga family in Ferrara.[103] According to Massimo Danzi, Tebaldeo's *disperata*, "Già cum suavi e mansueti carmi" in particular shows specifically the same experimentation with the genre as seen in Beccari's text.[104] Moreover, Danzi argues that Siena and il Saviozzo also appear in Tebaldeo's poetry, where, once again the same regions and courts in Tuscany, and Emilia Romagna constituted his geographical and historical background.[105] Indeed, the two poets shared much of the same culture and language. The above mentioned poem

and a second *disperata*, "Lingua mia stanca in tanto lamentare," clearly
identified as "disperata seconda" in some of Tebaldeo's editions, will be
the focus of my analysis because they are two accomplished examples of
Quattrocento *disperata* that not only became sources for other writers,
but also significantly merged the genre and court traditions.[106] Moreover,
both poems contain several of the fixed *topoi* that we have been discussing
thus far, with few variations and unique elements that add a fresh interpretation of the genre.[107]

"Già cum süavi e mansüeti carmi" features a unique beginning
where the speaker warns that as of now, it is more appropriate to arm himself with a more rigid style, coupled with cruel verses: "hor de un rigido stil
convien che s'armi" (v. 3, 448) and "forza é che usi anchor io verso crudele"
(v. 5, 448). The poet openly acknowledges that the *disperata* truly calls for
a harsher style, and that he is hereafter ready and able to employ it. The
beginning is indeed strong and sets both the tone and the mood for the
remainder of the poem. Furthermore, as if to warn the reader, he reminds
that despite its content on Love, in this particular genre, the usual sweet
and docile stanzas – "süavi e mansüeti carmi" (v. 1, 448), are no longer
warranted. Hence, Tebaldeo consciously shifts his stylistic and linguistic
approach to fully interpret the genre, and he creatively underscores this
effort in his first few verses.

A second reference to the genre is found in the seventh line, where,
by cleverly displaying its resilient feature, Tebaldeo pays homage to the
disperata tradition. He damns the stars, closely echoing Beccari's "Le stelle
universali e i' ciel rotanti," and addresses the Furies, rather than the Muses,
because they are more suited to assist him:

> Che a voler imprecar male a le stelle,
> Chi soccorrer pò meglio il mio intelletto
> Che le maligne Furie, al ciel ribelle?
> (vv. 19–21, 449).

Since he has lost his time, heart and spirit, he is left with only his tongue,
which will never fall silent. On the contrary, it will go on damning everything and everybody. Furthermore, it is with this single, yet all-encompassing malediction, that the speaker will find his revenge, thus underscoring the power of a desperate and miserable damnation:

> Perduto ho il tempo in l'amororsa traccia,
> Il core, il spirto e sol la lingua resta,

> Che insin che la forza non vo' mai che taccia;
> Maledicendo disperata e mesta
> Homini, dèi, terra, aqua, aëre e foco,
> Farà le mie vendette in parte questa.

(I have lost time in Love's tracks,/And my heart and spirit, only my tongue is left,/Until I have the strength, I don't want it to ever be quiet;/Desperate and sad, damning/Men, gods, the earth, water, air and fire,/It will avenge me all around) (vv. 49–54, 450).

Like other *disperate*, in the verses that follow he describes a series of apocalyptic wishes in which the world is catapulted in a complete human and natural turmoil, including incestuous relationships, such as Oedipus's, "e ogni figliol la madre,/come il thebano infortunato, impregni" (vv. 59–60, 450); infants dying in the cradle and being poisoned by the maternal milk; the earth swallowing humanity; mythological figures incarnating into agents of devastation; as well as all animals devouring humans (vv. 85–87, 451). The speaker then wonders whether he has cited enough destruction, because he forewarns that much worse will take place:

> Non scio se basta, e de dir poco io temo:
> Venga peggio, se pò, dopoi che a torto
> Per ben far piango, ardo, suspiro e gemo.

(I do not know if it is enough, and I fear to say little:/The worse is yet to come, and then, if I am wrong/I am right to cry, burn, sigh and moan.) (vv. 106–108, 452).

The *disperato* reflects on his own words, which are insufficient in expressing the tragic cataclysm that will shortly engulf the universe. This premonition is also a self-reflection on his own role in announcing and forewarning the devastation that he foresees, but cannot prevent. Indeed, he takes on the role of the poet-prophet charged to announce the end of the world, and the violent annihilation of all living beings.

Like in other *disperate*, Tebaldeo's second *disperata* also includes mythological figures transforming into catastrophic agents (vv. 112–126, 983). It envisions a series of tragic events, this time preceded by the conventional anaphora "voria," a constant rhetorical device central to the genre. Indeed, twenty-two tercets contain either "Voria," "Vorei," or "Vore," while four tercets begin with "Li altri vorian," in order to underscore even further the distance between the speaker and the rest of the world, and between his wishes and those of others:

> Altri vorian solazi, soni e canti,
> Et io vorei veder, misero e tristo,
> Ciascun morir in doglia, in pene e pianti.
> Altri di roba e fama far acquisto,
> Et io di sangue el mundo e l'aere pregno,
> Di rabia e pestilenza e fame misto.
> Altri vorian chi signoria e chi regno,
> Et io ciascun cum la testa sepulto,
> Dal ciel cader ogni pianeta e segno.

(Others want solace, music and songs,/And I wish to see, miserable and sad,/Everybody dying in pain, in sorrow and cries./Others want clothes and fame,/And I wish to see the world and the air filled with blood,/And rage and pestilence and hunger./Others want a Signoria and a kingdom,/And I wish to see everybody with their head buried,/And every planet fall from the sky.) (vv. 82–90, 981).

Some themes are common to both *disperate*. For example, they turn against Love, here in the first, "Già cum suavi e mansueti carmi" (Already with a pleasing and gentle solemn poem):

> Crudel signor, signor ingrato e avaro,
> Che per cibo a la mensa altro non hai
> Che sangue de' toi servi e pianto amaro!

(Cruel lord, ungrateful and miser lord,/The only food you have at your table/Is your servants' blood and their bitter weeping!) (vv. 112–114, 452).

And in the second, "Lingua mia stanca in tanto lamentare" (My tongue, tired of so much lamenting): "Amor bugiardo, o falso e iniusto cielo" (Deceitful love, false and unfair sky) (v. 128, 983). Love is the villain and is blamed throughout both compositions as the source of the narrator's despair. Love conspires with Fortune in order to fool and mislead men, a *topos* that emerges often in the poetry of despair investigated in this book. Tebaldeo openly denounces their union as it strengthens even more their vicious hold on humanity:

> Secretamente il forte braccio hai tolto
> Di Fortuna, e cum essa te acordasti,
> Ché sempre a inganni il tuo pensiero è vòlto.
> Lasso, quanti per te regni son guasti,
> Quante città son divenute ville,
> Quanti homin' degni a tristo fin tirasti!

(Secretly, you have taken the strong arm/of Fortune, and with it you made a pact,/Your mind is always turned to deceit./Miserable, how many reigns failed for you,/How many towns became villages,/How many respectful men did you push to a wretched end?) (vv. 124–129, 452–453).

Furthermore, in this poem Love and Fortune ally as enemies against the poetic persona, who in turn damns this punitive union.

However, other traits of the genre, such as fierce, wild animals and maledictions are not so prevalent in Tebaldeo's *disperate*, with a few exceptions in the second, where the speaker briefly calls upon lions, bears, and snakes to come and devour everybody, but in a fairly conventional image:

> Vorei veder lioni, orsi e serpenti,
> Cum rabia circundar ogni contrada,
> Divorar e smembrar tute le genti

(I would like to see lions, bears and snakes,/Surround every village with anger,/Devour and dismember everybody) (vv. 58–60, 979).

The maledictions are relatively tamed as well. As mentioned, in the first *disperata* there is only one malediction ("maledicendo disperata e mesta/homini, dèi, terra, aqua, aëre e foco"); and toward the end of the second one there is a direct damnation against the day he was separated from Love, "Io maledico il dì ch'i' fui diviso/Dal mio signor e disperato moro;" (vv. 166–167, 987), followed by one against his own consuming desire, "Sia maledeta mia bramosa voglia" (v. 172, 987).

Both *disperate* end with a passionate salute to death. In the first, "Volentier moro per finir mio male" (I die gladly to end my ills) (v. 184, 454), and in the second, "Adio, ti laso, e più viver non voglio!" (Farewell, I leave you, and I no longer want to live!) (v. 187, 989). These conventional conclusions stress, I would argue, that Tebaldeo's use of the genre seem to reaffirm the urgency that some court poets felt compelled to try their *dispositio* skills in all lyric forms. Thus, rather than creatively arranging the *disperata topoi* and securing a new model, Tebaldeo mostly exploits its constant ones. Despite some of the archetypical themes and the variety of catastrophic scenarios, his *disperate* never really reach the tragic tones of earlier models that the poet might have wished to emulate.

Several other of Tebaldeo's *capitoli* comprise features of the *disperata*, namely a thorough description of the narrator's misery, but do not include all of its thematic and structural features, the belligerent tone, and the many catastrophic events and tirades that are unvarying predilections of the *disperata* speaker.[108] Tebaldeo's restrained and *précieux* style seldom expresses the hopelessness that haunts the *disperato* as encountered in earlier examples because his audience was more refined and longed for romantic narratives rather than violent and realistic outbursts. I suggest that Tebaldeo, Serafino, and Cariteo eagerly adopted the genre in order to skillfully adapt it to a particular context—the audience and the cultural-historical circumstances of the Northern and Southern courts, which in turn thoroughly moderated its meaning.

Tebaldeo might have written other *disperate*, but the manuscripts and early-modern editions of his work do not establish his clear authorship.[109] For example, the famous Italian Manuscript of 1543, discussed above, features three *disperate* attributed to Tebaldeo. The first, "Passionato core or trista mente" is identified as "Disperata dil predicto Tibaldeo," yet his editor Jean-Jacques Marchand reproduces it as a "rima dubbia"—of dubious attribution, because its authorship cannot be determined for certain.[110] Although it cannot be confidently attributed to Tebaldeo, this text is undoubtedly a *disperata* with many fixed *topoi*, vituperations, and direct attacks against love pangs.

The second and third *disperate*, "Se mai nel lamentare sospiri caldi" and "Dapoi che la caduca e fragil vesta" are instead two melancholy *capitoli* and categorized as such by Tania Basile, because they, indeed, lack most of the genre's *topoi*.[111] Nonetheless, the Parisian manuscript confirms, again, the fortune of the *disperata* in France and Tebaldeo as one of its main interpreters. It also confirms the editors' and collectors' many interpretations of long lyric forms that over the years employed the *terza rima*, including *capitoli*, *canzoni*, elegies, and *disperate*, hence determining their circulation and fortune. Altogether, Tebaldeo's *disperate* are sound exemplars of the genre, but rather than shock and horrify the audience, as il Saviozzo's or Beccari's texts do, they entertain and, therefore, contribute to his fame as a well-rounded poet, thoroughly accomplished in a wide range of lyric forms.

Serafino de' Ciminelli, Known as L'Aquilano

Serafino's poetry was vastly popular and imitated because of his personality and his usage of Petrarchan language, dramatic attitudes, and popular themes. Serafino began his literary career at the Naples court, between 1478 and 1481, where he was in close contact with the poets of the Aragonese circle, including Cariteo.[112] He was well known amongst his contemporaries, especially for his *strambotti* and for the melodies he sang with his lute.[113] His fruiftul lyric production successfully entertained Italian and French courts because of its musical pulse, brevity, passionate themes, and facile diction.[114] He often traveled from court to court in Milan, in Urbino, in Mantova, where princes solicited his artistic talents; but also in Venice, Genoa, Rome and Naples, where he interacted with many of the Italian poets discussed in this study.[115]

There are several attribution dilemmas that surround Serafino's poems, which according to Antonio Rossi stem from his popularity: as soon as the poet composed rhymes, they would be dispersed throughout Italy. However, Rossi does not mention his *disperate*, although a series of thirteen *strambotti* titled "Ferma disperatione" deal with despair as well as with some of the *disperata*'s *topoi*.[116] These *strambotti* demonstrate how the *disperata*'s content was adopted to shorter, more popular forms by the Italian poets all the while the longer form was still very much in vogue.

In his *Opera dello elegantissimo poeta Serafino Aquilano; quasi tutta di nuovo riformata, con molte cose aggionte. Nella quale si contengono tutte le infrascritte cose, cioe. Sonetti clxv, Epistole vii, Disperate iii, Barzellette xix, Egloghe iii, Capitoli xx, Strambotti xxvii*, although the *disperate* are clearly identified as separate from the *capitoli*, two out of three were not composed by Serafino.[117] In fact, "Disperata Prima" is the only *disperata* that Serafino actually wrote, because "Disperata II" is in truth il Saviozzo's "Cerbero invoco, e'l suo latrare," and "Disperata III" is il Pistoia's "La nuda terra s'ha gia messo il manto," both reproduced with very few variations.[118] Furthermore, Serafino's *disperata*, "Disperata Prima," has yet to be published in a modern edition, despite its literary and cultural value and legacy.[119] Nested in his *canzoniere*, and well situated between short genres—sonnets first, and *strambotti* last, this *disperata* received much attention during the fifteenth and sixteenth centuries because of the popularity of its author.

As court poet *par excellence*, Serafino undoubtedly capitalized on his position and the respect it commands. The first tercets depict the image of a heralding trumpet, a loud instrument that demands attention and respect, as well as an important court icon.[120] It also symbolized the role of the poet who "trumpets" or predicts universal truths, to which everybody has to pay attention:

> Hor sù, stanco mio cor, suona la tromba
> Del doloroso pianto et fa tal suono
> Qual fulgure che Iove irato fromba.

Gridate, spirti mei, tanto che 'l tuono
Ad pianto muova l'acqua, l'aere e i sassi,
Poi che pietà m'ha posto in abandono.
Qual nelle branche una columba stassi
D'una aquila affamata i' resto vivo,
Spectando ogni hor che morte il cuor trapassi.
Sospiro in versi et con il pianto scrivo
Quel che mi decta il tormentato cuore
Carco d'affanni et di soccorso privo

(Now, now, my tired heart, play the horn/Of the painful weeping
and make noise/Just like irate Jupiter flings his lightning./Shout,
my spirits, so much so the thunder/and cries will move the water,
air and rocks,/Since pity abandoned me./As a dove remains in the
mouth of/a hungry eagle, I remain alive,/Waiting every hour for
death to pierce my heart./I sigh in verse, and with my weeping I
write/That which my tormented heart dictates/Filled with grief
and deprived of all help) (vv. 1–12).[121]

This beginning evokes the first lines of il Carretto's two *disperate*, "Esci
fuor voce, e con tua tromba spacha" and "La tromba suona io son verso
al giudizio," discussed earlier in this chapter: the first as a symbol of a
powerful, tragic voice; the second as the sound of judgment day; hence,
strengthening the intertextual ties between the work of the two popular
poets. In Serafino's first verse, the speaker encourages his heart to herald his weeping, a line that comes across as more constrained, and that
develops an image that acquires both clout and volume in the second and
third verses, thus creating a tragic opening tercet in which the word light-
ing, "fulgure," confers power. Although Serafino's *disperata* presents some
moments of intensity—all related to death, it never fully deploys, however, the genre's main *topoi*, such as the maledictions, infernal or sinister
settings, nor the long list of cataclysmal scenarios. Indeed, in this short
composition, Serafino reveals a much more temperate approach to the
genre. Even though its position in the *canzoniere* does bestow upon it a
more dramatic effect—after the *Capitoli*, and before the *Strambotti*, and of
course, the first of the three *disperate*—the text never really reaches high
tones or moments of despair.

More closely imitating the genre, Serafino evokes death as a recurring theme, as in the following verses: "I strido, e chiamo morte a tutte
l'hore," (I scream and call for death at all hours) (v. 15); "Lasciar vorrei qui
tra terrestre spoglia," (I would like to leave here my earthly form) (v. 16);

and "Hor satiati Fortuna che mi struggi,/Satiati anchor che a morte mi condanni" (Satiate yourself, Fortune, who consumes me,/Satiate yourself again, since you condemn me to death) (vv. 22–23). Death and thoughts of suicide are paired in order to add a sense of calamity to the poem. The poetic persona threatens to tear up his life (vv. 34–36), and he wishes for a cruel death that mirrors the cruelty of his earthly existence (vv. 40–42). He then, again, within the tradition of the genre, calls a wide variety of monsters and mythological figures in order to be taken, torn to pieces and transformed into stone:

> Harpie, hidre, centauri con fracasso
> Cerbero irato m'habbi per vendetta
> Stracciamdomi per fin ch'io resti lasso

> (Harpies, hydras, centaurs with uproar/Irate Cerberus, you have torn me up with revenge/In order to leave me miserable) (vv. 52–54).

Cerberus is theatrically summoned to finish him, a motif that often recurs in the *disperata*, where the infernal monster violently snatches the *disperato*, as in il Saviozzo's "Cerbero invoco."[122] He then wishes for more physical and gruesome pain, as his soul is torn from his chest.[123] Despite his screams and cries, he does not expect assistance or compassion, because nothing could truly alleviate his pain from Love's harmful presence:

> Amore ne fa di me spietato guasto,
> E mi costringe mille volte a morte,
> Morte a Fortuna ognihor mi da per pasto

> (Love makes of me a ruthless disaster,/And forces me to die a thousand times,/Death feeds me to Fortune at every hour) (vv. 28–30).

Although Love makes him suffer, and does not let its grip, Serafino never really reaches the tragic notes of despair that we witness in other *disperate*. His final verses are also quite moderate, attempting to persuade the reader that the lover-persona will continue to suffer, as his pain will never diminish, "Et ognihor cresce il duol, ne mai vien manco." (v. 85) Two imperatives, "look at me" and "think" (vv. 83–84) engage the readers, commanding their attention to focus on his pain, which he is forced to endure to eternity. Compelling us to witness and feel this agony allows the poet-persona to fully enlist the audience's trust and to respond to their expectations, while also creating a poem whose function is entertaining and cathartic.

OPERE

Dello elegantissimo

Poeta Seraphino Aquilano
nuouaméte con diligétia
impreſſe cō molte co
ſe aggiunte.

S onetti.	CLXV.
Æ gloghe.	III.
E piſtole.	VII.
C apitoli.	XII.
D iſperate.	III.
S trambotti.	CCCLXIIII.
B arʒelette.	XIX.

Figure 5. Opere Dello elegantissimo Poeta Seraphino Aquilano
nuovamente con diligentia impresse con molte cose aggiunte.
(By permission of the Bibliothèque nationale de France.)

As has been stated before, Serafino's poetry was vastly popular and imitated because of his personality, and usage of Petrarchan language, dramatic attitudes, and popular themes. Moreover, his style, witticisms and fluid concepts were venerated and imitated. Although his *disperata* remains fairly unknown today, it contributed to his fame as one of the most admired poets of the late Quattrocento and to the circulation of his work in the many early-modern editions of his *canzoniere* and in the Italian anthologies.[124]

Benedetto Gareth, Known as Cariteo

Cariteo's standing and the impact of his poetry in the kingdom of Naples and in Italy are quite remarkable. According to Pèrcopo, his poems widely circulated in Italian courts in manuscript form where they immediately met admiration throughout the early-modern period.[125] Moreover, they nurtured the next generation of Neapolitan poets, including Rota, Tansillo, and di Costanzo.[126] Cariteo was born in Barcelona but moved to Naples between 1466 and 1468, where he followed the Kings of Aragon. He was first nominated the keeper of the Great Royal Seal and shortly after Secretary of State to Ferrante II (Ferrandino). Thus, his life and pursuits were tightly connected to the Aragon dynasty and the Naples court, where he befriended other poets and humanists including Pontano, Panormita, and Sannazaro, joining their Accademia Pontaniana. Naples was not only the capital of the Kingdom of Aragon, but also one of the primary centers of intellectual activity and humanism in the fifteenth and early-sixteenth century.[127]

Italy became Cariteo's second homeland, and it is in Italian that he composed his work, *Opere del Chariteo*, which included his *canzoniere Endimione*, that features sonnets, ballads, madrigals, *canzoni* and sestinas, as well as *strambotti* and political songs.[128] His work was first published in 1506, and then in 1509, with the addition of more poems. In these collections, love verses written in honor of his beloved Luna intermingle with encomiastic poems written in celebration of the political exploits of the Aragon monarchy.[129] Cariteo's fierce attachment to his kings, his membership in the Accademia Pontaniana, and the strong humanistic culture surrounding the court of Naples undoubtedly inspired his literary vein. According to Wilkins, in the last thirty years of the Quattrocento, Cariteo's poetry and its new followers can be credited for beginning a new phase of Italian Petrarchism that quickly spread to other literary communities.[130]

Cariteo's *Endimione*'s table of content does not list *disperate*. However, his poetry began a phase of significant transformations in the genre because he adapted its content to other lyric forms at which he excelled, thus securing a legacy to poets of the late Quattrocento and early-Cinquecento. In the vast collection based on the first two editions of his *Rime* (1506 and 1509),[131] several *canzoni* adopt specific *disperata topoi*, but do not draw on others, including the full-blown maledictions.[132] Remarkably, *Endimione*'s very first *canzone* is an example of Cariteo's style in adopting the *disperata*, beginning with a hymn to the genre's iconic setting:

> Tra questi boschi agresti,
> Selvaggi, aspri e incolti,
> Ov'io son solo, & altri non mi vede,
> Posso far manifesti i miei tormenti occolti

(Among these rural woods,/Wild, harsh and untamed,/Where I am now, and where others do not see me,/I can reveal my secret torments) (vv. 1–4, 19–20).

The speaker wanders in the desolate and harsh forest; here, all alone, he can make his torments known and escape the woman who was offended by his declaration of love: "che del parlar d'amor tanto s'offende" (v. 13, 20). The second *canzone* starts with a similar setting, but it more closely imitates Petrarch's model, including his sonnet "Solo e pensoso":

> Errando sol per antri horrendi & foschi,
> Et per deserte piagge, aspre e noiose,
> Sterili, ove giamai pianta non nasce;
> ...
> Mi mena Amor

(Wandering alone in horrid and dark grottoes,/And through deserted beaches, harsh and boring,/And barren, where no plant ever grows;/ ... /Love guides me) (vv. 1–6, 27–28).[133]

However, here too, the poetic persona is drawn to these specific sites by his despair, which overwhelms him with false hope and desire, "Con dubbia speme & con certo desio,/Misero!" (vv. 35–36, 29). Luna, his Goddess, is the source of his melancholy and despair, a role that Laura had for Petrarch's persona. Thus, Cariteo included some of the *disperata topoi* in his poetry while also borrowing from Petrarch's system, including his and his poetry's devotion to a single woman, whose beauty and praises fill the *Endimione*.

Death, a common *disperata topos*, has a primary role in Cariteo's *Rime*. Verses that call for and allude to death abound in various ways, but never really reach the tragic tones that we encounter in most *disperate*, where hopelessness is palpable and real, and unattached to a particular beloved. Death is a wish, a welcomed finale, and talking about death, as Cariteo so poetically states, is a delight and amusement: "Parlar di morte è 'l mio magior diletto" (v. 15, 52), and "Abbrevia, morte, dunque il tuo camino,/Ch'anz'il destin morire è il mio destino" (Thus, shorten your path, death,/Rather than destiny, death is my only destiny) (vv. 49–50, 53).

In his "Cantico di Chariteo de dispregio del mondo" (Cariteo's song disparaging the world) (291–297), despite the stark, descriptive title that expresses a total disdain for the world, the poetic persona laments life, war, humanity's struggles, and false earthly treasures, such as fame and wealth. Although the poem is descriptive, it is not really a narration of the poet's labors, which ultimately renders it artificial and unmoving. Certainly, there are few exceptions that echo some of the *disperata* attitudes in which the poet-persona laments his existence, even if Cariteo's tone and attitude are noticeably milder and restrained (vv. 7–9, 291). Only in his "Canzoni di Chariteo" are there verses that reach the graver despair that is familiar to the readers of the *disperata*. These six stanzas[134] were included in the 1506 edition, but not in the 1509 edition of his *canzoniere*.[135] "Canzone IV" is a captivating example of how Cariteo adapted the *disperata* content to his *canzoni*:

> Quanto qui legi scritto,
> Ti manda quell'afflitto – e sventurato,
> Che vive desperato – in vita obscura,
> Lontan da tua figura – & di sua vita

(What you read written here/Has been sent to you by an afflicted –and unfortunate man,/Who, *disperato*, lives –a dark life,/Far from your presence –and from his life) (vv. 1–4, 433).

The reference to the "desperato" is a direct allusion to the *disperata* persona and to his place and role in the literary tradition. The poem then describes the day of the *innamoramento* and the many sorrows this day has caused, which push him to seek his suicide:

> Ne si pô la salute – ricovrare,
> Se non con lo sperare – presto uscire
> Di doglia, col morire: – io son già satio
> Di patir tanto stratio!; – & più desio

> Di questo male mio, – si duro & forte,
> Sanarme con la morte, – & romper l'anni,
> Et esser for d'affanni – & di dolore

(I cannot recover–my health,/Without the hope–to soon escape/
My sorrows, with death–I am already gratified/To suffer so much
torture!;–and with more desire/From this evil of mine,–so harsh
and cruel,/To find sanity in death,–and to disrupt my age,/In order
to get out of my sorrows–and my grief) (vv. 16–20, 434).

His hope to die soon and to "find sanity in death," alludes to suicide, and
further suggests that his life end so that he may be put out of troubles and
pain. The poet nevertheless clearly avoids realistic descriptions of physical harm and death and even how he would wish to die. Furthermore,
although the thought of death is present, the poet-persona is more attuned
to the Petrarchan model of the *amant martyr* than to the *disperato,* who
calls for a catastrophic and violent death. The song ends with a description
of more love pangs and the desperate state of his soul:

> L'alma colma da pene – & tormentata;
> Ma presto desperata – la vedrai:
> Chè sofrir più non pô tanti aspri guai!

(My soul filled with sorrows–and tormented;/But soon in despair–
you will see it:/Because I can no longer suffer such harsh sorrows!)
(vv. 35–37, 434).

Therefore, to despair is an integral component of this poem but certainly
not a recurring theme in Cariteo's *canzoniere*.

"Canzone V" is also fairly tame, apart from two verses where the
narrator elegantly accuses Love to push him to suicide, to despair, and to
throw himself into hell. Despair, again, is tightly linked to death, hell, and
love sorrows:

> Perchè mi fuste duce – & ferma guida
> Ad esser homicida – di me stesso,
> Conducendomi spesso – ad desperarme,
> E ad precipitarme – ne l'inferno?

(Why were you my master–and firm guide/To kill myself,/Pushing
me often–to despair,/And to throw myself–in hell?) (vv. 7–10, 435).

Finally, in "Canzone VI", the last of the series, the poet directly addresses
the beloved in very severe terms, "Ungrateful and cruel", (v. 1, 436). At
first, the beloved is actually depicted as if she were herself surrounded by

the *disperata*'s iconic landscape, in the company of savage animals and snakes and away from her fellow humans:

> Tra le fere nutrita, – & tra serpenti,
> Non tra l'humane genti; – o cruda, acerba,
> Indomita & superba – & aspra & dura
> Più ch'altra creatura, – al mondo nata
> (vv. 2–5, 436).

A stark description follows, in which she is portrayed as harsh and acerbic, unwavering, haughty, and cruel. Cariteo clearly evokes the *disperata* and pairs it with an unforgiving description of the woman, again, intimately linking despair to unrequited love. He also thoroughly develops the *disperata* *topos* of contentment in death and in dark places, as in the following verses:

> Anzi vivrò contento – & glorïoso;
> E, 'n loco tenebroso- & infoelice,
> Serrò lieto & foelice

(Actually, I will live content–and full of glory;/In this tenebrous and doomed–place/I will be glad and happy) (vv. 52–54, 438).

While Pèrcopo and Parenti fail to note the influence of the *disperata* on Cariteo's *canzoni*, instead underscoring the Classics, Petrarch, and his Academy colleagues such as Pontano and Sannazaro, Cariteo clearly adopts several of the *disperata*'s *topoi*, and adapts them with sophistication to the tastes of his audience at court. Marco Santagata notes the absence of forms in *terza rima*, such as *capitoli* and *disperate*, in the Neapolitan lyric production, and adds that these genres were mostly devoted to moral and religious topics, unlike in the Northern courts, where Tebaldeo and Serafino, for example, use them in abundance.[136] However, Cariteo used the *canzone* form, clearly adopting Beccari's *disperate*, and thus nurtured and contributed to the *disperata* genre because he infused his *canzoniere* with its *topoi*, attitudes and language, albeit "genteel-ized" in order to respect his immediate milieu and practices. As one of the favorite poets at the Naples court, he was expected to be a model for other writers and intellectuals; thus, he wrote poems that were refined and pleasurable. Furthermore, he was intimately entwined with the Aragon kings and their court; hence, his vocabulary and approach to poetry are more restrained—something we have already seen with Tebaldeo and Serafino.[137] Even though the genre depicts a world turned upside down, threatened by apocalyptic events, and completely void of order and sense, the poems by these three authors depict a world where Love and its rules reign, and subjugate the desperate lover.

Although the *disperata* poems of Tebaldeo, Serafino, and Cariteo are visibly milder, more restrained, and less violent than the previous paradigms, French critics in particular consider them to be the main exemplars of the genre, probably because they were greatly anthologized, circulated, and imitated in France. Their cultural and literary relations, as well as their allegiance to and development of court lyric are crucial to the differences in the approach and interpretation, but also transmission of the genre.[138] Their position and role at court lent their language and style a more sophisticated flair. Moreover, as well-established courtiers *par excellence*, they were favored by their patrons and assigned to important political and intellectual endeavors,[139] which transpires in their poetry. If the lack of order in other *disperate* demonstrates a need on the part of the author to represent a reality devoid of law, as Russell compellingly argues, these three poets, on the other hand, worked to pursue and establish order, with Love as the ultimate ruler, just like in Pertarch's *Rime*.[140] They not only utilized Petrarch's code, but also propagated it even further, thus perpetuating the image of the well-rounded poet-functionary. Fundamentally, they are Petrarchan poets who followed their master's experience of love and its implications, such as suffering, martyrdom, jealousy, unrequited desire, dissatisfaction, frustration, and melancholy. However, the elegiac world that they portray is that of the *disperata*: secluded, infernal and barren, and eager to welcome their obsessive calls for death and defiant despair, which contributed to the genre's development. As Cariteo's verse proclaims, "In this tenebrous and doomed–place/I will be content and happy", the oxymoronic *état d'être* of the *disperata* is omnipresent and palpable in the dark and in solitude, where the *disperato* can better despair about his misery and desolate soul. Some of these elements will nurture and transmit the *disperata* genre to the next generation of poets in Italy, as well as in France some fifty years later. Again, we can see how the Petrarchan tradition and the *disperata* merged in the context of court lyric. In fact, it is in these three poets' literary production that the two best converge and expand. Furthermore, their life and work are paradigms for most court writers in both Italy and France. Indeed, despite the differences in time and country, the *disperata*'s traits became distinctly recognizable and could be transferrable from text to text and be relevant, because, historically and culturally, these two countries were tightly intertwined. They both contended with religious and political conflicts, and they shared the same literary culture embedded in Classicism, Petrarchism, and in the new themes that would gradually become more dominant.

NOTES

[1] See Vecchi Galli, "La poesia cortigiana tra XV e XVI," 103.

[2] See Antonio Rossi, *Serafino Aquilano e la poesia cortigiana*, and Vianey, *Le Pétrarquisme en France*, 15–58.

[3] For a thorough review of the latest significant works on courtly poetry, see Vecchi Galli, "La poesia cortigiana tra XV e XVI secolo," and Tobia Toscano *Letterati Corti Accademie*.

[4] See Antonio Rossi, *Serafino Aquilano e la poesia cortigiana*.

[5] See Malinverni, "La lirica volgare padana tra Boiardo e Ariosto," and Carla Rossi, *Il Pistoia*, 5–11.

[6] See Carla Rossi who explains her intent to examine il Pistoia's work in relation to the cultural program of the satirical poetry from Tuscany, which was then exiled to the Northern courts, in *Il Pistoia*, 8–9. For Deschamps and Vannozzo, see Levi, *Francesco di Vannozzo*, 304–307.

[7] See Alison Cornish, "*Translatio Galliae*: Effects of Early Franco-Italian Literary Exchange," 309–330.

[8] Plumb, *The Italian Renaissance*, 21.

[9] Ibid., 24.

[10] For extensive bibliographies on court poets, see *Europa delle corti. Centro studi sulle società di Antico Regime* at www.europadellecorti.it and *Le corti nell'Italia del Rinascimento* at www.rm.unina.it.

[11] See for example Alessandro d'Ancona, "Del secentismo nella poesia cortigiana del secolo XV," 63–181, and Malinverni, "L'edizione e il commento dei Sonetti e Capituli di Panfilo Sasso," 368.

[12] Manacorda, "Galeotto del Carretto Poeta lirico e drammatico monferrino (14---1530)," 12.

[13] See Tissoni Benvenuti's discussion on the "koinè cortigiana" in *Il Quattrocento settentrionale*, 135–137.

[14] More technically, Italian court poetry has also been riddled with false attributions as in the case of several *disperate* here discussed.

[15] D'Ancona notes that all court writers divided their *canzonieri* utilizing the same genres, that is "Sonetti, Capitoli, Egloghe, Sestine, Strambotti, Disperate, Barzellette, Epistole, Canzoni," in "Del Secentismo nella poesia cortigiana," 155.

[16] Vecchi Galli, "La poesia cortigiana tra XV e XVI secolo," 96–97.

[17] See for example Baldassarre Castiglione's *Il Cortigiano*, which became very popular.

[18] On the Italian academies, see *Italian Academies of the Sixteenth Century*, and Michele Maylender, *Storia delle Accademie d'Italia*. On the French academies, see Frances A. Yates, *The French Academies of the Sixteenth Century*, Robert J. Sealy, *The Palace Academy of Henri III*, and Edouard Frémy, *L'Académie des derniers Valois*.

[19] See for example Weber, "La Condition sociale des poètes et l'influence de la vie de cour," in *La Création poétique*, 63–106, Robert J. Knecht, "A New Parnas-

sus," 211–225, Jacqueline Boucher, *La Cour de Henri III*, 131–135, and Balsamo, "Les Italiens de la Cour et les Lettres sous le règne de Henri IV," 77–95.

[20] "La 'Disperata', attribuée ici à Tebaldeo, est différente de la pièce contenue sous ce titre dans les éditions précédentes des œuvres de cet auteur. Elle figure dans le recueil des œuvres de Serafino dell'Aquila, sous le titre de 'Disperata 3a'. La 1ère pièce, 'Cerbero invoco', attribuée ici à Serdini, figure également, sous le titre de 'Disperata 2a', dans ce même recueil. Elle est attribuée à Antonio da Bacchereto par G. Volpi dans 'Giornale storico della letteratura italiana', XV, 45 et par F. Flamini dans la 'Lirica toscana del rinascimento,'" 638–639.

[21] Antonio Rossi notes in fact that it was easy to attribute to Serafino verses that were not his, which complicates matters of authorship pertaining to various *disperate*, but mostly to "La disperata" by il Pistoia. See *Serafino Aquilano e la poesia cortigiana*, 15. For Serafino, see Serafino Ciminelli, *Opera dello elegantissimo poeta Serafino Aquilano*, 1544.

[22] D'Aubigné, *Le Printemps*, Weber ed. 301–305. D'Aubigne's *Stances* will be discussed in Chapter Five.

[23] As we shall see, the implications of the falsely attributed *disperata* are significant.

[24] First stanza by Il Pistoia: "La nuda terra s'ha già messo il manto/di fiori e d'herbe, e ogni cor s'allegra,/et io pur hora comincio il gran pianto." His last: "A lei perdòno quanto mai m'offese./Anima, passa fuor di tanti affanni!/Mia morte a tutto il mondo sia palese,/che un sol exempio schiva molti danni." In Carla Rossi, *Il Pistoia*, 243 and 248. All references to il Pistoia's *disperata* will be based on this edition.

[25] For example, the Bibliothèque nationale's edition, *Opere dello elegantissimo Seraphino Aquilano nuovamente con diligentia impresse con molte cose aggiunte* (1516), http://gallica.bnf.fr/ark:/12148/bpt6k704444/f2.image. See Figure 5.

[26] Pèrcopo, "Una disperata famosa," 701. Pèrcopo provides as well the variances of the versions found in the Italian libraries, which all call it "La disperata" as if *the one and only*, and also to provide it with a title. See also Carla Rossi, *Il Pistoia*, 5.

[27] Carla Rossi, *Il Pistoia*, 5.

[28] Many of the *disperata* authors worked and moved at the court of Isabella d'Este Gonzaga, and at the cultural and literary circles not only in Mantova, but also in Ferrara, where, due to political and literary alliances, the poets entertained close interaction and fruitful exchanges. See Luzio and Renier, *La coltura e le relazioni letterarie di Isabella d'Este Gonzaga*.

[29] Carla Rossi, "La 'Disperata' capitolo conclusivo dei *Sonetti faceti* del Pistoia," 43–61. Pèrcopo wrote the article, "Una disperata famosa," yet he does not include the text in his edition of il Pistoia's *I sonetti faceti*, despite the fact that he used it to establish that the *codice ambrosiano* belonged indeed to Cammelli. Vittorio Rossi discusses Il Pistoia in *Il Quattrocento*, 814–815.

[30] Carla Rossi highlights the intertextualities with the Latin writers, with

Petrarch's *Rerum vulgarium fragmenta*, and with Tebaldeo's and Serdini's *disperate*. See *Il Pistoia*, 249–251. While these intertextualities are important, I will concentrate mostly on those between all the *disperate*, thus between the early modern Italian and French writers of the genre.

[31] It is the lyric *reverdir*, celebrated by the poets of the Sicilian School and by the French *troubadours*. All references to Il Pistoia's poetry will be based on Carla Rossi's edition, *Il Pistoia*, 243–248.

[32] Antonio Salvazo's *contro-disperata* is a direct response to this famous *disperata*. It is an example of religious retort to the many maledictions and curses contained in the genre: "Se la nuda tera muta ora 'l manto/verdigiante ognor, e più s'alegra,/per primavera, et mi da l'altro canto;/ ... /Quanti zercano 'l scuro e strane grote,/et io lume del sol clarido e frescho,/per consolar le vogie avian già rote." Pèrcopo, "Una disperata famosa," 717–718.

[33] For a catalogue and significance of animals in the tradition of early-modern poetry, see Malinverni, "Note per un bestiario lirico," 7–31.

[34] This verse eerily echoes Théophile's poetry, as we shall see in Chapter Six.

[35] According to Pierre Fontanier, "*L'Interrogation* consiste à prendre le tour *interrogatif*, non pas pour marquer un doute et provoquer une réponse, mais pour indiquer, au contraire, la plus grande persuasion, et défier ceux à qui l'on parle de pouvoir nier ou même répondre. Il ne faut donc pas la confondre avec *l'interrogation* proprement dite, avec cette *interrogation* du doute, de l'ignorance ou de la curiosité, par laquelle on cherche à s'instruire ou à s'assurer d'une chose." In *Les Figures du discours*, 368.

[36] For a complete biography see Girolamo Tiraboschi, "Sassi Panfilo Modenese," 22–34. See also Malinverni, "Sulla tradizione del sonetto 'Hor te fa terra, corpo' di Panfilo Sasso," 123–165.

[37] This volume also contains another copy of Yd 617 described above.

[38] While Luigi Lechi notes the first publication of this *disperata* in 1499 in *Della tipografia bresciana nel secolo decimoquinto*, 70, the Bibliothèque nationale's volume is from 1503 (Milan: Pedro Martire di Mantengati). See also Antonio Rossi, *Serafino Aquilano e la poesia cortigiana*, 126. Malinverni notes three printings: 1499 (Brescia: Misinta); 1502 (Brescia: Misinta); and 1503, which is the edition printed in Milan. See his "Sulla tradizione del sonetto 'Hor te fa terra, corpo' di Panfilo Sasso," 137.

[39] See Malinverni, "Sulla tradizione del sonetto" where he provides also a list of Sasso's work and includes the "Disperata contro l'amore," which, however, does not appear in Tiraboschi.

[40] Malinverni, "Sulla tradizione del sonetto."

[41] See, for example, Malinverni, "L'Edizione e il commento dei Sonetti e Capituli di Panfilo Sasso," 361–89. Malinverni discusses the thematic unity between sonnets and *capitoli* about love, and mentions Sasso's eclogues, 381. However, he does not once reference the *disperata*, which also is a poem about love.

[42] Tiraboschi, "Sassi Panfilo Modenese," 22.

[43] See Malinverni, "Sulla tradizione del sonetto," 124, and Giulio Bertoni, "Comunicazioni e Appunti. Sasso Sassi allias Panfilo Sassi," 272.

[44] See Ferdinando Gabotto, "Francesismo e antifrancesismo in due poeti del Quattrocento (Panfilo Sasso e Giorgio Alione). Gabotto analyzes Sasso's political poems in light of the events of his time, while noting as well that many other poets, including Tebaldeo, Serafino, Galeazzo di Tarsia, il Pistoia, and Cariteo were afflicted by and wrote about these events, 283. Sasso himself was against the French faction.

[45] All references to Sasso's *disperata* will be based on the Parisian manuscript, which has no page number.

[46] This stanza is reminiscent of Petrarch who often wrote about the specific moment of his *innamoramento*, and the many offences this caused.

[47] Frederic Jameson, "Magical Narratives: Romance as Genre," 135–163. See also Arthur F. Marotti who offers a compelling analysis of sonnet sequences in terms of "the more general socioeconomic and sociopolitical encoding of love poetry," in "'Love is not Love': Elizabethan Sonnet Sequences and the Social Order," 397.

[48] See for example Malinverni, "L'edizione e il commento dei *Sonetti e capituli di Panfilo Sasso*," 374–375, d'Ancona, "Del Secentismo nella poesia cortigiana," 154, and Antonio Rossi, *Serafino Aquilano e la poesia cortigiana*, 125.

[49] See Antonio Rossi, *Serafino Aquilano e la poesia cortigiana*, 126–127.

[50] See for example Vianey, *Le Pétrarquisme en France*, 37–45; Hugues Vaganay, *Le Sonnet en Italie et en France au XVIe siècle*, and his "Un modèle de Desportes non signalé encore: Pamphilo Sasso."

[51] In the Département des manuscrits occidentaux, site Richelieu.

[52] Zampetro de L'Eremita's *disperata*, "Misera sorte mia piu che altra al mondo," Tebaldeo's *disperate*, "Passionato core o trista mente," "Se mai nel lamentare sospiri caldi," and "Dopoi che la caduca e fragil vesta," and il Carretto's *disperata*, "La tromba suona io son verso al giudizio."

[53] See Donato Bramante, *Sonetos*, Francisco Merino Morales, ed. Morales also speaks to the importance of this manuscritpt, noting that it is an "importante florilegio poético recopilado en Milán hacia el 1495–1496, y que contiene los testimonios más interesantes de la poesía en la corte sforzesca, escrita entre los años 1490 a 1494," 23.

[54] Renier, "Saggio di rime inedite di Galeotto del Carretto," 241. In this essay, Renier states that this Parisian manuscript not only includes the most poems by Carretto, a total of twenty-six, but also their most accurate transcription. A second manuscript containing the same poems by Carretto is the Magliabechiano II, II 75.

[55] Carretto, *Poesie inedite di Galeotto del Carretto*, 442–447.

[56] See Manacorda, "Galeotto del Carretto," 47–125 and Giuseppe Turba, "Galeotto del Carretto, tra Casale e Mantova," 95–169. See also Luzio and Renier, *La coltura e le relazioni letterarie di Isabella d'Este Gonzaga*, where the authors discuss Isabella d'Este's relationship with Tebaldeo and Carretto, amongst other poets.

[57] Carretto, *Poesie inedite di Galeotto del Carretto*, Spinelli, ed. All references to this *disperata* will be based on this edtion.

[58] See Manacorda, "Galeotto del Carretto," 47–125; Turba, "Galeotto del Carretto tra Casale e Mantova," 95–169; Renier, "Saggio di rime inedite di Galeotto del Carretto"; and "Galeotto del Carretto," Roberto Ricciardi, *Dizionario Biografico degli Italiani*.

[59] Cf. Renier, Saggio di *Rime inedite di Galeotto del Carretto*, 241, Spinelli, *Poesie inedite di Galeotto del Carretto*, 64–65, and finally Malacorda, *Galeotto del Carretto*.

[60] Page 124, Ms. It. 1543 in the Bibliothèque nationale, Site Richelieu. All references to this *disperata* will be based on this manuscript.

[61] See pages 120 to 124, where his *disperata* starts.

[62] See Manacorda, 82.

[63] See Tissoni Benvenuti, *Il Quattrocento Settentrionale*, 122.

[64] Vecchi Galli, "La poesia cortigiana fra XV e XVI secolo," 111. Vecchi Galli also comments on this manuscript and the Fior. Naz. II.II.75, and their importance in disseminating not only the poems, but also the regional vernaculars, in particular between Milan and Bergamo, 116.

[65] In addition to his poems, Carretto also wrote four plays, including one of the first Italian tragedies, *La Sofonisba* (1546), dedicated to Isabella d'Este. See Renier, *Saggio di Rime inedite*, 233–234.

[66] Vecchi Galli, "La poesia cortigiana tra XV e XVI secolo," 103.

[67] See Cian, Flamini, Antonio Rossi, and Vittorio Rossi. See also Pasquini, "Il Saviozzo e la poesia cortigiana del Quattrocento," in which he talks about the legacy of il Saviozzo's *disperate*, 319–322. I will analyze the *disperate* that are most significant to the genre, although many more examples can be found in the *canzonieri* of the fifteenth and sixteenth centuries.

[68] See Pèrcopo, "Una disperata famosa," 702, and Vittorio Rossi, who comments on the *disperata* writers as "facitori di tali stranezze" – "makers of such odd things" in his review of Cian's *Le rime di Bartolomeo Cavassico*, 219.

[69] See Cian, who provides examples of manuscripts that contain *disperate*, xc-ccxxxv.

[70] Rigolot, "Quel genre d'amour pour Louise Labé," 304.

[71] Tissoni Benvenuti, "La tradizione della terza rima," 306

[72] Biancardi, ed. *Il Canzoniere Riccardiano*, 10–13.

[73] Ibid., XLIX.

[74] Petrarch, "Benedetto sia 'l giorno e 'l mese et l'anno/e la stagione e 'l tempo et l'ora e 'l punto/e 'l bel paese e 'l loco ov'io fui giunto/da' dei begli occhi che legato m'ànno." vv. 1–4, 139.

[75] See Biancardi, *Il Canzoniere Riccardiano*, xiii, and Flamini, *La lirica toscana del Rinascimento*, 403–410.

[76] "Sia maledetto l'anno, il mese e il giorno,/il punto, l'ora, il tempo e la stagione,/il loco e il bel paese, che cagione/mi fu di far veder tuo viso adorno!/E

maledetto el primo scorno,/ ... Maledette le voci coi sospiri/... Sia maledetta la lingua e la mano" 36.

[77] Pasquini sees Il Saviozzo's *disperate* as the main influential texts that facilitated this spread. See his "Il Saviozzo e la poesia cortigiana nel Quattrocento," 319.

[78] See Giovanni Pozzi and Giulia Giannella, "Scienza antiquaria e letteratura: Il Feliciano," 469–470. See also Franco Pignatti's contribution, "Felice Feliciano."

[79] Andrea Comboni, "Rarità metriche nelle antologie di Felice Feliciano," 65. This article provides an extensive bibliography of Feliciano's work and an account of his many roles as an important intellectual in Verona and Venice at the beginning of the Quattrocento. For an historical and literary background, see also Alessandra Mulas, "Epistole e prosimetri inediti del Feliciano," and Serena Spano Martinelli, "Note intorno a Felice Feliciano." This article offers a comprehensive list of Feliciano's work, including two prints housed at the Bibliothèque nationale in Paris.

[80] See Spano Martinelli, "Note intorno a Felice Feliciano," 230, and Pozzi and Giannella, "Il Feliciano," who claim the poet was persecuted by poverty, 466.

[81] Feliciano's *disperata* is found in Russell, "Intenzionalità artistica della disperata," 183–192, reproduced from ms. It. 1029, housed at the Bibliothèque nationale in Paris. All references to Feliciano's *disperata* will be based on Russell's edition.

[82] Ibid., 172.

[83] Feliciano dedicated much of his time to collecting poetry and his own letters. He assembled twenty epistles devoted to the humanistic theme of friendship. See Pozzi and Giannella, "Scienza antiquaria e letteratura: Il Feliciano," 467.

[84] Ibid., 471.

[85] Ibid., 470.

[86] Wiese, 385–386. Verses 1–120 will be based on this edition. Verses 124 to 160 will be based on Ernesto Lamma, "Intorno ad alcune rime di Leonardo Giustiniani," 375.

[87] Ibid., 375.

[88] Cian, *Le rime di Bartolomeo Cavassico*, lxxxciii.

[89] The pioneers are undoubtedly Vianey, *Le Pétrarquisme en France*, Vaganay, *Le Sonnet en France et en Italie*, as well as Jacques Lavaud, *Un Poète de cour au temps des derniers Valois. Philippe Desportes.*

[90] Vianey, *Le Pétrarquisme en France*, 8, Balsamo, *Les Rencontres des muses*, and DellaNeva, *Unlikely Exemplars* and "An Exploding Canon."

[91] Giovanni Parenti, *Benet Garret detto il Cariteo*, 145.

[92] See DellaNeva, *Unlikely Exemplars*, 125, and in particular, her chapter on the role of anthologies, 91–121.

[93] Vianey, *Le Pétrarquisme en France*, 13.

[94] See for example Vaganey, *Le Sonnet en France et en Italie*, Mia Cocco, *La tradizione cortese e il petrarchismo nella poesia di Clément Marot*, 79–115; Marius Piéri, *Pétrarque et Ronsard*, Lavaud, *Un poète de cour*, Giulio Marzot, "Il tramite

del Petrarchismo, Arturo Meozzi, *Il petrachismo europeo*, and Pierre de Nolhac, *Du Rôle de Pétrarque*. See also the works already cited.

[95] See Luzio and Renier, *La coltura e le relazioni letterarie di Isabella d'Este Gonzaga*. This work divides the cenacles into "Gruppo mantovano, ferrarese, lombardo, veneto, emiliano, dell'Italia centrale e meridionale." 104–115, 146–47, 202, 208–211, 242–71.

[96] For a historical and literary account of the many centers and salons, see Robin, *Publishing Women*.

[97] See Antonio Rossi, who notes that this relationship is important "per intendere l'intero corso della poesia cortigiana dagli anni 1490–1495 in poi, influenzata in misura determinante appunto dal connubio Tebaldeo-Serafino." *Serafino Aquilano e la poesia cortigiana*, 113.

[98] Ibid., 106–113, and Marchand, "I sonetti del Tebaldeo in morte del Serafino."

[99] See in particular Marco Santagata and Stefano Carrai, *La lirica di corte nell'Italia del Quattrocento* and Toscano, *Letterati Corti Accademie*.

[100] Massimo Danzi calls Tebaldeo "campione della poesia di corte." See his "Sulla poesia di Antonio Tebaldeo," 259.

[101] See Vittorio Rossi, *Il Quattrocento*, 804–805.

[102] Antonio Rossi, *Serafino Aquilano e la poesia cortigiana*, 113. See also his study of their respective intertextualities, 107–111.

[103] For more on these cultural and literary connections, see Danzi, "Sulla poesia di Antonio Tebaldeo," 261.

[104] Danzi, "Note e discussioni," 270.

[105] Ibid., 276.

[106] Marchand, "Le disperate di Antonio Tebaldeo," 163–164. All references to Tebaldeo's poetry will be based on the Tania Basile's and Jean-Jacques Marchand's edition. "Già cum suavi" is in volume II 1, *Rime della vulgata*, Basile ed. and "Lingua mia stanca" is in volume III 2, *Rime estravaganti*, Marchand, ed.

[107] In *Opere de miser Antonio Tebaldeo da Ferrara. Sonetti, dialoghi, disperata, epistole, egloghe, capitoli, etc ...* housed at the Bibliothèque nationale. The *disperata* is indeed "Ia cum suavi e mansueti carmi". See Figure 1.

[108] Marchand makes a difference between an elegiac *capitolo*, like the majority of Tebaldeo's *capitoli*, and a narrative *capitolo*, and notes that the *disperata* is a bit of both: "*Strictu sensu* dunque la disperata non apparterrebbe al genere narrativo. Tuttavia, la disperata tradizionale è anche tutta giocata su un'ampia prolessi ipotetica che assume dimensioni narrative." "Le disperate di Antonio Tebaldeo," 163.

[109] See Basile, *Per il testo critico delle rime del Tebaldeo*, especially pages 329–333 which provide a list of Tebaldeo's manuscripts.

[110] III 2, pages 1182–1188.

[111] II 1, pages 401–406, and 433–439. For more information on manuscripts and publications, see pages 11–125. In the aforementioned 1511 edition, "Se mai

nel lamentarvi fusti caldi" is also titled "*Capitulo primo*" and it immediately follows the "*Disperata*".

¹¹² See Marco Santagata, *La lirica aragonese*, Pèrcopo, *Le Rime di Benedetto Gareth detto il Cariteo*, CCXLVIII-CCLII, and Carlo Dionisotti, "Fortuna del Petrarca nel Quattrocento," 98–99.

¹¹³ See Vincenzo Calmeta, *Vita del fecondo poeta vulgare Serafino Aquilano*. This collection focuses in particular on praising Serafino and his poetry.

¹¹⁴ In France, Serafino's *strambotti* inspired the *madrigal*. See Cocco, *La tradizione cortese e il petrarchismo*.

¹¹⁵ Luzio and Renier, *La cultura e le relazioni letterarie di Isabella d'Este Gonzaga*, 269–271; Antonio Rossi, *Serafino Aquilano e la poesia cortigiana*, 93–102; and Tissoni-Benvenuti, *Il Quattrocento settentrionale*, where she calls Serafino's *rime* true "best sellers" between 1502 and 1513, 1164.

¹¹⁶ There are in fact more than fifty editions of Serafino's poetry: see Antonio Rossi, *Serafino Aquilano e la poesia cortigiana*, 11, and his extensive biography and bibliography in his *Serafino Aquilano. Strambotti*, LIII-CXIX. The thirteen *strambotti* "Ferma desperatione" are on pages 147–157. See also Vecchi Galli, "Su una edizione poco nota di Serafino Aquilano," 87.

¹¹⁷ Serafino, Vinegia: Bartolomeo detto l'Imperador, et Francesco suo genero, 1544. All references to Serafino's "Disperata Prima" will be based on this edition. As mentioned above, the Bibliothèque nationale owns a similar edition reproduced in Figure 5, *Opere dello elegantissimo Seraphino Aquilano nuovamente con diligentia impresse* (1516) at Gallica: http://gallica.bnf.fr/ark:/12148/bpt6k704444/f2.image

¹¹⁸ Pasquini explains that Serafino borrowed il Saviozzo's "Cerbero invoco" because he was very fond of this *disperata*, which would then explain this false attribution to Serafino. See his "Il Saviozzo e la poesia cortigiana nel Quattrocento," 321.

¹¹⁹ Mario Menghini published the first modern edition of Serafino's poetry in *Le Rime di Serafino de' Ciminelli dall' Aquila*, with his sonnets, eclogues, and his *Rappresentazione allegorica e le epistole*. I can only speculate that, maybe, his second volume, which never materialized, might have included Serafino's *disperata* together with the remaining *rime*. More recently, Antonio Rossi edited *Serafino Aquilano, Sonetti e altre rime*, but again, did not mention his "Disperata Prima" while he did discuss and include the other poems written in *terza rima*, such as his *capitoli*, 19–21.

¹²⁰ The French poets as well use the term "hurler" or scream their despair, as a loud mean to demand attention and amplify their hopelessness and grief.

¹²¹ References to Serafino's *disperata* will be based on the 1544 edition of his *Opera*.

¹²² Serafino's verse is similar to il Saviozzo's verse in his female-voiced *disperata* "O specchio di Narciso, o Ganimede" which states "Oimè, oimè, che Cerbaro è già presso,/le Furie e gli altri spirti tapinelli/presa m'han pei capelli:/oimè, ch'io ardo e vommene in inferno!" (vv. 185–188, 99) Both poets depict an image of Cerberus' hunger and anger, who is very eager to snatch the desperate lover.

[123] An image that will recur in d'Aubigné's poetry.

[124] On Serafino's fame, see also Stephen D. Kolsky, "The Courtier as Critic".

[125] Pèrcopo, *Le Rime di Benedetto Gareth*, CCXXXIX.

[126] Indeed, the Academy represented a coveted center for young intellectuals from Italy and Spain. See Parenti, *Benet Garet*, 10.

[127] See Mary Hollinsgworth, *Patronage in Renaissance Italy*, 182–183, Carol Everhart Quillen, "Humanism and the Lure of Antiquity," 48–49, David Abulafia, "The South," 208–225, and Nuovo and Coppens, *I Giolito e la stampa nell'Italia del XVI secolo*, 161.

[128] For an analysis of the metric of Cariteo's *Endimione*, and his *canzoni* in particular, see Dionisotti, "Fortuna del Petrarca nel Quattrocento," 95–100; Enrico Fenzi, "La lingua e lo stile del Cariteo," and his "Cariteo: il fascino del nome."

[129] For Cariteo's political poems, see my "Cariteo's 'Aragonia.'" For a detailed biography and analysis of his work, see Parenti, *Benet Garret*, and Pèrcopo's introduction in *Le Rime di Benedetto Gareth*. All references to Cariteo's poetry will be based on this edition

[130] Wilkins, *Sudies in the Works and Life of Petrarch*, 283.

[131] For a detailed description of these two editions see Pèrcopo, LVII–CXVIII.

[132] Although some poems contain the word "maledico" or "maledetta sia", the other fixed *topoi* of the genre are missing. See for example *Canzone VXVII*, where Cariteo writes "Che maledetta sia di quel Sydonio/L'ombra perversa & sonte (funesta)/Perfida alma, crudel, superba & dura," vv. 49–51, 181.

[133] For a reading of the *topos* of solitude sought in "loca deserta" and Propertius, see Claudia Fanti, "L'elegia properziana nella lirica amorosa del Cariteo," 24 and 34. The coveted solitude found in deserted places, as in Petrarch's notorious sonnet "Solo e pensoso i più deserti campi" (95), is sought out by Cariteo more for love motivations than for despair triggered by several other causes, as in the *disperata* genre. French poets as well will adopt and adapt Petrarch's sonnet, for example Du Bellay, "Seul et pensif par la deserte plaine", Desportes, "Solitaire et pensif dans un bois écarté," and Baïf, "Solitaire et pensif par les lieux plus sauvages". On this topic, see Robert Griffin, "'Solo e pensoso': The Context of Petrarchan Melancholy," and Luzius Keller, "'Solo e pensoso,' 'Seul et pensif,' 'Solitaire et pensif': mélancolie pétrarquienne et mélancolie pétrarquiste," and Weber, *La Création poétique*, 307–327.

[134] Pèrcopo notes that the six *canzoni*, so called by Cariteo himself, are indeed "stanze." See note 1, 427. The Italian *stanze* will be imitated by the French Renaissance poets, as discussed in the following chapters.

[135] For a detailed content of each edition, see Parenti, *Benet Garret*, 3–7, and Fenzi, "Cariteo: il fascino del nome," 49.

[136] Santagata, *La lirica aragonese*, 261. For the *Endimione*, see 270–277.

[137] Cariteo in particular was greatly committed to writing political propa-

ganda in order to secure the Aragon kings' influence in Southern Italy. See Jerry H. Bentley, *Politics and Culture in Renaissance Naples*, Benedetto Croce, *Storia del Regno di Napoli*, and my "Cariteo's 'Aragonia'".

[138] Antonio Rossi reviews the many "influences" of Cariteo over Serafino, as well as over other court poets, arguing that Cariteo prepared the environment for court lyric to flourish especially in the last decades of the Quattrocento. *Serafino Aquilano e la poesia cortigiana*, 97.

[139] Fanti for example, notes that Cariteo's literary experience was soundly anchored in the study of the Classics, which is what the refined and educated community of the court and the Academy demanded. Cariteo's readers were mostly intellectuals. "L'elegia properziana nella lirica amorosa del Cariteo," 23–24.

[140] Russell, "Intenzionalità artistica della disperata," 169.

Chapter Four

The *Disperata* in the Cinquecento

> Ma Fortuna al timor mostra il sentiero
> erto ed angusto e pien di tanti inganni,
> che nel piú bel sperar poi mi dispero.
>
> Isabella di Morra

The *Disperata* in the Cinquecento

Although Serafino and Tebaldeo wrote *disperate* in the more traditional *capitolo* form, Cariteo's *canzoni* presaged a shift to other lyric forms in the Cinquecento. In fact, starting in the second decade of the sixteenth century, the authors began to transfer the *disperata*'s content, themes, and language to other forms, including the popular sonnet, as we shall see in the poetry of Angelo di Costanzo, Bernardino Rota, Luigi Tansillo, and Isabella di Morra.[1] Their poetry also marked the return to Petrarch's *Canzoniere* and its genres, which Pietro Bembo proclaimed to be the foremost model to be imitated. In his *Asolani* (1505) and *Rime* (1530), Bembo urged the restoration of the sonnet, the *canzone* and the *sestina*.[2] Thus, Petrarch's *Canzoniere* remained the fundamental point of origin of the poetry of the Cinquecento. Furthermore, since his *Canzoniere* only featured five forms – the sonnet, the *canzone*, the ballad, the *sestina,* and the madrigal—other lyric genres, including *capitoli ternari*, slowly started to fall out of favor.[3] More significantly, Bembo advocated a return to more philosophical and platonic topics that could be expounded in shorter forms, thus further devaluing longer ones.[4]

Although single-authored works continued to be circulated in both manuscript and print—as seen with Pietro Aretino, Nocturno Napolitano, Sannazaro, Tansillo, and other successful poets—the Giolito anthologies, whose "Libro Primo" was published in 1545, denoted an important event in literary history. Not only did Petrarchism, and the sonnet in particular, spread greatly, but Italian poetry as a whole became a printing phenomenon. Circulated widely, Italian poetry made its mark in sixteenth-century literary culture, especially in France and Spain.[5] Also, because the popularity of an author was closely associated with using a variety of genres, including the *disperata*, authorship, genre, and fame became increasingly entwined.

In this chapter, I discuss three poets, Pietro Aretino, Eurialo Morani d'Ascoli, and Isabella di Morra, and their *disperate* as good examples of interplay between the *disperata* and its Cinquecento forms. Furthermore, I revisit the *disperata femminile*, this time the ones authored by Morra, as well as the interplay between genre and gender. These poets' *disperate* embody the genre's passage from the fifteenth to the sixteenth century: Aretino uses the genre in a fairly conventional way, while Morani uses a long series of stanzas meant to elicit feelings of despair, and Morra uses sonnets and *canzoni* meant to express a deep-rooted patriarchal marginalization.

Pietro Aretino's *Opera Nova*

One of the few Cinquecento authors to write *disperate* in the *capitolo ternario*, Pietro Aretino (1492–1556) was an important cultural and literary figure of the European Renaissance. He was a poet and painter whose work, including several collections of poems, comedies and epistles, achieved great popularity during the mid-sixteenth century. On his frequent journeys through Perugia, Siena, Rome, Venice, and Mantua, he acquired many friendships, alliances, and patrons but also many enemies, due mostly to his polemical and satirical work.[6] Aretino wrote in a great variety of genres, including *strambotti*, sonnets, *canzoni*, *capitoli*, lauds, stanzas, essays, *I Ragionamenti* (1534–43), as well as plays, including *La Cortigiana* (1525) and *Orazia* (1546).[7] He addressed poems to great European figures, such as Pope Paul III, Francis I of France, and the Habsburg emperor Charles V, demonstrating an interest in politics and diplomacy.[8] His lyric poems were first published in his *Opera Nova del Fecundissimo Giovene Pietro Pictore Aretino* (Venice, Antonio Zoppino, 1512), which contains fifty-six *strambotti*, twelve sonnets, four *barzellette*, four *capitoli*, one eclogue, and one *disperata*. Like other Quattrocento and early-Cinquecento works, this volume is divided into metric compositions, increasing the popularity of the *canzoniere*.[9] Published in Venice, the printing capital of sixteenth-century Italy, this volume is a significant moment in the transmission of the *disperata* because of the popularity that Aretino would encounter later on. The intertextualities with Tebaldeo and Serafino in particular are noticeable. They also represent a continuum with the court lyric, whose language and traits persisted well into the sixteenth century.

Although Aretino's work continues to appear in modern anthologies and be printed in modern editions, his "Desperata" remains widely unknown and is yet to be included in scholarly discussions. It begins with a peaceful ode to nature in the springtime, and it closely echoes the first lines of il Pistoia's *disperata*, especially in expressions like "la nuda terra," which attest to Aretino's debt to the genre's tradition and his proclamation to be part of it:

> Vego già preparar il verde amanto
> a primaver, e gli uccelletti in fronde
> di tronco in tronco far lor terso canto.
>
> ...
>
> La nuda terra allo sparso sudore,
> buon seme producendo, gioglia rende,
> restaurando ogno'om delle perse ore.

(I already see Spring preparing its/green mantle,/and the little birds in the trees/singing from one branch to the other their distinct song./ ... /The naked earth has spread its sweat,/thus producing good seeds and joy,/and restoring all men of lost hours.) (vv. 1–15, 69).

To this idyllic beginning, the poet-persona juxtaposes his sorrow, which absorbs the whole universe in a fairly conventional way of the *disperata*, including the repetition of familiar *topoi* and use of the genre's standard elements (vv. 17–18, 69). The frantic sequence of sighs, pain, martyrdom, cries of grief, and the listing of nature's components, such as the sky, air, earth, and sea, are efficiently contained in two verses in order to communicate immediately what is distressing the speaker, but also his intent to place his *disperata* in the genre's tradition. Other formal and rhetorical *topoi* of the *disperata* are methodically replicated as well. The conditional "vorrei," (to wish), opens a sequence of tercets, and recurs twenty-one times throughout the one hundred verses. The speaker wishes that his miserable body would become food for the wild dogs; that the sun, stars, and the moon would be catapulted into the Earth in order to shatter its habitat and reverse the world order. He also calls for fierce animals, including dragons, to devour and annihilate humanity. In a colorful image, he wants thieves and spies to devastate forests and cities and for fights to break out regularly among men. He also calls for fantastic calamities to engulf not only the Earth, but the seas as well, a theme that makes this *disperata* particularly unique:

> Pioggie vorrei veder, baleni e toni,
> e fulminar dal ciel sagitte e sassi,
> e templi con teatri spezi e 'ntoni.
> In mar vorrei veder gli scogli e' massi
> urtar le barche, e mandar presto in fondo
> la merce coi nochier aflicti e lassi.
> Vorrei l'acque veder girar a tondo
> a l'universo la secunda volta,
> en fame, en pesta, en guerra el ciel e 'l mondo.

(I would like to see rain, wales and tunas,/and thunder from the sky strike rocks,/and temples with broken theaters./In the sea, I would like to see cliffs and rocks/hit boats, and soon sink/helmsmen with their goods, afflicted and tired./I wish to see the waters/inundate the universe for a second time,/with hunger, plague, and the sky and the world at war.) (vv. 37–45, 70).

Together with aquatic disasters, metaphors of war and mythology pervade the text, and a host of dramatic scenarios take place, in which human tragedies, animal upheavals, and natural catastrophes permeate every tercet without relief. This prompts the speaker to declare that without any more pity or hope, he wishes to see men die by spears and swords and for their blood to turn into a frightening sea:

> Senza pietà vorrei veder né speme,
> morir gli omini per terra a lance e spade,
> el sangue fussi un mar quando piú freme
> (vv. 52–54, 70).

Aretino's *disperata* capitalizes on the *topos* of an imaginary apocalypse that engulfs the whole universe. Unlike other *disperate* with their desolate desert settings, this text draws on several catastrophic images of seas, rivers, lakes and swamps, as seen in the following tercets:

> Vorrei veder per fiumi, fossi e laghi,
> cader gli omini per fame, orridi e brutti,
> e di mangiar l'un l'altro fussin brami

(I wish to see in rivers, pits and lakes,/men fall because of hunger, horrid and ugly,/eager to eat each other) (vv. 61–63, 70).

Verses 70 to 75 also elaborate on the devastation of deluges, as waves, rivers, seas, springs, and swamps turn into blood, and the fish devour all humanity, which he wishes to see being buried alive: "e, messi nel sepulcro, ancor, sien vivi" (v. 75, 71). The poet-persona's verve is particularly focused on all that is water, which becomes a metaphor for all the devastation and despair that engulf his world, which no human intervention can stop, and where men are hopeless and helpless. Indeed, it is as if the seas, rivers, and lakes serve to confirm yet again humanity's vulnerability and powerlessness. Throughout his *disperata*, Aretino is particularly keen on demonstrating how all aspects of the universe are at work to destroy men, their surroundings, and their livelihood.

After more gruesome descriptions of violent fatalities, the speaker makes a final wish for death to come and take everybody:

> E l'impia morte poi alla schermaglia
> esca colla suo falce e fiero strale,
> e privi ognun di vita e no gli caglia

(That the impious death chase the skirmish/with its sickle and straight arrow,/and deprive of life everybody, without any care) (vv. 94–96, 71).

Furthermore, the striking, final verse is a dramatic wish for every day to be Judgment Day, thereby ending the narrative with a sweeping gesture of destruction and doom.[10]

> Gli dèi, gli omini, le piante a fiero male,
> E gli animal vadin in precipizio,
> E manchi l'emisperio a un batter d'ale,
> E vorei ogni giorno el gran iudizio.

(I wish to see the gods, men, trees in proud evilness,/And animals fall in a precipice,/And the hemisphere fall in an instant,/And that everyday be judgment day.) (vv. 97–100, 71–72).

Although Aretino does not employ the full traditional *disperata* repertoire, he does concentrate on the genre's *topos* of destruction—the complete annihilation of the universe and its inhabitants. He portrays the apocalyptic visions with repetition and deviating little from the established conventions. With the exception of the destructive power of water and few verses that echo il Saviozzo's vigorous and realistic lines, such as the following, Aretino keeps to the script and to the most conventional traits of the *disperata*:

> Vorrei veder questa misera spoglia
> ligata in mezo a doi rapaci cani,
> e esser cibo a lor sfrenata voglia

(I wish to see my miserable corpse/tied up between two voracious dogs,/and be the food for their wild hunger) (vv. 28–30, 70).

Evidently, he wished to firmly place his poem within the genre's tradition, tercet after tercet, by imitating specific vocabulary and images, as well as to place his *Opera Nova* within the tradition of the Petrarchan *canzoniere*, including the variety of forms.

However, Aretino's publication was not just an homage to already well-established traditions, but it was also a way to introduce his work to the Italian literary scene. Although, as already mentioned, anthologies would become increasingly popular in the Cinquecento because of their variety, as well as their relatively moderate price and manageable format, the single-authored collections or *canzonieri* continued to be published because they remained an important tool for authors to reach readers and fame.[11] Moreover, the *canzoniere* was considered a superior accomplishment, one that was only achieved by writers who had either already established their fame, as Santagata claims,[12] or by those who needed to establish it, as in Aretino's case. On the other hand, some of the poets who were anthologized remained fairly unknown and did not publish single-authored collections, as demonstrated by the long indexes of Giolito's and his rivals' anthologies.

The fact that the *disperata* continued to appear on the title page of the Cinquecento *canzonieri* demonstrates its transmission into the sixteenth century. According to Dionisotti, in order to write well in the Renaissance, a poet had to first have studied and digested the poetry and meters of the Duecento and Trecento, which includes also the meter and conventions of the *disperata* genre.[13] Aretino's *Opera Nova* follows the format of other court poets' collections, such as Serafino's and Tebaldeo's, who used the *disperata* as a way to show poetic range. Furthermore, writing a *disperata* that deliberatively employs recognizable vocabulary and images is Aretino's way to prove his skills in utilizing the popular Renaissance Italian genres. However, although Aretino's other writings would find much fortune in Italy as well as in France,[14] his *Opera Nova* did not meet great success,[15] and most scholars consider it to be an "opera giovanile," a work of his youth, one conceived to inaugurate his entry into the literary scene.[16]

Eurialo Morani d'Ascoli's *La Vita disperata*: Staging Despair

There are only few documents available to help reconstruct Eurialo Morani's life (ca. 1485–90–ca. 1554), but we know that, like other *disperata* writers, he too was a poet-functionary, traveling from one court to another in order to accomplish his diplomatic duties and to seek fame. From Ascoli, Morani moved to Siena, and then to Rome, and finally to Bologna. In Rome, he served as the city of Ascoli's ambassador to the Pope, a charge that highlights the political and nomadic nature of his life. In 1538, he published *La Vita disperata*, a series of sixty-five octaves, staging a life riddled with darkness and despair. This work finally brought Morani some acclaim.[17] *La Vita disperata* was also included in the second volume of *La seconda parte delle stanze di diversi autori* by Lodovico Dolce, a collection that found much fortune in both Italy and France, and which, as Vianey notes, greatly contributed to the popularity of the *disperata* in France with poets such as Desportes, as we shall see in the following chapter.[18]

Although *La Vita disperata* does not feature all of the *disperata*'s traditional components, it is the perfect paradigm of how the genre developed into a sequence of stanzas capturing a life filled with failures and disappointments, ultimately revealing a chronic existential hopelessness. In fact, rather than calling it *Disperata*, Morani titles it "A Despairing Life", narrating how despair infects all aspects of his existence. Therefore, Morani freely borrows from the *disperata*, but also modifies the model. Hence, as in the history of all genres, the reader can see, once again, the *disperata*'s adoption, its expansions, and its variations.[19] Morani's own preface, which he paradoxically dedicates to himself, provides insight into his long composition entirely devoted to literary despair. His poverty, blamed on the avarice of the wealthy, drove him to dejection and insanity, and it pushed him to publish a text in which he would lugubriously hide, burying himself and his miseries.[20]

The poem is virtually a social commentary that recounts all of the injustices that the poet experienced and endured, one by one. Morani's words also uncover a deep-rooted rebellion that triggers his refusal to continue an existence that is no longer tolerable. Sandro Baldoncini notes that *La Vita disperata* is "a great allegory of grief."[21] Indeed, written like a confession, the poem, or as he calls it "la predica delle mie angoscie"—"a homily of my anguish," is provoked by his melancholic humors ("miei umori melanconici", 57), and it is dedicated, not to an important Prince or Lord, but to himself, because nobody else could understand such tragedies and misfortunes: "Così adunque sotto il nome d'Eurialo e all'ombra d'Eurialo esce ora la disperata vita d'Eurialo secura di sapersi con più viva forza dalla invidia e dalla malignità diffendere che dalla povertà non ha saputo infino a ora." (And thus, under the name of Eurialo and in the shadow of Eurialo comes the desperate life of Eurialo, sure of being able to defend itself with renewed strength from envy and malice, as it was not able to defend itself till now from poverty.)[22] The *disperato* of the poem is Eurialo, and along with in his shadow, he describes his desperate life, so much so that his pain forces him to curl up into himself. Furthermore, his work is meant to both recognize and honor a life of hopelessness, thus radically inscribing its author's name in the tradition of literary despair.

Like many of the poets already discussed, Morani too was considered a "minor" literary figure, one among many,[23] but his *disperata* created a model of despair that would be later adopted and elaborated upon at the end of the French Renaissance. In fact, his poetry fully develops the personal crisis and the dark pessimism that we encounter in the poetry discussed in the following chapters. The *disperata* elements all come into place, but they are arranged differently and further amplified. Each element receives more attention and textual space. At five hundred and twenty verses, this is the longest *disperata*. Each stanza develops painful details that are expertly elaborated upon, always with an eye to the macabre and meant to shock. They are then repeatedly alluded to throughout the poem in order to expound on their meaning and darkness.

The first stanzas introduce the poet-persona's wretched existence and blame impious Fortune for the speaker's current condition. The words, "Poscia che," "Given that," suggest that an intimate conversation is taking place, as if the speaker was in the middle of a conversation with his readers, who are fully expected to understand the reasons why his life is full of despair:

> Poscia che così vuol l'empia Fortuna
> Ch'io sia per povertade in odio al sole,
> Mirar non voglio più stelle né luna,
> Né più già mai sentire vive parole
> Ma voglio un lembo de la notte bruna
> Per vestir queste membra afflitte e sole;
> Et voglio fabricar, solo, in un bosco,
> Un antro che m'assembri, oscuro e fosco.

(Given that wicked Fortune wishes/For me to be in poverty and
hate under the sun,/I no longer want to see the stars and the moon,/
And no longer hear living words/But I want a patch of the dark
night/To cover these afflicted and lonely limbs;/And I want to
build, alone, in a forest,/A grotto that embraces me, dark and sinister.) (I, 59).[24]

The poetic persona, Eurialo, then wishes to build a dark cavern that will
host many catastrophic events. He immediately invokes the entire universe
(the sun, the stars, and the moon) as a *locus* of despair, a theme common
to the *disperata*. He also assembles other aspects of the genre—Fortune,
the beaten body, and the search for solitary places—in order to establish and then break down an idyllic setting, building stanza by stanza in
intensity and hopelessness. Thus, Eurialo weaves death, poverty, and sorrow together to include more and more aspects of his life, universe, and
lyric imaginary, from microcosm to macrocosm, but also from imagined
to real. The chosen verb tense is the future tense because this allegorical
journey has to unfold before the readers' eyes. Indeed, Morani describes a
descent into hell that takes place in and around his doomed cavern, which
becomes his whole world.

The second stanza stages the traditional *disperata* monsters and
Furies,

> i dolorosi mostri;
> E quante Furie son tra gente morta
> Porterò io ne i miei dogliosi chiostri

(the painful monsters;/and many Furies that are amongst dead
people/I will take with me in my painful paths) (II, 59).

In the third stanza, the iconic grotto reappears and its darkness becomes
one with the speaker's pain; "L'antro fia oscuro e oscuro il mio dolore,/e 'l
sasso piangerà come fa il core" (III, 59). The *disperato* encounters a myriad
of mythological figures that further drive his desire to bury himself in the
dark grotto and in his grief (IV, 60). The grotto becomes a mythic place,
populated by nocturnal birds that fill the sky with their ominous voices and
with death. The speaker's own reflection will scare both his surroundings
and the night. His pain, "la mia doglia acerba e dura" (IX, 61), is omnipresent, because it has become his sole companion in this grand journey.

Stanza by stanza, the speaker tells his life story. One important variation from the tradition of the *disperata* is that the conditional "voria"
turns into future in Morani's poem, "vorrò", "I will/I will want." In fact,

the future tense rather than the conditional tense seems to better articulate his dooming fate and the many unfortunate events that will keep his life under Fortune's malignant and never ending spell. Remarkably, many of the French poets will adopt the future tense in order to express the same hopeless fate that awaits them, as a myriad of apocalyptic scenarios will engulf them and their world. This tense change from conditional to future marks an important evolution in the *disperata*, as the persona no longer wishes these events. Rather, he knows that they *will* come true, and thus, they become more threatening and real. Furthermore, the future tense is more persuading than the conditional: the reader is provoked to feel this sense of looming tragedy and feel fear. What the speaker wishes the most is to stage his despair for all of humanity and nature to see and to touch, and for his imagination to flow freely in the cavern's darkness, a powerful symbol of his hopeless life of isolation and sorrow.

Moreover, his many destructive wishes—that the world be devoured by fire and filled with pain and weeping (XIV, 63); that Perseus and Medusa spread sorrow and show to the world his sad and desperate life (XVI, 64); and matricidal scenes (XXII, 66)—all conspire to shock the reader. The *disperata* Furies and wild animals, including panthers, tigers, lions, wolves, bears, and poisonous snakes, will compete to annihilate the whole of humanity (XXIII–XXVII, 66–67), while macabre, ingenious scenes continue to unfold. Out of the dark tombs will come skulls and bones, which will end up at the doorstep of his cavern, happy to have found such a fitting a site:

> Le teste e l'ossa de le genti morte
>
> ...
>
> Ove dimoreran liete, conforme
> Mirando il mio nero antro a le lor forme (XXIV, 66).[25]

Death is everywhere. Dead people not only fuel the poet's imagination, but they also delight him. He then calls on more calamities by using the subjunctive, a tense that will also be widely employed by the French poets: "Et or disperazione, or crudeltade/venghino quivi a insanguinar le spade" (And now desperation, now cruelty/that they come to stain with blood the swords) (XXX, 68). He fervently wishes to see the whole human species disappear, hence the assertive "vorrò" foreshadows the future lurking over the speaker's will. However, although wild beasts usually eat men and women in this genre, in *La Vita disperata* it is the speaker who devours them: "Poscia divorerò, sparsi fra sterpi,/orsi, lupi, leon, aquile e serpi"

(XLI, 72). His hunger and anger are such that he will end up thirsting for his own blood and craving his own flesh and soul:

> Et una dipsa, nel mio teschio inchiusa,
> Morderà sì ch'io berrò po' il mio sangue;
>
> ...
>
> Anzi io berrò, da la gran sete oppresso,
> Col sangue proprio l'alma di me stesso

(And a dipsa, enclosed in my skull,/will bite it so that I will drink my own blood;/ ... /actually I will drink, afflicted by a deep thirst,/ with my blood my own soul) (XLIV, 73).[26]

And later on: "che mia fame è tale/ ch'io mangiarò del proprio petto il core" (my hunger is such/that I will eat my heart from my own chest) (LVIII, 78). Morover, unlike in previous *disperate*, it is no longer Cerberus who is hungry for the speaker's body and soul. In a striking reversal of roles, it is the *disperato* himself that shows an enraged hunger that increases the intensity of the poem as well as its effect on the reader.

Masochism intermingles with sadism in the psychology of self-destruction. While still pursuing the obliteration of everything and of all of those who surround him, the speaker calls for the harshest punishments upon himself. He summons all the fury of Hell, even though he is not or does not consider himself to be a sinner. Although other *disperati* blame the beloved for all adversities, here the source of blame is poverty and misfortune. The vocabulary is particularly harsh, and many of the stanzas project a universe reigned by ruthlessness and horror, accentuated by the alliteration of the consonants "R" and "S" as in the following verses:

> Perseo ...
> Che, sparso, spargerà sì gran romori
> Che giungeran fino al balcon soprano
> U mostreran la doglia alta, infinita
> De la mia trista disperata vita.

(Perseus ... /Who, scattered, will scatter such great noise/That it will reach even the highest places/Where the greatest pain of my infinitely/Sad and desperate life will be shown.) (XVI, 64).

In many other stanzas the vocabulary creates realistic images characterized by anxiety and violence. Beginning with stanza XLIV, the poetic persona accelerates his race toward self-destruction, pushed by his desire to make an example of his despair, a *topos* we often find in the *disperata*:

> Perch'io sia d'ogni strazio al mondo essempio,
> Strappin coi crin la carne e le cervella
> Sì che l'alma, se può, da me si svella

(So that I may serve as an example to the world,/And that my flesh and brain be torn off/So that my soul, if possible, be dismembered) (XLIX, 75).

Furthermore, the speaker stresses the fact that he is the only person to have suffered to this level, so much so that Cruelty takes pity on him: "Ch'un pover uomo ha doglia sì infinita/Ch'ha pietade di lui la crudeltade" (LXI, 79). Death is preferred to his present state, and indeed, in a rhetorical question he states that he has no reasons to live amongst mortals when his poverty makes him suffer so much: "perché viver debb'io più tra mortali?/E ogni or soffrir di povertà gli strali?" (LXII, 79).

Like other *disperate*, in the end, the poem is meant to go on and narrate the poet-persona's despair, so that others can weep even after his death: "E udendo, deh, piangete, anime pie,/La lunga istoria de le pene mie" (LXV, 80). Although the maledictions are not spelled out, the entire poem sequence is written as an arrangement of vituperations that curse his life, poverty, and suffering. As has been stated before, *La Vita disperata* echoes the many texts I examine in this study, but it also expands on the genre by integrating new elements, such as the transition from the conditional tense to the future tense in order to depict an apocalyptic doom, as well as the speaker's infuriated hunger, rather than Cerberus's or other monsters' in order to symbolize the magnitude of his despair. Furthermore, this role reversal also embodies Morani's intense desire to represent his grief in all of its facets and cruel consequences, skillfully expounded in his preface as well. Finally, it is obviously the past that incites the poet to find refuge in a deserted and sinister cavern, descend into its infernal underbelly, lose himself in his despair, and give free expression to the many looming and dark scenarios that fuel his imagination.

Isabella di Morra: A Woman's Despair

Unlike in the female-voiced *disperate* by il Saviozzo, da Prato, and degli Alberti, in which the male author controls the woman's speech, her body, desire, and despair, in Isabella di Morra's poetry the speaker is the protagonist of her own narrative and in full control of her own representations. Morra's poems are filled with solitude and despair like other authors of the *disperata*, but in writing about her personal condition, the distinction is that it's a woman's personal condition that she experiences and therefore is able to represent with accuracy and authenticity. In her interpretation of the *disperata* genre, its major themes are skillfully adapted to her ten sonnets and three *canzoni*. Furthermore, issues of genre and gender at times mesh and at times diverge: for one, Morra, was a young intelligent woman under the strict supervision of her brothers who did not approve of her literary gifts and who kept her prisoner in their family castle of Favale in Southern Italy. Because of her father's absence, she had no support, no protection, and no means to visit and socialize in the nearby courts and literary circles, despite her noble rank. Hence, Morra greatly missed the opportunities afforded to other early modern women writers. In brief, as a young person, she lacked social interaction and suffered from solitude; as a daughter, she missed her father's safeguard; and as a woman poet, she missed the benefits and acclaim that a literary community would have undoubtedly bestowed upon her poetic talents. If she were a man, none of the above would have happened. In fact, her brothers were free to move around the Kingdom as they pleased, to entertain friendships, and even to leave Italy.

Isabella di Morra was born in ca. 1520 in a small castle in the Southern Italian region of Basilicata. Her father, the humanist Giovan Michele di Morra, provided his children with a solid education, including Isabella and her sister.[27] As with most poets in this study, for Morra, too, the historical and socio-cultural backdrop was particularly harsh: by 1498, wars between France and the Kings of Aragon and their ally, the Emperor Charles V, ravaged the Kingdom of Aragon and its capital, Naples. The long-standing dispute over the hegemony of Southern Italy and, in particular, over the crown of Naples greatly penalized Southern Italy and its economic growth.[28] In 1528, because of his allegiance to the French King, Francis I, Giovan di Morra was exiled to France, where, together with one of his sons, he spent the rest of his life. This political exile greatly hindered Morra's youth and short life. Moreover, her father's exile has a haunting presence in her poetry because it left a young daughter imprisoned within the walls of the family castle and abandoned to the guardianship of three begrudged brothers. In this forsaken part of the country, as Morra herself calls it, "vili ed orride contrate" (I, v. 3, 46), human contact was scarce.[29] Her only social and intellectual interactions were with her tutor and with another poet, the Spaniard Diego Sandoval de Castro, with whom she exchanged letters and poems. However, when her brothers intercepted the correspondence, they accused her of having a romantic liaison with Castro. Consequently, they stabbed her to death, killed her tutor, and a few months later, they killed Castro as well. Morra was only twenty-five.[30]

Of upmost importance to my discussion is Morra's publishing history.[31] Despite the death of its author, her poetry reached the prestigious Giolito's press in Venice, where in 1552, the polygraph Lodovico Dolce included them in his *Rime di diversi illustri signori napolitani, e d'altri nobilissimi intelletti; nuovamente raccolte, et non piu stampate.*[32] Two subsequent editions of this anthology would feature Morra's poems, bringing her previously unknown poetry wide-spread fame. It was, in fact, printed alongside poems by other authors from the same geographical area, such as di Costanzo, Rota, and Tansillo, who were well-renowned not only in Italy, but also in France.[33] All three editions of *Rime di diversi illustri signori napoletani* circulated in France, and it was one of the anthologies that attracted and inspired neo-Petrarchan poets.[34] This collection singled out the Neapolitan region as particularly productive and innovative, and its popularity greatly increased the reach of Morra's verses. Remarkably, as Robin points out, Morra was one of the first Neapolitan poets ever to be published by a prestigious commercial press in Venice despite her obscure beginnings.[35]

Only three years later, in 1559, Morra's thirteen poems were again published as a complete *canzoniere* in the groundbreaking anthology by Lodovico Domenichi, *Rime diverse d'alcune nobilissime, et virtuosissime donne,* the first anthology of poetry written by women.[36] With this volume, Morra became one of the most repeatedly anthologized women poets of the Cinquecento. Domenichi organized her poems in order to compose a miniature *canzoniere* that followed her tragic, short existence, thus fashioning a spiritual itinerary in which suffering is at the forefront of her *poesis*, from her first sonnet to the last *canzone*, where she turns entirely to her faith.[37] Domenichi modeled Morra's short *canzoniere* after Petrarch's *Rime Sparse*, thus positioning her work in the Petrarchan tradition.[38] In other words, Domenichi presented Morra's poems as altogether profoundly Petrarchist, even if, as I will show, Petrarch's poetry is not its only source. It is just the starting point of a combination of linguistic and lyric features that make up her "uncultivated and frail style"—"stil ruvido e frale"—to use her modest words (XI, v. 4, 70), in which the *disperata* plays a crucial role.[39]

Most significantly, Morra's complete *canzoniere* was anthologized, which is significant in two important ways. It meant her poetry was circulated, firstly, alongside poets from her own geographical area and, secondly, alongside poets of her own gender. This is a crucial moment of my discussion of the *disperata*, because, not only were many poets who used the genre, including Serafino, Cariteo, Napolitano, di Costanzo and Tansillo, from or had visited Naples, but also because, once again, gender intersects with genre. Morra carried the genre forward and bolstered it with the voice of a talented female poet, adding a new and authentic perspective—that of a woman's despair.

Thanks to the connections with both her father and her tutor, Morra's education benefited from the strong humanistic tradition widely rooted in the Neapolitan region, whose capital was one of the most progressive and prosperous courts in all Renaissance Europe.[40] Moreover, I would like to suggest that Morra was familiar with the genre and had read il Saviozzo's *disperate* because his poetry circulated in Naples as early as the beginning of the Quattrocento.[41] His verses were also included in a prominent volume, the *Libro de Aragona*, known as *Raccolta Aragonese* (1476), that was sent by Lorenzo il Magnifico to Ferrante I of Aragon in 1477. This gift was a precious anthology of Italian poets mostly from the Tuscan region, featuring authors from the School of Sicily to the then contemporary Florence.[42]

Morra is not the only early-modern woman writer to author poems in which despair is present, but her voice is very much unique in its hopeless nature, and it is very germane to the poetry I investigate in this book. Her sonnets and *canzoni* skillfully paint the portrait of a young woman whose aspirations, desires, and maturity—both literary and personal—are perfectly articulated with nuanced language and style. Juliana Schiesari has investigated women's canon of melancholia, loss and mourning, and in particular Morra's poetry. She argues that some Cinquecento women, including Morra, "found ways to reformulate loss, [...] by writing out a poetics of mourning."[43] More recent studies have characterized Morra's poetry as a lament, and they have mostly compared it to Petrarch's and other Petrarchan women's mourning, such as Vittoria Colonna, Gaspara Stampa, and Veronica Gambara.[44] Morra succeeded in representing mourning and loss, but it was despair that mainly pervaded her poetry, thereby significantly contributing to the *disperata* tradition. Petrarch's language and code, however, were insufficient to express her deprivations and her state of complete abandonment, as well as the haunting sense of geographical and existential imprisonment.[45] Instead, it is in the poetry of the *disperata* that Morra found a suitable and stimulating model. Fortune, maledictions, death, and infernal settings, as well as other motifs are woven together and fashioned in such a manner to convey her most intimate desires and feelings, but also her immense state of isolation and hopelessness.[46]

As Sara Adler argues, Morra's *canzoniere* "represents the best of the genre" because of its unconventional traits.[47] These unconventional traits largely draw from the poetry of the *disperata* and its tradition. Most of all, they draw from a strong sense of the self, which transpires through a voice whose voluminous nuances are neither artificial nor superficial. On the contrary, the poet-persona's voice is clearly and loudly asserted in a memorable verse through the pronoun I, coupled with her name and directed to her father, the man who, in fact, bequeaths his name to his family members: "io tua figlia Isabella"—"I, your daughter Isabella" (III, v. 2, 50). Her speech is also emphasized as a result of her own sense of being a writer, as in the first poem, "Scrissi con stile amaro, aspro e dolente"—"I wrote with bitter, harsh and sorrowful style" (I, v. 1, 66), or "dirò con questo stil ruvido e frale"—"I will speak with my uncultivated and frail style" (XI, v. 4, 70), and then again in a prayer, "Questa grazia signor mi sia concessa/ Ch'io mostri col mio stil te a me stessa" (This grace my Lord grant me/ So that, through my style, I may reveal you to myself) (XII, vv. 21–22, 78). This affirmation of the literary self, in clear terms, allows the poet and speaker to define herself on the page and in her writings, an assertion that is vastly lacking in the *disperate femminili* by male authors.

Morra's deeply personal distress is painstakingly spelled out in each of her poems, which draw mostly from her personal, familial, and geographical circumstances. As a young woman who had never known romantic love, Morra lived a marginalized life, far from any type of social and literary community and surrounded by her immediate inhospitable landscape.[48] In her "uncultivated and frail style," she narrates a tragic story in which Fortune holds a crucial role and appears as both a cruel persecutor and a stern adversary, responsible for much of her loneliness and hardships, a role Fortune also plays in many *disperate*.[49] The figure of "La fortuna," inherited from a long tradition starting with the Romans, was perceived as unpredictable, variable, and even capricious during the Medieval and Renaissance times; a spiteful female figure who turns the wheel according to her whims.[50] Whereas at times Morra's poems express moments of hope and dreams, invariably, Fortune takes them away and instead denies all possibilities that would set the poet-persona free from her current misery. Starting with the very first sonnet, Fortune is blamed for her cruel "assaults":

> I fieri assalti di crudel Fortuna
> scrivo piangendo, e la mia verde etade;
> me che'n sí vili ed orride contrate
> spendo il mio tempo senza loda alcuna

(I write weeping about Fortune's cruel and fierce assaults/and mourn my young and tender age;/I, who live in such vile and horrid land/and spend my time without any praise) (I, vv. 1–4, 46).

Fortune is furthermore reproached for a life spent in the company of irrational people of unrefined habits, in which the woman and the poet are left marginalized and forgotten, instead of a life lived in serenity and praises that she feels she deserves. This theme recurs often in the descriptions of both the locale and the people that surround her, "fra questi aspri costumi/di gente irrazional, priva d'ingegno" (among the harsh customs/of irrational people, devoid of intellect) (XI, vv. 7–8, 71). As in the *disperata*, here, too, Fortune deprived the speaker of the means for a serene life, in this case, of a father who could have helped her grow and exist in the status due her noble family: as the daughter of an Italian baron in a position to receive respect, a suitable husband, and a much brighter future. Instead, she is forced to accept that Fortune has condemned her to her father's perpetual absence, as voiced in her third sonnet, where she dares to hope to see him returning from his long exile. However, she has to resign herself to a reality of longing:

> Ma la mia adversa e dispietata stella
> non vuol ch'alcun conforto possa entrare
> nel tristo cor, ma di pietà rubella,
> la calda speme in pianto fa mutare

(But my adverse and merciless fate/does not allow any comfort/in my heart, and has no pity,/thus, my temperate hope turns to tears) (III, vv. 5–8, 51).

Thus, against Fortune she despairs and complains, and as already mentioned, Fortune becomes the principal target of her invectives:

> Contra Fortuna alor spargo querela
> ed ho in odio il denigrato sito,
> come sola cagion del mio tormento

(Thus, against Fortune I complain/and I abhor this denigrated place,/as the only cause of my sorrow) (III, vv. 12–14, 52).

Rather than damn herself, or her own past actions, the poet-persona damns her fate, the main culprit of all of her grief, as in her fourth sonnet where, despite a hopeful beginning, Fortune, personified as a "diva," soon annihilates all of her fervent hopes, "speme viva" (VI, v. 6, 54), and rejoices in the young woman's low condition, "malgrado de l'acerba e cruda Diva,/ ch'ogni or s'esalta del mio basso stato" (VI, vv. 7–8, 54). The complaint continues in the sixth sonnet and expands into a complete condemnation against Fortune, which is responsible not only for her misfortunes, but also for those of Francis I and his losses against Charles V:[51] "Fortuna che sollevi in alto stato,/ogni depresso ingegno, ogni vil core" (vv. 1–2, 58). In a moving curse from woman to woman, "Son donna, e contro de le donne dico" (I am a woman and against women I say) (v. 9, 58) as "la Fortuna" is feminine in the Italian language, she accuses her of persecuting all of those who were born with a kind heart and good intentions, like herself.[52] Instead, Fortune favors those who are cruel and void of intellect. As often seen in the *disperata*, the poet-persona is forced to shout her sadness, repeatedly warning the reader that those who befriend Fortune are monsters, and that Fortune will extinguish all hope for a promising future. Morra's case is unique, as, stunned with despair, she often cries out through her ink: "E spesso grido col mio rozo inchiostro." Her words and damnations are genuine and elicit in the reader frustration and anger.

Morra's ill fate appears again in her eighth sonnet as a particularly haunting presence. She blames it as the origin of all evils, "ché Fortuna, che mai salda non stassi,/cresce ogn'or il mio mal, ogn'or l'eterna" (VIII, vv. 7–8, 61), and she blames it again in sonnet IX as both her father's and her own adverse fate: "l'aspra Fortuna e lo mio fato avaro" (IX, v. 4 and v. 6, 63). Fortune is personified many times, and the frequent descriptions of her in human-like terms serve to increase Fortune's looming presence throughout the *canzoniere*.

Often, the uncertainty of the future intensifies the poet's anxiety and despair, a feeling skillfully expressed in Morra's last sonnet where she is forced to accept that her fate will not improve, nor will it loosen its grip. Thus, she must abandon all hope: "che nel più bel sperar poi mi dispero" ––"and then, in the most beautiful hope, I despair" (IX, v. 12, 65). Fortune's attacks engender Morra's mournful verses—"Scrivo piangendo." Her promising youth, her intellectual aptitude, and aristocratic rank are experienced without notice and are wasted amidst empty and unkind surroundings, in complete solitude. Furthermore, her fate continually presents her with new obstacles in a vicious cycle of misfortunes that oppress her relentlessly. Since birth, Morra feels persecuted and plagued by this external force that makes her powerless, limiting her actions and thoughts, and thoroughly preoccupying her writings.

Morra feels as though she is the only one singled out by Fortune, and thus, the only one that ever complained as much against it. As all the other *disperata* speakers, she stands alone as the most ill-fated human being. Her current miserable state, "stato," is often reiterated in order to articulate her dismal condition of abandonment and pain, which in turn justifies her harshness against Fortune, just like in il Saviozzo's "Cerbero invoco e il suo latrare," in which he asks his song to herald his miserable state: "Direte loro il mio misero stato" (v. 130, 222), for which he also accuses fate, Fortune, and destiny (vv. 136–138, 222). Morra's marginalized condition is often repeated in an existential way to assert herself to herself, and on the page, as in the following examples, where Fortune places her in unfavorable circumstances and takes pleasure in her miserable condition: "ch'ognor s'esalta del mio basso stato" (IV, v. 8, 54). The lack of a father, a ghost-like presence throughout Morra's slim *canzoniere*, causes the daughter to suffer in abandonment, "qui posta da ciascuno in cieco oblio" (XI, v. 11, 71). Therefore, she cannot find a dignified place as a woman: "Qui non provo io di donna il proprio stato" (XI, v. 34, 72).

In Morra's verses, gender again intersects with the *disperata*, because the speaker's identity as a woman has to be restated, first, as proof of life mainly to herself, and second, so that her status is not forgotten. The reader is reminded that she is a woman who deserves the *proper* circumstances and environment in order to thrive not only as a woman, but also as a daughter, a sister, and a writer, rather than being forgotten by the world in "cieco oblio." However, the recognition she so longed for, and deserved, was unfortunately not experienced while she was still alive. Morra died not knowing that her poems would reach influential booksellers and editors, first in Naples and then in Venice, and not knowing that she would meet her "proprio stato" as a woman and as an author in a community of writers from her region and from her sex in the pages of successful anthologies.[53]

In the last three *canzoni*, the poet-persona's bitter and painful lament is again caused by tribulations brought on by Fortune: "I wrote with bitter, harsh, and sorrowful style [...] against Fortune" (X, vv. 1–4, 66). In an intimate reflection on her past, Morra is now forced to accept that to hope was indeed foolish. Starting with this poem, she accepts her disappointments, turns her thoughts to the future and to the realization that hoping is vane: "Dunque ogni altro sperar, fratello, è vano" (X, v. 14, 67). In fact, in her last three *canzoni*, Morra shifts her attention to spirituality and concedes that fighting Fortune is no longer useful, nor is it something she desires. Since Fortune has clipped the wings of her propitious longings and hopes, with a simple word of explanation—"Poscia", "Since"—the poet will instead recount her life struggles and sufferings.

> Poscia che al bel desir troncate hai l'ale,
> che nel mio cor sorgea, crudel Fortuna,
> sí che d'ogni tuo ben vivo digiuna,
> dirò con questo stil ruvido e frale
> alcuna parte de l'interno male
> causato sol da te fra questi dumi,
> fra questi aspri costumi
> di gente irrazional, priva d'ingegno
> ove senza sostegno
> son costretta a menare il viver mio,
> qui posta da ciascuno in cieco oblio.

(Since you have clipped the wings of my beautiful desire,/that was rousing in my heart, cruel Fortune,/so that of all of your goods I am deprived,/I will speak with my uncultivated and frail style/of all of the sides of this internal evil/that you alone cause, in this place,/among the harsh customs/of irrational people, devoid of intellect/where, without support/I am forced to lead my life,/abandoned here in blind oblivion.) (XI, vv. 1–11, 70–71).

As in the *disperata*, here too, Morra bitterly evokes the first days of life. Fortune has been cruel since birth:

> Cosí, a disciolta briglia
> seguitata m'hai sempre, empia Fortuna,
> cominciando dal latte e dalla cuna

(Thus, unrestricted/you have always persecuted me, impious Fortune,/starting with the milk and the crib) (vv. 20–23, 71).

Morra's personal narrative sadly embraces her family members as well: her father is unable to help his own daughter, her brothers are unable to help their mother, and the King of France is unable to help the Morra family, despite its loyalty. The loss of the father is once again mourned, yet his absence weighs heavily on her writing, as a ghost. France is her last resort and its King is the last person who can rescue her; thus, she looks to France and promises Fortune to forgive her should Fortune allow her poetry to reach the King, in a final, desperate pleading:

> Ogni mal ti perdono,
> né l'alma si dorrà di te giamai
> se questo sol farai
> (ahi, ahi, Fortuna, e perché no 'l dêi?)
> che giungano al Re gli sospir miei.

> (I forgive you every damage,/and my soul will never complain again against you/if only you will allow/(alas, alas, Fortuna, and why should you not?)/my sighs to reach the King.) (XI, vv. 67–71, 74).

In Morra's *canzoniere*, the many adjectives used to describe Fortune—cruel, impious, pitiless, unrefined—become an obsession for the poet-persona, who combines this with other *disperata* themes.[54] Since Love as the culprit and addressee of various maledictions is replaced by Fortune, Fortune fulfills the need of the *disperata* speaker to blame somebody or something. Fortune is held responsible for causing the loss of a father, a unified family, a community, a refined society, and maybe even literary promises. Fortune has instead abandoned her in solitude, surrounded only by brutes who would eventually take her life.

Another *disperata topos* emerges in the seventh sonnet, where a desert-like and stark landscape envelops the poet's emotional and physical space. This scenery, that so much characterizes the genre, is fully adopted by Morra, whose interpretation and expression is all encompassing and singular. Her existential despair bursts out in all of its anguish, absorbing both nature and the reader. One of the crucial aspects of Morra's poetry is that she develops what is almost a geographical map, guiding readers as they walk and discover her mental landscape. Here, the mental landscape materializes in an intimate invitation to follow along her footsteps for as far as her voice can carry us:

> Ecco ch'una altra volta, o valle inferna,
> o fiume alpestre, o ruinati sassi,
> o ignudi spirti di virtute e cassi,
> udrete il pianto e la mia doglia eterna.
> Ogni monte udirammi, ogni caverna,
> ché Fortuna, che mal salda non stassi,
> cresce ogn'or il mio mal, ogn'or l'eterna.
> Deh mentre ch'io mi lagno e giorno e notte,
> o fere, o sassi, o orride ruine,

o selve incolte, o solitarie grotte,
ulule, e voi del mal nostro indovine,
piangete meco a voci alte interrotte
il mio piú d'altro miserando fine.

(Now, yet again, oh infernal valley,/oh mountainous river, ruined
rocks/oh broken spirits deprived of virtue,/you will hear my weeping and eternal sorrow./Every mountain will hear me, and every
cave,/everywhere I pause, everywhere I walk;/for Fortune, who
never rests,/intensifies my ills, making them eternal./Alas, while
I lament day and night,/oh beasts, rocks, horrid ruins,/oh uncultivated woods, solitary grottoes,/oh ominous birds, and you, who
know our suffering,/cry with me in high, incessant voices/my miserable end, equal to no one.) (VII, 60–61).

The speaker includes numerous details that shorten the distance between
her surroundings and the readers so that they feel like they are there. An
intermingling of harsh and deserted settings, fierce animals, secluded grot-
tos, and nocturnal birds are summoned to partake in her misery. In four-
teen verses, Morra weaves together several *disperata topoi*, and matches
them to her distinctive and desolate voice. Furthermore, this sonnet
closely echoes Tansillo's "Valli nemiche al sol, superbe rupi," discussed in
the following chapter, especially in its depiction of a very similar, forsaken
landscape. There is also a keen resemblance in vocabulary and in the speaker's solitude and despair. Morra's last two verses in particular are analogous
to Tansillo's last tercet:

che tra voi vengo a deplorar mia fede
e spero al suon di desperati stridi
se non piega il ciel, mover l'inferno.

(and I come among you to deplore my faith/and with the sound
of desperate screams, I hope/to move hell, if not bend the sky)
(vv. 12–14, 270).[55]

As in the *disperata*, here too the speaker demands that nature partake in her
despair and cry with her, "piangete meco," assertively, so that her voice can
be carried across the infernal valley. Irene Musillo Mitchell compellingly
argues that in this sonnet, "seething with hostile essences and filled with
the pain of the condemned [...] Isabella has reached the nadir of despair."[56]
Indeed these images abound in the dreadfulness that characterizes the *disperata*'s iconic settings and its speaker's attitude and hopelessness.

As mentioned, the *disperata* depiction of nature stretches across the expanse of Morra's *canzoniere*, from her very first sonnet, "in vili ed orride contrate (v. 3, 46), to the third sonnet, "così deserto è lo infelice lito" (v. 10, 51) and "il denigrato sito" (v. 13, 52), to the seventh above. It also expands into the eighth sonnet, where the river Siri, whose waters are turbulent and shores stony, adds to the desolation of the surrounding milieu. Indeed, the river is portrayed as a wound, cutting the land and isolating Morra's castle from the rest of the world.[57] Finally, in her three *canzoni*, her feelings of tremendous isolation stretch without relief in a crescendo of despair. In the first *canzone*, the depths of her internal solitude match the prison she has been forced to inhabit, "in questo inferno solitario e strano/ ogni disegno mio facendo vano" (in this isolated and strange hell/all my hopes become useless) (XI, vv. 48–49, 73), as her seclusion prevents her from planning her future and from daring to hope.

In her last two *canzoni*, the poetic persona turns to God and the Holy Mary, as all earthly desires have been denied, and, thus, she abandons them. In the last *canzone*, Morra eagerly returns to the ominous setting of the *disperata*, delighted to find it, and to immerse herself in it again. Her mood is finally lifted because she no longer dwells in the harshness of her present. Rather, she looks straight past it, with all hopes and desires turning toward her deep faith:

> Quel che gli giorni a dietro
> noiava questa mia gravosa salma,
> di star fra queste selve erme ed oscure,
> or sol diletta l'alma

(That which in the past/troubled my burdensome body,/to stay in these solitary and dark woods,/now, it alone pleases my soul) (XIII, vv. 1–4, 84).

In fact, the speaker's personal transformation takes over her surroundings, and henceforth, they too appear friendly and inviting:

> Per voi, grotta felice,
> boschi intricati e rovinati sassi,
> Sinno veloce, chiare fonti e rivi

(For you happy grotto,/tangled woods and ruined rocks,/rapid Sinni, clear springs and rivers) (XIII, vv. 90–92, 88–89).

She is happy and content to be in the dark forest (XIII, v. 15, 85). Morra's depictions of nature are as realistic as the landscape neighboring her home, which was indeed desert-like, barren, and secluded. Aldo Zaccone notes that when walking in this area, it is easy to find Morra's lyric portrayals as the eye runs over the great rocks on which the family castle was built, and then down to the precipices and caves by the riverbank, and further into the valley.[58]

In Morra's everyday reality, the world order is turned upside down, another central *topos* of the *disperata*. In a deeply patriarchal society, her father's sudden departure and absence had a series of negative consequences, leaving the daughter in a state of anxious awaiting.[59] The poet describes the wreckage her father's exile has caused: "O cosa non più udita,/privar il padre di giovar la figlia!" (Oh it is something never heard,/ to deprive a daughter of her father's support!) (XI, vv. 18–19, 71). As has already been stated, he could have provided her with material and spiritual support, rather, she is forced to live without him: "ove senza sostegno/ son costretta a menar il viver mio" (XI, vv. 9–10, 71). His absence also affected her other siblings and her lonely mother: "Baston i figli de la fral vecchiezza/esser dovean di mia misera madre" (XI, vv. 56–57, 74). Tobia Toscano suggests that the father's exile caused the Morra family to lose its political hegemony and prestige, which destabilized the brothers' social rank and accelerated their hate toward their sister, and thus, a true *delitto d'onore*.[60] This, of course, caused the family dynamics to turn upside down.

In her last *canzone*, the tragedy of her family is again bitterly recounted, focusing in particular on a state of catastrophic circumstances in which the universal and the personal are woven together. Her father's absence inverted the family order because the brothers took the place of the father, which negatively affected the sister. Her world was in every way turned upside down, a reality that is skillfully depicted in the following verses,

> Alzato a mezo il polo
> il gran pianeta co' bollenti rai,
> ch'uccide i fiori in grembo a primavera,
> s'alcuno vide mai
> crucciato il padre contra il rio figliulo,
> così contemplo Cristo, in voce altera

(High up in the celestial pole/the great planet, with simmering rays,/kills the flowers in mid spring,/if anybody has ever seen/the father angry with the wicked son,/thus I contemplate Christ, with a lofty voice) (XIII, vv. 61–66, 87–88).

The high temperature of the sun scorches the earth, kills the flowers, spring, and the promises that come with spring. Moreover, the father is

enraged against the son, the familial peace overturned, signaling an apocalyptic end—images often found in the *disperata*, but that here accurately
describe Morra's stark reality.

At times, the poet-persona allows herself to hope, only to soon realize that all hope is vain, "che nel più bel sperar poi mi dispero" (IX, v. 14,
65). This striking play of words, "sperar" and "dispero," fully expresses her
terrible recognition that daring to hope is to despair. In another verse as
well, the futility of hope is adroitly reiterated, this time by including all of
humanity, "Dunque ogni altro sperar, fratello è vano" ––"It is thus point-
less for us all, my brothers, to continue to hope" (X, v. 14, 67). Her authority in matters of despair is authentic and immense, and thus, she feels that
she can indeed promulgate such advice to all with this verse, expressing a
deep-seated finality. Moreover, despair takes the shape of torment, "come
sola cagion del mio tormento" (III, v. 12, 52), and of an eternal struggle,
"udrete il pianto e la mia doglia eterna" (VII, v. 4, 61).

Despair and death are interwoven from the first to the last poem
of Morra's *Rime*. Death is a form of liberation, a reprieve from the earthly
prison that holds the poetic persona's soul, "se non col corpo, almen con
l'alma sciolta" (I, v. 10, 47). And when the bitter end is near, Isabella, the
daughter, trusts the river to inform the father of her sorrow: "fa' tu noto
il mio duolo al Padre caro" (VIII, vv. 1–4, 61–62). Death is welcomed by
this *disperata* also as the beginning of the end of suffering, and the imperative tense, "make my pain known to my dear Father", is used to further
involve the river in her death, because it has to become an example to other
hopeless souls, "esempio miserando e raro" (VIII, v. 7, 63). Moreover, just
like despair, death is blatantly evoked in most of her poems, as in most
disperate. Morra portrays death as something the poet-persona does not
fear and as the final aspiration and liberation from this world's afflictions:

> Con ragione il desio dispiega i vanni
> ed al suo porto appressa il bel pensiero
> per trar quest'alma da perpetui affanni

> (With reason, desire spreads its wings/and takes my fine thoughts
> to its port/to remove my soul from perpetual burdens) (IX,
> vv. 9–11, 65).

However, unlike for the great majority of *disperati*, suicide is never evoked,
nor wished by Morra's persona. Rather than contemplating hell and its
horrors, she is eager to meet her creator and sit by the Virgin Mary, a
thought that brings her much comfort.

When Morra starts turning to more mystical considerations of her trials, she turns to death: "che dolce vita mi saria la morte" (because death will be a sweet life) (XI, v. 36, 73), an image fully developed by the *disperata* poets.[61] Indeed, in the very last *canzone*, Morra directs her full attention and writing toward God and the Holy Mother. Her faith presents an escape and the ultimate refuge. Accordingly, the *canzoniere* concludes with the speaker intimately addressing her own poem, "canzon," and appeasing it, because once in heaven, all misery will disappear in the company of the Queen of the Heavens, Goddess of all gods:

> Quanto discovre e scalda il chiaro sole,
> canzon è nulla ad un guardo di lei,
> ch'è Reina del Ciel, Dea degli dei

> (That which the bright sun reveals and warms/song, it is nothing compared to the gaze of the one,/who is the Queen of Heaven, Goddess of the gods) (XIII, vv. 106–108, 89).

Unlike the *disperate* from the previous chapters, Morra's song is intended to welcome the author into a better afterlife through her faith and to become a retort to this earthly, wretched despair. Ultimately, Morra's faith triumphs over despair. As mentioned, she doesn't recur to thoughts of suicide: she merely welcomes death as it will lead her to a life in the love of God, sitting by the Queen of all skies, where her despair will finally subside.

In conclusion, Morra's lyrics and language superbly reflect the geographical reality of her native province, and the cultural marginality in which she was forced to live. Petrarch's language had proven to be insufficient to define and communicate the solitude and exile in which Morra spent her days, forgotten by everybody, "qui posta da ciascuno in cieco oblio." Indeed, it is the language of the *disperata* that better communicates her reality. From the genre she also borrowed at liberty a number of suggestive *topoi*, including the maledictions against Fortune, the infernal atmosphere, the geographical-cultural landscape, the emphasized and persistent despair, as well as the notion of death as the final refuge and triumph over her desolate condition. Her profound reflections on her own writing, from the first sonnet, "Scrivo piangendo" (v. 2, 46), to the eighth, "Scrissi con stile amaro, aspro e dolente" (v. 1, 66), to the last *canzone*, demonstrate a conscious effort to assert her whole self into her writings and to project an existential reflection into the only space she had at her disposal, the page. Her voice, insistent and whole, faithfully adapts the *disperata* genre to her sonnets and *canzoni* and when we read them, we

witness an authentically gendered despair due to the paternal abandonment and the isolation from social and literary activities that plagued her
short life. Morra's "rozo stile" superbly reflects the rough geographical and
emotional reality of her native province and the socio-cultural isolation in
which she was forced to live.

NOTES

[1] Quadrio mentions a sonnet by Bartolo Partivalla, written at the end of the
seventeenth century, "Lungi o penne, addio Muse, arco superno" as also being a
disperata, since its title is "Desperation." *Della storia, e della ragione*, 568.

[2] Pietro Bembo, *Prose della volgar lingua*. For an English translation, see Bembo,
Lyric Poetry.

[3] See Dionisotti, "Fortuna del Petrarca nel Quattrocento," 109–110. In
these pages, Dionisotti traces "l'assoluta prevalenza in Italia, fin oltre la metà del
Cinquecento, del sonetto." 110.

[4] See for example Vittorio Rossi: "Soffocata in Italia dal petrarchismo orto-
dosso del Bembo, si muove oltremonte, ma inseguito di nuovo nelle opere di Di
Costanzo, Rota e Tansillo." 170.

[5] See Vaganay, *Le Sonnet en Italie et en France*. For the fortune of the Italian anthologies and the circulation of single-authored works, see Richter, "Printers and Poets"; Branca, "Le raccolte di rime e le collezioni di classici"; Tomasi,
"Alcuni aspetti delle antologie liriche del secondo Cinquecento"; and Bullock,
"Some Notes on the Circulation of Lyric Poems in Sixteenth-Century Italy."

[6] For an extensive biography, see Edward Hutton, *Pietro Aretino the Scourge
of Princes*. See also www.treccani.it/enciclopedia/pietro-aretino

[7] See *Le più belle pagine di Pietro Aretino*, Massimo Bontempelli, ed.

[8] For example, Aretino wrote letters to Francis I ("*Al re di Francia*"), to
Charles V ("*A lo Imperadore*"), and to the Pope ("*Al papa*"), among other missives.

[9] See Aretino, *Poesie Varie*, Vol. 1. All references to Aretino's *disperata* will be
based on this edition, 69–72.

[10] Judgment Day will be an important *topos* in the neo-Petrarchans' poems.

[11] See Marie-Françoise Piéjus, "Lecture et écriture selon des anthologies poétiques," 339, and Amedeo Quondam, *Petrarchismo mediato*.

[12] See Santagata's analysis in *La lirica aragonese*, 172–173.

[13] Dionisotti, "Fortuna del Petrarca nel Quattrocento," 95. The same can be
said of the French poetry of the fifteenth and sixteenth century, because French
poets closely studied, and consequently digested, the poetry and metric of the
Italian writers from the Middle Ages to the Renaissance.

[14] See Balsamo, *Les Rencontres des muses*, 194, 210 and 269; Rosanna Gorris
Camos, "'Je veux chanter d'amour la tempeste et l'orage': Desportes et les Imitations de l'Arioste," and especially Bruna Conconi, "Sulla ricezione di Pietro

Aretino in Francia." Aretino also wrote another *disperata*, whose vituperations are thrown against popes and cardinals of the Roman court. Specific characters are herein mentioned in a series of "terzine velenose e rabbiose," (poisonous and angry tercets) as Luzio calls them. This *disperata* is more of a satirical poem in which the poet-persona curses Pope Clement and wishes for the city of Rome to be ruined. He also curses important political figures, such as the French King Francis I and the Holy Roman Emperor Charles V: "Vorrei che fusse legato pe pazzo/El nostro messer Carlo imperatore/Che lassò re Francesco ire a sollazzo" (cited by Luzio, 4). See Luzio, *Pietro Aretino nei primi suoi anni a Venezia e la corte dei Gonzaga*, 4, and note 1, 4.

[15] Giuliano Innamorati, *Pietro Aretino*, 115, and 93–123.

[16] See Aquilecchia's introduction to *Aretino Poesie varie*, 10–11.

[17] Emilio Debenedetti, "Notizie sulla vita e sugli scritti di E. M. da Ascoli," 5. For a detailed biography and bibliography, see also Morani, Aurelio (Eurialo Da Ascoli) in *Dizionario Bibliografico degli Italiani*, www.treccani.it at enciclopedia/aurelio-morani

[18] *La Seconda parte delle Stanze di diversi autori, Novamente mandata in luce.* Three more printings were to follow in 1572, 1580, and 1589. See Vianey, *Le Pétrarquisme en France*, 385.

[19] See Jauss's "L'historicité d'un genre," 86.

[20] "poich'è la povertà mia, nata dall'avarizia dei Ricchi, disperato e pazzo a un medesimo tempo mi doveva fare, essendomi venuto il capriccio di pubblicare quello che forse e senza forse m'era molto meglio, a mio potere, di nascondere e sepellire meco istesso nel fondo delle miserie." *La Vita disperata* is edited in a modern edition by Sandro Baldoncini, 39–80, 57. All references to Morani's poetry will be based on this edition.

[21] Ibid., 53–54.

[22] Ibid., 58.

[23] See Debenedetti, "Notizie di Eurialo Morani da Ascoli," 29.

[24] *La Vita disperata*'s stanzas will be referenced as stanza number and page.

[25] This and other stanzas by Morani are echoed in d'Aubigné's *Stances* discussed in the following chapter, as well as in other French poets of the end of the sixteenth and beginning of the seventeenth century.

[26] A dipsa is a small, poisonous snake from Medieval times.

[27] See Croce, *Isabella di Morra e Diego Sandoval de Castro*, 13–15, and Robin, "Morra, Isabella di (ca. 1520–1545)," Juliana Schiesari, "Isabella di Morra (c. 1520–1545)," and Valeria Finucci, "Isabella di Morra." See also Laura Anna Stortoni, *Women Poets of the Italian Renaissance*.

[28] For more historical information, see Croce, *Storia del Regno di Napoli*, Giovanni Coniglio, *Il Regno di Napoli al tempo di Carlo V*, Abulafia, "The South," and J.R. Hale, *Renaissance Europe*, 37–41.

[29] Isabella Morra, *Rime*, Maria Antonietta Grignani, ed. All references to Morra's poetry will be based on this edition, and indicated with poem, verse, and page number.

[30] A detailed account of Morra's short life is provided by Marcantonio di Morra, the son of Isabella's youngest brother, in his family memoir, *Familiae nobilissimae de Morra historia* (1629). See Croce, *Isabella di Morra*, 9–12.

[31] For a detailed account of Morra's publishing history, see my "Reading the Afterlife of Isabella di Morra's Poetry," Robin, *Publishing Women*, 73–78, and her "Descriptions of the Fifteen Volumes in the Giolito Anthologies Series: 1545–1560," 219–242, and Toscano, *Diego Sandoval di Castro e Isabella di Morra Rime*, 11–12.

[32] For the publication history of this anthology, see Toscano, *Letterati Corti Accademie*, 183–200 and Balsamo, ed. *Ma Bibliothèque poétique*, and its website http://www.fondation-italienne-barbier-mueller.org.

[33] Grignani has called attention to the compelling similarities between Morra's lexis and that of the poets from her region throughout her edition of Morra's poetry.

[34] See also Vianey, *Le Pétrarquisme en France*, 380–381, Balsamo, "Les Poètes français et les anthologies lyriques italiennes," and DellaNeva, *Unlikely Exemplars*, 97. For the various editions of this anthology in which Morra's poems appear, see my "Reading the Afterlife of Isabella di Morra's Poetry," and Robin, *Pubishing Women*, 228–232.

[35] Robin, "Morra," *Encyclopedia*, 275.

[36] Domenichi's anthology was published in 1559, in Lucca by Busdrago. For more information on the history of women's publishing in Italy, including Morra, see Robin, "Women on the Move:" also at http://www.jstor.org/stable/10.1086/673416 and Virginia Cox, *Women's Writing in Italy 1400–1650*.

[37] For more on Domenichi's anthology, see Deanna Shemek, "The Collector's Cabinet. Lodovico Domenichi's Gallery of Women," Piéjus, "La Première anthologie de poèmes féminins: l'écriture filtrée et orientée," and Angela Piscini, "Domenichi, Lodovico."

[38] See Kennedy, "Petrarchan Textualitiy Commentaries and Gender Revisions."

[39] Giovanni Caserta notes that "frale" is one of Morra's favorite adjectives, and it seems to reflect the uncertainty and vulnerability of her life. See *Isabella Morra e la società meridionale del Cinquecento*, 106.

[40] Grignani, Morra, *Rime*, 31, and Grignani, "Per Isabella di Morra," 527. See also Nuovo and Coppens, *I Giolito e la stampa*.

[41] See Pasquini, "Saviozzo, Simone Serdini detto il," 322.

[42] See Vittore Branca who argues that this book was an attempt to establish a more varied and vast canon alongside Dante and Petrarch, "Le raccolte di rime e le collezioni di classici." See also my "Cariteo's 'Aragonia,'" 1, Pasquini, "Saviozzo, Simone Serdini detto il," 322, Contini, *Letteratura Italiana del Quattrocento*, 129–133, and Verhulst, "Fonction sociale de la poésie du Quattrocento."

[43] Juliana Schiesari, *The Gendering of Melancholia*, 166. See also her "Petrarch's 'Ladies' and Sappho's 'Sirens.'"

[44] See Sara Adler, "The Petrarchan Lament of Isabella di Morra," Levarie Smarr, "Substituting for Laura: Objects of Desire for Renaissance Women Poets," Gabriele Niccoli, "Romancing the Father: Writing as Weeping, Loss as Identity in Isabella di

Morra's Rime," and Ruggero Stefanelli, "Il Petrarchismo di Isabella di Morra."

[45] Morra's poetry also borrows Dante's macabre representations of *Inferno,* but mostly, Dante's *Rime petrose*, a group of four *canzoni* which celebrated Dante's frustrated love for an unidentified lady, compared in each of them to a stone, sometimes precious because of her beauty, and sometimes harsh because of her coldness toward her lover. See Durling and Ronald L. Martinez, *Time and the Crystal Studies in Dante's Rime Petrose.*

[46] Schiesari does not consider other models for Morra's writing, except for an overturn of Petrarch's code.

[47] Adler, "The Petrarchan Lament," 202.

[48] Unlike the poets I have discussed thus far, Morra did not partake in a circle's or court's social and intellectual interactions, friendships or alliances, an aspect that characterizes her poetry as deeply subjective and unique.

[49] In Beccari's *disperata* as well, Fortune is mainly adverse fate.

[50] See Hanna Fenichel Pitkin, *Fortune is a Woman*, 138–139.

[51] Scholars agree that this sonnet was written after Francis I's defeat at Crépy against Charles V in 1544, when the French King had to relinquish to Spain Naples and its kingdom in the Treaty of Crépy. See Grignani, 57, and Irene Musillo Mitchell, ed. and trans., *Isabella Morra Canzoniere*, 9.

[52] See Nunzio Rizzi, "'E donna son, contra le donne dico': il canzoniere di Isabella di Morra," who notes that in Morra's *canzoniere*, Fortune has an exclusively prosecuting function, 21.

[53] Niccoli sees Morra's "stato" as "an inability to reconcile aspects of the self (personal/textual) into a relatively coherent and acceptable sense of self" as well as the search for identity formulated in the context of lack, loss, and separation. "Romancing the Father," 163 and 165.

[54] See Caserta's analysis of recurring adjectives, *Isabella Morra*, 106–107.

[55] Luigi Tansillo, *Rime*, 270. For more intertextualities between Morra and Tansillo see also Tansillo, *Rime*, 992.

[56] Musillo Mitchell, *Isabella Morra Canzoniere*, 10.

[57] See Croce's description of the countryside that surrounds the Morras' castle in Favale, *Isabella Morra*, 20–22, and Aldo Zaccone, "I luoghi morriani: sulle tracce d'Isabella."

[58] Zaccone, "I luoghi morriani," 142.

[59] This aspect places Isabella as one of the heroines of Ovid's *Heroides* who anxiously awaits her beloved, just like in her third sonnet, vv. 1–4, 50. Rosati calls this scenario, "una scenografia dell'attesa, fatta di sguardi sempre tesi sull'orizzonte marino, di giornate interminabili e notti insonni consumate nei soliti lavori femminili." "Epistola elegiaca e lamento femminile," 41.

[60] Toscano, *Diego Sandoval di Castro e Isabella di Morra*, 14.

[61] As, for example, Cariteo, who claims, "Parlar di morte è 'l mio maggior diletto" (Chapter Three) and Napolitano, "che a morte a un tristo più che vita piace" (Chapter Five).

Chapter Five

The *Disperata* in France

Me doy-je plaindre ainsi comme je fais?

Philippe Desportes

The Cinquecento in France

Angelo di Costanzo, Luigi Tansillo, and Bernardino Rota

"Ce fut la plus belle époque du pétrarquisme français, la plus féconde, la plus originale." (It was the best period of French Petrarchism, the most fruitful, the most original.)[1] This is how Vianey describes the second wave of Petrarchism in France, dominated by poets such as Angelo di Costanzo (1507–91), Bernardino Rota (1509–74), and Luigi Tansillo (1510–68), which also greatly affect the *disperata* genre as it crossed into France. To these three poets, I will add Nocturno Napolitano, whose work, including a *disperata*, had a significant impact on French poetry. The works by these Neapolitan writers undoubtedly represent a continuum with Morra's *disperate* as all five poets share rich geo-cultural and literary traditions.[2] They owe their reputation and popularity in France mainly to the Italian anthologies, including the *Libro terzo delle rime di diversi illustri signori napolitani*, published by Giolito in Venice in 1552, and *I fiori delle rime de' poeti illustri nuovamante raccolti et ordinati da Girolamo Ruscelli*, published in Venice in 1558. One goal of these volumes was to print the work of the best poets.[3] These works then became strong models for other emulators. The *Rime di diversi illustri signori napolitani* in particular marks "a shift in emphasis from the Bembist school in Venice to the Neapolitan group," as Richter points out.[4] This anthology's three editions and their successful circulation drew attention to the writers from the Naples region and their prominent, new place in literary culture. The continued presence of Di Costanzo, Rota, and Tansillo and the number of their poems featured in the anthologies are a clear indication of their fame. As mentioned, Morra's poetry too was included in this volume, as the book seller Marcantonio Passero had assembled her verses following the police investigation in her family castle and had distributed them to the successful polygraphs Dolce, Giolito, and Domenichi.

Di Costanzo, with his sixty-six poems, is the first poet featured in the 1552 edition of *Rime di diversi illustri signori napoletani*.[5] His poetry, along with that of Tansillo and Rota, features themes and language that express despair and several of the *topoi* and psychological attitudes found in the *disperata*. The anthology, therefore, represents a vital link between the genre and the French poets examined in this study, and it is, thus, worthy of a brief discussion before focusing on the transnational nuances of the adoption and adaptation of the *disperata* poetry in France. The following sonnet by Tansillo is a remarkable example of the *disperata*'s content adapted to a shorter form, while its essence remains intact:

> Valli nemiche al sol, superbe rupi
> che minacciate il ciel; profonde grotte
> onde non parton mai silentio e notte;
> aere, che gli occhi d'atra nebbia occupi;
> precipitati sassi, alti dirupi,
> ossa insepolte, erbose mura e rotte,
> d'uomini albergo et or a tal condotte,
> che temon d'ir fra voi serpenti e lupi;
> erme campagne, abbandonati lidi,
> dove mai voce d'uom l'aria non fiede,
> ombra son io dannata in pianto eterno
> che tra voi vengo a deplorar mia fede
> e spero al suon di desperati stridi
> se non se piega il ciel, mover l'inferno.

(Oh valleys, enemy of the sun, superb rocks/which threaten the sky; deep grottoes/from where the silence and the night never leave;/land, that occupies the sky with dark fog;/fallen stones, tall cliffs,/unburied bones, broken, grassy walls/shelter to men, and now my destination/near which snakes and wolves fear to come;/secluded lands, abandoned shores,/where no human voice is ever heard,/I am a shadow damned to eternal weeping/and I come among you to deplore my faith/and with the sound of desperate screams, I hope/to move hell, if not bend the sky.)[6]

The entire sonnet stages the sense of space found in the *disperata* landscape, its main elements, and its inhabitants—the wild animals—as well as the speaker's canonical attitude. The speaker is nothing but a shadow, damned to walk these valleys, but hoping at least to move Hell with his desperate cries. Horror is materialized in the macabre image of unburied bones steeped in darkness and silence, which also pervade the whole sonnet. The poet-persona's inner solitude and despair are projected onto the poem in which even the alliteration of the consonants "R" and "S" express harshness, bitterness, and horror. The ideal setting and psychology of the *disperata* are perfectly crafted to blend with the genre and its uninterrupted development and movements.[7]

As already stated, because the sonnet, the *canzone*, and the *sestina* were some of the preferred genres in Petrarch's *Rime*, Bembo urged their restoration in his *Asolani* and *Rime*.[8] Shorter lyric forms, thus, were to be chosen by poets. Although Petrarch's imitation remained the fundamental point of origin of the poetry of the Cinquecento, and certainly gained strength during the century as Bembo reasserted its importance, the *disperata* maintained its position in some of the sixteenth-century sonnets and *canzoni*. In fact, the literary production by Tansillo, di Costanzo, and Rota, although still bound to some aspects of Petrarch's code, deviates in part because it was inspired by the poetry of the *disperata*.[9] Continuously present are its attitudes and rhetoric, barren landscapes, dark and lonely refuges, such as caves and remote forests, and a penchant for indulging in hopelessness. Above all, this lyric production is characterized by a deeper and more visceral despair in love, which marks the transition from the early to the later Cinquecento, but also from Italy to France. Erika Milburn persuasively argues that Tansillo "is a transitional figure, bridging the gap between the rigid traditional Petrarchism espoused by poets such as Bembo, and the more flexible and open style of the Baroque."[10] Thus, the *disperata* reaches France not only through a direct reading of poems by il Saviozzo, il Pistoia, Serafino, Tebaldeo, Aretino, and Nocturno, but also through the highly anthologized and admired di Costanzo, Tansillo and Rota, who had already adapted its themes to their sonnets, which were vastly read and imitated at the French literary circles and courts.[11]

The *Disperata* in France

The French poets found a creative way to channel anguish and anxiety into poetry, often disguised as "love poetry." Thus, it is in France that the *disperata* becomes not only a poetic model, but a way of writing one's existence; of navigating the trials of personal and collective trauma; and of narrating despair. This chapter and the following will discuss the many examples of intertextuality in themes and psychology, attitudes and language, *topoi* and images, in order to trace the genre's emergences and variations in France and its transnational relevance. Here, I show how poets appropriated the models into their own style and language, adapting them to poetic forms that better suited French conventions. As mentioned, Weber, Dubois, and Mathieu-Castellani, and more recently, Roland Guillot, have called attention to the presence of the *disperata* in France as a new lyric model, and as a strong intertext from 1570 to 1620.[12] These compelling analyses constitute the point of departure for my tracing of the genre in France, particularly in the works of French poets such as Philippe Desportes, Agrippa d'Aubigné, and Clovis Hesteau de Nuysement, among others. Although numerous scholars have skillfully outlined Petrarch's and his Italian disciples' poetry as an essential and bountiful intertext for the French poets, my analysis shows that the *disperata* complemented and, in some instances, even changed Petrarchism and its intertextual manifestations in France.[13] Both models went hand in hand, as the *disperata* provided additional images as well as a psychological attitude that met the French poets' particular circumstances in their war-torn country, deeply divided by religious and civil unrest. Once again, literary culture is confronted with historical circumstances that, just like in Italy, negatively impacted the poets' lives.

The *disperata* delivered a viable and strong frame of despair to the French poets who lived and wrote during the French Wars of Religion (1562–98) and to the next generation.[14] They were, as readers of the *disperata*, witnesses both to the profound crisis of the speaker, his reaction and ensuing violent damnations, his cries of despair, and to horrific historical events of unprecedented violence in their own lives, including civil strife, personal and social anguish due to the killings, mutilations, and unspeakable loss caused by the wars that ravaged France for much of their lives. From the first War of Religion in 1562, to the Edict of Nantes in 1598, writers integrated images of war and language of violence into their texts. Just like the *disperata* speakers, who cast themselves in opposition to natural and human rejoicing and to main-stream engagement in social interaction, the religious wars grouped poets as separate and marginalized from their opposite faith faction. In particular, Protestant and Huguenot writers forged an unwavering identity that conflicted with the Catholic resistance.[15] Throughout these years, both parties solidified their intolerant claims, as well as their militant identities, and both depicted themselves as being persecuted and damned by the other, as we shall see in some of the French poems. Like the *disperato*, who feels persecuted by Fortune, Love, and poverty, the French poets of the end of the Renaissance portray themselves as victims, and as such project their violent outbursts and anxieties into their poetry, and onto their audience: violence given for violence felt.

The poetry of the *disperata* hence provided a convincing and self-contained model for reacting to these tragic events. It also delivered a lyric system in which despair and anguish engaged with a well-established and recognizable *toile de fond* that could be immediately embraced and adopted. After all, the *disperata* poets from the Trecento to the Cinquecento were reliable sources. Furthermore, as already discussed, the *disperata* allowed its speakers to assert themselves and persuade the audience of their immesurable grief and unique position as a *disperato* or *disperata*.[16] Readers of French poems, too, become entangled witnesses because the text is gripping and emotionally demanding. Thus, French authors employed the *disperata* as a model in order to secure the readers' attention and interest, creating a poetic space in which to loudly express oneself, be heard, and communicate both violence and its fear, personal emotions, and the desire to conquer and overcome history's brutality. Furthermore, for both writer and reader, poetry brings catharsis and consolation, in particular at the French court, where the audience becomes fully immersed in idyllic, solitary landscapes inhabited by savage beasts, threatening shadows and ghosts.[17] As Alexander argues, "Shared trauma depends on collective processes of cultural interpretation."[18] The court and its writers collectively experienced the civil conflicts, as expressed by d'Aubigné's all encompassing "tout," and his catalogue of recognizable elements:

> Tout gemist, tout se plaint, et mon mal est si fort
> Qu'il esmeut fleurs, costaux, bois et roches estranges,
> Tigres, lions et ours et les eaux et leur port,
> Nimphes, les vens, les cieux, les astres et les anges.
> Tu es loin de pitié et plus loin de ma mort.

(Everything is moaning, everything is lamenting, and my ill is so strong/that it moves flowers, hills, woods and strange rocks,/Tigers, lions and bears and the waters and their harbor,/Nymphs, winds, skies, the stars and the angels./You are far from pity and even farther from my death.)[19]

The familiar "estrange" setting, inhabited by wild animals, provides the perfect stage on which to despair, and where war and love commingle and seduce while writing and reading oneself through and into despair.

Despite the difference in time and space between the French and Italian poets, the French poets were inspired by the morbid and sordid context of the *disperata*, which transcended form, meter, and language. Furthermore, the vastly Italianized court of Henri III of Valois, which

eagerly welcomed an additional Italian lyric model to the already assimi-
lated Dante, Petrarch, Boccaccio, and Ariosto, favored the appropriation of a new source.[20] The Italian poets of the *disperata* synthesized and
harmonized these models, but also added an element of despair that felt
right at home at court. For instance, in both Petrarchism and the *disperata* the speaker is by definition a rejected lover, and the inaccessibility
of the beloved or object of desire is the *sine qua non* condition of these
two systems. However, in the latter, unrequited love is bluntly damned,
and violence is legitimized as a *topos* in which the Eros-Thanatos mindset is pushed to morbid and somber extremes. Moreover, personal experiences and emotions take center stage, as the "je" confidently appropriates the lyric space and consumes the pages with words that resonate with
the grave circumstances and traumas of each individual. As Gros and
Fragonard explain although imitation of predecessors was still in vogue,
personal feelings and details particular to each individual prevail, as poets
started to develop new personal myths and new representations of the self
in order to express the intensity of individual suffering.[21]

As the *disperata* transitioned from Italy to France, the transformation of its content continued into other forms such as sonnets, odes, *complaintes*, *plaintes*, elegies, and *stances*, in order to accommodate France's
literary culture and genre's historicity, as well as each poet's personal taste
and style. Yet, these poems embrace all of the genre's distinct elements
previously discussed—confession, maledictions, passion, aggression, violence, free spirit, self-accusation, masochism, sadism, and finally, the ultimate wish for a violent and lonely death.

The Italian anthologies by Giolito, Ruscelli, and their rivals provided poetic models,[22] not only by established authors such as Petrarch,
Bembo, Serafino, Tebaldeo, Cariteo, and di Costanzo, but also by lesser-
known poets, who, despite their lack of notoriety, nonetheless had their
poems printed side-by-side and, therefore, associated with those of the
masters.[23] Thus, anthologies presented novelty and abundance, but also
diversity in a plethora of examples.[24] As DellaNeva notes, the anthologies
published between 1540 and 1550 are "'canon-expanding' documents that
are characterized by their inclusiveness rather than their exclusiveness."[25]
As a written form and a volume structured to follow specific criteria, the
anthology became an authentic and irreplaceable vehicle in the diffusion
of early-modern Italian poetry and the cultural, intellectual, and linguistic
patrimony it embodied.[26] In France as well, the *recueils collectifs* such as,
for example, the *Recueil de diverses poésies* (1597, 1599, and 1600) and *Les*

Muses rallies (1598) provided an opportunity to lesser known authors to see their poetry circulated.[27] As already mentioned, as the popularity of these volumes shows, Renaissance writers in both France and Italy enjoyed not only reading new sources, but also exercising their skills in a variety of well-established genres.[28] Therefore, the ways in which the *disperata* was first adopted and then adapted, as determined by the author's style, tastes, and verve, constitute an important phase in its history and transmission, as it gained in both substance and status.

French Genres and the *Disperata*

As previously discussed, genre dynamics are directly related to the transmission of the *disperata*, at first when form and content are inextricably connected, and, second, when form and content are no longer entangled. In the beginning, form and content were entwined in the *capitolo ternario*, the form for which the *disperata* became renowned and codified with specific themes, attitudes, language, and metric. Similarly, imitation and genre are closely intertwined as well. After all, imitation starts with the emulator's very first choice of selecting a genre: this genre and its conventions come into play immediately, as the poem follows its form, metric, and inner mechanisms, albeit more meticulously or more loosely. For example, unlike their predecessors, Desportes, d'Aubigné, and Nuysement did not always favor the sonnet, but rather, they elected longer and more pliable genres that are also better suited for the *disperata*'s unique content.[29] Therefore, this choice marks the beginning of a more comprehensive assumption of the *disperata* as one of the intertexts to be imitated and molded into French genres, where its generative and organic nature grafted onto lyric forms that were already being employed by the poets from the School of Lyon, the Pléiade, and neo-Petrarchism.

The notion of genre is particularly important to my discussion of transnational intertexuality as well because it embodies convention, tradition, and a heavily inscribed code within an established, national literary system, which are imposed upon a writer by his or her readers and are institutionalized by the national literatures, in our case, Italian and French.[30] Genres, then, hold meaning and investment, as writers inscribe their voices in a genre's tradition in order to partake in it. As previously discussed, a hierarchy is established when writers use, consume, and propagate a specific genre, whereby certain categories become more relevant, while others are disregarded, or even completely dismissed. As Clément

Moisan convincingly argues, genres also create declassifications within a hierarchy of literary values by reassigning a genre a lower status and classifying another.[31] In the case of the *disperata*, by assuming various forms, the genre's content not only survived, but blossomed and thrived, often gaining more intensity, singularity, and verve.

When borrowing a genre from previous periods and from different traditions, a process of adaptation to the current period and its culture is necessary, whereby the adoptive writers' voice, style, tastes, and whims are adapted to the demands of their audience. Furthermore, when borrowing a specific genre, for example the love sonnet, the newly imitated poem is no longer the same sonnet.[32] In fact, while *imitatio* does come into play, it is mostly *dispositio* that is a determining factor, as the new adoptive linguistic system and metric structures might be significantly different. As Pigman explains, "A reader can feel justified in expecting a text to assert its difference from its model and to make use of that difference."[33] Moreover, lyric forms are not only re-inscribed in the newly adoptive literary tradition, in this case the French Renaissance, but they also provide a lyric continuity between past and future. Martines convincingly argues that genres follow particular "stylistic and formal conventions. In part, therefore, they bear the echoes of past voices." However, he notes that when other poets adopt these genres later on, they "are adapting and adjusting the earlier voices to their own requirements."[34] In this case, the poetry of the *disperata* was adjusted to French tastes, and its subject, treatment, and attitudes were adapted to lyric forms that better suited the French language, culture, and context.

Unquestionably, because of its heavy reliance on the subject matter, the *disperata* genre came to be known as "the" composition dedicated entirely to the narration of despair. The content and the ways in which it is narrated, as we have seen, determine whether a poem is truly an example of *disperata*. As Mathieu-Castellani argues, in fact, all lyric genres can rely on a narrative structure with specific elements such as verb tense, explicit locution manners, as well as on the relationship between these elements and the speaker.[35] Thus, a French sonnet, an ode, or a *stance* might contain a narrative format that comfortably accommodates and transmits the *disperata* content.

Just like in Italy, in France too a positive force behind the spread of the *disperata* was the remarkable popularity and vogue of the love *capitolo* (*capitolo amoroso*), which had evolved from the fourteenth through the sixteenth century, and which reached its peak with court poets such as

Serafino, Tebaldeo, Sasso, Aretino, Ariosto, and di Costanzo.[36] Mellin de
Saint-Gelais brought the *capitolo* to France while experimenting with it
as a vehicle for the *terza rima*.[37] His position as royal librarian at Francis
I's Fontainebleau allowed him to handle many Italian books and anthologies, as the King was exceptionally fond of Italian art and literature.
Furthermore, in France, as Luigia Zilli notes, the *terza rima* is considered "à juste titre comme la plus italienne qui soit aux yeux de la culture
française." (rightly so, the most Italian according to French culture).[38]
However, the *terza rima* did not really become popular in France, as a
brief review of French translations of Ariosto shows, as, with the exception of one attempt, most translations of *Orlando furioso* were in prose,[39]
including Desportes's *Les Imitations de l'Arioste*.[40] Nonetheless, at the time,
the *terza rima*, was instrumental in establishing the Italian literary tradition and its culture. Just a few examples include Dante's *Divina Commedia*,
Petrarch's *Trionfi*, Boccaccio's *Caccia di Diana* and *L'Amorosa visione*, as
well as Ariosto's *Orlando furioso*.[41] These works were not only admired for
their meter, but also for their content.[42] Furthermore, the *terza rima* was
favored in the translation of the Classics, and systematically used during
the second half of the fifteenth century.[43] As it relates to the *disperata*, as
has already been stated, it greatly contributes to its internal vigor, as its
open meter and propulsive driving force are meant to connect each tercet
with a regular rhyme, and to increase the strength of its content. Its interlocking rhymes also provide a solid unity to the long composition. Hence,
the variety of images and *topoi* that the desperate speaker recounts are fully
intensified by the meter, one tercet at the time.[44]

Just like the *disperata*, in France as well there are genres that depend
rather rigidly on their content due to their specific domineering theme.
Two noteworthy examples are the *plainte* and the *complainte*, in which
the speaker complains (*se plaint*) of somebody or something. In his *Art
Poétique francoys* of 1548, Thomas Sebillet (1512–89) writes that some
genres are listed or fall under more popular genres. For example, he notes
that "complaintes et deplorations sembleroient estre comprises soubz
l'élégie [...] car l'élégie proprement veut dire complainte." (Complaints and
laments seem to be comprised under the elegy [...] because elegy means
precisely complaint.)[45] Thus, the elegy comprises other analogous genres,[46] including *complaintes*, similarly to the *capitolo* or *canzone* in Italy.[47]
As already noted, in the sixteenth-century Italian *canzonieri* and anthologies we find *disperate* listed as *capitolo*, *canzone*, or *elegia*,[48] rather than *disperata*, denoting precisely that the form was privileged over the content,

hence perpetuating a long-lasting ambiguity in relation to the *disperata* generic status.[49] Furthermore, this type of classification established a hierarchy that was thereafter perpetuated in the literary tradition.[50]

The *Disperata*'s Timid Entry into Renaissance France

Jacques Peletier du Mans, Joachim Du Bellay, Olivier de Magny, and François d'Amboise

In France, the theme of the love complaint—*la plainte amoureuse*—became a poetic commonplace encompassed by several genres, including the first wave of *disperata* poetry starting with Jacques Peletier du Mans (1517–82), who published "Le chant du desesperé" in 1547. Joachim du Bellay (1522–60) followed soon after with, first, an ode titled "Chant du desesperé" in 1549, and in 1552, with another ode titled "La Complainte du desesperé." The following year, in 1553, Olivier de Magny (1529–61) published his "Chant du desesperé," and in 1572, François d'Amboise (1550–1619) published his *Desesperades*.[51] Although these poems are inspired by the *disperata*, after all their titles all use a derivative of the word despair, they are predominantly anchored to the tradition of the love complaint.[52] For the most part, they lack crucial components of the *disperata* genre, such as the maledictions, the catalogue of natural elements, infernal landscapes, wild beasts, and the presence of an eerie nature. Moreover, its hopeless mood and violent images are significantly tempered, as the overall tone of these poems never reaches the tragic and anguished levels found in the Italian sources nor in later examples of French *disperate*, such as d'Aubigné's *stances*.

Peletier's "Chant du desesperé" begins forcefully with a malediction against his birth, "O la male heure ou je fu né!/O que je suis infortuné!" (Oh the evil hour when I was born!/Oh how unfortunate am I!" (vv. 1–2, 99).[53] It then describes his birth, which initiated the speaker's misfortunes, inlcuding the lack of work, a vexing discomfort of his living conditions, and his enemies (v. 53, 100). The poem then moves toward thoughts of death:

> Cessez malheurs, cessez
> Ou mourir me laissez
> ...
> Oste moy hors d'icy,
> O mort, s'il est ainsi

(Stop misfortunes, stop/Or let me die/ … /Take me out of here,/Oh death, if it must be so" (vv. 55–60, 100).

Throughout though, Peletier's despair remains lighthearted, and although his poem depicts unhappiness and hardships, the poetic persona never mentions the word "despair," nor uses tragic vocabulary or dark attitudes and tones. The bleakest moments of the poem are those that convey a physical and spiritual distress, as in the following verses:

> Mon corps se consume et se ronge,
> Mon esprit travaille et songe
> Endurer je ne puis,
> D'estre ce que je suis.

(My body is being consumed and eaten away,/My spirit labors and dreams/I can no longer endure,/To be who I am.) (vv. 13–16, 99).

Furthermore, the poem does not employ any of the *disperata*'s essential *topoi*, apart from the initial malediction, and concludes with the speaker's resignation. Unlike the *disperato*, who does not cease to complain, nor to damn something or somebody, nor sees an end to his despair and continues to make his voice and cries heard until after his death, Peletier's persona instead stops his plaint because he concedes that the more he protests, the more his sorrows grow:

> Mais je cesse de me douloir,
> Attendant des Cieux le vouloir,
> Car tant plus je me lamente,
> Et plus mon mal s'augmente.

(But I cease to complain,/Waiting for Heavens' will,/Because the more I complain,/The more my ills increase.) (vv. 61–64, 100).

Thus, at the poem's very end, the poet-persona consciously ceases to hurt and to lament. In summary, the theme of *le désespoir amoureux*, cherished by the Pléiade and most Renaissance poets, is here extensively developed at the expense of the *topos* of hopelessness.[54]

Peletier's song closely resonates in Du Bellay's ode of despair. Du Bellay's "Chant du desesperé" and later on his "Chanson du desesperé" are dominated by sadness and melancholy rather than by despair as an all-encompassing existential pain. Moreover, the tone remains contained throughout these two compositions. In the "Chant," the speaker laments several aspects of his life in a state caught between life and death:

> Mes plaintes sont funebres,
> et mes membres transiz:
> Mais je ne puy' mourir,
> Et si ne puy' guerir

(My laments are funeral,/and my limbs numb:/But I cannot die,/Nor can I heal) (vv. 15–18, 71).[55]

His excessive complaint (v. 51, 72) enumerates the poetic persona's personal feelings, including languor, pain, regret, and fear. These are expressed throughout the poem, which culminates with a call for death (vv. 61–62, 73). Despite the finality of it all, the mood, however, stays light and uplifting, complemented by the music of nightingales and other birds singing in the forest. In fact, Du Bellay compares his song to that of a "cygne poétique" (v. 43, 72), rather than to a wretched cry. Thus, the "Chant" remains a complaint about a vague displeasure that never materializes and that does not reach hopeless intensities to the point of total damnation.

Three years later, Du Bellay published a longer ode, which he titled "La Complainte du desesperé." Differentiating it from his earlier "Chant" by writing a much longer composition, he laments unreservedly the flight of time and old age.[56] Although deploying the themes of nature, mythology, illness, regret, and death, this poem too never reaches the *disperata*'s dramatic breadth. For the most part, the speaker evokes a fairly serene youth and happier times:

> De mes ans plus vigoureux
> ...
> Que mes jours les plus heureux
> (vv. 129–132, 71).

Contrarily, he blames old age for his current state of deep sadness:

> Et mile souciz cuysans
> Avancent de ma vieillesse
> Le triste hyver qui me blesse
> Devant l'esté de mes ans
> (vv. 135–138, 72).

However, toward the very end of the poem (vv. 409–414, 79), Du Bellay unmistakably refers to some of the *disperata*'s main *topoi*, as the poetic persona damns his birth as the beginning of his unhappy life. Moreover, a subdued melancholia, "tristesse profonde," pervades this ode even if the poet-persona continues to make hopeful meditations and nostalgic remembrances.

In both poems, the speaker evokes settings that are welcoming rather than threatening, and nature itself is melancholic and idyllic:

> Je me trayne par les champs,
> Le soucy, qui m'accompaigne,
> Ensemence la campaigne
> De mile regrets tranchans

(I wander through the fields,/The worry that accompanies me,/ Sows through the countryside/A thousand piercing regrets) (vv. 291–294, 76).

The grottoes are wild, but never haunted by the poet's dark ghosts, and just like nature, the animals encountered by the poetic persona are friendly and sympathetic to his melancholy, rather than threatening and wild. In fact, Du Bellay's depictions of nature are akin to those found in pastoral literature, expressing with regret the longing for a simpler life. The speaker sings his misfortunes in a lyric, bucolic setting, encountered also in d'Amboise's eclogues. And although suffering is present, despair—as in lack of hope and the wish for personal ruin that carries a troubling finality—is not, because, as Weber convincingly argues, this is essentially Du Bellay's "bercement de la souffrance par le chant." (the soothing of his sufferance through his *chant*).[57] However, the culmination of the poem increases in intensity with the poetic persona's pleas for his death to come quickly in order to end his "vie desperée" (v. 493, 82), and a malediction against life is severely voiced: "Maudicte donq' la lumiere,/Qui m'esclaira la premiere" (vv. 409–410, 79).

In sum, the images developed by Du Bellay are for the most part not drawn from the *disperata* tradition, the invectives are lacking, and the sorrow never reaches the deep nuances of heartbroken despair. Mario Richter states that "La Complainte" especially expresses Du Bellay's spiritual crisis caused in part by the physical deterioration due to his old age.[58] The reader, therefore, is left with a sense of the speaker's melancholia and his vague dissatisfaction with life and its current circumstances.

Just like Du Bellay's poems, Magny's "Chant du desesperé" evokes melancholia. The poetic persona conjures his troubles, torments, sadness, and deep bitterness:

> Soucy me guide, & avec moy habite
> Douleur, tristesse, & desespoirs frequentz
> Et tous les maux qui leur sont subsequentz

(My worry guides me, and I carry/Pain, sadness, and frequent
despairs/And all the ills that ensue) (vv. 22–24, 180).[59]

He then laments his enemies and their wrongdoings, and he compares
himself to unfortunate mythological lovers, a *topos* also encountered in
the *disperata*. In wondering what causes him to be so miserable, he blames
his misfortunes, but does not resort to maledictions, nor does he evoke
the *disperata*'s wild animals or its canonical infernal settings. He is more
concerned with sharing his immeasureable unhappiness and soliciting the
reader's compassion: "O pauvre moy tant malheureux tenu" (v. 93, 182),
and again "O moy chetif! ô moy plus qu'incensé" (v. 99, 182). The "Chant"
ends with a plea to the gods to finally put an end to his suffering, implor-
ing death to come quickly. Therefore, in his *plainte*, Magny demonstrates
his familiarity with the *disperata* genre and with some of its distinctive
expressions of despair, while overall he remains fairly timid in its adoption. As Jules Favre argues, in Magny's "Chant," the reader must not take
too seriously Magny's despair, as "ce chant n'est qu'une plainte purement
littéraire" (this *chant* is purely a literary compaint).[60]

About two decades after Magny's poem, François d'Amboise published his *Desesperades, ou Eclogues amoureuses, L'une marine, l'autre forestiere, esquelles sont au vif dépaintes les passions et le desespoir d'Amour*
(1572).[61] The title clearly acknowledges the *disperata* and its tradition,
but also positions itself in the tradition of the love complaint that laments
passion and *le désespoir amoureux*. Furthermore, the two *desesperades*,
"Clionette Thassalogue, ou Eclogue marine," and "Le Chasseur desespere,
Theralogue, ou Eclogue forestiere," are embedded in the piscatory and pastoral eclogue tradition and differ to a certain extent from each other. The
first, with 238 verses, is a complaint voiced by the fishermam Franciot, a
clear reference to the poet's first name, against Clionette, the capricious
beloved whom he addresses throughout the poem. Her name is also a nod
to the classical tradition, as Clio was the muse who assisted writers and
guided their stories. She could also be an allegory of poetry. For the most
part, Franciot focuses on the pangs that Clionette's betrayal instigates,
which also cause him to lose sleep, "Tant mon amour me brule" (v. 79, 99).
He naively offers her the fish from his catch in exchange for her love, and
he tenderly evokes the moment of the *innamoramento* in a bucolic setting,
"Je t'ay veu sur la rive estant jeune fillette" (I saw you on the bank when
you were a young girl) (v. 154, 101). He then even lists his own qualities
in order to convince her of his worth and loyalty. However, Clionette can-

not be dissuaded; therefore, Franciot enumerates all the places he could go and what he could do in hopes of finally forgetting her. However, the only solution seems to be death:

> Mouron donc: sus mouron ...
> et pour mieux m'abimer
> se rompe mon vaisseau
>
> ...
>
> seul soy-je infortuné, seul puisse-je mourir

(Let me die, thus, let me die ... /and in order to better destroy myself/that my boat break/ ... /and alone, let me be ill-fated, and alone let me die) (vv. 213–224, 103).

Hence, immediately thereafter, he decides to kill himself by jumping from a rock into the sea, under the very eyes of the beloved Clionette, and finally end his misery.

D'Amboise's eclogue is an exploration in Love's betrayal and its devastating repercussions, describing how Clionette turned her back on Franciot and how her infidelity drove him to thoughts of suicide. The lamentable experience is analyzed in minute details, with nostalgia, and continues as well into the other eclogue, "Le chasseur desespere," even if voiced by a different speaker, the huntsman Ambrosin, this time a reference to the poet's last name. This second eclogue is longer, with 384 verses, and again alludes to a real love story and past lover. Although the unfortunate hunter is also pursued by misfortune, he focuses the reader's attention on unrequited love, the culprit of all of his unhappiness and suffering. The *désespoir amoureux*, however, feels more acute here, and several of the *disperata topoi* are actually deployed throughout.

Once again, the poetic persona accuses the beloved of pushing him to seek death: "Je mourray, je mourray, ma cruelle l'ordonne" (v. 73, 106). He also compares himself to all of the unfortunate mythological lovers, and, just like in the *disperata*, his suffering is equal to no one. With a series of anaphoras, he singles out his own wretched condition, clearly echoing the *disperata*'s assertive expression of setting himself apart from the world, with "Un autre... moy"—"Un altro" and "Io solo":

> Un autre est bien, moy mal, un autre a paix, moy guerre,
> Un autre vole au ciel, moy j'enfonce en terre
>
> ...
>
> Un autre a esperance, et je me desespere

(The other is well, I am not well, the other is at peace, I am at war,/
The other flies toward the sky, I sink in the ground/ ... /The other
hopes, I despair) (vv. 161–165, 108).

The speaker also calls for several cataclysms in order to put an end to his
desperate state, preceded by the conditional tense that culminate in hell
and its abyss:

> Je voudrois voir les cieux contre eux tourner en rage
> Se deffaire l'un l'autre, et le pere des feus,
> Avec la sœur tomber dans les abismes creus
>
> (I would like to see the skies turn against each other with rage/
> Unravel each other, and the father of fires,/And with his sister fall
> in the allow abyss) (vv. 178–180, 109).

The apocalyptic images heighten the poem's tone and gravity (vv. 175–194,
109), while at the same time deploying a lyric crescendo in which the earth
and water are overwhelmed by the poetic persona's uproar: "Le ciel, la
flamme, l'air, l'eau, la terre perisse,/Puisqu'il faut que je meure occis par
l'injustice." (That the sky, fire, air, water, and earth perish,/Since I must die
at the hand of injustice.) (vv. 193–194, 109)

The *disperata*'s tradition is, again, brought into play with calls
for wild animals and frightening monsters to come eat and destroy the
speaker:

> Que ne vient un lion pour de moy s'aviander ?
> Que ne vient un tygre, ou quelque hideuse fere,
> Que ne vient quelque monstre affin de me deffaire
> Et entomber mon cors de trop vivre ennuyé ?
>
> (Why can't a lion come to eat me?/Why can't a tiger, or other hid-
> eous beasts come,/Why can't a monster come in order to undo me/
> And bury my body, that is so tired of living?) (vv. 200–204, 109).

This death sentence is instigated by the injustices of his condition as desperate lover. Furthermore, the "Que" and rhetorical questions echo the
subjunctives and language of the *disperata*, where the speaker wishes for
countless calamities to strike his world and end his miseries. As already
mentioned, d'Amboise uses the conditional tense in several lines of this
poem, as, for example, in the following verse: "Je voudrois voir par tout
couler le sang humain" (I would like to see human blood flow everywhere)
(v. 175, 109), without deviating much from the *disperata* model. While

evoking his suicide, Ambrosin adds a personal detail, giving this *desesper-ade* an image rendered unique by being set within a hunt:

> Mon épieu qui souloit les feres enferrer
> Je veux en desespoir dans mon cueur le fourrer,
> Ça donc, ha! Qu'est-ce cy? Helas! que veu-je faire?
> Me veux-je donc meurtrir au gré d'une meurtrière?

> (My sword that used to cut through iron/I want it to pierce my heart in despair,/Now now! What am I saying? Alas! What do I want to do?/Do I want to murder myself because of a murderess?) (vv. 231–234, 110).

He calls all of nature—its trees, mountains, valleys, planes, and so on, to witness his pitiful death because of Love, and finds comfort knowing that his end is near. Death is the final stage of his suffering, and in this case, it is also meant to extinguish love and desire (vv. 377–384, 114–115).

One element that sets this eclogue apart from the *disperata* is that the lover-persona provides a detailed description of the beloved, her body, beauty, and seducing traits, thus deploying the vast lyric tradition of the Renaissance that culminates in Petrarch and the neo-Petrarchan poets. The classical conventions of pastoral poetry come into play as well, especially when the long monologues evoke pastoral images, and the single voice of the fisherman and the hunter laments the beloved's cruelty in this pastoral setting.[62] The bucolic scenes give way to a game of double pursuit in which the lover-persona becomes the prey himself, hunted and tracked down by Love, while coveting the young woman. Furthermore, instead of the *disperata*'s favored deserted and ominous landscape, d'Amboise prefers a bucolic and melancholic one in which to sing his *désespoir amoureux* in temperate tones. This is an important distinction which shows that d'Amboise seems reluctant to fully embrace the inconsolable and wretched attitude and tone of the *disperato*. Furthermore, the lovers in each poem, Franciot and Ambrosin, while focusing on their love laments, accept the beloveds' refusals and rebuffs without violent rebellion.

In both of his poems, d'Amboise depicts at length a nostalgic longing for happier times, as seen in Du Bellay's poems, and lost love. What resurfaces the most is the speaker's hope for his beloved to come back to him. Therefore, hope is still alive, unlike in the *disperata*, where the speaker is utterly hopeless. In fact, as Dante Ughetti notes, the tension between consolation and despair is palpable throughout d'Amboise's poems, and tends to die down in contemplation.[63] More than a *desesperade*, if we were to translate the term to *disperata* in Italian, d'Amboise's eclogues present the reader with an expectation that the young woman will come back to the lover-persona, in which case, all troubles would be gone. Furthermore, the bucolic setting and lengthy reminiscing about happier times seem to soothe the speaker, as well as convey the anticipation of an imminent reunion with the beloved.

Overall, d'Amboise's eclogues are a confluence of Renaissance traditions, including the classical, the Pléiade, Petrarch's code, with Renaissance genres—the pastoral, the *complainte amoureuse*, and the *disperata*. Moreover, the lone edition of *Desesperades* as a whole is a *canzoniere* that features a sonnet, a portrait, two eclogues, and seven elegies. These compositions are unified by the theme of doomed love in which shepherds, and in this case a fisherman and a hunter, sing love songs to lament their passion for a young, beautiful shepherdess, echoing also *Arcadia* and *Galatea* by Jacopo Sannazaro (1458–1530).[64] Alice Hulubei examines the eclogue genre's origins and development in France, in addition to d'Amboise's *desesperades*.[65] She notes, in fact, that the French poet gives his two *desesperades*, "ce lyrisme d'origine italienne qui consiste, non pas dans l'analyse du sentiment, mais dans la peinture des effets hyperboliques provoqués par un amour malheureux." (this lyricism of Italian origins that, rather than analyzing feelings, paints the hyperbolic effects caused by an ill-fated love.)[66] Furthermore, Weber included the second eclogue, "Le chasseur désespéré," in Appendix II of his edition of d'Aubigné's *Le Printemps*, right after Appendix I, which presented what he thought to be Serafino's "Disperata Terza," although it is really il Pistoia's *disperata*.[67] The French critic, thus, identified Serafino as an intertext for *Desesperades*, thereby establishing a persuasive link between Serafino's *disperata*, d'Amboise's eclogues, and d'Aubigné's "Stance I." However, Hulubei and Weber both agree that d'Amboise's poems are eclogues dominated by a maritime and forestal setting.[68] Hence, d'Amboise mostly draws his inspiration from the Classic and Italian pastoral elegy, with its origins in Theocritus and Virgil's eclogues, although adopting few of the *disperata's topoi* as well, thus blending both models and skillfully building on both traditions.

Altogether, the *Desesperades* represent an important moment in the *disperata* tradition in France, engendering a continuum with the *plaintes amoureuses* of Peletier, Du Bellay, and Magny. It is also significant because it is clearly a recognition of the *disperata's* place in the French literary tradition by well-known canonical writers, with the exception of d'Amboise perhaps, whose work is still rarely analyzed. However, in these French poems, nature is a companion, and it is not threatening nor unpleasant. Rather, it inspires in the speaker a tenacious melancholy meant to soothe the speaker's broken heart, complementing the nostalgia for a better past. Weber calls it "le sentiment tout moderne de la mélancolie,"[69] a different feeling from the expressions of despair found in the *disperata* genre. Therefore, although all four poets acknowledged the *disperata* tradition, they seemed reluctant to fully adopt it. Taken collectively, this first wave of *disperata* in France contemplates despair as a romanticized state that fuels the poets' imagination and creativity. Moreover, it emerges with milder, melancholic tones and a nostalgic temperament whose monologues are devoid of full-fledged hopelessness.

In addition to the *disperata*'s continuum with the *plainte amoureuse*, the last three decades of the Renaissance witness the emergence of Mannerism and Baroque. Scholars of this period have convincingly shown that this new aesthetic characterized not only artistic production, but literature as well.[70] Dubois, Mathieu-Castellani, and more recently Michael J. Giordano, for example, have closely studied Mannerism and Baroque, and they recognize individualism as one of the main traits of these new aesthetics.[71] This "émergence du moi" is already present in the *disperata*, hence this model's tradition intermingles with Mannerism and Baroque, as each French poet developed a personal *poesis* in order to more effectively express suffering and despair and to convince the reader.[72] The French writers borrowed these aspects of the *disperata*, which they subsequently transformed into their preferred lyric forms. In fact, the *disperata*'s specific elements, mostly dealing with content and rhetoric, resurface in French poems that not only feature despair, but craft and narrate it in a particular way, as the writings of the three following poets demonstrate. In the poems by Philippe Desportes, Agrippa d'Aubigné, and Clovis Hesteau de Nuysement, we can trace the *disperata*'s evolution and transformations, as well as its transnational developments and progress.

Philippe Desportes and Nocturno Napolitano

How was the *disperata* adopted, and consequently transformed and adapted in France for another readership with perhaps different expectations? In order to address this question, I will discuss the remarkable connections between Philippe Desportes (1546–1606) and the Italian poet Nocturno Napolitano (ca. 1490–ca. 1552). These connections are important in two ways: first, they have yet to be fully examined as an important

source of Desportes's imitation practices, and, second, as a concrete example of the circulation of the *disperata* in France.[73] Although Nocturno's
books were widely disseminated in Italy, with 111 editions from 1518 to
1530—most of them published between 1518 and 1520—not much is
known about his life,[74] perhaps because he has often been wrongly identified with either the poet Marc'Antonio Epicuro or the poet Antonio
Caracciolo.[75] Nocturno was born in Naples around 1490, and he traveled
mostly to the courts of Northern Italy. In Mantua, he sought the patronage of the Gonzaga family, as several of his encomiastic and eulogistic
poems attest. Indeed, like many of his contemporary fellow court writers
and artists, including Desportes, Nocturno "vivait de sa plume." As I have
discussed in the previous chapters, the *disperata* moved through transmission channels such as the courts: the foremost early modern site for the
concentration and dissemination of power, and where the *disperata* poets'
topoi and stylistic approaches progressed from one text to the next.

Several studies have amply demonstrated how deeply Desportes was
concerned with the form and structure of his lyric discourse, the flow and
organization of his work, and the esthetical arrangement of the genres he
employed. As Olivia Rosenthal notes, "Le discours lyrique, chez Desportes,
se fonde aussi sur la variation des formes, variation qui débouche sur ce
qu'on pourrait appeler une politique des genres." (Desportes's lyric discourse is based also on the variation of forms, variation that leads to genres'
politics.)[76] For Desportes, as for many other Renaissance poets, genre was a
major factor not only in the fertile process of composition itself, but also in
the process of creating and uniting an *œuvre* and its presentation to its readership and patrons. Early-modern editors, too, were fully invested in the
arrangement and ordering of the many forms that would compose a volume for obvious marketable reasons. When looking at the "table des mat-
ières" in many editions of Desportes's *Premières Œuvres*,[77] we can observe
that he cleverly alternated a wide variety of forms in various combinations
over forty-two years, suggesting that he was notably concerned with poetic
genres and paid particular attention not only to the order of sonnets, a
genre for which he is well known, but to the order of other forms as well.
And despite the fact that all sonnets written after 1573 can be linked to
Desportes, as Max Jasinski notes,[78] remarkably, out of 600 of Desportes's
poems, only half are sonnets—the rest are odes, *chansons*, *complaintes*,
stances, dialogues, *discours*, epitaphs, elegies, and even *Rymes tierces*, the
French equivalent of the *terza rima*. Desportes was indeed one of the few
French poets who used the *terza rima*.[79] *Les Amours de Diane* contains two

poems titled "Rymes Tierces," and elsewhere we find a total of thirty-three tercets in *terza rima*, suggesting that he was well versed in this meter.[80]

Desportes's own copy of Nocturno Napolitano's *Opera Amorosa*,[81] published in 1521 (Figure 6), serves as a useful example in demonstrating his keen attention to Italian genres and the ways in which he adopted and transformed them. This volume, currently housed at the Bibliothèque nationale in Paris (Y 1166) contains Desportes's signature on its title page,[82] as well as his annotated words and passages, underlinings, and marks that demonstrate that Desportes was particularly enticed by both a variety of images, ideas, words, and expressions about love and its pangs, and by the diversity and possibilities that Italian lyric forms afforded. Nocturno's *canzoniere* comprises five different ones: thirty-nine *strambotti*, one *capitolo*, one epistle, four sonnets, and a *disperata*, offering a sound balance between short and long poetic forms. Because these are clearly identified and highlighted on the volume's title page, it is evident that they were an important element in the conception, design, presentation, and reception of a sixteenth-century *canzoniere*.[83] Indeed, from the very first page the reader is made aware of the variety the volume offers as a demonstration of Nocturno's dexterity and creativity in the plethora of forms and their lyric possibilities.[84] I am also suggesting that this title page becomes a written promise meant to define the volume's *horizon d'attente*, in which the favored form is the *strambotto*, with thirty-eight placed at the beginning of the *canzoniere* and one placed at the very end as its solid culmination.[85] There are also four sonnets,[86] and in between, three different long, narrative forms: an *epistola ad amicam*, a *capitolo ad amicam*, and a *disperata*. Hence, since the *disperata* is not only listed separately from the *capitolo*, but also has a prominent space on the page with the caption "Et una disperata," we have clear evidence of its reputation in both Italy and France. Nocturno's *canzoniere* was largely inscribed in this tradition, while at the same time it fully acknowledged its literary debt to Petrarchism. This particular edition, as Desportes's signature attests, is also a fine example of what the French Renaissance poets were reading and using as a source of inspiration.

As has been stated before, *capitoli* especially, and *disperate* in smaller number, were well represented in the single-authored *canzonieri*, as well as in the anthologies that circulated in France.[87] Vianey suggests that the French poets, and Desportes in particular, wrote elegies in imitation of the long genres found in the editions of the Quattrocento and Cinquecento: "les longues élégies en rime tierces intitulées capitoli ou disperate, occu-

Figure 6. Opera nova amorosa di Nocturno Napolitano.
Ne la quale si contiene Strambotti Sonetti Capitoli Epistole
Et una disperata. Libro primo.
(By permission of the Bibliothèque nationale de France.)

paient presque autant de place que les sonnets." (the long elegies written in *terza rima* titled *capitoli* or *disperate* occupied as much place as the sonnets.)[88] Desportes's intertextualities with these poets have been thoroughly documented, and scholars were able to pinpoint the precise source texts of his poetry.[89]

Let us now turn to Nocturno's *disperata* in which the poet-lover damns the day he was born, the world, all natural elements, and in particular his beloved for all of his misfortunes. His anguish and despair are equal to none, and his hopeless life is doomed to a tragic end. He never finds a promising resolution, rather, in the poem's final verses, the poetic persona calls for the most violent death to end his miserable existence. Although this *disperata* has very unique characteristics, it also follows the genre's main structure and *topoi*. First, each tercet begins with the same anaphora: "Se/Hor/Che," "If previously/Now/Because," as to clearly express the difference in position, attitude, and "stato d'animo" before and after falling in love. Second, the first tercet establishes the pattern for the entire composition:

> Se alzai mia voce mai per trovar pace
> Hor alziola in battaglia cruda e fera
> Che a morte a un tristo piu che vita piace

(If I ever raised my voice to find peace/Now I raise it in harsh and fierce battle/Because death is dearest than life to the unhappy) (vv. 1–3).[90]

As early as the first tercet, the narrator claims that a sad man prefers death to life, thus setting the disconsolate tone of the poem. In the second tercet, the narrator also remarks that "un lieto ama il giardin, misero il bosco," touching on one of the genre's most recurring *topoi*: "a happy man loves the garden, a miserable man loves the woods." Traditionally, the garden is a serene, green, lush, and sunny space, while the woods are dark, secluded, and solitary, and where, as Nocturno explains, a widower turtledove flies over a dead branch ("che un veduo Tortorin vol secco ramo" v. 15). Thus, rather than a serene *locus amoenus*, the speaker is quick to depict an arid and harsh landscape, more likely to welcome the *disperato*.[91] Darkness is preferred to light because the sane man favors light, whereas the ill one prefers the dark, "che luce brama il sano, e oscuro, l'egro" (v. 108). Because life is fear and hate, death becomes an obsession, fervently desired by those who were born in unhappy circumstances, "che morte chiama, chi è mal nato al mondo" (v. 63). Thus, the motif of death as the object of desire continues to emerge in the *canzonieri* of the Cinquecento and will intensify in the verses of the French poets. Hell is portrayed as a coveted place:

> S'io cercai lieto giunger sempre in porto
> Hor lieto cerco giunger ne lo inferno
> Che a' miseri non è poco conforto.
> Se qui pace, o salute, i' non discerno
> Hor son certo che almen lì è n fermo stato
> Che cui vi entra non mor, ma sta in eterno.

(If I used to seek a harbor/Now I am happy to look for hell/ Which is not a small comfort to the miserable souls./If here, peace or health I don't find/Now I am sure that at least I will be in idle state/Because who enters there does not die, but lives in eternity.) (vv. 133–138).

Finally, the narrator pictures himself dead and already buried, with a dramatic epitaph on his tomb:

> Di Noturno e qui il corpo e l'alma in fiamma
> Giace appresso Pluton per donna ingrata
> E se penando ben mai non sfiamma
> Gode che anchor sua fe' vien celebrata.

(Here are Nocturno's body and soul in flames/He lies near Pluto because of his ungrateful lady/And while continuing to suffer in eternal flames/He rejoices, as his faith is still celebrated.) (vv. 142–145).

Although the structure is very ordered and controlled, the *disperata* elements are randomly scattered throughout the text, as death, earthly and eternal pain, despair, and betrayal become binding ingredients. Furthermore, it is in the middle of the poem that the very *raison d'être* of the *disperato* and his cry come alive:

> S'io non feci ad alcun, torto o menzogna
> Hor voglio farlo a tutti, e più a chi me ama
> Che pace, a chi vol guerra, non bisogna.
> S'io cercai laude, precio, honor, e fama
> Hor cerco infamia, vituperio e scorno
> Che un disperato altro, che mal, non brama.

(If I never did anything wrong or said a lie to anybody/Now I want to, and even more so to those who love me/Because those who want war do not need peace./If I used to seek praises, distinction, honor, and fame/Now I seek infamy, invectives, and disgrace/Because a disperato only seeks ills.) (vv. 91–96).

The speaker thereby defines for himself and for his audience what a desperate man wants and seeks, limiting his scope to infamy, vituperation, disgrace, and humiliation, because a desperate man only desires evil. In a strong and persuasive verse, Nocturno effectively provides the very definition of the *disperato*; as the *disperato* dares not wish for hope or happiness, he becomes an exemplar of the genre. Although it does not contain the violence and rage found in other models, Nocturno's poem does not deviate much from the genre's main tone and *topoi*. Undoubtedly, this is also what attracted Desportes because of his own temperate style and mild images.

Furthermore, throughout his poem, and with the repetition of the anaphora "If previously/Now/Because," the speaker describes with great passion his life before he met his ungrateful lady, and his present life, now that he is under her harmful spell. This anaphora pulses at regular intervals, creates a rhythm of despair throughout the text, and builds a crescendo that is accelerated by the alternation of the verb tense between past and present. The ensuing tension is heightened and pushed forward by the *terza rima*, while the anaphora persists from beginning to almost the very end, with the exception of the last five lines, out of 145, at which point the speaker finally gives in and accepts his beloved's cruelty, even if, or maybe precisely because, it sets his body and soul on fire, "Di Nocturno è qui il corpo e l'alma in fiamma."

Let us now turn to the markings Desportes made in his own volume of Nocturno's *disperata* and to the parts of the text that clearly held his attention. The French poet emphasized the first seven verses with a vertical line. He also underlined verse 20, "Hor viver bramo mesto immortal gridi" (I now live amongst immortal cries); marked with a star and a line the following two lines, "Hor tristo giaccio in una oscura cava/Cha ognun che ha contra il ciel, convien tai nidi" (Now I lie sad in an dark cave/Because who is against the sky, prefers these places) (vv. 23–24); and underlined two more verses: "hor lieto corro al fin qual celler pardo/Chel pensar dil ben vecchio e dolor novo" (Now I happily run toward the end/Because I used to think of good things, but now there is new sorrow) (vv. 32–33). I can only speculate that these twelve verses caught Desportes's attention because they are intense and filled with captivating images, but also with characteristic *disperata topoi*: a death wish, lying in sadness in a dark grotto, and a morbid attraction toward death.

A similar beginning can be found in the first three verses of one of
Desportes's *stances* in *Les Amours d'Hippolyte*:

> Si je languy d'un martyre incognu
> Si mon desir, jadis tant retenu,
> Ores sans brides à son gré me transporte

(If I suffer of an unknown martyrdom/If my desire thus far has
been contained,/Now it transports me without restraint) (vv. 1–3,
341).[92]

The anaphora "If I/If/Now" is suggestive of Nocturno's verses and captures thoroughly the meaning of his first tercet in representing the *amant
martyr*'s pangs: an anguish that can no longer be tamed and a physical
desire that consumes his every thought and action. Ultimately, the poet-
persona is overwhelmed and transported by his martyrdom. Furthermore,
the fourth verse of the *stance*: "Me doy-je plaindre ainsi comme je fais?"
(Must I complain as I do?) creatively and skillfully employs one of the
foremost motives of the *disperata*, that is to complain about life's and
Love's adversity, and lament one's misery in detail and at length. Thus, in
this *stance*, Desportes borrows the linguistic structures of the *disperata*'s
first tercet, namely the anaphora, as well as its main theme and attitude,
the amorous despair, in which the narrator mourns his unfortunate predicaments, blames the beloved, and seeks a violent death. Moreover, the
emphasis seems to shift right away, after the first three lines, as if to summarize the *disperata* in a powerful, compact verse, "must I complain as I
do?" Indeed, with this fourth line, Desportes seems to linguistically distance the remainder of his text from Nocturno's poem, but he actually
connects it meaningfully to what the *disperata* is all about. In other words,
with a single verse, the French poet encapsulates the *disperata*'s unique
subject matter and redefines it using a very strong and beautiful rhetorical
question: "Me doy-je plaindre ainsi comme je fais?" The answer, of course,
is yes, he has to complain because that is the nature of the poem. It is also
the way in which he communicates love and despair within the very tradition of the Italian *disperata* in which the French poet seeks to insert his
own text.

Some sixteen verses later, at the end of the *stance*, Desportes returns
to the *disperata*'s subject matter and introduces death as a conclusion much
preferred to living with little courage. As mentioned, some of Desportes's
underlining and marks in Nocturno's text emphasize verses that deal with

death and its bountiful, hopeful relief from suffering and from life itself, as echoed in his own lines: "Cherchon la mort, plustost qu'en nous cachant/ Vivre, et monstrer qu'ayons peu de courage." (Let's seek out death, rather than hide/Living, and showing that we have little courage.) (vv. 23–24, 342)

Hence, although the French poet moves away from the *disperata* as early as the fifth verse, he starts and ends his *stance* by coming back to it. I want to emphasize that in his borrowing and interpretation of the *disperata*, Desportes refused to play by its rules and conventions, nor did he use its traditional form and meter. Instead, he borrowed what appealed to him the most: its essence and main ideas, such an active pursuit of death; its attitude; a paramount anaphora; its content; and the formal, narrative nature of the poem that can be easily transferred into a *stance*, which is also a narrative genre. He preferred to exercise and translate his *dispositio* skills in a genre at which he excelled: the *stance*. After all, this form also had its origins in Italy and was quickly and widely circulated by the Italian anthologies.[93] Desportes was one of the first French poets to use this emergent genre, and he did so abundantly throughout his published work.[94] Vianey notes that "sous le règne de Desportes un des spectacles auquel on assiste est celui de voir nos poètes faisant des stances, parce que les Italiens en font [...] mais essayant d'avoir une stance française." (under Desportes's reign, we can witness our poets composing *stances*, because the Italians write them [...] but trying to compose a French *stance*."[95] His imitation and adaptation of the Italian *strambotto*, or octave, also influenced his use of the *stance*, to the point that, by the end of the century, French poems formed by different lengths of stanzas, four to six *alexandrins*, are called *stances* as well.[96] Furthermore, the choice of the *stance* as a lyric form better reflects a grave and passionate tone, which in turn fits well in the *disperata*.[97]

Finally, the *stance* allowed Desportes's readers to notice and appreciate how he differentiated himself from Nocturno's *disperata* and produced a distinct poem instead.[98] Moreover, by simply addressing its content, Desportes was able to engage it meaningfully and initiate a direct intertextual dialogue, rather than quarrel with its strict original form and exceptionally rigorous components. If, as Mathieu-Castellani eloquently explains, genres are sort of "relays" that allow one work to be in relation with other works,[99] then Desportes wrote a *stance* that undoubtedly constitutes a solid relay for future French *stances*, such as those written by d'Aubigné, only few years later, in which the *disperata* makes a grand reappearance.

Théodore Agrippa d'Aubigné's *Stances*

Théodore Agrippa d'Aubigné (1552–1630) was a Huguenot poet who also frequented the court, mainly between 1573 and 1576, when he became the squire of Henri de Navarre, the future King Henri IV.[100] In his autobiographical work *Sa Vie à ses enfants*, d'Aubigné wrote much about his youth, his education as a Protestant, and the tragic events he witnessed and experienced.[101] His mother's death, which occurred while giving birth to him, inspired his name, Agrippa, from the Latin *aegre partus*, which became a metaphor for the bitterness he often encountered in a Catholic France. While traveling with his father, who died when the poet was eleven, they saw the impaled heads of the Huguenot leaders at Amboise.[102] D'Aubigné himself survived many battles and escaped the Saint Bartholomew's Day Massacre in 1572. He lived an existence of ruptures and traumas that feverishly haunt his verses. His poetry becomes the site of war, of its representation and the impossible quest to survive it. Although Petrarchan language and images are present throughout his lyric poetry, and Ronsard's texts constitute a strong intertextual model, d'Aubigné forges a language and images that are unprecedented in both their intensity and violence.[103] Furthermore, though masked by love lyric, his poetry expresses extensive grief and vigor. The many facets of despair in d'Aubigné's *canzoniere* are fashioned by a fragmented spirit, instability, sacrifice, broken promises, breaches in relationships, hopelessness, darkness, violence, blood, wounds, and last but not least, an accumulation of body parts. Hence, more than any other sixteenth-century French poet, d'Aubigné refashioned and spread the poetry of the *disperata*, adding his furor and anger, but also his human vulnerability and sorrows. In his verses, his contemporaries could find their struggles. As Jean-Raymond Fanlo notes, d'Aubigné's writings "affirment la transparence du texte aux événements ou à l'émotion." (state the text's transparency toward events or emotions.)[104] Indeed, despite its dark intensity, d'Aubigné's poetry presents the reader with unprecedented honesty and clarity.

　　Although I will mostly discuss d'Aubigné's *canzoniere, Le Printemps*, which comprises *L'Hécatombe à Diane*'s one hundred sonnets, and his fifty-two *Stances et Odes*, his work also includes *Les Tragiques* (1616), *Histoire Universelle* (1619–26), and *Sa vie à ses enfants* (1630).[105] History, whether personal or collective, informed his thought and work. Indeed, d'Aubigné was appointed the official historian of the Huguenot cause in 1603 by the Synod of Gap.[106] His poetry, like his life, is mostly preoccupied with Love and war, for which the poet crafts varied and beautiful metaphors. As he boldly claims: "J'accorderois bien ma lire/À la guerre et à l'amour" (Ode XIII, vv. 77–78, 99),[107] unequivocally pledging his dual commitment to war and to Love which, in his work, go hand in hand.

In the introduction to d'Aubigné's *canzoniere Le Printemps*, Bernard Gagnebin suggests that *Le Printemps* is Agrippa d'Aubigné's youth, while winter is the song of his old age : "*Le Printemps*, qui aurait dû être le poème de l'amour, s'achève en poème de la douleur et de la déception." (*Le Printemps*, which should have been a love poem, ends as a poem of pain and disappointment)[108] In fact, the title itself immediately destabilizes the lyric tradition, as the spring in this instance is not a season to rejoice, a time of youth and love, of rebirth, hope, and *reverdir*. Rather, it is a season of despair, of multiple endings, of martyrdom and death, just like what we read at the beginning of il Pistoia's *disperata*, "La nuda terra s'ha gia messo il manto" (243). Furthermore, d'Aubigné's poetry too blends Petrarch's lyric tradition with multiple memorials to persecution and anger, as his many representations of violence and brutal images demonstrate.[109] Starting in his "Préface" to *L'Hécatombe*, he warns his readers with the following verses:

> Tu (mon livre) es du fons des orages,
> Des guerres et des voiages
> Avorté avant les jours,
> D'une ame plaine d'angoisse

(You, my book, come from deep within the storms,/From wars and trips/Aborted before time,/From a soul filled with anguish) (vv. 43–46, 4–5).

The poet explains where and how the book was conceived, or rather, aborted, with unapologetically direct terms. *Le Printemps' poesis* is infused with harsh realism in order to traumatize the audience and to demand its complete attention so as to evoke the deepest and darkest emotions and fears. As Mathieu-Castellani has justifiably remarked: "Lire Aubigné, c'est d'abord recevoir un choc." (To read Aubigné is at first to receive a shock.)[110]

Let us look now at how the poetry of *Le Printemps*, love poetry by all intents, is speckled with *disperata topoi* and language. From the beginning, the reader is confronted with an unbearable reality that is so genuine, and hence extremely destabilizing, as in the first *stance*:

> Tous ceulx qui ont gousté combien de morts on treuve
> Couvertes soubz les fleurs d'une longue amitié,

> Ceux qui en bien aimant ont bien seu faire preuve
> De leurs cueurs et non pas d'un regard de pitié,
> Ceulx qui affriandoient comme moy leurs pensées
> D'un poison ensucré, loyer de leur printemps,
> Qu'ils lisent mes regrets et mes larmes vercées,
> Et mes sanglots perdus aux pertes de mon temps.

(All of those who have tasted how many deaths can be found/Covered under the flowers of a long friendship,/Those who, by loving well, have fully proven/Their heart's worth and not their regard of pity,/Those who like me sugarcoated their thoughts/with sweet poison, their springtime pursuit/That they read my regrets and my spilled tears,/And my sobs lost to the losses of my time.) (Stance I, vv. 1–8, 3).[111]

As a warning, we are advised to doubt the many fatalities camouflaged by friendship and Love. Thus, it should be obvious to the attentive reader that this poetry is not about Love, at least not of the happy kind; rather it is poetry about deception and heartbreak that fully involves the audience. The very first verses of the collection are only meant as a warning for those who have greatly suffered. Indeed, if one has not fallen in and for love, if one has instead wisely resisted Love's assaults, then, the speaker warns, they are forbidden to read his poetry, his anger and cries: "je leur deffends mes vers, mes rages et mes cris" (Stance I, v. 12, 3). His words, he continues, are restricted to those who suffer and have suffered, as they alone understand and believe "l'aigreur de mes maulz" (Stance I, v. 16, 3). In the *disperata* poetry, the reader has to see and believe what the poetic persona feels and voices. Furthermore, the lover-persona wishes to spend the rest of his days crying and suffering, "Faisons un dur combat et noïons en nos larmes/Le reste de nos jours en ces sauvages lieux" (Stance I, vv. 23–24, 4).

More than any other French author, d'Aubigné's sense of space matches the *disperata's*. The landscape that fuels his verses closely echoes the genre's "luoghi deserti e solitari," a *topos* that recurs often in his poetry and that becomes the *locus amoneus par excellence*: "Ces rochés egarés, ces fontaines suivies/Par l'echo des foretz respondront à nos voix" (These lost rocks, these fountains followed/By the echo of the woods will respond to our voices) (Stance I, vv. 27–28, 4), because it is the beloved who confined him to these sites: "Celle qui confina mes regretz en ces lieux" (Stance I, v. 66, 5). And again,

> Je cherche les desertz, les roches egairées,
> Les foretz sans chemin, les chesnes perissans,

Mais je hay les forestz de leur feuilles parées,
Les sejours frequentez, les chemins blanchissans.

(I seek the deserts, the lost rocks,/The woods without paths, the
dying oaks,/But I hate the woods paraded with their leaves,/The
crowded places, the white paths.) (Stance I, vv. 93–96, 6).

D'Aubigné's odes also portray the signature *disperata* scenery: "A ce bois,
ces pretz et cest antre/Offrons les jeux, les pleurs, les sons" (To these
woods, these meadows and this cavern/Let's offer the games, cries, and
sounds) (Ode XX, vv. 1–2, 121).

In his introduction to *Le Printemps*, Weber provides a subtle analysis of d'Aubigné's first *stance* and its similarities with Serafino's "Disperata
Terza." However, as I have previously shown, this is really il Pistoia's *disperata* "La nuda terra s'ha già messo il manto," problematically attributed
to Serafino. It has already been noted how this *disperata* came to be known
and circulated as "The disperata"—the one—as a prototype of its genre
because of its comprehensive list of *topoi* and popularity. One of the collections in which this text appears is housed at the Bibliothèque nationale
in Paris and it is titled: "La Disperata (di Serafino dell'Aquila)" (1526),
further creating confusion.[112] One can see also that thanks to Serafino's
greater fame and popularity in both Italy and France, and because of his
use of the genre, it would have been easy to accredit him this text. Also,
one wonders if the resemblance between Serafino's last name, Ciminelli,
and that of il Pistoia, Cammelli, contributed to this confusion and misattribution.[113] Finally, as an important testament to court culture, it particularly resonated with the French writers as well because of Serafino's popularity as court poet.[114]

Despite the mistaken attribution, Weber's analysis of d'Aubigné's
first *stance* is key to acknowledging the importance of the *disperata*'s intertextuality not only with d'Aubigné's verses, but also with other French
texts. Weber notes that the main elements of d'Aubigné's first *stance* belong
to the Italian *disperata*: "La recherche d'un décor sauvage et sinistre, le désir
de voir tout s'assombrir, se corrompre et mourir autour de soi." (The search
for a savage and sinister decor, the desire to see everything darkening, spoil-
ing and dying around oneself.)[115] Stephen Murphy's analysis of the myth of
Diane and the *disperata* is compelling as well, as it emphasizes the genre's
main elements in d'Aubigné's *stances*.[116] Moreover, d'Aubigné not only
adopts these vital elements, but he also captures the very essence, spirit,
and attitudes of the *disperato*. He gathers much tension, suggests a mul-

titude of dark thoughts, and expresses unbearable raw emotions, thereby creating a direct intertextuality with the Italian texts. If we recall the categories from the previous chapters, we see that d'Aubigné's first *stance* is a true *disperata*, and perhaps the only accomplished and comprehensive example written by a French author. All of the genre's elements and traits are concentrated here and pushed to an extreme, in which visceral and painful images, fierce maledictions, untamed hopes, and apocalyptic scenarios come together and bleakly burst out. Hence, his verses take the relay from the *disperata*. The realism, brutality, and authenticity of his poems remind us of the Italian texts from the previous chapters. Furthermore, what he celebrates the most—pain, persecution, lost love, war, blood, rage, and mistrust—is also present in most *disperate* which provide the perfect plethora of images, *topoi*, and attitudes that help the rejected lover to voice, or rather *scream*, his pain and rejection in excruciating detail, despite using Petrarchan language, well familiar to the precious milieus of the French court in which d'Aubigné was expected to participate.

In other poems of despair, the speaker first seeks the listener's full attention and sympathy; his words become a call for action on behalf of all dejected lovers:

> Sus! Tristes amoureux, recourons à nos armes
> Pour n'en blesser aucun que nos seins malheureux,
> Faisons un dur combat et noïons en nos larmes
> Le reste de nos jours en ces sauvages lieux.

(Shush! Sad lovers, let's take up our arms/In order to injure only our miserable chests,/Let's fight hard and let's drown in our tears/The rest of our days in these wild places.) (Stance I, vv. 21–24, 4).

As in the *disperata*, here too the lover-persona does not want to hurt anybody except himself. Violence against the self is indeed a *sine qua non* and a crucial attitude. As a rejected, humiliated lover, just like the *disperato*, d'Aubigné, "Pressé de desespoir" (Stance VIII, v 1, 25), is condemned because of his religious affiliation. First, he is isolated from his motherland, France, because of his protestant beliefs,[117] and second, by his fiancée Diane, whose uncle broke their engagement "sur le différent de la religion."[118] Fundamentally, his religious beliefs chastened him in at least two ways: in love and in society. Moreover, this double separation and personal loss became a malediction that directly impacted his life and set him apart. So, too, with the *disperato*, who cries "solo io" "only I," he stands alone and cannot be part of any joyous experience.

The engaging interlocking of d'Aubigné's personal history—that of a militant Protestant living at court, with the great literary and cultural traditions of *The Bible*, Seneca's tragedies,[119] Petrarch and the Italian and French Petrarchists, and the *disperata*, produced highly dramatic lyric compositions. However, when focusing on the *disperata*'s presence in particular, his *stances* brim with an underlying anguish that he so poetically calls my evils' acerbity ("l'aigreur de mes maulx", Stance I, v 16, 3). Furthermore, it is not only the "décor sauvage" that moves the poetry of the *disperata*, it is also its general and deep sense of despair, expressed in realistic, morose terms. Despair for d'Aubigné becomes an obsession, a *raison d'être*:

> Aux plus subtilz demons des regions hautaynes,
> Je presteray mon cors pour leur faire vestir,
> Pasle, deffiguré, vray miroer de mes peines;
> En songe, en visions, ilz lui feront sentir
> Proche son ennemy, dont la face meurtrie
> Demande sang pour sang, et vie pour la vie.

(To the most skilled demons of the highest regions,/I will lend my body to cover them,/Pale, disfigured, true mirror of my anguish;/In dreams, in visions, they will make it feel/Its enemy nearby, whose wounded face/Demands blood for blood, and a life for a life.) (Stance IV, vv. 73–78, 19).

Over and over the narrator returns to his despair, never stepping away too far, despite his many wanderings:

> Pleurez, o rochers, mes douleurs
> De vos argentines fonteines
> Pour moy qui souffre plus de peines
> Que je ne puis trouver de pleurs,
> Pour moi douloureux qui ne puis
> Plorer aultant que j'ay d'ennuis!

(Cry, oh rocks, for my pangs/With your silvery fountains/For me who suffers more sorrows/Than I can find tears,/For me, distressed, who cannot/Cry for all of my sorrows!) (Stance XII, vv. 25–30, 34).

While following the speaker in a constant search for solitary and deserted places, we see that he struggles to find peace and a reprieve from his anguish. His despair never leaves him, as he carries it within himself: "Je fuis contre la source et veulx par mon absence/De moy mesme fuyr, de moy

mesme laissé" (I run away from the source, and I want with my absence/
To run away from myself, so tired of myself) (Stance III, vv. 59–60, 14).
D'Aubigné is persecuted by his despair, but at the same time, despair nour-
ishes his creation, as does all *disperata* poetry. In fact, in his first *stance*'s
204 verses, it is almost as if despair and furor come together to take over
the page and then induce a palpable discomfort into the reader, so that the
speaker and his audience are sunk in a universe engulfed in distress:

> Le lieu de mon repos est une chambre peinte
> De mil os blanchissans et de testes de mortz
> Où ma joie est plus tost de son object esteinte :
> Un oubly gratieux ne la poulce dehors.
> ...
> Dans le cors de la mort j'ai enfermé ma vie
> Et ma beauté paroist horrible dans les os.
> Voylà commant ma joye est de regret suivie,
> Commant de mon travail la mort seulle a repos.

(My resting place is a room painted/In a thousand white bones and
skulls/Where my joy is soon extinguished by its object:/A gracious
oblivion does not push it out./ ... /In death's body I enclosed my
life/And my beauty seems horrible among the bones./Here's how
my joy is followed by regret,/How death only rests in my work.)
(Stance I, vv. 49–64, 5).

Hell is also the lover-persona's comforting setting, and often he wanders
in there:

> errant par les brisées
> Des Enfers esgairez et les Champs Elizées
> Rien ne regretteroit (Stance XVI, vv. 31–33, 42).

Moreover, blood and body go hand in hand in d'Aubigné's poetry, and this
aspect moves it closer to the *disperata*, such as the one written by Carretto,
"Canzone facta per il predecto. Disperata."[120] Here too the poetic persona uses a very visceral language and portrays the body as the site of
anguish, often characterized by bloody images. To stress the importance of
"trumpeting" the truth and illustrating the many humiliations and aches
inflicted on the poet by the beloved become an essential part of Carretto's
poem as well:

> Esci fuor voce, et con tua tromba spacha
> La terra, el fuoco, l'aria, l'acqua e sassi,
> Et con lamente a' lati, al ciel tè attacha.
>   (vv. 1–3, 42).[121]

Carretto's *disperata*, thus, starts with a cry that has to come out ("Esci fuor voce"), accompanied by a tongue that splits ("spacha") everything it finds: the earth, fire, air, water and rocks, the usual accumulation of natural elements. It proclaims the truth ("el ver"), because, although all hells are fierce, nothing compares to Love's hell.

Another distinct component that can be found in d'Aubigné's *Le Printemps* is Carretto's use of corporeal and realistic themes and images, something that belongs to the genre but that is particularly manifest and powerful in this *disperata*. The torn, bleeding body takes center stage and, once again, causes great discomfort to the reader. In d'Aubigné's Stance XVII, for example, the body is destroyed, the spirit is then haunted by the body, and the corporeal and spiritual mesh in a perfect, albeit tormented symmetry:

> Le cors vaincu se rend, et lassé de souffrir
> Ouvre au dart de la mort sa tremblante poitrine,
> Estallant sus un lit ses miserables os,
> Et l'esprit qui ne peult pour endurer mourir,
> Dont le feu viollant jamais ne se termine,
> N'a moien de trouver un lit pour son repos.

(The vanquished body surrenders, and tired of suffering/Opens its trembling chest to death's stinger,/Laying down on the bed its miserable bones,/And the spirit that cannot die in order to endure,/Whose violent fire never ends,/Cannot find a bed to lay down and rest.) (Stance VII, vv. 7–12, 23).[122]

Here is Carretto's *disperata*:

> L'acerbo sdegno e 'l dolo interno ch'io
> Portato ó già gran tempo in pecto chiuso,
> Scoppiar conviemmi con stil acro e rio.
> Et per piú dire il mio martir diffuso,
> Dico ch'amor spietato aspro et protervo
> Fu quel ch'à nel petto questo infuso.

(The bitter disdain and the internal pain that I/Have carried in my closed chest for a while,/Better burst out with sharp and adverse style./And in order to tell of my great martyrdom,/I declare that cruel, harsh and arrogant love/Was the cause of what I carry in my chest.) (vv. 10–15, 42).

A similar image is deployed, although treated in different terms by d'Aubigné. The chest ("pecto" in Italian, "poitrine" in French) is the site of immeasurable pain, a receptacle that is agonizingly closed for Carretto and opened up by death in d'Aubigné. Each poet describes an unimaginable agony, both physical, "il dolo interno" and "sa tremblante poitrine," and spiritual, "il mio martir diffuso/ ... amor spietato aspro et protervo" and "Et l'esprit qui ne peult pour endurer mourir,/ ... N'a moien de trouver un lit pour son repos." We encounter this image again in Stance XVII: "Et son esprit venteur repeu de son dommage/Estalle un estommac gravé de mille coups" (vv. 7–8, 44).[123] The body is thus mutilated, charred, petrified, and yet still alive in order to withstand more torture and trials. We find the same brutal images in il Saviozzo's *disperate*, where the narrator's body is infected, "il corpo infetto" (v. 1, 69). A very compelling metaphor is fashioned, and it is one that moves from the Italian to the French text in order to portray the *disperato's* psychological and spiritual degradation, wherein the dreadful condition of the body has become a given.

Fire is another element that often invades d'Aubigné's verses, consuming all that surrounds the poetic persona:[124]

> Tu me brusle et au four de ma flame meurtriere
> Tu chauffes ta froideur : tes delicates mains
> Atizent mon brazier et tes yeux inhumains
> Pleurent, non de pitié, mais flambantz de cholere

(You burn me and in the ardor of my murderous flame/You warm up your coldness: your delicate hands/Kindle my flame and your inhuman eyes/Cry, not because of pity, but flaming with rage) (Stance VI, vv. 9–12, 22).

Desire and deprivation burn the body, "Bruslant le cueur, le cors, hostie à ton courroux" (Stance VI, v 18, 22), and yet never hurt nor kill.[125] On the contrary, they often envelop the poetic persona in a calming embrace; as fire does no harm to fire, neither does it make an already tormented state worse:

> Je suis l'Ethna bruslant en ma flamme profonde
> Tu es le Nil heureux qui espanche ton unde
> Sur la terre qui meurt de la soif de tes eaux ;
> Noie les feuz, mignonne, embrazeurs de mon ame,
> Ou me laisse brusler ton Nil dedans ma flamme,
> Que je noye en tes pleurs, ou seche en mes flambeaux.

(I am Etna burning in my deep flames/You are the joyful Nile that pours your wave/Over the earth that dies thirsting for your waters;/

Drown the fire, my lovely, that sets my soul on fire,/Or let me burn
your Nile inside my flame,/So that I may drown in your tears, or dry
up in my fire.) (Stance XVIII, vv. 97–102, 57).

Although fire is a recurring metaphor and fuels many verses in Petrarch's
and his followers' poetry, d'Aubigné's depictions are invigorated and more
tragic, just like we encounter in Feliciano's *disperata*. Here too, the speaker
evokes Mount Etna, whose eruptions nobody is able to tame. Flames
and water, in the form of tears, engulf him as well. He addresses his song
directly, "Maledetta canzon da Dio e da Santi" (v. 271, 191). It is a *disperata* damned by God and by the saints, written and consumed by the volcano, and again, its own tears cannot put out its own fire because both fire
and tears provide a welcomed release to the speaker. His "damned" song
carries his voice and personifies him, and he is condemned to cry forever:

> Maledetta canzon da Dio e da Santi,
>
> ...
>
> nel scoglio fluctuante sopra i lidi
> di Ethna, ch'al gran foco ognor si avampi,
> e negli averni ombrosi campi;
>
> ...
>
> in questi luoghi oscuri,
> non voglio ch'el tuo canto mai si tempre,
> ma che tu piangi, piangi, sempre, sempre.

(Song damned by God and by the Saints,/ ... /on the floating cliff
above the shores/of Etna, where a great fire always burns/and lives
in the shady avernus;/ ... /in these dark places,/I don't want your
singing to soften,/But you must cry, cry, forever and ever.) (vv. 279–
300, 191–192).

Let us now return to d'Aubigné's poem, where the speaker himself personifies Mount Etna; he has become the volcano burning in its own fire,
and his beloved, embodied by the great river Nile, is asked to extinguish
the fire with an imposing imperative: "Noie les feuz, mignonne." Again,
d'Aubigné's verses adopt the *disperata*, but adapt it by pushing the inherent despair and wretchedness to a never ending existential crisis that,
just like fire, burns the poet-persona eternally or, just like water, dries his
flames, creating a very poetic, albeit bleak ending to his *stance*. Although
both Feliciano and d'Aubigné used an antithesis that occurs quite often
in Petrarch and his followers, both poets added a tragic masochism and
challenging attitude: Feliciano's persona wants his song to go on and cry

forever, and d'Aubigné's prefers to continue to suffer, whether by burning or drowning.

Death is omnipresent in *Le Printemps*, and its narrator is never afraid to die, as in the following sonnet in which a tragic passing is preferred to despair and damnation. Here too, the *disperata* is a powerful intertext:

> Si ceux là sont damnez qui, privez d'esperance,
> Sur leur acier sanglant vaincus se laissent choir,
> Si c'est damnation tomber en desespoir,
> Si s'enferrer soy mesme est une impatience,
> N'est-ce pas se damner contre sa conscience,
> Avoir soif de poison, fonder tout son espoir
> Sur un sable mouvant? hé! Où peut-il avoir
> Pire damnation, ny plus aigre sentence?
> Un mesprisé peut-il craindre son dernier jour?
> ...
> Je meurs pour avoir mieux,
> Puis que de deux malheurs il faut choisir le moindre.

(If those, who, deprived of hope, are damned,/Defeated, they let themselves fall on their bloody sword,/If it is damnation to fall in despair,/If to transfix yourself is eagerness,/Is it not to be damned against one's conscience,/To crave poison, and build all of one's hopes/On quicksand!/Ha! Where can there be/A worst damnation, or a more bitter sentence?/Can a despised man fear his last day?/ ... /I die to have better,/Since of the two evils I must choose the lesser.) (*L'Hécatombe* LXI, 82).

All of hell's fire is better than unjust love, and death is preferable.[126] The first quatrain is of particular interest to our discussion. It is almost as if the poet was directly addressing the *disperata* speaker:

> *ceux là* sont damnez qui, privez d'esperance,
> ...
> si c'est damnation tomber en desespoir (emphasis mine).

The "if" has a rhetorical limitation, both because the speaker is damned and also because the poet, too, is desperate and deprived of all hope. It is almost as if he already knew the *disperato* intimately, understood his desperation, and shared in his constant state of damnation because he is one himself. The first verse's "sceux là" designate the Italian *disperati*, those who are damned and who damn, who are deprived of hope, and thus are *désespérés*, and who fall into despair because they are indeed condemned. Il Saviozzo's verse "poiche fuor di speranza io son condutto" (v. 55. 70), which literally translates to "since I am forced out of all hope" is a recurring *topos* in the Italian *disperata* and an integral part of the definition of its speaker. Furthermore, just like in Desportes's *stance*, d'Aubigné provides the genre's definition in the very first quatrain of this sonnet. The *disperata* supplied d'Aubigné with additional language and images that allowed him to better express his obsessive despair since the Petrarchan and French Renaissance traditions were no longer sufficient to re-enact the traumas that plagued his life and community.

D'Aubigné's obsession turns into suicidal thoughts, just as with the *disperata* speaker. These thoughts often recur in his work, where suicide is a welcomed, albeit violent act that brings an end to all suffering, as in this final stanza:

> Frape doncq', il est temps, ma dextre, que tu face
> Flotter mon sang fumeux, bouillonnant par la place,
> Soubz le cors roidissant.
> Haste toy, douce mort, fin d'un'amere vie,
> Fay' ce meurtre, l'esprit, ma rage te convie
> Aux umbres fremissant.

(Strike then, it is time, my right hand, so that you cause/My smoldering blood to float, foaming all over,/under my blushing body./ Hurry up, sweet death, end of a bitter life,/Finish this murder, the spirit, my rage invites you/To the trembling shadows.) ("Stance XVI," vv. 55–60, 43).

As seen in previous chapters, the *disperata* portrays many instances of suicide. Il Saviozzo, for example, refers to ending his life in very chilling terms and tone: "ché quanto me medesmo abbia schernito/del ben che 'nfino a qui Dio m'ha prestato" (that which I myself have mocked/the good that God has lent me until now) (vv. 75–76, 75). The double "me medesmo" echoes in the French "ma dextre/mon sang," as both poets stress the personal nature of suicide, over which they have full control, as well as of their existential tragedy over which, on the contrary, they do not. Thus, the only solution is to deliberately cause one's own death.

Darkness is also part of the *disperato*'s realm and existence. His thoughts, his present, and his future are dark and disconsolate. In the following verses, the subjunctive resonates the *disperata*'s many "vorrei."

> Que du blond Apollon le rayon doré n'entre
> En ma grotte sans jour, que jamais de son euil

> Nul planete ne jette un rayon dans mon antre,
> Sinon Saturne seul pour incliner mon deuil.

(The blond Apollo's golden ray may not enter/My dark cave,/And no planet may throw a ray in my grotto,/Only Saturn can in order to give way to my morning.) (Stance I, vv. 201–204, 10).[127]

Tebaldeo's "Disperata seconda" contains about twenty-five anaphoras with the verb "want". Here, we find not only the conditional "vorrei," but also the desire to unleash a dark scenario in which men are under sinister and threatening skies, and crippled with fear, they try to find refuge in dark grottoes:

> Vore'veder li cieli inimicarsi,
> Da fulgur', toni e saete percossi,
> A terra ruinar disfati e arsi.

(I want to see the skies all upset,/By lightnening, thunder and bolts,/And strike the earth undone and scorched.)[128]

Eurialo Morani, too, claims: "Et voglio fabricar, solo in un bosco,/Un antro che m'assembri, oscuro e fosco" (And I want to build, alone, in a forest,/A grotto that embraces me, dark and sinister). (vv. 7–8, 59).

Images that portray a world upside down often recur in the *disperata*, and become another element that d'Aubigné borrows, not only in his love lyric, but also in his *Tragiques*.[129] Since d'Aubigné's love is always without hope: "Amour qui n'est qu'amour, qui vit sans esperance" (Stance XXI, v. 1, 69), the beloved is portrayed as a sadistic predator, thirsty for the *disperato*'s blood. This theme is very common to the *disperata* as well, for example, Carretto's lady is also a cruel warrior and an insatiable beast, "un aspra mia crudel guerriera" (v. 17, 42).[130] Not only is the beloved a warrior, just like d'Aubigné's Diane, she also physically tortures the poet-persona. She is portrayed as an insatiable animal, as perpetually bloodthirsty, and sadistically boasting of his dead, beaten body. D'Aubigné describes his beloved Diane as a destructive sadist as well, whose only pleasure is to see her lover's complete, subjugated suffering:

> Diane, ta costume est de tout deschirer,
> Emflammer, desbriser, ruiner, mettre en pieces,
> Entreprinses, desseins, esperances, finesses,
> Changeant en desespoir ce qui fait esperer.

(Diane, your custom is to tear everything apart,/Burn, fragment, ruin and shatter,/Plans, intentions, hopes, delicacies,/

Changing into despair that which gives hope.) (*L'Hécatombe*, vv. 1–4, 111).

Diane beats him and only wants to see him suffer: "Et n'as autre plaisir qu'à me faire endurer." (*L'Hécatombe*, v. 8, 111).

Throughout *Le Printemps*, Diane is portrayed as the beloved in the *disperata*: the worst enemy, a blood-thirsty beast, "sanguynaire" (Stance XIV, v. 7, 37), and the cause of all evils and pain:

> Vostre presence me devore,
> Et vostre absence m'est encore
> Cent fois plus fascheuse à souffrir

> (Your presence devours me,/And your absence is even/A hundred times harder to endure) (Stance X, vv. 43–45, 29).

The speaker also accuses her of having ruined his life. The theme of martyrdom, both in love as *l'amant martyr* and in religion as *le martyr huguenot*, remains one of the main *topoi* of d'Aubigné's poetry. As a double, painful deception in love and religion, two important identities of late sixteenth-century France, this trumped love cannot be given up. Indeed, "pressé de desespoir" (Stance VIII, v. 1, 25), d'Aubigné demands that his beloved herself open up his chest, take his heart in her hands, and end his martyrdom, once and for all:

> Belle, pour estancher les flambeaux de ton yre
> Prens ce fer en tes mains pour m'en ouvrir le sein,
> Puis mon cueur haletant hors de son lieu retire,
> Et le pressans tout chault, estouffe en l'autre main
> Sa vie et son martire.

> (My lady, to satisfy the flames of your rage/Take this sword in your hands and open up my chest,/Then, take my gasping heart out of its place,/And squeezing it all warm, suffocate in your other hand/Its life and its martyrdom.) (Stance VIII, vv. 6–10, 25).

The beloved is also compared to the *disperata*'s wild animals, as in Carretto's verse "Costei sichome insatiabil fera" (v. 19, 92), but the French poet pushes this image further, and convincingly accuses her of being crueler than them, and of being,

> Plus cruelle que tout ce que puis nommer,
> Tigres, ours et lions, serpens, monstres estranges:
> Tu ris en me tuant et je meurs pour aimer.

(More cruel than anything I can name,/Tigers, bears and lions, snakes, strange monsters:/You laugh while killing me and I die to love.) (Stance III, vv. 95–100, 15).

The gathering of many of the *disperata*'s elements, such as forests, strange rocks, animals, monsters, and death, converge in this *stance* in order to portray Diane's harshness.[131] With powerful verses that defy tragedy, d'Aubigné claims, "Plus heureux mort que vif" (Stances I, v. 189, 9), and "Dans le cors de la mort j'ai enfermé ma vie" (Stances I, v. 61, 5). Death is more of a reality than life, thus his poetry of life is a poetry of despair. Moreover, his poetry longs to damn and to be damned in a destructive cycle that has no end: "Je maudy mon vouloir, mon desir et mes yeux" (I damn my will, my desire and my eyes) (*L'Hécatombe*, v. 10, 83).[132] The feverish rhythm and concentration of the above elements depict a lady who is not only harsher than anything the lover-persona can enumerate (v. 98), but also harsher than the sum of all of these threatening elements. And unlike Petrarch's speaker, d'Aubigné's is not willing to accept her refusals, therefore he rebels and damns her.

Thus, if in *Le Printemps*' first *stance* we already find many of the *disperata* traits, then throughout his lyric collection we see that d'Aubigné convincingly demonstrates, like other *disperata* poets, that unrequited love is a macrocosmic experience, one whose apocalyptic tragedy haunts the poet just as the Wars of Religion threaten his life.[133] As the above examples show, it is not only the *disperata*'s landscape that we encounter in *Le Printemps*, it is also its deep despair; its wild animals and other emblematic components; Love's malice; the beloved's cruelty; darkness; a perverse mutilation that is both corporeal and spiritual; and a deep existential crisis that calls out for blood, death and suicide.[134] In other words, all is at war, and nature, Love, the elements, the cosmos and the narrator and his beloved are thrown in a vicious spiral damned to eternity. What is most remarkable about d'Aubigné's poetry is that his verses are infused with *disperata topoi*, language, and images, yet, unlike the *disperata* in which the name of the beloved is not divulged, his poetry is entirely devoted to one woman, Diane, just like Petrarch's *Canzoniere* is to Laura, and many of the Petrarchists' beloveds—for example Cariteo's Luna and Scève's Délie—are as well.[135] This again demonstrates d'Aubigné's ability to mesh the literary traditions and compile a noteworthy text in which the poetry of the *disperata* becomes an agent of connection and interconnectivity between the Italian cultural and literary traditions (Dante-Petrarch-Petrarchism-*disperata*) and the French tradition.

As a scholar of history, d'Aubigné dutifully recorded facts not only in his *Tragiques*, but also in his *Sa vie à ses enfants* and his *Histoire Universelle*. However, it is really in his *Printemps* that his personal history as a poet comes alive and intersects with France's history,[136] where his love-torn lyrics are also inspired by the overall violence of the Wars of Religion and civil unrest.[137] Indeed, at the end of the sixteenth century, Love is intimately and cruelly linked to these tragic circumstances. Collective trauma and social despair cannot be separated from personal sufferings, something that d'Aubigné has skillfully and creatively merged in his lyric work where he drew attention to and emphasized the trauma that engulfed his country's life. After all, d'Aubigné and the poets of his generation had only known a France at war and had experienced very few moments of peace. Caught between the Catholic Henri III and the Protestant Henri IV, their courts and their political and cultural influence, these poets dealt with several serious conflicts, experienced war more than peace, and were themselves historians. They also originated from a poorly treated noblesse troubled by both internal and external power struggles.[138] As they wrote history, disguised perhaps by Love's language, they also relived and re-enacted its injustices, as we shall see in more details in the following chapter. Their work still carries the heavy burden of the melancholic and rejected lover's tradition, in which the lover now faces traumatic historical and social challenges. D'Aubigné's response is once again symbolic of his times, and it embraces all of the above hardships:[139]

> Tout cela qui sent l'homme à mourir me convie,
> En ce qui est hideux je cherche mon confort:
> Fuiez de moy, plaisirs, heurs, esperance et vie,
> Venez, maulz et malheurs et desespoir et mort!

(All that fancies a man to die suits me,/I look for comfort in what is hideux:/Flee from me, pleasures, hours, hope, and life,/Come come, evils and misfortune and despair and death!) (Stance I, vv. 89–92, 6).

Obsessed with death and real life's horrific events, the lover-persona wishes for pleasure, time, and hope to flee from him. This wish is in an intimate dialogue with the many "vorrei" of the *disperata*, whose writers also felt the burden of unrequited love, social conflicts, and a deep existential crisis. In both, the language of Love is permeated by disappointment and desolation, thus unraveling a reality in which the love story becomes entangled with history's brutality that poets are compelled to share.

Clovis Hesteau de Nuysement's Triangle:
A Woman-to-Woman Tale of Despair.

Clovis Hesteau de Nuysement (ca. 1555–ca. 1623) belonged to the circle of King Henri III, together with Ronsard, Dorat, Jamyn, Passerat, Du Perron, Desportes, and others, and he was the secretary of the Duc François d'Alençon, the King's younger brother. Like many poets at court, and the King himself, he was particularly fascinated by the teachings of Paracelsus (1493–1541), a physician, botanist, and astronomer, mostly known for his contributions to chemistry and hermetic alchemy, to which we shall later return.[140] The majority of Nuysement's life remains unknown. His *Œuvres poétiques* (1578) are followed by more than 40 years of silence, when in 1620, he published *Les Visions hermétiques* and *Poème philosophic de la verité de la Phisique mineralle*, followed a year later by *Traittez de l'harmonie et constitution generalle du vray sel*, and in 1624 by *Poème philosophic sur l'azoth des philosophes*. In these latter works, Nuysement's interest turns completely to alchemy.[141]

Although much of his amatory poetry is inspired by the *disperata*, as I will also discuss in the following chapter, it is Nuysement's female-voiced *disperata* "Plainte de Telie à Eco" that best embodies the intricacies of the intersection between gender and the *disperata* genre in France. Here, he creates a dialogic triangle between his Muse Telie, Echo, and his authorial persona. Furthermore, Nuysement takes a different approach from the models of il Saviozzo, da Prato, and degli Alberti previously discussed. Instead of using the ventriloquized female voice in order to create distance from his female character, the French poet identified with her, going so far as to give her authorial credit in several of his poems.

The third volume of Nuysement's *Œuvres Poetiques*, titled *Divers poemes* (1578), which comprises sonnets and longer forms, features several poems about Telie, including a poem written "by her."[142] She is the poet's Muse with whom his persona often dialogues, an imaginary goddess who becomes the subject and dedicatee of his poems. In "Plainte de Telie à Eco," he ventriloquizes Telie's complaint to another woman, the nymph Echo, and borrows her voice to mourn her lost love and acute longing for Tirsis.[143] Although Nuysement clearly appropriates Telie's voice in this particular composition, it is important to note, however, that first, Telie effectively lent her voice to the poet in several of the sonnets at the beginning of his *Livre II*,[144] which is itself dedicated to Telie, the Goddess and Muse, who embodies the mysteries of Love. She thus, not only inspires him, but also authorizes him to write about Love. This clever literary device has a twofold objective: first, it validates the author's ventriloquization of her voice, and second, it appropriates her authority and knowledge in matters of female desire and despair. Remarkably, two sonnets by real-life women endorse this device. Indeed, it was not unusual for members of Henri III's court to write letters or poems in order to promote or defend a work before it was published.[145] Hence, the "Sonets dediez a l'autheur," written by two fairly influential women, are strategically placed at the end of the first book, thereby also sanctioning Nuysement's whole *canzoniere*.[146] These, together with a third poem in Latin, penned by Nuysement but credited to Telie, "Telia ad lectorem," are key to understanding the Muse's role in Nuysement's *canzoniere*, and the permission she granted him to speak on her behalf throughout the collection, including her *plainte* to Echo.

The first sonnet, "Plusieurs ont creu l'amour estre une passion," is authored by Françoise de la Rochefoucaut, an educated noblewoman of Catherine de Medici's entourage, who states that Telie, so eruditely celebrated in Nuysement's poems, is but a simple imagination of her author: "Car Telie en ses vers si doctement chantee/N'est sinon qu'une simple imagination" (vv. 10–11, 204). Nonetheless, despite Telie's imaginary manifestations, he has been able to perfectly portray Love's effects and its powers as to touch everyone:

> Toustefois il a sceu si vivement despaindre
> Les effects de l'Amour, que triste l'oyant plaindre,
> Il contraint un chacun à pleurer son malheur
> (vv. 9–11, 204).

Thus, even though he did not experience the pangs of Love himself, the poet is able to move his readers through Telie and her representations, and thus experience her feelings. The second sonnet, written by Catherine de Mallesse, also an educated noblewoman of the poet's circle,[147] praises Nuysement and affirms his deftness in matters of Love:

> S'il est honestement d'une Idee amoureux,
> Croyez le neantmoins en aymant bien heureux,
> Pour n'estre moins aymé de sa chaste Telie
> (vv. 9–11, 205).

Similarly, these verses reiterate the idea that, although the poet himself is not in love, the chaste Telie loves him, and thus we, as readers, must believe him and his poetry. Consequently, both sonnets suggest that Love and Telie approve of the poet's attempt to write about Love itself and its challenges. While in the sonnets the Muse is portrayed as imaginary and as an idea, these two sonnets by real, not fictional women validate the poet's skills in speaking of Love as both real and credible.

Finally, the third sonnet authored by Telie, but obviously ventriloquized by Nuysement, is dedicated to the readers ("ad Lectorem"), thereby subverting the literary tradition of dedicating one's work to a Muse. Rather than the poet addressing his Muses or Furies, it is through Telie's voice that Nuysement dedicates his verses to the reader, again, appropriating the female voice in order to sing his literary virtues and skills. Telie takes an active role throughout the *canzoniere*, addressing the readers, praising the poet's greatness, and glorifying herself for having spread Love's ardors and for having her beauty celebrated everywhere by the poet: "Bienheureuse moi qui ai pu répandre tant d'ardeurs,/Alors que ma beauté célébrée brillera désormais pour lui seul" (vv. 11–12, 206).[148] Telie, therefore, joins the two noblewomen in both authorizing and praising Nusement's poetry. She enthusiastically transfers her agency, authority, and voice to him. Thus, I suggest that Nuysement writes some of his poems with and through Telie, as a joint-gendered endeavor that can more effectively depict Love and its pangs.

Although Telie is also the subject of other poems in *Livre III*,[149] it is in "Plainte de Telie à Eco" that Nuysement fully assumes her voice, her love, desire, and despair. Indeed, he completely takes over her persona as if he and she were one, fusing his voice and actions to hers. Echo, one of the better known and more frequently employed mythological figures in the Renaissance, represents *l'amante désespérée* who, because of her unrequited love for Narcissus, hides and pines away, crying until she is nothing but a voice. However, in a rewriting of Ovid's myth of Echo and Narcissus, the latter has no presence and no voice in Nuysement's *plainte*. Indeed, in a uniquely gendered turn, Narcissus is completely excluded, and the tale focuses instead on Telie, on Echo's ethereal manifestation, and on their intimate dialogue in which the female voice has a central role.[150] While Echo is unable to speak of her despair, Telie's ventriloquized voice becomes Echo's voice as well, because she not only narrates her own story, but she also represents or "re-echoes" Echo's story, who is therefore no longer silenced. Furthermore, Telie also ventriloquizes the voice of her lover Tirsis, thus leaving no textual space to male voices, suggesting that the feminine voice is all the more crucial.

Traditionally, Echo adds an element of erudition to a poem, as mythology played a significant role in Renaissance literature and culture.

Here, though, she also adds an element of sophistication, because female physicality is substituted by her voice, as in da Prato's Eulogia (Chapter Two). Furthermore, Echo serves as a metaphor for the poet.[151] In fact, in this *plainte*, she embodies the poet's alter-ego and his power of speech, as he is the one who "voices" the lover-persona's complaint, in this case Telie's. Finally, in most literary depictions, Echo can only re-echo with her own voice what she hears, as if she were allowed to only repeat male speech, a fitting metaphor for all women in the early-modern period whose voice was not supposed to be heard outside the domestic domain.[152] In the female-voiced *disperate* discussed in this study, with the exception of Morra's, the female voice is "publicly" heard and re-echoed only through the male author. Despite these various literary representations, in the *disperata*, Echo is usually staged as the poet's listener, and as the embodiment of a voice, often meshing the two roles. For example, Sasso wonders why he cannot become the miserable Echo, "Perche non divento io la misera Eccho" ("Disperata contro l'amore" v. 91) so that he can better embody the nymph, who in turn can empower his despair. Likewise, in Nuysement's poem, Echo is pursued by Telie's weeping and power of speech, "accens de ma voix," which in turn, as la Rochefoucaut has noted, attempt to move the reader.

In "Plainte de Telie à Eco," Echo is a disincarnated voice, and thus has no visual presence, but it is also one that listens and responds, albeit only with her invisible company, to the distressed Telie. Since Echo is a desperate lover *par excellence* herself, she can better understand Love's miseries, and identify and sympathize with other unfortunate lovers. She too seeks darkness and wanders in the secluded forest surrounded by wild animals, just like the *disperata* speaker. Furthermore, Echo is designed to literally "echo" other voices' feelings, further emphasizing these feelings of acute hopelessness.

The *plainte* opens with the *disperata*'s traditional setting in which the distressed Telie wanders in the middle of rocks, caverns, and woods begging for her hostess, Echo, to answer and to listen to her mourning:

> Hostesse des rochers, des antres, et des bois,
> Respons, je te supplie, aux accens de ma voix;
> Entens ces tristes plains que lentement je crie
> (vv. 1–3, 158–159).

Although Telie does not see Echo, she hopes to be heard by her and to be able to hear her response. The entire *plainte* centers on the agency and power of "la voix," as the only way through which the male poet can appropriate Telie's tragic love story for the shepherd Tirsis, as well as for his readers' attention.[153] Nuysement operates well within intertextual and intratextual contexts, because he was a skillful adaptor of the *disperata*, and like il Saviozzo, degli Alberti, and da Prato, he too contended with writing the experience of women in a plausible and compelling manner. The Renaissance, indeed, created an increased interest in appropriating, defining, and examining female experiences, which resulted also in the codification of women's behavior and speech.[154] These texts demonstrate this interest, prompted undoubtedly by a humanist and literary revival of Ovid's *Heroides* and of the elegy as a prolific genre.[155] Ovid's text institutionalized the female voice and gave its heroines the power of speech so that they could directly declare their truth, without the mediation of a male voice.[156] Furthermore, Ovid's female characters are afflicted by unrequited love and abandonment, as are those of the female-voiced *disperata*, and their words constitute their very *raison d'être*.[157] In this *plainte* in particular, the ventriloquized female voice narrates her tragedy, loss of love, and despair, but mostly, her loneliness.

Telie asks Echo for advice, "Sur le bort de cet antre, et me dy, je te prie" (v. 4, 159), and describes how her body is viscerally affected by her misery, which distresses even her voice:

> gesné, va gesnant le canal de ma voix,
> Laquelle est comme l'eau qui voulant saillir toute
> Horz du vaze, est contrainte à sortir goutte à goutte
> (vv. 10–12, 159).

The importance of the voice is emphasized throughout the poem, not only as the lover's signifier, but also as her vital sign and only means of communicating despair. If at first Telie's voice is hindered, in the end it is forced to overflow and express her sorrows. Even the animals seem to echo her sadness, again emphasizing the role of the voice and its inflection, "D'un accent tout plaintif, semblent plaindre mes maux/Et sentir comme moi mon lamentable encombre" (vv. 14–15, 159). Telie's voice conveys her misfortunes and further represents a way for the writer to exert power over his woman-to-woman lament.

Nature also responds to her *plainte*, because it, too, takes part of the speaker's sorrow:

> Des grands saulles feuillus, mourans, se vont cacher
> Sur le fest soleillé d'un esgaré rocher,

> Où ruminans à part, de leurs voix enrouees,
> Halettent (gemissans) mes douleurs endurees
> (vv. 18–21, 159).

Thus, the first twenty-four verses of the poem introduce a voice as a mean to articulate despair, connect with Echo and nature, and seek their compassion. Telie's voice is not alone; rather, alongside Echo, it is literally replicated by nature onto which it is projected, and which is touched by her cries, "L'oyseau qui me regarde est de mon mal touché" (v. 21, 160). The landscape, the birds, and the animals that inhabit the verses that follow are traditional to the *disperata* poetry, and here, the "I" of the woman in love is forcefully asserted as the only important character who speaks and suffers, "Je me repais d'ennuis, je m'abreuve de larmes,/Je sens du Ciel vangeur les punissantes armes" (vv. 27–28, 160). Nothing matters more than her tragic circumstances.

Telie then goes back in time and describes her *innamoramento* with Tirsis, and Love's winning fire, "feu vainqueur" (v. 38, 160) that conquered her, but also burned her with an immense ardor. She loses herself, and it is here that her ventriloquized voice is lost by Love, and consequently lodged in her beloved: "Puis m'ayant hors de moy ma franchise ravie" (v. 43, 161). Likewise, Tirsis's proposals to Telie are also emphasized by the verb "retell," with the repetition of the welcomed intentions: "Les amoureux propos, qu'au plus frais des umbrages/Il m'aloit redisant" (vv. 47–48, 161). The two voices, hers and his, become a powerful symbol of love, and it is important to note that here it is Telie that ventriloquizes her male beloved's voice to her confidante, Echo. In fact, Tirsis starts carving words on a tree, which Echo and the reader receive by means of Telie's narration. Furthermore, unlike in the Italian female-voiced *disperata*, there are no physical descriptions of the male lover; the emphasis is again on his ventriloquized voice and on his profound love for Telie, as Love entangled them together (vv. 43–46, 161). Unlike the female protagonists of the Italian *disperate*, Telie's love is fully reciprocated, and her desire is satisfied, if only for a moment.

Sadly, Tirsis's carved words foreshadow a looming tragedy, preceded by a vivid description of future calamites:

> Aussi tost on verra toute la mer glacee
> ...
> Aussi tost on verra ce dont tout est enclos
> Se brouiller pesle mesle en un second caoz

(Soon we will see the frozen sea/ ... /Soon we will see that which is enclosed/Blur confusedly in a second chaos) (vv. 51–54, 162).[158]

The depiction of a *monde renversé* prophesizes Tirsis's death, as Diana and the forest nymphs, jealous of the two lovers' bliss, damn Telie's life, and slay her beloved: "Et pour mieux assouvir leur effrenee envie/En malheurant mes ans, luy osterent la vie" (vv. 71–72, 162). The *disperata's* damnations and their terrible effects are fully expressed in these powerful words, "en malheurant mes ans." Telie's dreams, love, desire, and her lover's life are damned to end. Furthermore, the final words are accompanied by a grandiose and dramatic scene where Tirsis rips his heart out of his chest and offers it to his beloved as proof of his eternal love. Before drawing his last breath, in a feeble voice he again pledges his eternal love to her:

> Tien, tien, chere Telie
> Que vivant j'ay aymé plus que ma propre vie,
> Recoy mon triste cueur pour gage de la foy
> (vv. 75–77, 163).

Telie then gathers the strength to talk, albeit with a "voix tremblante," and to vow her eternal love (v. 83, 163). It is her turn now to foresee an immense cataclysm, very analogous to the ones we find in the *disperata* and in other poems by Nuysement:[159]

> Puis detestant le sort, la nature, et les Dieux,
> J'eslevay ma clameur vers la voute des Cieux,
> Criant à haute voix: 'O mal-heureuse Lune,
> Pourquoi prens tu plaisir à ma triste infortune?
> Ainsi l'on te ravisse en te privant d'amy
> Le bel Endimion dessus l'alme endormy!
> Ainsi puisse Medee, ou quelque enchanteresse,
> T'arracher hors du Ciel par sa voix charmeresse!

(Then, abhorring fate, nature, and the Gods,/I raised my clamor toward the celestial vault,/Screaming out loud: 'Oh damned Moon,/ Why do you enjoy my sad misfortunes?/That you may be robbed of your beloved/The beautiful Endymion asleep under a tree!/That Medea, or another enchantress,/Tear you away from the Sky with her enchanting voice!) (vv. 97–104, 163–164).

Once more, the poet emphasizes the power of the voice, "criant à haute voix," this time screaming damnations against the moon, the nymphs of the forest and of the sea. As the tragedy unfolds under the readers' eyes, the poet provides his female voice with more and more power. In fact, the closer we get to the end of the tale, the louder the female voice gets, demanding our attention and compassion.

Telie turns to Echo with more intimate confidences:

> Voilà donc, chere Eco, la vangeresse plainte
> Qui sailloit lentement de ma poitrine attainte;
> Voilà donc les souspirs, les sanglots, les regrets,
> Heritiers des plaisirs qu'aux antres plus secrets
> Nous cueillions de l'amour; voilà ma douce flame
> Estainte dans l'obscur d'une poudreuse lame

(Here, it is dear Echo, the vengeful lament/That was slowly rising from my suffering chest;/Here are the sighs, sobs, regrets,/Heirs of the pleasures that in the most secrets caves/We received from love; here is my sweet flame/Extinguished in the darkness of a dusty sword) (vv. 115–120, 165).

These considerations are inspired by the *disperata* and in particular by the motif of retrospectively contemplating one's life, spent in misery and sorrow, secretly pining. Furthermore, this pause provides the poet and his female speaker an opportunity to reflect on the pain, on Love and its miseries, but also to further involve the reader in the text with an intimate "nous." The poem concludes with a bitter reflection, similar to Morra's universal deliberation about humanity's misery and misfortunes, in which there is a realization that despair has henceforth replaced hope: "Car tout ce que comprend ce large firmament/Dans son rond est suject à soudain changement" (Because all that is included in this vast firmament/In its roundness is subject to sudden change) (vv. 129–130, 165). Drawing upon the first-person authority, Nuysement clearly places his poem in the feminine domain, even when Tirsis speaks, and does so through Telie's voice. Furthermore, Echo never speaks—neither the reader nor Telie ever hear her voice—yet she is present throughout, and we can assume that she is listening to Telie's "vangeresse plainte" because of the dialogic nature of the narration, which inscribes a listener-confidante dialectic by regularly invoking her.

This poem, diligently imitating the *disperata*, aptly employs its canonical landscape and sense of space, its maledictions, acutely adversarial fate, gloomy atmosphere, furors of Love, presence of the animals, apocalyptic visions and foreshadowing, and the tragedy of lost love, as well as its despair and death. However, Telie replaces a wish for suicide with the power of her voice to narrate her grief and sad story to Echo, because in this poem, the act of narrating is more important than anything else, including ending her sorrows with her own death. Furthermore, although at the end of the *disperata* its author usually tasks the poem to spread his or her despair, here, Telie instead confides in Echo, whose role is to re-echo her tale of despair throughout the forest. Echo, and not the poem itself, will disseminate forever Telie's *plainte*, so that she too will get a chance to speak and narrate despair.

By impersonating the voice of an imagined Muse, Nuysement borrows her lament and focuses specifically on the female experience of despair, a practice also found in other female-voiced *disperate*, including those by il Saviozzo, degli Alberti, and da Prato. Remarkably, in Nuysement's *plainte*, Telie's ventriloquized voice first narrates a beautiful story (vv. 1 to 47); then it appropriates Tirsis's voice in order to lament his love and mourn his death (vv. 48 to 56). Finally, Telie takes over the narration once more (vv. 57–75), and her beloved's voice is yet again heard in his last breaths (vv. 75–82). The first-person authoritative voice then restarts (vv. 83–114) and strengthens, so that the narration is intensified by harsh invectives. The final address to Echo (vv. 115–130) is meant to ensure her attention and compassion, as well as the reader's. Hence, above all, Nuysement appropriates both lovers' voices with the intention to tell their heartbreaking experiences equally, but also engender them as one with his own narrating authority. Furthermore, by lending Telie's voice to Echo and excluding Narcissus's voice and presence all together, he destabilizes the Ovidian myth, as well as the literary culture of the time that looked at Classical writings as one of the main sources of imitation. Instead, he offered a new woman-to-woman tale of despair. La Rochefoucauld promised as much in her sonnet.[160] Hence, the female voice is single-handedly recounting the story and is certainly more "telling" than the male voice.

As has been stated before, Nuysement practiced alchemy, as did several other writers of the court of Henri III, where "nul qui brigue le renom de savant, n'a plus le droit d'en [alchemy] ignorer" according to Albert-Marie Schmidt.[161] The poet-alchemists questioned the longstanding tradition on which gender role distinctions were based,[162] and they struggled with notions of otherness, dissolution, conjunction, and hierarchy.[163] In this *plainte*, Nuysement, "le plus grand des poètes-alchimistes français,"[164] combines his passion for alchemy and poetry and challenges the established notions of gender distinctions in female and male voice textual enactments. Indeed, several of the above questions central to alchemy unfold in the text, blurring the lines between male and female voices, because the narrating voice is the mean of expression through which readers become acquainted with Telie, Echo, and her lover Tirsis. Serge Hutin explains alchemy's crucial concept of *dualisme sexuel*: all oppositions, all likes and dislikes found in the world originate from the opposition of two complimentary principles, the male and female, adding that the union between man and woman and the opposition of the generating and of the fecundated principles become the ultimate explanation.[165] Moreover, as Perry Long has convincingly shown, poet-alchemists were concerned with "the mutable sexuality of the alchemical process,"[166] a concept that is suggestive of Nuysement's ventriloquism of the female voice. Like in alchemy, gender difference is essential, but easily mutable, a fundamental concept that frames my exploration of the French poet's creation of Telie, her borrowed voice, but also Tirsis's voice. Indeed, as in an alchemical experiment that fuses opposites, Nuysement conjoined the female and the male voices as one narrating voice.[167] Even Tirsis's last words seem to express an important stage of the alchemical process, "tout [...] est sujet à soudain changement," because alchemy focuses on the process of perpetual change, and for Telie and her beloved, love and desire quickly dissolved into death and despair.

Finally, unlike il Saviozzo, da Prato and degli Alberti, Nuysement does not create a distance between himself and the persona; he does not judge, nor does he want to impart a lesson. Rather, he stages a collective, all-encompassing female despair in a *plainte* that skillfully stages the *disperata*'s main themes. The result is a ventriloquized voice that seems credible and inclusive, authoritative and authentic, and that combines a cacophony of voices devised to blur gender distinctions between Telie, Echo, Tirsis, and the author himself. In this manner, Nuysement created a convincing version of female despair that might, as Mallesse states, persuade us to believe him—"croyez-le neantmoins."

NOTES

[1] Vianey, *Le Pétrarquisme en France*, 9. See also Balsamo, *Les Rencontres des muses*, 232–234.

[2] As mentioned in the previous chapter, many are the intertextualities among these poets, especially those between Tansillo and Morra.

[3] As an indication of the importance of this anthology, in the 1555 edition, 33 sonnets by Rota, 32 sonnets by di Costanzo, and 23 by Tansillo were featured. Toscano notes that the 1552 anthology is also credited as having brought back the Neapolitan lyric production. *Letterati Corti Accademie*, 9, and 183–200.

[4] Richter, "Printers and Poets," 86, and Robin, *Publishing Women*, 41–78, and 228–232.

[5] Di Costanzo's poems were included in many of the Italian anthologies. See Longhi, "Una raccolta di Rime di Angelo di Costanzo." For di Costanzo in France, see L. E. Kastner, "Desportes et Angelo di Costanzo," and Vianey, "Une Rencontre des muses de France et d'Italie demeurée inédite." See also Paola Farenga, "Di Costanzo, Angelo."

[6] Tansillo, *Rime*, 270.

[7] Although Tansillo, di Costanzo, and Rota also wrote *capitoli*, madrigals, elegies, *canzoni*, and eclogues, the sonnet is undoubtedly their preferred form of the *disperata*. For all three poets, see Luigi Baldacci, *Lirici del Cinquecento*, Flamini, *La lirica del Rinascimento*, Giulio Marzot, "Il tramite del petrarchismo dal Rinascimento al barocco," Arturo Meozzi, *Il petrarchismo europeo*, Aldo Scaglione, "Cinquecento Mannerism and the Uses of Petrarch," 122–155, and Giuseppe Toffanin, *Storia Letteraria d'Italia. Il, Cinquecento*.

[8] Pietro Bembo, *Prose della volgar lingua, Gli Asolani, Rime*.

[9] Vittorio Rossi, *Il Quattrocento*, 170.

[10] Erika Milburn, *Luigi Tansillo and Lyric Poetry in Sixteenth-Century Naples*, 1.

[11] Dubois argues that these poets' work gives a more important role to melancholy, solitude as well as the "désespoir amoureux (la *disperata*)" in *La Poésie du XVIᵉ siècle*, 60. See also his *Le Maniérisme*, 198. Also of great importance is the publicity work by editors such as Girolamo Ruscelli, who claim that these poets are foremost models to be read and imitated. See DellaNeva, *Unlikely Exemplars*, 58. Furthermore, as an example of how widely imitated these poets were, see the case of Desportes, thoroughly studied by Rouget in "Philippe Desportes, médiateur du pétrarquisme français."

[12] See Weber's introduction to d'Aubigné's *Le Printemps*, 13–14, noting the theme of "le désespoir amoureux, cultivé dans la Disperata de Seraphino et Tebaldeo" and later on found in some of Tansillo's sonnets. See also his *La Création poétique*, 327–333, Alice Hulubei, *L'Eglogue en France au XVIᵉ siècle*, Dubois, *La Poésie du XVIᵉ siècle*, 60, and Mathieu-Castellani, *Eros Baroque*, 27, and her "Les enfants de Pétrarque," 1540–1640, 634, and Guillot's introduction and notes to Nuysement's *Œuvres poétiques*.

[13] See also Mathieu-Castellani, "Les Enfants de Pétrarque," Balsamo, "'Du florentin les lamentables voix': Mythe pétrarquien et modèle pétrarquiste en France au XVIe siècle," as well as G.W. Pigman III, "Versions of Imitation in the Renaissance," 1–32, Meozzi, *Il Petrarchismo europeo*, Robert Melançon, "La Fin du pétrarquisme en France," Kennedy, *The Site of Petrarchism*, and Richard Griffiths, "Some Uses of Petrarchan Imagery in Sixteenth-Century France."

[14] For historical perspectives on the French Wars of Religion, see Natalie Zemon Davis, *Society and Culture in Early Modern France*, Barbara Diefendorf, *Beneath the Cross: Catholics and the Huguenots in Sixteenth-Century Paris*, Mark Greengrass, *Governing Passions: Peace and Reform in the French Kingdom, 1576–1585*, Robert Knecht, *The French Wars of Religion, 1562–1628*, and *The French Civil Wars in Perspective*, and J.H.M. Salmon, *Society in Crisis: France in the Sixteenth Century*.

[15] See Scarlatta and Lidia Radi, *Representations of Heresy*.

[16] As seen in the female-voiced *disperata*.

[17] Cf. Russell, who also notes "La stereotipizzazione nella forma del contenuto (of the *disperata*) oltre a facilitare l'espressione dei pensieri intimi rende possibile l'immedesimazione del lettore nella situazione rappresentata e garantisce in questo modo la funzione catartica e consolatoria del componimento." 170.

[18] Alexander, *Trauma, A Social Theory*, 3.

[19] D'Aubigné, *Le Printemps Stances et Odes*, 15.

[20] For the Italianate climate at Henri III of Valois's court, see my "Reading Philippe Desportes in *Les Rencontres des muses de France et d'Italie*," Balsamo, *Les Rencontres des Muses*, 10–15, Jacqueline Boucher, *La Cour de Henri III* and *Société et Mentalité autour de Henri III*, and Gros and Fragonard, *Les Formes poétiques*, 118.

[21] Gros and Fragonard, *Les Formes poétiques*, 122.

[22] See for example Dionigi Atanagi's anthology *De le rime di diversi nobili poeti toscani, Raccolte da M. Dionigi Atanagi*, Libro Primo.

[23] See DellaNeva, *Unlikely Exemplars*, Balsamo, "Les Poètes français et les anthologies lyriques italiennes," Quondam, *Petrarchismo Mediato. Per una critica della forma "antologia,"* Franco Tomasi, "Alcuni aspetti delle antologie liriche del secondo Cinquecento," and Maria Luisa Cerrón Puga, "Materiales para la construcción del canon petrarquista: las antologías de Rime (libri I-IX)."

[24] DellaNeva also notes that anthologies provided "a treasure-trove of second-rate (and sometimes third-rate) poems to use as models, in addition to or instead of the *Rime sparse* of the canonical authority, Petrarch." *Unlikely Exemplars*," 14. See also Robin, *Publishing Women*, 219–242, and Vianey, *Le Pétrarquisme en France*.

[25] DellaNeva, "An Exploding Canon: Petrarch and the Petrarchists," 192.

[26] In addtion to cited works, see also Vianey, "L'infuence italienne chez les précurseurs de la Pléïade."

[27] See Gros and Fragonard, *Les Formes poétiques*, 112, and Frédéric Lachèvre, *Bibliographie des recueils collectifs de poésies du XVIe siècle*.

[28] See DellaNeva, "Reflecting Lesser Light: The Imitation of Minor Writers in the Renaissance," and "An Exploding Canon."

[29] For example, Balsamo notes that "La composition d'un sonnet, vers 1550, était une claire référence à Pétrarque. La primauté du sonnet constituait une forme du modèle pétrarquien, même si des thèmes adaptés du poète italien pouvaient être exprimés en d'autres formes." "'Du Florentin les lamentables voix,'" 121.

[30] In Italy, for example, we have seen how Bembo's work shifted the literary production back to genres used in Petrarch's *Canzoniere*, mainly the sonnet.

[31] Clément Moison, "Les Genres comme catégorie littéraire," 70–71.

[32] For a study on the Renaissance French sonnet, see Rigolot, "Qu'est-ce qu'un sonnet?", François Jost, "Le sonnet: sens d'une structure," 57–65, Balsamo, "Sonnets italiens et impressions françaises," Vaganey, *Le Sonnet en Italie et en France*, and Michel Jourde, "L'Imaginaire et l'histoire: sur la situation du sonnet en France vers 1550."

[33] See Pilgman, "Versions of Imitation in the Renaissance," 27.

[34] Martines, *Strong Words*, 267.

[35] Mathieu-Castellani, "Les Modes du discours lyrique au XVIᵉ siècle," 132.

[36] See for example *Fioretto di cose nove nobilissime et degne di diversi auctori noviter stampate cioè: Sonetti Capitoli Epistole Egloghe Disperate Strambotti Barzellette et una contra disperata*. See also Vianey, "Marcello Philoxeno et Mellin de Saint-Gelays," who traces some of Saint-Gelais's intertextualities with Philoxeno and Ariosto.

[37] Luigia Zilli, "Mellin de Saint-Gelais et la *Terza Rima*," 387. Zilli notes that in Italy, Saint-Gelais "découvre surtout le charme poétique et la discipline technique du sonnet, du *strambotto* et du *capitolo* in *terza rima*." 387. See also her edition of Saint-Gelais, *Sonnets*. Other scholars argue that it was Jean Lemaire de Belges that first composed poems in *terza rima*. See Victor Graham in his edition of Philippe Desportes, *Les Amours de Diane*, 184. For Saint-Gelais's role as an innovator in French poetry, see DellaNeva, *Unlikely Exemplars*, 125–149. DellaNeva convincingly argues that Saint-Gelais was the first French poet to capture the importance of the Italian anthologies as a source for his poetry, 149. See also John A. McClelland in his edition of Pontus de Tyard's *Les Erreurs amoureuses*, 108.

[38] Zilli, "Mellin de Saint-Gelais," 388. Gros and Fragonard also note that the *terza rima* is an "indice de modernité," as in Lemaire de Belges's *Temple d'honneur et de vertu* and *Concorde des deux languages*. In *Les Formes poétiques*, 75.

[39] See Balsamo, *Les Rencontres des Muses*, 108–110. For the verse translation by Jean Fornier, see Vaganay, "Le premier essai de traduction de Roland Furieux en vers français."

[40] See Gorris, "'Je veux chanter d'amour la tempeste et l'orage': Desportes et les Imitations de l'Arioste," 179; Alejandro Cioranesco, *L'Arioste en France des origines à la fin du XVIIIᵉ siècle* and "Les Imitations de l'Arioste de Philippe Desportes," Enea Balmas, "Note sulla fortuna dell'Ariosto in Francia nel Cinquecento," and Alice Cameron, "Desportes and Ariosto: Additional Sources in the *Orlando* and

the *Liriche*." See also Lavaud, *Les Imitations de l'Arioste par Philippe Desportes*.

[41] These Italian masterpieces had been translated and imitated in France since their original publication in Italy. The process of translation in particular was an important undertaking that not only required linguistic knowledge of the source and target language, but also of the many well-established lyric conventions in both countries. See Balsamo, "Traduire de l'Italien," 90.

[42] See Gorris, "*Le Roland furieux* [...] devient ainsi [...] un immense réservoir de rêves amoureux, de sentences, d'images, de plaintes et complaintes, de martyres de la folie amoureuse, de victimes d'une maladie inguérissable." "Desportes et les imitations de l'Arioste," 181.

[43] See Tissoni Benvenuti, "La tradizione della terza rima e l'Ariosto."

[44] For a fine analysis of the *terza rima* in France, see Kathleen M. Hall, "Pontus de Tyard and His 'Disgrace'," 108. Hall claims that "Disgrace" is the equivalent of Du Bellay's "Chant du Désespéré" and of the *disperata*, 103. Although written in *terza rima*, this poem is a very abstract complaint about love, and thus, does not have any of the realistic images that characterize the *disperata*. It can be found on pages 108–110 of the aforementioned edition of Tyard's *Les Erreurs amoureuses*.

[45] Thomas Sebillet, *Art Poétique francoys* (1548), 178.

[46] For a study of the French elegy in Renaissance France, see John E. Clark, *Elégie: The Fortunes of a Classical Genre in Sixteenth-Century France*.

[47] See also the excellent discussion on "élégies" by Roland Guillot and Michel Clément in the Introduction to Flaminio de Birague, IX-LIII, where they define the "élégie biraquienne:" "l'élégie semble pouvoir s'habiller de divers manteaux: selon qu'elle est églogue, complainte, pêcherie, despérade, ou épitre." (XXVIII).

[48] See Vecchi Galli, "Percorsi dell'elegia quattrocentesca in volgare," 54–55. Vecchi Galli notes that the *disperata* influenced the Italian elegy's meaning and vocabulary. Indeed, the personnification of Death, Love, and Fortune, which started in Antonio Beccari's *disperata*, is also found in many Italian and French elegies. Furthermore, il Saviozzo's *disperate* also inspired some of the Quattrocento and Cinquecento elegies. 56.

[49] See for example Nicolò da Correggio's case, whose 44 *capitoli* in *terza rima* are in fact *disperate*, eclogues, epistles, *dipartite*, *primavere*, and other genres. Gentili considers his "Serà pur ver che ognor contrarii venti" a true *disperata*. See "Il Capitolo in terza rima in Niccolò da Correggio: non solo elegia," 118.

[50] For more on genres' evolution and hierarchy, see Herman P. Salomon, "Observations on the Definition, Evolution, and Separation of Genres."

[51] See also Pierre de Ronsard, "Discours d'un amoureux desespéré," in *Œuvres Complètes*, Paul Laumonier, ed. 85. These dialogues do not have anything in common with the *disperata*.

[52] See Weber, *La Création poétique*, 400.

[53] Jacques Peletier du Mans, *Œuvres poétiques*, 99. All references to Peletier's poems will be to this edition.

[54] See Weber's excellent analysis of this poetic commonplace in his *Création poétique*, 400–413.

[55] Joachim Du Bellay, *Œuvres Complètes*, 71. All references to "Le Chant du desesperé" will be to this edition.

[56] In *La Monomachie de David et de Goliath*, Ernesta Caldarini, ed. 68–91. All reference to this text will be to this edition.

[57] Weber, *La Création poétique*, 413.

[58] Richter convincingly shows that both "Le Chant" and "La Complainte" are a testimony to the poet's violent spiritual crisis, as well as a physical state of prostration. *La Poesia lirica in Francia nel secolo XVI*, 20–22, and 146–160.

[59] Olivier de Magny, *Les Amours*, in *Œuvres poétiques*, Françoise Charpentier ed. 180–183. All references to Magny's "Chant" will be to this edition.

[60] Jules Favre, *Olivier de Magny*, 164. Magny's "Chant" is more comparable to Sannazzaro's *Arcadia*, rather than to the *disperata*.

[61] *Ensemble quelques Elegies du mesme sujet, extraites du sixième et settième livre de la Clion*, in François d'Amboise, *Œuvres complètes*, 95–115. All references to d'Amboise's poetry will be to this edition.

[62] For a definition of the pastoral and its forms, see Berckson and Ganz, *Literary Terms*, 193–195.

[63] Ughetti, *François d'Amboise*, 111.

[64] See Ralph Nash, ed. *Arcadia and Piscatorial Eclogues* and for a duscussion on the bucolic and piscatorial genres, Erik Fredericksen, "Jacopo Sannazaro Piscatory Eclogues and the Question of Genre."

[65] Hulubei, *L'Eglogue en France au XVI*ᵉ *siècle*.

[66] Ibid., 573, and 575.

[67] Weber, ed. *Le Printemps*, Appendice II, 306–315.

[68] Ibid., 14.

[69] Weber, *La Création poétique*, 403. Weber also provides an excellent analysis of Peletier and Du Bellay's songs of despair, 399–413.

[70] See Rousset, *La Littérature de l'âge baroque en France*. Rousset argues that the main themes found in baroque architecture and paintings are also the ones that dominate the literature of this time, 181–182.

[71] Dubois, *La Poésie Baroque*, Vol. I, 21. See also his *Le Maniérisme* and *Le Baroque: Profondeurs de l'apparence*. Mathieu-Castellani has published extensively on the Baroque; see *Eros Baroque, Les Thèmes amoureux dans la poésie française*, and *Mythes de l'Eros baroque*. Her *Anthologie de la poésie amoureuse de l'âge baroque* is a collection of poetry in which the *disperata* emerges regularly. See also Michael J. Giordano, "Reverse Transmutations: Béroalde de Verville's Parody of Paracelsus in 'Le Moyen de parvenir,'" Rigolot, *Poésie et Renaissance*, and in particular the section "La poésie dite 'maniériste' et 'baroque,'" 329–359, and Marcel Raymond, *Baroque et Renaissance poétique*.

[72] See my "The Continuity of Baroque Poetic Vision."

[73] See my "Philippe Desportes's Copy of Nocturno Napolitano's *Opera Amorosa*."

[74] Zampieri, "Il Notturno Napolitano." This article thoroughly documents Nocturno's first editions and reprints of both his lyrical and theatrical works.

[75] See Crescimbeni, *Dell'Istoria della volgar poesia scritta da Giovan Mario Crescimbeni*, 118–19, 305, and 381, and Pèrcopo, "Marc'Antonio Epicuro."

[76] Olivia Rosenthal, "Philippe Desportes. Esquisse d'une poétique des œuvres," 359.

[77] There were fourty-four editions between 1573 and 1615.

[78] Max Jasinski, *Histoire du Sonnet en France*, 105.

[79] See Vianey: "Les tentatives faites pour introduire chez nous telles quelles des formes purement italiennes, comme la rime tierce ou le *strambotto* demeurèrent isolées." *Le Pétrarquisme en France*, 11.

[80] Rouget, "Desportes et les inflexions métriques de la voix lyrique," 308. Rouget also points out that Desportes strived to follow strictly "l'homostrophie qui va dans le sens de la rigueur et d'une relative simplicité." 295.

[81] *Opera Amorosa de Nocturno Napolitano ne la quale si contiene Strambotti. Sonetti. Capitoli. Epistole. Et una disperata. Libro primo*, Rés. Yd 1166.

[82] See my "Philippe Desportes's Copy of Nocturno Napolitano's *Opera Amorosa*."

[83] Numerous title pages and table of contents list *disperata* and the *capitolo* as two genres; therefore, the *disperata* was considered a poetic genre in its own right.

[84] Nocturno's other nine volumes of his *Opera Amorosa* contain a great variety of lyric genres as well.

[85] Indeed, the *strambotto* is considered at the origin of the sonnet, and its French version, the *épigramme*, was put to effective use by poets such as Saint-Gelais and Maurice Scève. See Guillaume Colletet, *L'Art poétique I. Traité de l'épigramme et du sonnet*.

[86] Desportes's marking of "sonetto" between the two sonnets is meant to deliberately delineate the space of the sonnet, which is lacking.

[87] See Tissoni Benvenuti, "La tradizione della terza rima e l'Ariosto," 305, in which she mentions 25 by Tebaldeo, 44 by Sasso, and 5 by Correggio.

[88] Vianey, *Le Pétrarquisme en France*, 250.

[89] See note 4 in my "Reading Philippe Desportes in *Les Rencontres des muses de France et d'Italie*," and DellaNeva, "Reading Desportes through the Italians."

[90] *Opera Amorosa de Nocturno Napolitano*, 17. All references will be based on this edition.

[91] For the origins of the word and concept "locus amoenus", see Curtius, *European Literature and the Latin Middle Ages,* 192. See also his chapters 6 and 10 for an erudite discussion on nature and its role.

[92] Desportes, *Les Premières Œuvres*, Rouget and Bruno Petey-Girard, eds. 341–342. All references to Desportes will based on this edition.

[93] Poirier notes that the vogue of the *stance* in France was spread by the Italian anthologies. "Interstices à l'imaginaire maniériste: les stances de Philippe Des-

portes," 341. Some anthologies were entirely dedicated to *stanze*, for example *Stanze di diversi illustri poeti, raccolte da M. Lodovico Dolce* and *La seconda parte delle Stanze di diversi autori nuovamente mandata in luce.*

[94] See Poirier, "Interstices à l'imaginaire maniériste." Poirier notes: "Précisons tout de même que si Desportes semble avoir été l'un des premiers défenseurs de cette forme lyrique en France, plusieurs poètes l'ont imité." 345.

[95] Vianey, *Le Pétrarquisme en France*, 12.

[96] See Weber's introduction to d'Aubigné's *Le Printemps*, 12.

[97] See Gros and Fragonard, who note: "Les stances sont d'abord l'expression de l'émotion intime, de la passion, de toutes passions, alors que le sonnet intellectualise les sentiments." *Les Formes poétiques du Moyen Age à la Renaissance*, 114.

[98] Gros and Fragonard define the stance as: "... un genre neuf ... s'emploie au pluriel pour désigner un poème lyrique grave composé d'un nombre variable de strophes identiques." In *Les Formes poétiques du Moyen Age à la Renaissance*, 113.

[99] "La Notion de genre," 24.

[100] For biographical informations, see Weber, *La Création poétique au XVIᵉ siècle*, 601–733.

[101] See Mathieu-Castellani, *Agrippa d'Aubigné. Le corps de Jézabel*, 15–23, and Perry-Long, "The Representation of Violence in the Works of Théodore Agrippa d'Aubigné."

[102] The Tumult of Amboise took place on March 16, 1560, when Protestant leaders and militants attempted to storm the castle, but were instead defeated. Some of them were murdered, others drowned in the Loire, and others captured and hanged on the castle's iron hooks for everybody to see.

[103] See Patricia Eichel-Lojkine, 255–296.

[104] See Jean-Raymond Fanlo, "Topiques: l'œuvre inachevée," 63.

[105] *L'Association des Amis d'Agrippa d'Aubigné* maintains a very up to date and complete site about the poet, his life, his work, and publications. See http://www.agrippadaubigne.org/association.htm

[106] See André Thierry, *Agrippa d'Aubigné: Auteur de l'Histoire Universelle*, 35.

[107] Agrippa d'Aubigné, *Le Printemps II, Stances et Odes*. All references to d'Aubigné's *stances* and odes will be based on this edition.

[108] D'Aubigné, *Le Printemps I, L'Hécatombe à Diane*. All references to *L'Hécatombe*'s poems will be based on this edition.

[109] See Véronique Ferrer, "*Le Printemps* d'Agrippa d'Aubigné ou les épreuves du pétrarquisme," in particular 450.

[110] Mathieu-Castellani, *Agrippa d'Aubigné*, 7. See also her "Violences d'Aubigné."

[111] *Le Printemps, Stances et Odes*, 3. I adopt Weber's correction of "lient", verse 7, note 9, page 173.

[112] Rés – Yd – 621. This volume also contains *Sventurato pelegrino, Littera d'amore*, and *Sonetti*.

[113] See also Antonio Rossi, *Serafino Aquilano*, 14. As mentioned, Serafino's

poetry was immediately dispersed and reprinted in anthologies, and more editions of his work were published after his death.

[114] As Vianey, Vaganay, and other scholars have shown, Serafino's, Tebaldeo's, and Cariteo's poetry provided a plethora of models for sixteenth-century French poetry.

[115] Weber, *Le Printemps*, 171.

[116] Stephen Murphy, "Diane et la *disperata*."

[117] See in particular d'Aubigné's *Les Tragiques*, in which he portrays a mother, France, feeding her Protestant and Catholic twin sons. In "Misères," 80.

[118] Gagnebin, introduction to *Le Printemps*, I, XIV.

[119] See Ferrer, "*Le Printemps* d'Agrippa d'Aubigné ou les épreuves du Pétrarquisme."

[120] *Poesie inedite di Galeotto del Carretto*, 42–47.

[121] This beginning is very similar to Serafino's *disperata* prima: "Hor sù stanco mio cor, suona la tromba" in which the poet's truth and miserable condition are heralded. However, in this poem, the trumpet announces the unfairness of the speaker's situation and of the ways that love treated him. It continues: "Che se mia lingua el ver contar pur deve,/Son molti inferni et ciascuno è forte,/Ma al par di quel d'amore ogni altro è lieve." (vv. 97–99, 45) And finally: "Et per por fine al mio parlar, con dolo/Che mi trasporta l'infiammata lingua,/El cui gran strido va per tucto a volo" (vv. 139–141, 46).

[122] This image is also developed at length in sonnet L, *L'Hécatombe à Diane*, 69.

[123] This *stance* is particularly rich with metaphors between the spirit and the body, while portraying the difficulties of understanding the androgyn myth. See Perry Long's gender reading in *Hermaphrodites in Renaissance Europe*, 164–171, where she shows how d'Aubigné's conflict toward court society, religious identity, and conformity "may have facilitated his ability to combine disparate philosophies in his own work," 164, and that this *stance* is one of the earliest examples of using alchemy and philosophy in the context of Petrarchism, 171. In turn, I argue that the meshing of these philosophies and conflictual viewpoints helped the poet cope with the traumas of the wars, something that was also experienced by Nuysement.

[124] "Les Feux" is also the title of his fourth book of *Les Tragiques*.

[125] Some of these images can be linked to the popularity of *art macabre* and religious devotion during Henri III's reign. See Kjierstin Aukrust, "'J'ouvre mon estomac': Agrippa d'Aubigné et le corps macabre."

[126] Death is a very common *topos* in devotional and mystical poetry. See for example Cave, *Devotional Poetry in France*, who claims that "Since the aim is thus to provoke meditation on death as a physical reality, they [the poets] will use all their resources in an attempt to shock and horrify; and once again their tone of voice will most often be aggressive, outward, turned, like that of the preacher." 156. Devotion and meditation are associated with the writers of d'Aubigné's generation, during the Reformation and the Counter-Reformation.

[127] See Rouget, "L'Éros et la démesure: la poétique des *Odes* et des *Stances* dans *Le Printemps*."

[128] Tebaldeo, *Rime estravaganti*, Marchand, ed. III, 2, vv. 37–42, 977.

[129] See *Hécatombe*, 117, for example. According to Jean Céard, in d'Aubigné's *Tragiques*, the *topos* of the world upside down is fully deployed, and it could be said that it is "le cœur même du livre." "Le Thème du 'monde à l'envers' dans l'œuvre d'Agrippa d'Aubigné." 118.

[130] "Che structo m'á dal corpo ogni mio nervo/Costei sichome insatiabil fera,/Pasciuta s'é mai sempre del mio sangue,/E di mie spoglie va superba e altera." (vv. 18–21, 42).

[131] This image, "plus dure que les rocs" also reminds the reader of Dante's *Rime petrose*. See Dante Alighieri, *Rime*, 561, and www.danteonline.it

[132] As I will discuss in the following chapter, other neo-Petrarchan poets share many intertextualities with the *disperata topoi*.

[133] See Arlette Jouanna, *The St. Bartholomew's Day Massacre*.

[134] In his persuasive article, Murphy finds five main characteristics of the *disperata* in d'Aubigné's poetry: the "paysage sauvage," the lover's complaints, the cosmic and metaphysical dimensions, the poet's contemplation of suicide, and finally, a real or imagined death in the form of an epithaph. "Diane et *la Disperata*," 121.

[135] For an extensive study on Scève and his Délie, see Giordano, *The Art of Meditation and the French Renaissance Love Lyric*.

[136] D'Aubigné's relationship with Diane is indeed a lived history recounted in his *canzoniere*. See Mathieu-Castellani's analysis in *Agrippa d'Aubigné*, 41–44.

[137] On d'Aubigné's militant culture see also Murphy, "Du Bartas, d'Aubigné et le triomphe militant." For a compelling discussion on d'Aubigné's religion and how it informed his life and writings, see Michel Jeanneret, "*Les Tragiques*: mimesis et intertexte."

[138] Fragonard distinguishes five generations of poets who witnessed the Wars of Religion at different times during the sixteenth century: the generation of the 1510s, of the 1530s, d'Aubigné's generation of the 1550s, of the 1570s, and of the 1580s–1590s. See *La Mémoire des guerres de religion*, 34–35. As far as peace goes, starting in 1560 with the Conjuration d'Amboise, a series of wars burst in France, followed by short periods of peace marked by the following treaties: Traité de Hampton-Court (1562), Paix d'Amboise (1563), Paix de Saint-Germain (1570), followed though by the bloody Saint Bartholomew Day's Massacre in 1572. Then came the Traité de Bergerac (1577), the Paix de Nérac (1579), and the Edit de Nantes (1598) signed by Henri IV, which constitutes the longest period of peace in France, although revoked by Louis XIV in 1685. For a concise history of the Wars of Religion in France, see Briggs, *Early Modern France 1560–1715*, 13–32.

[139] See also Weber, *Agrippa d'Aubigné Le Printemps*, note 31, 180.

[140] See Giordano's study in "Reverse Transmutations," 88–137.

[141] See Wallace Kirsop's unpublished dissertation, *Clovis Hesteau de Nuysement et la littérature alchimique en France*.

[142] Guillot, Nuysement, *Les Œuvres poétiques*, Livre III, 12–13.

[143] For the origins of Echo in literature, see Elbridge Colby, *The Echo-Device in Literature*.

[144] Ibid., 53. See Livre II, sonnets XXIIII, 233; XXX, 240; LXXVIII, 290–291; and *Prière*, 317–318.

[145] See Annie Charon, "Regards sur le livre à la cour de Henri III," 393.

[146] Women not only participated in all of the literary events of the court but they also had the most dynamic role in promoting works. See Charon, "Regards sur le livre," 394.

[147] On la Rochefoucaut and Mallesse, see Guillot, 204–205.

[148] I use Guillot's translation from Latin to French, 206.

[149] See "Reproches de Medee à Jazon à Telie," 68–94, "La jalousie de Canidie à Telie," 122–143, and "Acherontide à Telie," 144–157.

[150] Ovid's story alternates between Echo's and Narcissus's story, while, as I point out, Narcissus's side of the story is completely absent in Nuysement's *plainte*. For an analysis of Ovid's narrative and gender, see Floyd Gray's *Gender, Rhetoric, and Print Culture in French Renaissance Writing*, 31–46. Gray compares Ovid and Jeanne Flore who, in her 1531 *Comptes Amoureux*, gives Echo twice as much voice as Narcissus.

[151] See Colby, *The Echo-Devise in Literature*, 5.

[152] Many are the compelling studies that have been published in the last thirty years or so. See for example, Virginia Cox, *Women's Writing in Italy 1400–1650*, Susan Broomhall, *Women and the Book Trade in Sixteenth-Century France*, Nancy K. Miller, *Subject to Change. Reading Feminist Writing*, Ann Rosalind Jones, "Surprising Fame: Renaissance Gender Ideologies and Women's Lyric," and Evelyne Berriot-Salvadore, "Les Femmes et les pratiques de l'écriture de Christine de Pizan à M. de Gournay."

[153] The character Tirsis belongs to the pastoral tradition and is undoubtedly borrowed from Thyrsis, one of the characters in Virgil's "Seventh Eclogue," who is a shepherd-poet who lost a singing contest with Corydon. Nuysement places the two lovers, Telie and Tirsis, in idyllic pastoral scenes, especially in verses 57–68. Furthermore, Tirsis is also a character in his "Chant Pastoral à Mademoiselle d'Atry," Livre III, 29–48.

[154] Ray, *Writing Gender*, 10. For women's behavior and speech see for example Juan Luís Vives, *The Education of a Christian Woman*, Sperone Speroni, "Della dignità delle donne," Castiglione, *Il libro del Cortigiano*, and Nancy Armstrong, *The Ideology of Conduct. Essays on Literature and the History of Sexuality*, and in particular Ann Rosalind Jones's article "Nets and Bridles: Early Modern Conduct Books and Sixteenth-Century Women Lyrics."

[155] On the revival of the elegy in France, see Guillot and Clément's discussion in their edition of Birague, *Les Premières Œuvres poétiques*, ix–xiii, and Clark, *Elégie*.

[156] Rosati, "L'elegia al femminile," 73.

[157] As discussed in Chapter Two, many are the similarities between the *dispe-*

rata femminile and the *Heroides*. W. S. Anderson's analysis of Ovid's letters in his chapter "*The Heroides*" also applies to the texts discussed in my study.

[158] In this plainte, Denis Augier sees Nuysement's defiance of death, as well as his obsessions about his immortality. See his "Clovis Hesteau de Nuysement: un certain désir d'immortalité."

[159] See Chapter Six, but also see his poem "Les Gemissements de la France au Roy," Livre I, 120–141, and in particular page 138.

[160] "Car Telie en ses vers si doctement chantee."

[161] Schmidt, *La Poésie scientifique en France*, 318.

[162] As Perry Long explains, philosophical alchemy proposed alternatives to Aristotelian gender roles and to Catholicism. *Hermaphrodites in Renaissance Europe*, 139.

[163] Ibid., 141–146.

[164] Schmidt, *La Poésie scientifique en France*, 336.

[165] Hutin, *L'Alchimie*, 62.

[166] Perry Long, *Hermaphrodites in Renaissance Europe*, 163. See also her "The Chemical Wedding in the Works of Clovis Hesteau de Nuysement," and "Salomon Trismosin and Clovis Hesteau de Nuysement."

[167] Giordano notes, "Through various procedures of refinement (sublimation, crystallization, distillation), the alchemist could effect a fusion of opposites (*coincidentia oppositorum*) from which a new substance emerges in an absolute state of perfection." "Reverse Transmutations," 93–94.

Chapter Six

Disperata and Désespoir

> Je ne dis les autres, sinon pour d'autant
> plus me dire.
>
> Michel de Montaigne

"Les coups du desespoir"[1]

The late French Renaissance, namely the years between 1575 and 1610, was a period of rapid changes and intense reform, both political and religious: the waning Valois dynasty losing ground, and soon the crown, to the Bourbon monarchs; Catholics losing ground to Protestants; and the aristocracy to the new, emerging bourgeoisie. According to Mark Greenglass, the governing elite of France experienced a "profound sense of crisis."[2] During these decades, a group of talented poets surrounded the close-knit circle of Henri III de Valois and his brother, the Duc François d' Anjou and Alençon. Their court was the center of significant social and economic importance, where political services, favors, and poems were regularly exchanged.[3]

For writers in particular, the court became the *raison d'être*, a matter of livelihood and social wellbeing. For the King, the court poets were vital agents in the representation of his rule and kingdom.[4] According to Jacqueline Boucher, "Henri III [...] compris la force de la pensée et de la plume et son importance dans la direction de l'Etat."[5] Poets like Pontus de Tyard (1521–1605), Desportes, Nuysement, and occasionally, d'Aubigné made up the King's literary army.[6] Other poets related to Henri III's and subsequent kings' courts were Flaminio de Birague (ca. 1550–?), Siméon-Guillaume de La Roque (1551–1611), Béroalde de Verville (1556–1626), Jean-Baptiste Chassignet (ca. 1570–1635), Etienne Durand (1586–1618), Théophile de Viau (1590–1626), and Antoine Girard de Saint-Amant (1594–1661).[7] Called neo-Petrarchans, they adapted the *disperata* to their texts taking inspiration from the Petrarchan Quattrocento and from the Cinquecento poets featured in the Giolito anthologies.[8]

Mathieu-Castellani has traced the shift from Petrarch to Quattrocento and Cinquecento Petrarchism, which was highly popular in France. In much of her work she convincingly shows that in France, lyric production between 1570 and 1600 is neo-Petrarchan and not Petrarchist, because it is inspired by the Petrarchan poets and their imitations of the master, rather than by Petrarch's verses directly. That French poetry was inspired by Petrarchan poets, who also borrowed from the *disperata*, explains in part the fortune of the *disperata* in France.[9] In the neo-Petrarchan production, the desperate lover-persona is not constant, but fickle, evokes all sorts of calamities, rather than the perfection of Love, and is most at ease in an unpredictable and fluctuating environment, rather than in idyllic settings. Petrarch's discrete laments and mourning, as already mentioned, are transformed into poems of despair, where acceptance and toleration give way to rebellion and defiance. As Balsamo notes, in the Renaissance, the very name of Petrarch, the "Tuscan," the "sweet lover from Florence," brought to mind a form of perfection and constancy in love.[10] However, in the poems that follow, Love is no longer idolatrized and divinized. Rather, it is vehemently accused and blamed for the speaker's calamities.

Imitation continues to be the primary writing practice. In his preface of his "Œuvres," "Au lecteur salut," Nuysement addresses his readers, and he cautions them about the inspiration he took from "the most dignified" Italian and French poets "desquels admirant les œuvres, j'ay tasché retracer quelques traits."[11] As a close reader of the *disperata*, Nuysement was in a good position to explain the "enrichment" that the Italian readings brought him and his contemporaries. He then asks his readers not to take offence if his verses are imitated or enriched by other writers, because "le crime avoué sans gesne est digne de plus douce peine." (77) Simply put, Nuysement is asking forgiveness for his "imitations," and because of his honesty, he should be forgiven. This preface is not only a true manifesto of the art of Renaissance imitation that propels Nuysement's work in a direct *imitatio* continuum from the Ancient to the modern sources, but also shows, as Daniela Costa notes, that the French poet believed that literature is self-nourished and books are in a dialogue with each other.[12] Imitation was practiced in order to remain relevant, improve on the model, and build on the tradition by writing new, perfected versions. Neo-Petrarchans adopted the *disperata topoi*—images, language, attitude, and mood—as a package, engendering a renewal in the poetry of despair, thus making the most of the well-established imitative practices. La Roque eloquently illustrates the continuum of hopelessness in the following verse: "Comme amant désolé je n'écris que tristesse,"[13] expressing the cruel reality of an inconsolable lover who only writes sadness, but also, I would argue, only writes because of it.

Although all Italian *disperata* poets mingled at different courts—with the exception of Isabella di Morra—the French poets were strictly connected to one court, that of Henri III and Henri IV, whose historical and political circumstances directly impacted their creation. Thus, they were a group of close-knit writers whose literary culture, sources, and reception were very much alike. Theirs are community stories of despair. They used despair as an underlying, powering force, and at times, they confronted and subverted the Petrarchan code with clever variations, images, obsessions, and linguistic tropes.

As the French poets became eyewitnesses and victims of the trauma caused by the Wars of Religion, they began to connect the Italian *disperata* with a particular *goût noir* of the court and its ethos. As civil wars and turmoil devastated France, the *disperata* genre, its tropes, and context provided rich and fitting material to the court poets, for whom the *disperata* became a primary source, alongside the Classics, the Medieval tradition, Petrarch, and the French predecessors. It also provided the language and *topoi* to describe their *état d'âme de fin de siècle*, and became, as Guillot notes, one of the essential components of this wave of neo-Petrarchism.[14] Like Guillot, other French critics have more recently recognized the *disperata*'s intertext, and they have provided compelling analyses for poets such as Nuysement and Birague, hence building on the work of Weber, Dubois, and Mathieu-Castellani.[15] In fact, the *disperata* appears with more and more rigor in the prolific theme of *l'amant martyr*.

The *canzoniere* form continued to remain popular. Nuysement's *Livre Second*, titled *Amours*, for example, is a *canzoniere* that contains 101 sonnets, one *prière*, two *stances*, one dialogue and one ode, and is dedicated to the personified love between the martyr of Love and his cruel beloved.[16] A second example is Durand's *canzoniere*, titled *Méditations*, which also features a great variety of genres, with forty-eight sonnets, seven *chansons*, ten *stances*, four odes,[17] six elegies, a madrigal, a dialogue, a *complainte*, and a *discours*.

The *disperata* supplied a language of persuasion with its subjunctives, imperatives, assertive "je veux," invitations, and colorful expressions. This lexis suited the culture of the time, a period marked by a rhetoric of enticement that preoccupied not only writers, but also artists, diplomats, and of course, the kings.[18] As Greenglass claims, "This culture of 'persuasion' both empowered literary culture and 'literarized' political culture," as political and literary culture went hand in hand.[19] As mentioned, since many of the poets I discuss in this chapter had political or ecclesiastical offices that closely tied them to the courts, and whose role was to write about their patrons' grandeur and benevolence, their poetry also sought to persuade readers, win them over, and force them to be witnesses of the unbearable despair.[20] The culture of persuasion produced a specific persuasion of despair, as writers felt compelled to display the misery that engulfed their world. The historical events that so drastically changed their lives and epistemological beliefs turned into a collective trauma deeply embedded in everyday life and language.[21] As Alexander argues: "Members of collectivities define their solidary relationships in ways that, in principle, allow them to share the suffering of others,"[22] which, of course, is also their own. Poets felt it was their social responsibility to narrate trauma in a lyric language that could perhaps make sense of the sufferings to their community. Therefore, late Renaissance French poetry partook deeply of social and cultural trauma.

Building on Alexander's concept of collective trauma, we see that the French poets, the *porte-parole* of their community and of their time, blamed Love and the beloved as the cruel perpetrator, although the real antagonist was history. Montaigne's quote at the beginning of this chapter, "Je ne dis les autres, sinon pour d'autant plus me dire," illustrates the kind of imitation we find in the following pages.[23] French poets "tell the others" so as to better narrate themselves. Imitation, as previously discussed, evokes resemblance and transformation: through reading and writing, the French poets discovered the Classical, the Italian, and their own tradition. They also discovered each other because of the close-knit community to which this particular group of poets belonged. Henri III's court and Palace Academy, and the literary salons afforded them numerous opportunities for interaction and exchange of words and ideas.[24] Therefore, in the poems that follow, "the others" are to be discovered and recognized in newly rearranged words and images that in no way attempt to disguise the relation between the model and the new text. Rather, the latter aspires to draw a continuum. As Montaigne explains: "Je feuillette les livres, je ne les estudie pas: ce qui m'en demeure, c'est chose que je ne reconnois plus estre d'autruy;"[25] because what is left from his readings is his, and no longer distinguishable from ever belonging to others. Therefore, the French poets imitate eclectically their models, including the *disperata*, from which they namely adopt a sense of space in which the world is turned upside down and is inhabited by fierce animals and governed by the Last Judgment; a rhetoric—the affirmative "je veux," the maledictions, and other devices that effectively express their hopelessness and are inherent also to their baroque penchant;[26] and finally, the intimate entanglement between forlorn despair and Love, Fortune, and death.

The Apocalyptic World of the French *Disperata*

A central theme in the Italian *disperata*, the *topos* of the desert reappeared obsessively in the work of the aforementioned French poets.[27] French poetry from about 1570 to about 1620 abounds in depictions of "lieux solitaires," "déserts écartez," and "lieux peu fréquentez." The more secluded the place, the better suited to the soul of the *disperato*. From Petrarch to Ronsard, to Du Bellay, the search for solitude in nature and exile has been thoroughly developed in French Renaissance poetry.[28] Petrarch uses the *topos* of exile strictly in relation to Laura, because of both her physical and emotional distance. For him and the French neo-Petrarchans, as Marie-Claire Bichard-Thomine notes, "the exiled lover feels his heart in exile."[29] However, whereas before this setting served as a solitary place in which to lament unrequited love and call for death, the French neo-Petrarchans present new nuances and use it mostly to exile themselves from the beloved and her emotional unavailability.[30] Furthermore, the settings now change from a lyrical-classical to a predominantly macabre landscape.[31] Therefore, the addition of the *disperata* produces an *exil amoureux* that is particularly gruesome and sinister.

The neo-Petrarchan speaker seeks a favorable place in which to let his despair burst and flow, and in which to lament his disappointment and hopelessness. In fact, each of these poets' *canzonieri* feature portrayals of these scenes with almost perfect rigidity, as if there were only one space for the poet to release his plaint. In the following *stance*, focusing on the *disperata*'s *locus amoneus*, Nuysement establishes an ambiguous mood that recreates the *disperato*'s attitude and doom:

> J'erreray par l'obscur dans l'espaisseur des bois,
> Et redoublant le son de ma mourante voix,
> Je me plaindray au Ciel de ma triste infortune

(I will wander through the obscurity of the thick woods,/and doubling the sound of my dying voice,/I will lament my misfortune to the Sky) ("Livre II," vv. 4–6, 327).

He continues his wandering seeking repose from the harshness that afflicts him, again in the most secluded places: "Soit parmy les forests aux lieux plus escartez" ("Livre II," v. 82, 330). As I have suggested in previous chap-

ters, to wander in the dark—amplifying a dying voice, forcing it to become
louder and louder, while denunciating and damning Fortune or Love, or
the cruel beloved—this is really what the *disperata* is all about. Thus, as
early as the first stanza, Nuysement pledges his allegiance to the *disperata*
tradition, revealing that he carefully read it, internalized it, and made it his
own by portraying a rejected lover who seeks solace in this imaginary setting. Time and time again, in his *canzoniere* Nuysement wanders through
his "lieux escartez," hopeless and rootless:

> J'erre seul mi-transi dans ces lieux escartez,
> Et par le vain accent de mes vers rechantez,
> Je decelle aux rochers la poison qui me tue

> (I wander alone, half dead in these isolated places,/And with the
> hollow accent of my repetitive verses,/I disclose to the rocks the
> poison that is killing me) ("Livre II," vv. 12–14, 280).

His "Stances" and "Enchantements" are pervaded with eerie landscapes,
the *chiaroscuro*, and many *disperata* landmarks which embrace the speaker's screams and his poisonous unhappiness.

In this *fin de siècle* ravaged by war, religious conflicts, and persecution, the poet-lover seeks an illusory place in which to lament his suffering,
far from society, the beloved, and the banality of his world. Guillot notes
that this sinister and hostile setting harmonizes well with the desperate
lover, becoming a poetic vogue.[32] D'Aubigné's "lieux déserts" make a grand
reappearance in Béroalde de Verville's poetry, which vividly describes the
speaker's privileged place:

> Je veux seul, escarté, ores dans un bocage,
> Ores par les rochers, souspirer mon dommage,
> Et plaindre sous l'horreur du destin irrité,
> Je veux aupres des eaux tristement murmurantes,
> Et pres l'obscurité des grottes effrayantes,
> Soulager mon esprit de soucis tourmenté

> (I want, alone, here in a grove/and there by the rocks, to whisper my
> injuries,/and complain under the horror of an irritated destiny./I
> want to alleviate my spirit tormented by worries/nearby the sad,
> murmuring waters,/and in the darkness of the frightening grottoes)
> (vv. 1–6, 42).[33]

The space is described in similar verses and tone because the model is compelling, and poets felt seduced to not deviate from it. Béroalde continues,

and ponders questions that, rather than seek an answer, are burdened with rhetorical meaning:

> Dans quel antre escarté m'iray-je retirer
> Dedans quelle forest iray-je souspirer,
> En quel lointain desert asses grand pour ma plainte,
> Pleureray-je le mal dont mon ame est atteinte?

(In which forgotten grotto will I retire,/In which forest will I go to whisper,/In which far away desert big enough for my lament/Will I cry the evil that ravages my soul?) (vv. 1–4, 19).

In fact, questions of this nature are meant to persuade readers of the lover-persona's agony, rather than interrogate them about it. However, if in many *disperate* this interrogation is used to elicit the reader's attention and complete allegiance,[34] Béroalde's obsession on where exactly will he despair is taken a step further in order to underscore the importance of the exact place that will accept the speaker's cries, as if looking for and obsessing about it might provide some relief.[35]

Flaminio de Birague, as well, obsesses about wandering in cherished isolation, lured by a familiar scene found in the Italian *disperata*. He often opens his poems with the formula:

> Par le milieu des desers écartez,
> Dans la frayeur des Antres plus sauvages,
> Et sur le bord des pluis loingtains rivages,
> Je fuy les lieux des hommes habitez

(In the middle of the secluded deserts,/In the frightful, wildest grottoes,/And on the banks of the farthest rivers,/I run away from crowded places) ("Tome I," vv. 1–4, 98).[36]

Birague's many invocations to these deserted and harsh sites are nuanced by a macabre and ghastly tone.[37] Moreover, the speaker often paints horrific scenes where he will continue to wander and despair his "cruels malheurs" ("Tome II," 152–155).[38] Surrounded by tombs, secret demons, and frightening forests, the poet-persona laments his pain day and night. From melancholic roaming to distressed pleas for his complaint to be heard, the *topos* is skillfully enriched and perfectly staged. Moreover, since the beloved refuses to hear her admirer's words, the grottoes' shadows and darkness gather to receive the tortured speaker, just like in Morani's *Vita disperata*: "et voglio fabricar, solo, in un bosco,/un antro che m'assembri, oscuro e fosco." (vv. 7–8, 69) Birague creatively refashions the *disperata* in a shorter and compressed form, pervaded by haunting images, familiar lexis, and an eerie atmosphere.

Théophile as well crafts an ode bursting with the very particular settings found in most *disperate*. Like many *disperate* authors, he draws on his personal history, but it is a history heavily influenced by the Wars of Religion, an experience unique to the French writers. A converted Huguenot, Théophile was exiled from Paris, and thrown in jail because of his political and religious beliefs, which spurred an urging need to hide and isolate himself from the public and from the court.[39] His poem turns into the speaker's own ghost, doomed to wander even after his death.[40] In another example, Théophile's persona also ends up in a desert:

> Je viens dans un desert mes larmes espancher,
> ...
> Parmi ces tristes lieux trainant mes longs regrets,
> Je me promene seul dans l'horreur des forests,
> Où le funeste orfraie, et le hibou se perchent,
> Là le seul reconfort qui peu m'entretenir,
> C'est de ne craindre point que les vivans me cherchent,
> Où le flambeau du jour n'osa jamais venir.

> (I come to this desert to pour my tears,/ ... /In these sad places I drag along my great regrets,/I walk alone in the horror of the woods,/Where the ominous osprey and owl rest,/There the only comfort that can appease me,/Is to not fear that the mortals will be looking for me,/Where the day's torch never dared to come.) ("Première Partie," vv. 5–14, 154).

Among the ominous night birds, his erratic search for solitude and darkness acquires the determination of a persecuted man who at last finds solitude and repose.

The motif of hiding and refuge is also present in the work of Pontus de Tyard, who served as Henri III's counselor and chaplain.[41] His *canzoniere, Les Erreurs amoureuses*, is one of the first lyric collections in France that shows significant intertextualities with the *disperata*. In the following *chanson*, the speaker seeks a cavernous mountain in which to grieve with violent ardor:

> D'une ardeur violente,
> En voix piteuse et lente:
> Je veux semer

> Le deuil qui accompaigne
> Mon ennuy trop amer.
>
> (vv. 5–9, 204).

Sheltered in the forest, he wishes to scatter his deep, bitter sorrow. The pain is voiced throughout his song, in pitiful laments and sharp sighs (vv. 37–45, 205), whereby the speaker calls for his death. Finally, he too addresses his song and shuts himself down:

> Avec moy, chanson rude,
> En ceste solitude,
> Amerement
> Pleure l'ingratitude
> Qui me tient en tourment

> (With me, my rough song,/In this solitude,/Bitterly/cry the ingratitude/That torments me) (vv. 64–68, 206).

Here he visibly resonates with Beccari's *disperata*, "canzon nova de pianto" and il Saviozzo's, "Canzon/ ... /Con le più disperate et tapinelle/anime parlerai: piange e suspira."

While using numerous ghastly elements and images, the seventeenth-century poet Saint-Amant repeats the pleasure he finds in the solitude of abandoned ruins in several of his stanzas. As a poet of the early Classicism, Saint-Amant used nature as both a welcoming and idyllic element in many of his works. However, in the following lines, he stages it as a macabre refuge, perfectly suitable to his apprehensions:

> O que j'ayme la solitude!
> Que ces lieux sacrez à la nuit,
> Esloignez du monde et du bruit,
> Plaisent à mon inquiétude!

> (Oh how I love solitude!/How these places sacred to the night,/Far from the world and from the noise/Are loved by my disquietude!) (vv. 1–4, 3).

The remote and silent world summoned here brings him back to the beginning of time and to a primitive condition of intimate isolation where he can find himself surrounded by nature's ravages. "La Solitude" is one of Saint-Amant's earliest-known compositions. Probably written in 1617, it demonstrates the persistence of the *disperata*'s influence during the early seventeenth century, as in twenty stanzas the poem develops numerous *disperata topoi.* Although some of the stanzas portray a romantic vision of nature, others significantly expand the *goût du désespoir* with macabre spectacles, fierce animals, and mythical characters, all steeped in deep solitude.[42] Throughout, the poetic persona never steps out of the *disperata* landscape and obsessively searches for a perfect place in which to let his words flow:

> Je ne cherche que les deserts,
> Où, resvant tout seul je m'amuse
> A des discours asses diserts

> (I only seek the deserts,/Where, dreaming all alone, I rejoice/With my eloquent discourses) (vv. 185–187, 8).

This crucial verse, "I only seek the deserts" visibly echoes d'Aubigné's "Je cherche les deserts," as well as the many other French poets of despair discussed in this book. The conversational, yet vastly assertive, "I only seek" constitutes an important complement to the model, because it underscores how these deserted settings have become the only suitable place in which the poet's hopeless state and thoughts can be freed, and then contained. As I have previously indicated, it is in this isolation and sinister world that the desperate soul finds it easiest to relive life's cruelest moments.

The adoption of the *disperata*'s familiar settings (hell, deserted nature, secluded spaces, and grottoes) is one of the most important aspects of intertextuality in neo-Petrarchan poetry.[43] If the "descente aux enfers" is a fusion of Virgil's and Dante's "Descensus Averno" with the *disperata*, the latter vastly embedded it into the everyday experience of the early modern poet, as an essential component of poetic despair. What is most significant, I argue, is that in the poetry of despair, there is little difference between terrestrial and infernal settings, as they are both invaded by desolation, solitude, and the macabre. Hell is on Earth, and thus, descending into hell is no longer a punishment, because, as Etienne Durand writes, "L'Enfer n'a point de peine à mes peines égale,/Ni point de feux aussi comme ceux que je sens" (Hell has no pain equal to mine,/Nor flames as those that I feel) (vv. 5–6, 76).[44] Moreover, the frantic search for a deserted site that promises to swallow the speaker, whether on Earth or in hell, provides a scenario that receives his boundless despair and dark *états d'âme*, where his only company are the sinister and fierce animals. Readers are once again cast in the role of reluctant witnesses to these dramatic scenes. Thus, Durand, a court poet of Maria de Medici's entourage between 1608 and 1618, attests to the persistence of many of the *disperata topoi* at the beginning of the seventeenth century.[45]

Another intertextuality we witness is with the arid settings that are inhabited only by fierce beasts and ominous birds, the *disperati*'s only companions. Their role is to complete the eerie atmosphere, as in Birague's sonnet, where the night birds see the beginning of a doomed love:

> Tous ces oiseaux qui sous la Nuit obscure
> D'un triste vol se plaignent lentement,
> Ne sont tesmoins du doux commencement
> De mon amour sainte, loyale, et pure

(These birds, who under the dark Night/Gently lament amidst their sad flight,/Are not witnessing the sweet beginning/Of my sacred, loyal, and pure love) ("Tome I," vv. 1–4, 32).

These nocturnal birds, as in Sasso's "Vol gli uccelli: che stridon la notte/ La nottula: la loccho: el guffo vanno,"[46] represent the ministers of death. Birague shows that he was an attentive reader, as his "Nuit" and "vol" closely echo Sasso's "volo" and "notte". The birds are not only witnesses to the speaker's despair but also moan with him, and for him. The presence of these birds foreshadows his doom, establishing therefore another main intertextuality between the poets of the *disperata* and the French neo-Petrarchans who do not rejoice with the birds' singing, but rather, mourn their laments.[47]

Another example of this intertextuality is found in La Roque's sonnet that, along with several other *disperata topoi*, imparts a particularly prominent role to the wild animals and nocturnal birds.[48] Two verses "Le seul objet d'une ame malheureuse" and "Et viens à vous pour lamenter mon sort" (The only object of an unhappy soul and I come to you to lament my destiny) are central to the entire sonnet, highlighting the importance and symbolism of these animals, the only objects and signs of an unhappy soul. In another sonnet, La Roque's speaker personifies the nocturnal bird who flees his own kind, a theme found often in both the Italian and French *disperata*:

> Je suis le triste Oyseau de la nuit solitaire,
> Qui fuit sa mesme espece & la clairté du jour,
> De nouveau transformé par la rigueur d'Amour,
> Pour annoncer l'augure au malheureux vulgaire

(I am the sad Bird of the lonely night,/That flees its own species and the day's light,/Transformed once again by Love's rigors,/And who bodes ill to the miserable commoner) (vv. 1–4, 62–63).

The speaker has metamorphosed into a nocturnal bird who shuns his own, living in light before, and now in darkness (v. 14, 63), forced to inhabit a universe steeped in the shadows that mirror his soul.[49]

Heavy with symbolism, the animals and birds from the neo-Petrarchans acquire a particularly lugubrious meaning. They do not serve as a merely decorative lyric element, rather, they foreshadow tragedy. In Nuysement's haunting poem "Enchantements," we see another example of intertextuality. Here, Nuysement gives his fierce beasts a prominent position: "Si les fiers animaux, si tant d'autres dangers" ("Livre III," v. 60, 100).[50] They inhabit their speaker's imagination and become objects that contribute to the overall morose character of doom that materializes in the text.[51]

As we have seen in the Italian *disperata*, many of the French *disperate* also depict an overturned world, where the family relations are torn by violence and subverted passions.[52] The speaker bitterly damns his crib as a symbol of the very beginning of a doomed life filled with empty promises. The disequilibrium, the desire for catastrophes and the calls foreshadowing the end of the world, mark a complete reversal of the natural order. Théophile's verses fully capture this reversal: "Tantost je prends le soir pour le matin,/Tantost je prends le Grec pour le Latin" (At times I take the evening for the morning,/and, at times, I take Greek for Latin) (vv. 47–48, 114). Paradoxically, in his "Epistre au lecteur," Théophile presents his œuvre as one that reflects his life truthfully, "assez conformes à ma vie, et très esloignez du bruict qu'on a faict courir de moy" (pretty close to my life, and very far from the rumors about me) ("Première Partie," 5). He also describes his world as damned by the Sky and the Earth ("Première Partie," 6), including the King Louis XIII. He explains that "les gens de lettre ne sçavent rien: la plus part des Juges sont criminels, passer pour honneste homme c'est ne l'estre point" (people of letters do not know anything: the majority of Judges are criminal, and to be perceived as an honest man means that you are not one) ("Première Partie," 6). In other words, Théophile is presenting a world whose order and principles are turned upside down, labeling it "ce rebours de toute chose"— this inverse of all things ("Première Partie," 6). Moreover, Théophile portrays a universe that often does not make sense, with images, objects, animals, human relations, and actions subverting their natural order and taking the hyperbole to extreme lengths in order to suggest the many impossibilities facing his existence.[53] The Italian *disperata* and the French neo-Petrarchan poets fully exploit this *topos* and weave it with countless new images and nuances.[54]

In the following ode, Théophile stages a realm that, as Streicher explains, has been affected by bad omens gathered on the page by a man who feels in danger:[55]

> Ce ruisseau remonte en sa source,
> Un bœuf gravit sur un clocher,
> Le sang coule de ce rocher,
> Un aspic s'accouple d'une ourse.
> Sur le haut d'une vieille tour
> Un serpent deschire un vautour,
> Le feu brusle dedans la glace,
> Le Soleil est devenu noir,
> Je voy la Lune qui va cheoir,
> Cet arbre est sorty de sa place.

(This stream goes back to its source,/An ox climbs up a steeple,/ Blood flows down this rock,/This viper mates with a she-bear./ High above an old tower,/A snake tears up a vulture,/Fire burns inside ice,/The Sun has turned black,/I see the Moon about to fall,/ This tree came out of its place.) (vv. 11–20, 164–165).

Each verse vividly puts in place an oxymoronic universe, whose disharmony is meant to draw in, rather than turn off readers. As this upside-down world unfolds before our eyes, it becomes clear that the fragmentary reproduction is a metaphor of the writer's intimate observations and painful realization that this "rebours" is determined to persist.

Nuysement also depicts an overturned world, and often calls for multiple cataclysms to end a chaotic cosmos, but a difference from the Italian *disperata* is that rather than affect the whole humanity, he calls for the cataclysms to strike only him: "Facent or mes mal-heurs" and "Pluton puisse à ma mort."[56] The subjunctive mode in "Facent" and "puisse," reflects the speaker's will to demand that despair ("mes mal-heurs") do evil. In another poem too, the subjunctive is used to project an apocalyptic view of the world, in which its elements are tragically subverted:

> Que les vents enragez facent precipiter
> Les estoilles du Ciel dans la mer une à une,
> Que Phoebus et Phoebé rendent sa face brune,
> Et que son foudre mesme il ne puisse eviter!

(That the enraged winds throw off/The Sky stars, one by one, into the sea/That Phoebus and Phoebe show his dark face,/And that he may not avoid his own lightning!) ("Livre II," vv. 5–8, 232).

An apocalyptic vision of gigantic proportions is also present in Jean-Baptiste Chassignet's poetry.[57] Very much aligned with the *disperata*, the following verses show the speaker's wish to experience a world engulfed by catastrophic events and imaginary calamities:

> Ce monde ...
> Un jour il doit finir et ce jour là s'appelle
> Jour de calamité, de plainte et de querelle.

(This world, ... /One day it must end, and that day is called/The day of calamities, laments and quarrels) (vv. 13–16, 512).

Just like the other *disperati*, this speaker displays a negative vision of the future, where all is doomed to a tragic end and where clashes and complaints prevail. The poem, appropriately titled "Le dernier jugement," continues with visions that jar the imagination,[58] in which families are in turmoil, and father, son, and brothers kill each other in a reversal of human bonds:

> Le filz delivrera au trespas rigoureus
> Son pere renié, le sanguinaire pere
> Fera mourir son filz, engence de vipere;
> Sans respecter le sang les parens se tu'ront
> Et frere contre frere en bataille entreront!
> (vv. 70–74, 514).

The entire family overthrows personal attachments and expectations as each member disregards sanguine relations and, instead, murders his next of kin. This is one of the *disperata*'s main traits, where the family's order is completely turned upside down creating the chaos in the speaker's world, as encountered in Morra's poems. At the end of the French Renaissance, though, it also reflects the reality of the civil wars where family members are pitched one against the other because of their religious beliefs and political allegiance.

In Chassignet's world, animals also contribute to its turmoil and are nurtured by a crescendo of jarring scenarios until its gruesome ending (vv. 102–172, 515–518). In this poem's 208 verses, the narrative closely mirrors the *disperata*'s calamity sequence. The effect of disturbing repetitions and the all-encompassing gravity of elements, such as "Tous les astres," is remarkably realistic. Furthermore, the reiteration of the word "mal-heur à" embodies a persuasive malediction, as in "mal à", that is "bad to" or "evil to," because in this day of doom, all can be damned and tragically upset.

These invectives greatly intensify the many images of a world already upside down, but being drawn directly from everyday life's experiences, they also reflect Chassignet's world which was a France torn by civil wars.

If the neo-Petrarchan poets readily embraced the *topos* of the world upside down, it was because these devastating scenarios fittingly conveyed the events of the end of the sixteenth and beginning of the seventeenth century. Many traumas plagued this period, such as the repercussions of the advent of the Reformation in a mostly homogenous religious country, the rejection of the rites of the Church previously integral to Europe's religious and cultural fabric, and all that was brewing in the political realm. Together, these constituted a drastic reversal of order and a blatant symptom of *le monde renversé*. According to Yves-Marie Bercé, the political and religious events that had perpetrated the world's order prompted the metaphor of a distraught and vacillating State, whose end was near.[59] As previously discussed, d'Aubigné had developed the theme of *le monde à l'envers* not only in his lyric poetry, but in particular in his *Tragiques*, undoubtedly providing an additional contemporary model for his fellow poets.[60] Sasso overtly wishes for this reversal in his verse: "Voria che andasse la terra sottosopra" ("Disperata contro l'amore," vv. 126). Furthermore, apocalyptic and Biblical images, and references to "judgment day" were widely spread.[61] The French poets witnessed an "upside down world" of apocalyptic doom every day, especially those who had embraced the Reformation, including d'Aubigné, Béroalde, and Théophile. Their poetry reflects this experience. Denis Crouzet establishes a compelling link between the brutality of the Wars of Religion, particularly the Saint Bartholomew's Day massacre and the fear of the Last Judgment.[62] Although all periods in history are plagued with apocalyptic fears, as Luc Racaut notes, "people were more afraid of the end of time in the sixteenth century than in any other time in history of Christendom"[63] because of the Reformation and the Counter-Reformation.

The Rhetoric of the French *Disperata*: "Je veux," "Rien de si malheureux que moi!" and "Maudit soi!"

Although the circumstances in late Renaissance France and in Trecento to Cinquecento Italy were similar in many ways, we will see the French poets change verb tense from conditional to more assertive. Both countries experienced wars, Church corruption, the Reformation and Counter-Reformation, and social upheavals. This world provided a plethora of suggestive fragments that burst into the *disperata*'s apocalyptic depictions and projections, fueled by the rhetoric of despair. The poets' assertive "je veux," "I wish," the subjunctive and imperative verb modes, the desire to split from the rest of humanity—"only I," in order to suffer alone as the most persecuted man on Earth, and the maledictions persist in images characterized by pessimism and collective trauma.

The Italian *disperata*'s conditional "vorrei," and its future equivalent "vorrò" reappear in the verses of the French poets with an assertive "je veux." The conditional tense had been abandoned for a more emphatic "I want/I will." In Nuysement's poem "Enchantements," clusters of "je veux" and "je me veux" abound for a total of seven in the first eighteen verses, thus echoing the *disperata*'s distinctive style and determination: "Je me veux rendre serf d'une eternelle peine" (I want to serve eternal sorrow) ("Livre III," v. 2, 95).[64] The verses that follow continue a desideratum that is as apocalyptic as the catalogues we find in the Italian *disperate*: "Je veux or' esprouver et le bien et le mal" (I want now to prove both good and evil) ("Livre III," v. 4, 96). However, Nuysement creatively predicts multiple cataclysms that again, rather than affecting the world and humanity, strike only him. In the following poem the future tense is used to emphatically foretell the speaker's own daring actions and untamed will:

> Je couvriray mon corps d'un long habit de dueil,
> J'auray autour de moy un drap et un cercueil,
> Tenant de l'une main la consacree image,
> De l'autre le cousteau; et pour luy faire outrage,
> L'approcheray du feu, ores frappant le corps,
> Ores picquant le cueur, ore gravant dehors
> Mille coups punisseurs ...

> (I will cover my body with a long, mourning cloak,/I will be surrounded by a cloth and a coffin,/Holding in one hand the consecrated image,/In the other a knife; and to provoke outrage,/I will put it by the fire, at times beating my body,/At times stabbing my heart, and at times carving/A thousand punishing blows ...) ("Livre III," vv. 191–197, 112–113).

The tenebrous tone and macabre notions mesh perfectly to create this haunting picture.[65] Moreover, the speaker's determination to inflict pain upon himself by martyrizing the body and burning it, unveils a masochistic desire to suffer physically and mentally as a last attempt to mask the emotional turmoil of his everyday existence. A recurring theme in the poetry of the *disperata*, self-inflicted punishment also entices the French poets, who capitalize intensely on its disturbing effect on the reader.

The assertive voice of the French poets, rather than the conditional tense of the Italian *disperata*, can be seen with Béroalde, who often uses the expression "je veux" to assert his voice: "Je veux donc sans espoir perir en mon malheur,/Je veux d'un coup mortel perçant mon triste cœur" (I want to die, without hope,/I want to pierce my heart with a fatal blow) (vv. 151–152, 39). As if responding to Nuysement's verse "picquant le cueur," this verse too compellingly shows that the heart is the site of despair, thus, the first to be hurt and slayed. Undoubtedly, the speaker's verbalization of his will, as well as his subjunctives, firmly place him in a position of power. Mathieu-Castellani argues that Béroalde's many "je veux" are integral to the baroque discourse, as it is authoritative, direct, and seeks to reassure its position and control.[66] Certainly, this position recurs in the Baroque, but it is also one of the *disperata*'s main traits, and it remains fundamental to the stance of the poet-persona as it allows him to emphasize his wishes, demands, desires, and actions. Likewise, in Tebaldeo's, Morani's, and d'Aubigné's *disperate*, the poet-persona's resilience is bursting to express and assert itself. Moreover, this relentless attitude of self-assertion allows the speaker to bestow some order upon his existence and to exert some control over his life. The French neo-Petrarchan poets purposely adopted this attitude because, as court poets in times of war, they exerted little control over their own circumstances and found that order was often out of reach.[67] Birague couples his "je veux" with the future tense:

> Je veux à tout jamais d'une plainte importune
> Remplir de pyteux cris l'air, la Terre, et les Cieux.
> Une ondoyante mer de mes pleurs je veux faire,
> Où singlera la nef de mes bouillans desirs,
> Qui aura pour Phanal ma flame ardente et claire,
> Et pour mes vers, le vent de mes tristes souspirs.

(I want forever, with an importunate lament/Fill with pitiful cries the air, the Earth, and the Skies./I want to make an undulating sea with my weeping,/Where the ship of my burning desires will sail,/My ardent and clear flame will be its light,/And my verses, the wind of my sad sighs.) ("Tome I," vv. 11–16, 164–165).

Again, we encounter the speaker's urge to make his *plainte* heard in a traditional coupling of "je veux" with the future tense ("singlera" and "aura"), as in Carretto's and Serafino's poems where the trumpet will herald their pain. Moreover, the first and final verses of this *complainte* are a perfect example of how deeply Birague's *poesis* is inscribed in the *disperata* tradition. The entire poem demands to be heard and believed—hear, say, narrate ("Oyez, Dites, Contez"), with a multiplication of imperatives, threatening futures, and demanding "je veux."[68]

The imperative was also used by the French writers to create credibility. For example, La Roque writes an evocative *complainte*:

> Vous forests à qui je raconte
> La fureur du mal qui me domte,
> Croyez qu'amour me fait parler

(You woods, to which I tell/The furor of the evil that subjugates me,/Believe that love makes me talk) (vv. 49–51, 132).

The reader and the forest are forced to believe ("Croyez") his unrequited desire is a *sine qua non* of his existence.[69] He then continues to demand that his despair be heard, witnessed, and broadly broadcasted.[70] Saint-Amant as well makes frequent use of the imperatives, as in the following verses where the mode becomes a sharp damnation against dead people, monsters, and all that lies within the sea:

> Que l'ire de Neptune outrage,
> Des gens noyez, des monstres morts,
> Des vaisseaux brisez du naufrage,
> Des diamans, de l'ambre gris,
> Et mille autres choses de pris

(That Neptune's rage outrage,/Drowned people, dead monsters,/Shipwrecks,/Diamonds, grey amber/And a thousand other things) (vv. 166–170, 7).[71]

The first line, "That Neptune's rage outrage" also accompanies other *disperata* motifs that are developed in other stanzas of the poem, shaping images filled with compulsion and despair, and thus transforming the speaker's wishes into dark visions that engulf his universe.

As I have shown, the frequency of "I want" or "I don't want," verbalized imperatives, futures, and the subjunctive mode all became a motif in itself that the French neo-Petrarchans adopted into their poems. These examples show that the French poets capitalized and expanded on the repertoire of linguistic and rhetorical formulas in order to paint a vision that reflected their world and that would persuade their readers of their despair. In fact, the forlorn poet-persona deploys a set of linguistic practices that describe his unique and lonely predicaments in the face of unspeakable calamities. La Roque as well finds himself alone and asks, as the unhappiest man on earth, to be abandoned to his fate:

> Et vous roches abandonnees
> Qui voyez le cours des annees,
> Roches que j'esbranle d'effroy,
> Escoutez ma douleur profonde
> Veistez vous jamais en ce monde
> Rien de si malheureux que moy?

(And you abandoned rocks/Who see the passing of time,/Rocks that I shake with fear,/Listen to my deep pain/Have you ever seen in this world/Anything as unhappy as myself?) (vv. 31–36, 114).

Demanding to be heard, "Escoutez," yet asking directly if anyone as unhappy as him has ever been seen, the poet-persona clearly stands out, alone, against the world, accompanied only by his *malheur*. In fact, it is his *malheur* that sets him apart.

As in Tyard's poem, where the speaker points out his uniqueness in the face of his incurable grief, "Or donc, puisqu'il n'y ha homme vivant au monde" and awaits death as the only solution to his miserable existence,[72] Birague addresses a number of natural entities (O desers ...ô plages ... ô rivages ... ô Astres ...O cieux...) and asks if a more miserable lover has ever been seen before: "Vistes vous onc Amant plus que moy miserable" ("Tome I," v. 14, 119), which, is not really an interrogative question, but rather a fervent statement crafted to convince the reader of his exceptional pain and of a cruel fate that only persecutes him.

In a wide range of lyric forms, Durand similarly paints a very macabre setting full of suffering and immediately establishes a somber mood. He asks the Shadows to confirm that nobody else suffers as much as he does:

> Ombres qui dans l'horreur de vos nuicts eternelles
> ...
> Venez asseurer qu'en sa pleine fatale
> L'enfer n'a point de peine à mes peines egale,
> Ny point de feux aussi comme ceux que je sens

(Shadows, who in the horrors of your eternal nights/ ... / Come to assure that in its fatal plane/Hell has no pain equal to mine,/Nor flames as those that I feel) (vv. 1–6, 76).

In another poem, Durand's speaker stands alone in the face of adversity:

Croy-moy, mon cher soucy, que dans ces tristes lieux,
Ces rochers envieillis qui soustiennent les Cieux,
Ny ces arbres brisez par le poid de leur aage,
N'ont jamais veu d'Amant qui souffrist davantage

(Believe me, my dear distress, that in these sad places,/Neither these
aged rocks that support the Skies,/Nor these trees broken by the
weight of their age,/Have ever seen a Lover who suffered more)
(vv. 87–90, 123).

Thus, when it comes to pain and despair, the *disperato* is equal to none,
be it alone in hell or on Earth, and forced to face his unique, unfortunate
condition.

   As I have shown in the previous chapters, the rhetoric of maledictions is one of the principal characteristics of the *disperata*, whether
against Fortune, Love, despair, the speaker's state, or even the parents who
gave him birth,[73] and they are passionately repeated by the French neo-
Petrarchans, thus persuasively expanding one of the genre's main *topoi*. In
a troubling tale of despair, for example, Nuysement asks how many times,
wandering as a bull blinded by the furors of love, has he damned his destiny and everything else:

Errant comme un taureau par amour furieux,
Ay-je maudit le sort, la nature, les Dieux,
Le Ciel, l'Air, l'Eau, la Terre, et Phoebus et la Lune!
("Livre II," vv. 2–4, 271).[74]

The question posed in these verses is strictly rhetorical and a direct reference to the *disperata* maledictions against Fortune, nature, the Gods,
the universe, and its elements. This malediction, carefully placed in the
first quatrain, becomes one of this poem's main components to which
other *disperata topoi* are related, culminating in the lover-persona's blatant
admission of his despair: "But, halas, I am now unhappier than anybody
else!"[75] In another instance, Durand's maledictions go as far as cursing his
own sight for exposing the object of desire,

Et dans ce triste enfer où mon âme se treuve
...
N'ay-je pas bien raison de maudire ma veue
Qui m'a comblé le cœur d'une rage incognue
Qui ne se peut guarir?
                                   (vv. 52–57, 79).

In a rhetorical question, the lover-persona asserts the reason that pushes him to damn as a legitimate expression of his all-encompassing rage that cannot be tamed.

As these examples demonstrate, the French neo-Petrarchans use maledictions in various degrees of power and with an assortment of meanings according to the intensity of their rhetoric, tone, and despair. These are an expression of verbal violence and aggression; words in which the invectives bring about evil, destruction, and often a tangible curse. Moreover, these maledictions, especially in a short genre like a sonnet, are a blatant form of verbal violence, but, as we have already seen in the Italian *disperata*, they also contribute to the overall darkness and gloom of the poem. These curses are not only a call for "mal-heur," but they are also charged with negative consequences for the speaker, thus pervading his texts and his world with nuanced hopelessness.[76]

Fortune, Love, and Death

In the poetry of the *disperata*, Love and Fortune are negative forces, the antagonists that work against the speaker's efforts to reach serenity. Death on the other hand, becomes the object of desire and an end to which aspire. Because Love and Fortune haunt the poetic persona, death is welcoming, and a sure end to one's sorrows. Most of all, death is truthful, loyal and not deceitful—in other words, all that Fortune and Love are not. Moreover, because death is everywhere and an everyday life occurrence, it is more predictable and acceptable; thus, it substitutes Love as the object of desire and assured gratification.

Fortune and misfortune continue to haunt the French poets, as *le sort* is often set against *l'amant martyr* and his desires, but we notice an even deeper resentment that builds in intensity and anger on the Italian model. Furor and Love go hand in hand, and the experience is gravely tainted by Fortune's negative power. In La Roque's *plainte*, for example, Love and Fortune conspire to shut down hope, in a whirlwind of broken dreams:

> Puis que l'absence me retire
> En ce desert, òu je soupire
> L'amour qui me rend furieux:
> Puis que le sort me porte envie,
> Je veux faire escouler ma vie
> ...
> L'espoir doit estre supprimé (vv. 1–9, 112–113).

La Roque pairs Love with destiny and hopeless desire in images that recur often in the poetry of the French neo-Petrarchans. Although possibilities still seem within reach, the speaker debunks them for himself and for the reader, who is then left with a sense of endless disappointment. In another of La Roque's poems, Love is blamed and damned, and the speaker accuses it of triggering all sorrows and furors:

> Tout ce qu'on peut voir icy bas
> D'horreur, d'ennuis & de trespas,
> De fureur, sur la terre & l'onde,
> Vient par cest enfant malheureux (vv. 7–10, 179).

La Roque again pairs Love with destiny and hopeless desire. Here, he does not deviate from the model where the ill-fated lovers employed fate's unfavorable side to serve as an example of martyrdom to all other lovers and to set themselves apart as uniquely unfortunate. In another example by Béroalde, the speaker feels outnumbered by Fortune's and Love's conspiracy against him, and he feels unprepared to even put up a fight against such negative force:

> Sous les forces d'amour vainement poursuyvant
> Une fortune aveugle, iray-je loing du monde
> joindre avec tant de maux une peine profonde?
> …
> que me faut-il donc faire
> Pour me rendre propice un destin si contraire
> (vv. 66–72,19–20).

In his poem "Les Visions," Saint-Amant is also haunted by an opposing fate, and thus, feels compelled to keep wandering:

> Moy, qui d'un sort rigoureux outrage à tous propos,
> Et qui ne puis gouster ny plaisir ny repos,
> …
> J'erre dans les enfers, je raude dans les cieux;
> (vv. 15–19, 33).

Whether inexorable or rigorous, Fortune is never on the poet-persona's side, not even by chance. Thus, the powerless speaker must contend with both Love and Fortune.[77] United in hostility, they conspire to destroy all of his desires and to disappoint all of his aspirations. In Durand, we see a close imitation of the *disperata* because he too rebels against the beloved's refusals, and like many other poets of despair, he too expresses his bitterness and disappointment, "Mais ce folastre Amour que j'eus par le passé/Est maintenant contraint à céder à l'outrage" (vv. 7–8, 170). Unlike in Petrarch's *canzoniere*, therefore, the French poet no longer patiently endures Love's frustrations. Furthermore, *l'innamoramento*, as already seen in the Italian poems, becomes the beginning of the end, where Love's rejections and humiliations cause alienation from the world. Therefore, we are faced once again with a subversion of the Petrarchan code as the lover-persona openly rebels against the beloved's cruelty. Opposite the hostility of Love and Fortune, he shows vulnerability and suffering, at times begging for consideration or condemning them with harsh terms, as in Birague's verses: "O Destin rigoureux! ô marastre Fortune,/Verserez-vous toujours sur moy mille malheurs?" ("Tome I," vv. 5–6, 142) and "Ferez-vous jamais tréve à mes griéves douleurs?/Finirez-vous jamais ma langueur importune?" (vv. 7–8, 142). However, Love and Fortune display no sympathy as they are relentless in their devastating path, where the poet-lover is doomed to contend with them as the two main culprits of his despair.[78] Poetry, then, becomes the site of rebellion, in which Love is accused and shamed of pushing the lover-persona to expose his deepest evils. In adopting their sources, the French poets greatly increased the dramatic tones, intentionally pushing readers to witness their unjust treatment.

As previously seen with both the Italian and French *disperata*, death turns into the object of desire and embodies the last wish that promises repose from despair. Death recurs in various manifestations in all of the texts examined, but mostly it is cast as a refuge and as a welcomed final destination. The *topos* of pleading for death reappears frequently in the French neo-Petrarchans' verses, as in this desperate call by Birague's poetic persona:

> Mort, asseuré refuge, et unique recours
> De tous desesperez, viens achever le cours
> De ma triste, dolente, et miserable vie

(Death, sure refuge, and final resort/Of all desperate souls, Come end the course/Of my sad, doleful, and miserable life) ("Tome I," vv. 12–14, 77).

Indeed, in order to terminate all other unrequited desires that have tortured the lover, the only wish that can plausibly be answered is to find an end to his miserable days. In many such examples, death is not an improbable phenomenon, nor a matter-of-fact, unavoidable event. Rather, it is something the speaker wants to embrace and hasten.

La Roque, for example, finds comfort in death, and instead of circumventing it, he ardently calls for it:

> Non je ne trouve pas que la mort soit cruelle
> Ma voix à son secours à toute heure l'appelle:
> C'est le dernier confort d'un cœur desesperé
> (vv. 9–11, 27).

Death is not portrayed as cruel nor meant to punish the speaker. On the contrary, it is desirable, the last consolation that will appease the poet-persona's final moments. Likewise, Saint-Amant reminds his readers that death is alluring to the miserable soul:

> ...je te decris mes travaux intestins,
> Où tu verras l'effort des plus cruels destins
> Qui troublerent jamais un pauvre miserable,
> A qui le seul trespas doit estre desirable
> ("Les Visions," vv. 3–6, 33).

Chassignet's fascination with death is evident from his *canzoniere*'s title, *Le Mespris de la vie et consolation contre la mort* (1594), where he unabashedly claims: "Je ne crain point la mort" (I don't fear death) (CCIV, v. 1, 256),[79] a verse that eloquently describes the speaker's constant state of mind, and where religion and despair commingle.

Death and its many manifestations bring solace in the poetry of the last decades of the Renaissance, and continue to maintain a macabre attraction in the early seventeenth century, where Saint-Amant similarly writes the pleasure he feels at finding the sites where despair meets death, luring the speaker in his last meanders, where solace and refuge can finally be found. Here, the poetic persona describes the consolation he feels at the sight of a lover's skeleton, whose life ended in this sinister place, accompanied by the bird of death:

> L'orfraye, avec ses cris funebres,
> Mortels augures des destins,
> Fait rire et dancer les lutins
> Dans ces lieux remplis de tenebres.
> Sous un chevron de bois maudit
> Y branle le squelette horrible
> D'un pauvre amant qui se pendit
> Pour une bergère insensible

(The eagle, with its funeral cries,/Mortal wishes of destiny,/Makes the goblins laugh and dance/In these places filled with darkness./ Under a timber of damned wood/There shudders the horrible skeleton/Of a miserable lover who hung himself/For an insensible shepherdess) ("La Solitude," vv. 91–98, 5).

The entire scene is a close imitation of the *disperata*, where death is a vision to be savored and actively sought out. In this case, another lover's death brings comfort to the speaker, who is cast as a voyeur and who finds pleasure in not only witnessing it, but also recounting it as a prized spectacle. Furthermore, the haunting specter of death is depicted in realistic and nuanced terms, because the *disperata* images, which largely inspired d'Aubigné, deploy violent and catastrophic scenes that closely mirror the everyday events of the French civil wars. Death remains the desired, final aspiration, one that does not frighten, but instead entices the speaker. It is a *topos* that haunts the poetry of despair in both Italy and France, one that becomes an obsession, as the *disperato* seeks death in every corner and at all times, as in Tyard's verses:

> Les tristes nuiz,
> La Mort, si ce tems dure,
> Finira mes ennuiz

(In these sad nights,/Death, if this time lasts,/Will end my sorrows) (vv. 61–63, 206).

In his *Soupirs*, Béroalde fully develops the theme of death and its many possibilities:

> Je veux donc sans espoir perir en mon mal'heur,
> Je veux d'un coup mortel perçant mon triste cœur
> Tomber ombre legere, & croistre miserable
> Le nombre des esprits de la plaine effroyable

(Thus, I want, without hope, to die in my misfortune,/I want, with a mortal blow that pierces my sad heart/Fall like a light shadow, and multiply miserably/The number of spirits of the frightening plane) (vv. 151–154, 39).

As Janis Pallister argues, in Béroalde's poetry "it is man's catastrophe to be born into this uncertainty; it is his boon to be delivered from it into the ironically more certain posture of death."[80] Hence, death is not in charge of man, feared and avoided or even postponed. On the contrary, as staged in the *disperata*, it delivers him from a life plagued by distress and presents a welcomed certainty that is in stark contrast to unrequited love and to a life of misery.[81]

Birague weaves death to despair ("Desesperé") and forcefully reclaims a *disperata topos*, the crib (berceau), in order to underscore the all-encompassing hopelessness he has had to endure since birth:

> Desesperé chetif du repos de ma vie,
> Je chemine à grands pas au sentier douloureux
> De l'Orque espouvantable, où le sort rigoureux
> Avoit dés le berceau ma jeunesse asservie.
>
> ...
>
> Ciel, pourquoy m'as-tu fait si tost naistre icy bas,
> Pour souffrir mille maux pires que le trespas,
> Et mourir, sans mourir, mille fois en une heure?
> Helas! Appaise un peu ton injuste rigueur,
> Ou bien pour m'affranchir de ma triste langueur,
> Fay que mourant soudain aussi ma peine meure.

(Desperate and tired of my life,/I walk fast toward the painful path/ Of the dreadful Orca, where the rigorous fate/Had overwhelmed my youth since the crib/ ... /Heaven, why did you give birth to me down here/To suffer a thousand ills worse than death,/And die, without dying, a thousand times in an hour?/Alas! Appease a bit your unjust rigor,/Or in order to liberate me from my sad languor,/ Make me die suddenly so that my pain dies too.) ("Tome I," 60).

While persevering in a painful journey that started at birth, the poet-persona himself claims to be desperate. Although this *topos* is already present in the Classics and Dante's "Inferno," here it replaces the traditional descent into hell, staged as a journey of the soul, and instead posits a despair that begins far earlier. The crib, a *topos* that reminds us of the many damnations encountered in the Italian texts, as in Carretto's "La misforma culla dove io giacque," becomes the symbol of the very beginning of the expiation of punishment for the *disperato*, who, since birth, is damned to wander in despair. Biragues's sonnet intensifies as it progresses, as each verse builds in hopelessness. Moreover, verses 10 and 11 culminate in an existential question, stating the obvious fact and universal truth that binds the *disperati* together: why be born to suffer?[82]

Another example of poetry of despair fully inscribed in the *disperata* tradition is a sonnet that Théophile wrote in exile.[83] The first four verses in particular express the speaker's inability to be free of his *malheur*:

> Quelque si doux espoir où ma raison s'appuie,
> Un mal si descouvert ne se sçauroit cacher;
> J'emporte malheureux, quelque part où je fuie,
> Un trait qu'aucun secours ne me peut arracher
> ("Première Partie," vv. 1–4, 154).

The entire sonnet is built and structured around the theme of despair, incorporating several of the *disperata topoi*: unspeakable sorrow, wandering in secluded and solitary places, as well as the ominous presence of wild animals. Moreover, the final tercet is meant to summarize not only the speaker's state, but also the overall theme of despair. His only comfort, which is no comfort at all, is to be left alone, where his immense grief can be freely articulated.

Tyrard's poetry contains this type of unadulterated despair as well. Many of the poems in his *Erreurs amoureuses* portray a distraught lover who sees despair as all-encompassing, a plain, raw feeling that cannot be escaped. In the following stanza, for example, the whole universe is embraced in his sorrow:

> Fuyant le jour de ce mien beau Soleil,
> Tout m'est obscur et rien ne void mon œil
> Que dueil, ennuy et funebres tormens,
> Tormens si grans que ma douloureuse ame
> Meut à pitié le Dieu qui tant m'enflame,
> Mesme le Ciel et tous les elemens

> (Fleeing the day of my beautiful Sun,/Everything is dark and my eyes see nothing/Other than mourning, sorrow and funereal torments,/Torments so great that my painful soul/Moved to pity the God that burns me so,/Even Heaven and all of its elements) (vv. 31–36, 133).

In another poem, despair is again the culprit of many evils, "Puisque tant est ma vie miserable/Que desespoir fait en moy son office" (vv. 10–11, 234). Furthermore, as seen in the many *disperate* that are charged to sing the speaker's misery well beyond his death, this song too has to continue and carry on his voice:

> Avec moy, chanson rude,
> En ceste solitude,
> Amerement
> Pleure l'ingratitude
> Qui me tient en tourment

(With me, rough song,/In this solitude,/Bitterly/Cry the ingrati-
tude/That keeps me in anguish) (vv. 64–68, 206).

The above examples show that the *disperata* continued to be relevant and
inventive in the poetry of the neo-Petrarchans who adapted its wretched
feeling, nuanced perceptions and tropes, and in particular its representations of Fortune, Love, and death. These French poems too were born
out of hopelessness, which provided meaning to much of the poetry of
despair.

Trends of Despair

The poems examined in these chapters show that despair is intimately
entwined with death, and in most cases, it unequivocally leads to death
as the speaker seeks his own end. Durand's statement is indisputable:
he calls to death because of his despair—"Alors desesperé vers la Mort
je m'addresse" (v. 9, 46). Despair is the underscoring drive of the many
intertextualities between the Italian and French poetry here analyzed; a
theme that is organic, generative, and most of all, narrated in the same
tortured way. The poetry from both countries finds meaning, sustenance,
and an existential *raison d'être* in the deepest despair. As these examples
compellingly demonstrate, this anguish is also an emotion experienced
both physically and mentally. The many faces of despair are portrayed
as the cause and meaning of the "mal-heur" that has inspired hundreds
of hopeless verses, skillfully expressed with indignations against Love,
regrets, bitter disappointments, and anger. Although only d'Aubigné, La
Roque, Nuysement, and Birague have been directly linked to the *disperata*,
this chapter shows that other French poets of the end of the sixteenth and
beginning of the seventeenth century were indeed close readers and imitators of the genre.

Despair is the common denominator of this poetry. It becomes an
expected word that conjures an expected feeling, as *desespoir* is engraved
over and over, so that writers and readers alike come to commonly understand it and share in its authority. Saint-Amant, like other poets, blames it
unequivocally: "pour les coups du desespoir" (v. 37, 4) and stages a lover
who, because of despair, finds solace in steep mountains that:

> Sont aux malheureux si propices,
> Quand la cruauté de leur sort,
> Les force à rechercher la mort!

(Are favorable to the miserable souls,/When the cruelty of their fate,/Forces them to seek death!) ("La Solitude" vv. 38–40, 4).

Thus, *le desespoir* becomes a familiar and permanent feature of this poetry, as if everybody should understand that, due to despair, lovers will unavoidably seek death. Furthermore, as the many poems examined in this study demonstrate, despair demands to be told. "Ainsi doncq'je diray ce qui me desespere" ("Livre III," v. 73, 100) writes Nuysement in forthright style that seems to sum it all up. Clearly, his despair needs to be recounted in his verses, demonstrating, in a cathartic manner, that by telling and retelling one can find some comfort. Despair also has to be communicated and made an example in order to warn other lovers not to make the same mistake and, rather, to learn from it. Nuysement expresses the feeling of being worn down by the strain of despair:

> N'esperant seulement fors en son desespoir
> Car, helas, ce cruel me mord, me lime et ronge
> Je ne suis plus moy-mesme, ains un frivole songe
> Qui erre ça et là sans force ny pouvoir

(Fiercely hoping only in his despair/Because, alas, this cruel one bites me, and files me down and gnaws at me/I am no longer myself, but a frivolous dream/Who wanders here and there without force nor power) ("Livre II," vv. 11–14, 311).

Despair erodes the poet-persona, causing him to lose himself in a tragic nonexistence, and forcing him to wander, *errant*, without purpose or will, as a ghost whose only force is fueled by hopelessness.

"Because of despair" is a line that, phrased in limitless ways, recurs often, and its understated, matter-of-fact nature makes it a poetic *sine-qua-non*. In truth, despair becomes a theme in literary culture, and a familiar *topos* with countless motifs of the poetry of the late Renaissance, featuring several variances acquired mainly from the poetry of the *disperata*.[84] The mournful compositions by Birague, Nuysement, Durand, La Roque, Tyard, Chassignet, Béroalde, Théophile, and Saint-Amant, but also Desportes and d'Aubigné, reveal that the *disperata* was indeed a major source of inspiration in late sixteenth- and early seventeenth-century France, when the poetry of despair emerged as particularly suitable for both writers and readers. When Birague wonders, "Formeray-je toujours tant de funebres plaintes?" ("Tome I," v. 1, 265), he adds his voice to Desportes's "Me doy-je plaindre ainsi comme je fais?" (Chapter Five), for which a confirmatory yes is solicited. Later on in the same sonnet, Birague also wonders if he will ever write a sonnet without complaints, "Traceray-je jamais un sonnet sans complaintes" ("Tome I," v. 5, 265). Again, the answer is predictable and expressive, encompassing so much more than his unassuming: "Helas! Je crois que non" ("Tome I," v. 7, 265). These, of course, are questions that could have been easily asked and answered in the sad complaints by the many poets read in this study, because, as Nuysement asserts in a verse that deeply captures the distress felt in both the Italian and French poems of the *disperata*: "Le cruel desespoir m'enchaisne sous sa loi" (Cruel despair chains me up with its laws) ("Livre II," v. 69, 323). Despair is both an emotion and a force that drive much of this poetry.

Although certainly Eros and Thanatos comingle in these haunting verses, in the poetry of this waning French Renaissance, Love joins despair in as persuasive a dichotomy as Eros and Thanatos, but one that is no longer shocking. The neo-Petrarchan poets' verses produce romantic horror stories, as time and time again the love narrative becomes entangled with the brutality of history. Love is nothing but an excuse—a fashionable and very amenable one at that. After all, the court longed for romance and for poems that depicted unrequited love inscribed in the Petrarchan tradition and blatantly embedded in its code. However, it was despair that fueled the imagination, the passion for writing, as well as a distorted vision of love, labeled "la fureur amoureuse,"[85] because the fury of Love was inextricably intertwined with the macabre. The macabre of the *disperata* is one of the main components of the Baroque, and it pervades the poetry of these decades.[86]

However, for the French neo-Petrarchans, "la fureur amoureuse" is a mask for other *fureurs* directly related to socio-historical factors that weighed on the poets of the last Valois King, who were forced to live and work during unstable times in the confines of the court.[87] Where Love was closely and cruelly linked to the Wars of Religion, to the overall violence that ravaged France, and to the collective and personal suffering, the *disperata* provided the French neo-Petrarchans images and language to recount the collective trauma of the wars, the violence it ensued, and the internal chaos and conflict that engulfed everyday life experiences. Although Petrarch and his code continued to be appreciated, the *disperata* became a remarkable model because of the many appealing paradigms it provided for writing about the civil wars, and for the later poets, the beginning of the Guerre de Trente Ans, and their inherent day-to-day life traumas. The poets of this chapter show that *l'amant martyr, le désespoir amoureux*, and *la plainte amoureuse* are all symptoms and hiding places for a grander *mal de siècle*, just as the Italian *disperata* poets had already expressed and written years earlier.

In conclusion, the Italian and French *disperata* exist within a continuum that intimately entwines French and Italian literary culture. When Beccari and his bitter resentment conjured the whole universe in deep hopelessness, he inspired Nuysement to write:

> Tout ce que les Cieux ont de maligne influence,
> Tout ce que les enfers ont d'aspre violence
> Sont ore à mon mal-heur fierement conjurez,
> Car tout ce qui est clos dans ce grand hemisphere,
> Le Feu, l'Air, l'Eau, la Terre et le Ciel m'est contraire,
> Tesmoingnant leurs efforts en mes maux endurez.

(All of the Skies' malign influence,/All of hell's bitter violence/Are now summoned against my misfortunes,/Because all that is closed in this great hemisphere,/Fire, Air, Water, the Earth and the Sky, is against me,/Witnessing their efforts endure in my ills.) ("Livre II," vv. 61–66, 323).

Both poets viewed despair as a universal force, encompassing all natural elements, and overwhelming the poetic persona. Furthermore, a myriad of negative feelings are summoned by despair, such as the indignation of Love, regret, bitterness, disappointment, and anger. Remarkably, in the above examples, French poets adopted a great variety of lyric forms, frequently using the longer ones including *stances, chansons,* odes, elegies, *plaintes* and *complaintes*, which allowed more textual space for a cornucopia of images that explicitly thematize despair.[88]

Many of the neo-Petrarchans were attracted by tropes of the ugly and the horrible, the fierce and the violent. Did despair taint their vision and force them to see and narrate only evil and unhappiness?[89] It seems like a plausible possibility. Despair was a fascinating and generative force, a subject and object to be studied, explained, and written through many of its mesmerizing facets. Certainly, the Italian and French *disperate* shared the same obsessions: and obsessions we must call them, not only because of their frequency and intensity, but also because of the many nuanced ways and tones in which they have been written and rewritten, as in the macabre landscapes, in the maledictions against Fortune, Love, and of course, through an assertive rhetoric and will.

The Italian *disperata* in France affords more ways of reading the neo-Petrarchans, and of discovering an intertext that has been greatly ignored until the last forty years or so, thus opening new pathways of inquiry to Renaissance scholars and readers. As a viable and generative model, the *disperata* poetry allows us to not only appreciate the poetry of despair, but also to couple it with historical and cultural texts that recount the period and its challenges. Finally, to identify and explore the *disperata* as one of the main intertexts allows us to also explore the many cultural and literary ramifications that ensue, thus providing new ways to open up transnational analyses and dialogues that further strengthen and entwine the considerable links between Italy and France.

NOTES

[1] "La Solitude," in *Œuvres Poétiques de Saint-Amant*, v. 37, 4. All references to Saint-Amant's poetry will be based on this edition.

[2] See Mark Greengrass, *Governing Passions*, 365.

[3] See Annie Charon, "Regards sur le livre à la cour de Henri III," 390.

[4] See Weber, *La Création poétique*, 63–106.

[5] Ibid., 134. See also Robert K. Knecht, "Henri III: The King and his *Mignons*," in *The French Renaissance Court*, 280–304, Philippe Erlanger, *Henri III*, and Emmanuel Le Roy Ladurie, *L'Etat Royal*.

[6] D'Aubigné lived at Henri III's court between 1572 and 1576 with the King of Navarre, future Henri IV. However, Henri III and d'Aubigné were not on good terms, which, according to Boucher, was the king's "grand échec." See "Un Climat favorable à la culture," in *La Cour de Henri III*, 135. See also Flamini's "Le rime di Odetto de la Noue e l'Italianismo al tempo d'Enrico III." Flamini concentrates in particular on Desportes, but his literary analysis applies also to other poets at court. Other poets of Henri III's circle were Dorat, Ronsard, Passerat, du Perron, Antoine de Baïf, and Amadis Jamyn.

[7] See also Balsamo, "Les Italiens de la Cour et les Lettres," 89–92.

[8] See Vianey, *Le Pétrarquisme en France*, and Mathieu-Castellani, "Les enfants de Pétrarque," 623–642, and *Mythes de l'éros baroque*, 14–15.

[9] See Mathieu-Castellani, "Les enfants de Pétrarque," 623–642, Balsamo, "'Du florentin les lamentables voix,'" and Melançon, "La Fin du pétrarquisme en France."

[10] Balsamo, "'Du florentin les lamentables voix,'" 119.

[11] Nuysement, *Les Œuvres poétiques*, "Livres I et II," 77. Nuysement's *Divers poemes* are in "Livre III."

[12] Daniela Costa, "Les Poètes de Henri III et Pétrarque," 381.

[13] *Poésies. Amours de Phyllis et Diverses Amours* (1590), 9. All references to La Roque's poems will be based on this edition.

[14] Ibid., 15.

[15] See Guillot for Nuysement, and Guillot and Michel Clément in *Flaminio de Birague, Les Premières œuvres poétiques*, Murphy, "Diane et la disperata," and Ferrer, "*Le Printemps* d'Agrippa d'Aubigné." See also Mathieu-Castellani's edition of La Roque's *Poésies Amours de Phyllis et Diverses Amours, Eros baroque*, 27–32, and *Les Thèmes amoureux dans la poésie française*, and Dubois, *Le Maniérisme*, 198–200, and *La Poésie baroque*.

[16] See Guillot in his introduction to Nuysement's *Les Œuvres poétiques*, "Livres I et II," 40.

[17] For a study on the French ode, see Rouget, *L'Apothéose d'Orphé. L'esthétique de l'ode en France*, 11–36. As in all the French lyric genres that adopted the *disperata*, in the ode as well Rouget sees a genre transformation and stylistic research that better suited the new spirit of the Renaissance, 25.

[18] Greengrass, *Governing Passions*, 39–40, and 365–366.

[19] Ibid., 368.

[20] See Costa, "Desportes et l'Académie du Palais," Balsamo, "Les Italiens de la Cour et les lettres," R.J. Sealy, *The Palace Academy of Henri III*, and Yates, *The French Academies of the Sixteenth Century*.

[21] See Denis Crouzet, "Le Règne de Henri III et la violence collective."

[22] Alexander, *Trauma. A Social Theory*, 7.

[23] Montainge, Livre 1, XXVI, "De l'Institution des enfans," 195.

[24] See Rouget, "Academies, Circles, Salons, and the Emergence of the Pre-Modern 'Literary Public Sphere' in Sixteenth-Century France," Sealy, *The Palace Academy of Henri III*, and Yates, *The French Academies*.

[25] Montaigne, Livre 2, XVII, "De la praesumption," 314.

[26] As previously mentioned, the baroque rhetoric is well defined by Mathieu-Castellani's criteria of "Les traits différentiels du discours baroque" in *Anthologie de la poésie amoureuse de l'âge baroque*, 22–27.

[27] See for example il Saviozzo: "Ma poi che piace al ciel che così sia/abitar vo' fra boschi e mutar forma,/menando vita indomita e restìa./E vo' che la pietà per me si dorma,/per monti alpestri e per diserte piaggi/vo' seguitar de' faüni la torma;" vv. 49–54, 219.

[28] For an analysis of the poet-lover and his relation to nature, see Weber, *La Création poétique*, 307–327.

[29] Marie-Claire Bichard-Thomine, "L'Amour en exil," 50.

[30] Ibid., 47–61. The author provides an important analysis of the theme from Ovid to the Pléiade, to Desportes and La Roque, noting that for the two French poets in particular, it is mostly the absence from the beloved that causes the speaker to feel exiled.

[31] The use of the desert has roots in the Classics, and Ovid in particular, which provides numerous examples of this type of exile in deserted places. See Curtius, *European Literature*, 92–94.

[32] Guillot, Introduction to Nuysement's *Les Œuvres poétiques*, "Livre III," 15. Dubois as well comments on the significance of this decor, where "Le macabre, le

morbide, l'horrible sont l'autre face de l'amour." *Le Maniérisme*, 198.

³³ François Béroalde de Verville, *Les Souspirs amoureux* (1588). All references to Béroalde's poetry will be based on this edition. I wish to thank Michael Giordano for sharing his copy of this book.

³⁴ See Fontanier, *Les Figures du discours*, 368.

³⁵ Théophile de Viau is also seduced by the cold horror of these secluded settings: "La froide horreur de ces forests,/L'humidité de ces marets,/Cette effroyable solitude,/.../Grands deserts, sablons infertiles,/Où rien que moy n'ose venir,/ Combien me devez-vous tenir/Dans ces campagnes inutiles?" (*Première Partie*, vv. 45–54, 135–136). In his ode titled "La Solitude," nature mirrors the *disperata* landscape, beginning with its opening line "Dans ce val solitaire et sombre" (*Première Partie*, v. 1, 16), and its "bois sombres" (v. 45, 18), inhabited by wild animals, "L'orfraye et le hibou s'y perchent/Ici vivent les loups-garoux." (vv. 25–26, 17). This ode is very similar to Saint-Amant's "La Solitude," which I shall soon analyze. Both poems stage nature as both an idyllic setting, and the *disperata* motif. See Richard A. Mazzara, "Théophile de Viau, Saint-Amant, and the Spanish Soledad."

³⁶ And again, "Parmy les froids rochers ceints d'horreur admirable" ("Tome II," v. 1, 77). See Birague, *Les Premières œuvres poétiques*. All references to Birague's poetry will be based on this edition.

³⁷ What Guillot and Clément have called "le registre de la *disperata* ou despérade." Ibid., "Tome II," 156–157. They draw many parallels between Birague's work, particularly his elegies, and the *disperata*.

³⁸ He also writes, "J'erreray fantastique/Aux effroyables bois,/Compagnon des Forets/Et des Daemons secrets." ("Tome II," vv. 9–12, 152) Guillot also highlights this "topique" or "registre' in Nuysement's poems in the *Introduction*, Livre *I et II*, 55, and "Livre III," 15.

³⁹ See Mazzara, "The Philosophical-Religious Evolution of Théophile de Viau," and Streicher's bibliography in Théophile's *Œuvres Poétiques*.

⁴⁰ See Beccari's "canzon nova de pianto" or il Saviozzo's "Canzon ... piange e suspira" who use a similar image.

⁴¹ Tyard often participated in Madame de Retz's salon together with Desportes and other neo-Petrarchan poets of the *disperata*. For more biographical information, see *Les Erreurs amoureuses*. All references to Tyard's poetry will be based on this edition.

⁴² See Françoise Gourier, *Etude des Œuvres Poétiques de Saint-Amant*. Gourier classifies this poem as "pré-romantique," because of the macabre, wild, and night birds, 178–180. She provides as well useful biographical information. See also Edwin M. Duval, *Poesis and Poetic*, 3–68.

⁴³ Guillot points out that "l'amour au désert," found in the *disperata* and in the French neo-Petrarchans, mostly experienced by "l'amant-ermite" finds its origin in the poetry of Propertius and Tibullus. See also his "L'exil de l'amour ou l'amour au désert," where he links "l'amour au désert" to an apocalyptic vision of

the world, which, as I argue, is inspired by the *disperata* as this genre amply combines both motifs.

[44] Etienne Durand, *Poésie complètes*. All references to Durand's poetry will be based on this edition.

[45] For a compelling discussion on the Italian influence on the poetry of this period, see Cecilia Rizza, "Persistance et transformation de l'influence italienne dans la poésie lyrique française de la première moitié du XVIIᵉ siècle." Rizza provides an analysis of Petrarch's, Tasso's, and other Italian writers' presence, but does not mention the *disperata*.

[46] See Sasso's *disperata*, Chapter Three, vv. 13–14.

[47] Birague writes elsewhere: "Le soir dessus mon toict les funebres oyseaux/ Annoncent mon trépas, et les malheurs nouveaux/Que je voy ja tomber sur mon chef miserable." "*Tome I*," vv. 9–11, 86.

[48] "Obscur valon, montagne sourcilleuse,/.../Rochers pierreux, & vous caverne hideuse/Où les Lyons & les Ours sont enclos:/Hiboux, corbeaux, augures d'Atropos,/Le seul objet d'une ame malheureuse:/.../Et viens à vous pour lamenter mon sort,/Flechir le Ciel, ou, s'il ne se peut faire,/Mouvoir l'Enfer, les Parques, et la Mort" (vv. 28–29). See also Mathieu-Castellani's notes 7 and 9, 29.

[49] Furthermore, this verse echoes Nocturno's and his use of "If/now" to describe his serene past and his wretched present (Chapter Five).

[50] Again, an enumeration of doves, turtledoves, sparrows, roosters, owl, scorpions, as well as crows, dragons, and tigers occupies verses 205 to 243, intensifying the speaker's anguish, and intimately exposing his incurable *mal d'amour* mirrored in the decor. See Mathieu-Castellani, *Les Thèmes amoureux dans la poésie française*, 357–383.

[51] Ibid., 368–371.

[52] See Sasso, "El figliol fai congiongere con la matre/Tanto gli accende de furor la mente/La sorella al fratel: la figlia al patre," vv. 167–170.

[53] See Chapter One and Curtius who comments on Théophile's use of this *topos*, *European Literature*, 97.

[54] For a history of the *topos* see Curtius, *European Literature*, 94–95.

[55] Streicher, in Théophile, *Œuvres poétiques*, 164.

[56] "Facent or mes mal-heurs, forceant ma destinee,/Irriter tous les Dieux invoquez en mes vœus,/L'air, la terre, et les eaux, la machine, et ses feus,/Influans ma misere injustement donnee./Pluton puisse à ma mort, pour ma fin terminee,/En coulevreaux retors eschanger mes cheveux,/Sur le dos d'un rocher serré de mille neus/Ciller mes yeux d'horreur comme au pauvre Phinee." "Livre II," vv. 1–11, 211.

[57] See Hans-Joachim Lope's introduction to Jean-Baptiste Chassignet, *Le Mepris de la vie et la consolation de la mort*, xclii. All references to Chassignet's poetry will be based on this edition.

[58] See vv. 21–34, 515–518.

[59] "La Fascination du monde renversé dans les troubles du XVIᵉ siècle," in *L'Image du monde renversé*, 9–15, 11.

[60] See Céard, "Le Thème du 'monde à l'envers,'" 118–127.

[61] See Odette de Mourgues's compelling discussion on the apocalyptic in *Metaphysical, Baroque, and Précieux Poetry*, 85–88.

[62] Crouzet, *Les Guerriers de Dieu*, I, and *La Nuit de la Saint-Barthélemy: un rêve perdu de la Renaissance*.

[63] Racaut, *Hatred in Print*, 27.

[64] See also Guillot's analysis in Nuysement, *Les Œuvres poétiques*, "Livre III," 95–96.

[65] *Enchantements* features several other *disperata topoi* that became conventional in the poetry of the neo-Petrarchans, such as the wild and fierce beasts and birds; deserted and infernal landscapes, as seen above; "l'errance" ("j'erreray par une obscure voye", "Livre III," v. 90, 102); an antagonistic Fate ("si l'ardent destin s'obstine contre moy" "Livre III," v. 43, 99); mythical characters; despair; and the writer's use of his own poetry to warn others ("Livre III," vv. 255–256, 120).

[66] See Mathieu-Castellani's second differential trait of the baroque discourse in *Anthologie*, 24, and "Eros furieux: La rhétorique baroque des *Soupirs amoureux*," 13.

[67] Théophile provides an additional example in his demand, "Le ciel pour chastier mes vices/Fasse un Enfer plus rigoureux," (*Première Partie*, vv. 89–90, 57). Here too, the subjunctive mode is used to express the poet's will and command to create a harsher hell than the narrator's current fate.

[68] Birague: "Desers inhabitez, orgueilleuses montaignes,/Torrens impetueux, et vous Antres segrets,/Vallons, forets, ruisseaux, rivages, et campaignes/Oyez le pyteux son de mes tristes regrets./.../Mais vous en ce pendant, desers, vallons, rivages,/Mons, campagnes, forests, et torrens furieux,/Prez, bocages, ruisseaux, et cavernes sauvages,/Dite adieu pour moy au Soleil de mes yeux." "Tome I," vv. 1–4, 25–28, 164–165.

[69] According to Mathieu-Castellani, this is the third differential trait of the baroque discourse, *Anthologie*, 25.

[70] La Roque: "Je ne mens point de mon martyre/.../Passans, temoins de la tristesse/.../Annoncez par toute la terre,/Qu'autant qu'il fut heureux en guerre/Il est miserable en amour," vv. 52–60, 132–133.

[71] This stanza is also an example of the *topos le monde à l'envers*.

[72] "Or donc, puisqu'il n'y ha homme vivant au monde/Qui sente ennuy prochain à ma douleur profonde,/Et qu'elle est incurable,/J'attens la seule mort pour m'estre secourable." vv. 73–76, 116.

[73] See Giustiniani, "Io maledico .../el giorno el puncto e lhora chio te vitte/.../Io maledico i miei pensier traditi/.../Io maledico tutto el mio parlare," vv. 124–130, 375.

[74] The entire sonnet gathers several *disperata topoi*: "Combien, combien de fois, d'une suitte importune/De soupirs embrasez, ay-je esventé les Cieux,/Et d'un double torrent ruisselé de mes yeux/Ay-je fait un sejour à quelqu'autre Neptune!/Combien ay-je invoqué, par les ombreux destours/Des bois remplis d'effroy, la

mort à mon secours,/Et souhaitté me voir Promethee ou Prothee!/Mais helas maintenant (dont je suis en fureur)/Je suis plus mal-heureux, cognoissant mon erreur,/Que ne furent jamais Prothee et Promethee!" "Livre II," 271–272.

[75] In another sonnet as well Nuysement damns his life, with a verse that becomes a profanity, since the very essence and agent of benediction, God, is joined to a blasphemy against life, his most precious gift to mankind: "Le Dieu se joint à elle et je maudis la vie," "Livre II," v. 13, 281. For a study on religious blasphemy, see Jean-Claude Schmitt, "Les images de l'invective," 11–20. Birague as well condemns the universal elements, "Et me plains contre vous, cruels astres des Cieux,/Qui seuls rendez ma vie en ce point mal-heureuse" ("Tome I," 269), accusing them to be the cause of his *mal d'amour*. Here too, he damns the very hour he was born replicating a familiar image: "L'heure qui me fit voir la grand lampe des Cieux/Soit maudite à jamais, puisque tant je souspire" "Tome I," vv. 13–14, 265.

[76] See Beaumatin, "La violence verbale," 21–25.

[77] Weber notes that destiny is not an abstract power, rather, it is the result of the dominion of the celestial world over the earthly world, and of the stars over our body and actions. *La Création poétique*, 41.

[78] See also il Saviozzo, "E per mille ragioni il ver discerno:/chi prende questo Amor falso a seguire,/uccide il corpo e lalma va all'inferno." vv. 112–114, 221.

[79] Chassignet's work is mostly grounded in religious concerns, but integrates as well some of the death visions of the *disperata*. See André Baïche's discussion on "Le thème de la mort: Chassignet et Sponde," 245–255, and Marc Bensimon, "La Porte étroite; Essai sur le maniérisme."

[80] Janis Pallister, "Béroalde de Verville's *Stances de la mort* and *Soupirs amoureux*," 59.

[81] This, I would argue, is a point of dissonance between Baroque and poetry of despair. As Dubois notes, "A l'âge baroque, elle [la mort] tient le gouvernail du monde, horrible, décharnée, présente en tous lieux, et persécutant sourtout la jeunesse et la beauté." *La Poésie baroque*, I, 23. In the *disperata*, on the contrary, death is called for and does not persecute.

[82] See in particular "Complainte III," 228–229, and "Complainte IIII," 268–270, and the following pages for Guillot's and Clément's analysis. As previously mentioned, both critics draw attention to the *disperata*'s presence in Birague's poems, who, in other texts as well is obsessed with narrating his despair, giving it meaning and reason: "Troublé du desespoir qui m'oppresse et m'entame", "Tome I," v. 1, 227.

[83] Streicher, *Œuvres poétiques*, 154.

[84] See the definitions by Beckson and Ganz, *Literary Terms*, 70, as well as Mathieu-Castellani's compelling distinction between "*thèmes, topos, motifs*" in *Thèmes amoureux*, 46–50. Thus, despair is the theme, as "*une grande unité,*" as well as the *topos*, as a group of motifs.

[85] See Guillot and Clément, Birague, *Les Premières œuvres*, "Tome I," CLVI. See also Mathieu-Castellani, "La Poétique de la fureur et l'esthétique des vers rapportés: l'exemple de Clovis Hesteau de Nuysement."

[86] See Marcel Raymond, *Baroque et renaissance poétique*, Rousset, *La Littérature de l'âge baroque en France*, and Dubois, *Le Baroque*.

[87] See Lucien Bély, "Les illusions perdues des Valois," 214–231.

[88] See Vianey who argues that Tyard used all the genres found in the Italian *canzonieri*, in *Le Pétrarquisme en France*, 121.

[89] In discussing Chassignet, Lope argues that "Si les poètes pétrarquistes s'efforcèrent à ne voir que le beau, Chassignet voit d'un œil fasciné les choses laides et périssables." *Le Mepris de la vie et la consolation de la mort*, (LVII). This is an important distinction that extends to all neo-Petrarchan poets of the time.

Conclusion

Changeant en desespoir ce qui fait esperer.

d'Aubigné

Au joug d'un desespoir; le desespoir me donne
La fureur, le regret, le despit, le courroux
La paleur et la peur, qui me conduisent tous
Sous le pouvoir fatal de la Parque felonne.

Nuysement

The *disperata*, maybe more so than any other Italian poetic genres, has fallen victim to two major calamities: first, Italian literary criticism of the late eighteenth and nineteenth centuries, which in general passed a negative judgment, and thus, greatly influenced the canon, subsequent generations of scholars, and readers.[1] Second, as an ancillary to court poetry—*poesia cortigiana* and *poésie de cour*, it also received unfavorable criticisms in both Italy and France.[2] Alessandro d'Ancona's article, "Del secentismo nella poesia cortigiana del secolo XV," is an example of such greatly influential scholarship that prejudiced many writers who used the *disperata* genre and prevented them from being published and circulated until recent years.[3] At the same time in France, the *disperata* poets were trapped by the negative views of some critics on imitation, plagiarism, Italianism and anti-Italianism.[4] If, as Amedeo Quondam convincingly argues, poetry became more and more a means of "social transmission," from the beginning of the sixteenth, and all the way to the eighteenth century,[5] this book focuses on how the poetry of the *disperata* has provided a model for the transmission of despair in lyric, yet realistic terms.[6]

This book reevaluates the importance of the *disperata* genre and of its intertextual ramifications in Italy and France. It also seeks to show the close connections between this poetry and the historical and social contexts in which it thrived. A close reading of the Italian and French texts reveals how authors adopted and yet subverted in creative ways the most important and highly conventional lyric code of the period in question, Petrarchism. Although Petrarch and the Petrarchan poets provided the tropes to speak about Love, their refined and restrained language proved to be insufficient in depicting the deepest hopelessness, acute grief, and marginalization shared by most of the authors discussed here. Thus, they turned to the *disperata*, which, instead supplied a code and language to narrate existential grief and collective trauma, disguised as unrequited love. The *disperata* provided a model for how to write despair and how to integrate it in the dominant lyric tradition. Moreover, the genre fused several literary and cultural traditions: Classical, court lyric, Dante's infernal landscape, regionalisms, Petrarch and Petrarchism, and the French tradition. It also embedded in the text history and the uncertainties of war, poverty, and the numerous civil and religious conflicts that plagued both countries.

The main goal of this book has been to establish the remarkable developments of the *disperata* by highlighting a comprehensive history of the genre, from its very beginning in the Trecento, through the Italian fifteenth and sixteenth centuries, to late Renaissance France. By studying the intersections between genre, imitation, and gender, I sought to highlight the differences between the texts and the unique ways in which they narrate despair. Furthermore, by connecting the *disperata* poems to the historical, social, and cultural contexts, I showed how these works remained relevant for several generations of poets in two countries. In the Trecento, writers including Antonio Beccari and il Saviozzo established the genre by generating images and linguistic patterns that immediately became a popular and highly-imitated model, with core traits, including maledictions, secluded and infernal landscapes, ominous birds and fiery animals, and loud calls for death, that came to define the *disperata*. During the Quattrocento, poets such as il Pistoia, Panfilo Sasso, Galeotto del Carretto, and others who remain fairly unknown to this day, such as Felice Feliciano, Rosello Roselli, Domenico da Prato, Antonio degli Alberti, and Leonardo Giustiniani, continued the tradition and enhanced it with their own individual nuanced touches, at times blending it with Petrarchan motifs and language, and at times subverting this dominant tradition with overlapping and variation of the genre. For example, the poet-lovers recognize the moment of the *innamoramento* as a life-changing experience, yet they immediately curse it, because it represents the beginning of the despair that pushes them to seek secluded and haunted places, and ultimately their own death.

Throughout this book, I have sought to show how genre, imitation, and gender deeply intersect. Gender becomes at times a central issue in the narration of despair. Some of the poems in particular, such as the female-voiced *disperate* and Isabella di Morra's sonnets and *canzoni*, clearly inscribe gender in their narrative. Whether in a ventriloquized voice or in Morra's authentic voice, despair prompts a new interplay between Eros and Thanatos. Moreover, Love is no longer the main obsession, rather, it is upstaged by despair as the generative force behind much of this poetry. Despair, therefore, assumes gendered nuances that commingle with genre and with imitation in intriguing manners, particularly when the female- and the male-voiced *disperate* are in an intratextual dialogue. Proficient in composing both gendered *disperate*, some of these authors expertly deploy despair in ways that are deeply integrated in both the culture and literary canon of the early modern period, yet destabilizing both at the same time. In the male-voiced poems in particular, gender is at play especially in the relationship with the beloved. She is no longer portrayed in all her beauty and glory, and she is no longer the object of contemplation and desire. Rather, she is cursed and, for the most part, physically absent from the text.

The Quattrocento also saw the birth of three poets whose popularity helped generate recognition for the genre: Serafino, Tebaldeo, and Cariteo. Their productivity, fame, and success at the main Italian courts, from the north to the south of the peninsula, and the frequency of their publications and circulation, allowed the *disperata* to gain ground and impress readers and writers alike. Most importantly, the latter started to adopt and adapt the *disperata* content to shorter, more popular lyric forms, such as the sonnet and the *strambotto*. Serafino's *strambotti* and Cariteo's *canzoni*, for example, multiplied the *disperata*'s distinct traits with unique representations of suffering and despair. Love was acknowledged but no longer celebrated, allowing Eros and despair to commingle in a multiplicity of grim ways. Thus, in Italy and France the poetry of the *disperata* grew in various, shorter forms, and its long, original form—the *capitolo* and *canzone*—were abandoned. Its narrative became more succinct and direct, yet still bequeathing a full expression and communication of despair.

In the Cinquecento, the *disperata* genre continued to spread through the Italian anthologies of Giolito and his rivals, and the popular poetry of di Constazo, Tansillo, and Rota, which features the *disperata* content. Similarly, poets such as Pietro Aretino and Isabella di Morra, and lesser-known authors such as Nocturno Napolitano and Eurialo Morani also adopted the genre, thus multiplying its intertextual connections. Through these works, the *disperata* moved to France, where it circulated at court and met great success, especially with the poets of the last decades of the 1500s. Thanks to critics including Weber, Mathieu-Castellani, and

Dubois, the genre was recognized in France as well. This book builds on this recognition, but reveals several other poets in both Italy and France whose *disperate* remain unpublished in modern editions and largely unread. My analysis brings attention to them, and closely examines them in their own right, but always with the intention of showing the overlapping and variability that contributed to and transformed the genre in unique ways.

Because of the *disperata* poetry's remarkable continuity and unique content, in France, poets of the courts of Henri III and Henri IV enthusiastically embraced it, imitated it, and also adapted it to their personal style and to better suit their particular culture and literary background. *Stances*, odes, *plaintes*, and sonnets by the neo-Petrarchan poets of the late Renaissance—Desportes, d'Aubigné, Nuysement, Birague, Béroalde, Chassignet, Durand, Théophile, La Roque, Tyard, and Saint-Amant—exhibit a strong intertextuality with the aforementioned Italian authors, because they openly, yet creatively, drew inspiration from their work. Indeed, their verses bring into play the collective trauma of long and violent religious conflicts that, once again, narrate despair overshadowing Eros, and coupling Eros to Thanatos in an intimate dance. Metaphors of despair, war, struggle, blood, and torn body parts abound. The *disperata* model offered a language and attitude of despair, but also a reaction that could fully sound the depths of despair, that Petrarch and Petrarchism could not provide. If Petrarch's poetry constituted one of the intertexts well into the late Renaissance, thenceforth the *disperata*, too, became a crucial component of French poetry. The two seem to coexist in the poetry of the neo-Petrarchans, thus sharing in the continuation of the lyric tradition that started in the Trecento.

Remarkably, the French poets simultaneously evoked and subverted Petrarch, once again, blending the two traditions in creative ways, with distinct traits inherited from their French predecessors, including the poets of the Pléiade. And while love lyrics continued to wow court audiences and readers alike, Love was often only a pretext. What the poets in this study have shown is that the inventive maledictions against Love and *le désespoir amoureux* are all chronic manifestations of the sixteenth-century *mal de siècle*, which fully unraveled in various ways by the poetry of the *disperata*. Thanks to wide spread imitative practices, the Italian cultural and literary tradition (Dante-Petrarch-Petrarchists-*disperata*) and the French neo-Petrarchan tradition were strengthened. Indeed, d'Aubigné, Nuysement, Béroalde, and other French poets, created a collage of *disper-*

ata motifs that pivoted around despair, and they borrowed and reworked those motifs to better fit to their tastes and those of their audience.

Finally, how did the *disperata* as a genre cease to exist? In Italy, critics agree that Pietro Bembo put an end to a host of lyric genres, including the *disperata*. His literary reforms and codifications, and his strict Petrarchism in matter of language and forms marginalized the *disperata*. Bembo's edition of Petrarch's *canzoniere* in 1501,[7] and the publication of his own *Rime* in 1530,[8] marked the triumph of Petrarchism and of the Petrarchan sonnet, and consequently, the decline of other genres including the *capitoli ternari*.[9] According to DellaNeva, "Bembo sought to vilify the Quattrocento poets who, in his mind, carried their Petrarchism to an extreme and corrupted their language with preciosity and impurities."[10] Malinverni calls Bembo's movement a blatant condemnation of the late fifteenth-century generation of poets.[11] Thus, the popularity of the Quattrocento poets including Cariteo, Tebaldeo, Sasso, and Serafino, and that of the subsequent Cinquecento generation started to fade away—and so did their *disperate*. Yet, as this book argues, the importance of these poets in the French lyric landscape cannot be underestimated. Eventually, however, codifications and stricter rules undermined the *disperata* in France as well. François de Malherbe advocated the severe laws of Classicism and put an end to the personal laments of the poetry of despair.[12] Thus, the seventeenth century's thirst for universality and moderation eventually euthanized the voice of the *désepéré*.

Just recently, a member of Ficino asked a fundamental question that preoccupies most scholars of the early modern period: "Did the great works of Donatello, Fra Filippo Lippi, and Michelangelo spring into being despite the social and political conditions of the times, or rather because of them?" (September 27, 2014).[13] This same question could be posed about the poets of the *disperata*. My answer would be both: despite *and* because. The poets of the *disperata* sprang into being *despite* the many and substantial constraints imposed on them—be it financial, social, political, or religious. Yet, also *because* of these constraints, they sought to express and transpose their collective trauma into their lyrics, even though they were still expected to wow and entertain their powerful—and temperamental—patrons and audience. Thus, a new poetry of despair emerged, flourished, and progressed.

NOTES

[1] For example, Pèrcopo, who brought to critical attention il Pistoia's "la disperata," that is the most famous and the most misattributed *disperata*, writes: "Ma letto cotesta tritera che ha scarso pregio artistico, non si comprende affatto la ragione di tanta popolarità. E una noiosa infiltrata di maledizioni e di imprecazioni, tutta luoghi comuni ed esempi mitologici, messa in bocca ad un pover'uomo che, disperato per la morte della donna amata, ha stabilito di uccidersi." "Una disperata famosa," 702. As Martines notes, it is only in the late nineteenth and early twentieth centuries that "'Minor writers' (the *minori*) such as Iacopone da Todi, Saviozzo, Franco Sacchetti, Leonardo Giustiniani, Antonio Cammelli, plus a host of 'Petrarchists' and 'bourgeois realists,' were fetched up from early printed editions and manuscript libraries, to be put on their way to respectability." *Strong Words*, 164.

[2] See for example Tiraboschi on Sasso: "E veramente nelle poesie del Sassi, e nelle Italiane singolarmente, vedesi il difetto comune a quasi tutti i Poeti, che vissero verso la fine del secolo XV, cioè, che questo in essi si scorge di fanstasia e d'estro, tanto comunemente hor manca di eleganza e di grazia." "Sasso Panfilo modenese," 29.

[3] D'Ancona, 63–181.

[4] Balsamo, *Les Rencontres des Muses*, and his "Du Florentin les lamentables voix," 123. See also Rigolot, *Poésie et Renaissance*, in particular 117–205.

[5] Quondam, *La locuzione* artificiosa, 14–15.

[6] See also Malinverni who notes, "lo zibaldone di rime," that is the poetic collection of various genres had the unique goal of pure social diffusion, "L'edizione e il commendo dei *Sonetti e Capituli* di Panfilo Sasso," 380.

[7] *Le Cose Volgari di Messer Francesco Petrarcha.*

[8] Bembo, *Rime* (1530).

[9] Tissoni Benvenuti, "La tradizione della terza rima," 306.

[10] DellaNeva, "An Exploding Canon," 190.

[11] Malinverni, "La lirica volgare padana," 695.

[12] Although Malherbe largely imitated Tansillo in *Les Larmes de Saint Pierre Imitées du Tansille* (1587). See *Les Œuvres*, and in particular his commentary on Desportes, Vol. IV, 249–473.

[13] Ficino is an international online seminar and bulletin board for the circulation and exchange of information about the early modern period and all of its manifestations.

Bibliography

Primary Sources

Alberti, Antonio degli, in Natalino Sapegno. *Poeti minori del Trecento*. Milano: Riccardo Ricciardi, 1952.

Amboise, François de. *Œuvres complètes*, I. Edited by Dante Ughetti. Naples: Edizioni Scientifiche Italiane, 1973.

Angiolieri, Cecco. *Rime*. Edited by Raffaella Castagnola. Milan: Mursia, 1995.

Aretino, Pietro. *Poesie Varie*. Vol. 1. Edited by Giovanni Aquilecchia and Angelo Romano. Rome: Salerno Editrice, 1992.

Aubigné, Agrippa de. *Le Printemps, L'Hécatombe à Diane et les Stances*. Edited by Henri Weber. Paris: Presses Universitaires de France, 1960.

——. *Le Printemps, L'Hécatombe à Diane*. Edited by Bernard Gagnebin. Genève: Droz, 1948.

——. *Le Printemps Stances et Odes*. Edited by Eugénie Droz. Genève: Droz, 1973.

——. *Les Tragiques*. Edited by Frank Lestringant. Paris, Gallimard, 2003.

Aquinas, Thomas. *The Summa Theologica*. http://www.sacred-texts.com/chr/aquinas/summa/sum275.htm

Beccari, Antonio. *Le Rime di Maestro Antonio da Ferrara.* (Antonio Beccari). Edited by Laura Bellucci. Bologna: Pàtron, 1972.

Bembo, Pietro. *Rime*. Venice: Giovan Antonio & Fratelli da Sabbio, 1530.

——. *Prose della volgar lingua, Gli Asolani, Rime*. Edited by Carlo Dionisotti. Turin: UTET, 1966.

——. *Lyric Poetry, Etna*. Edited and translated by Mary P. Chatfield, I Tatti Renaissance Library. Cambridge: Harvard University Press, 2005.

Birague, Flaminio de. *Les Premières Œuvres poétiques [1585]*. Edited by Roland Guillot and Michel Clément. Vol. 1 and 2. Geneva: Droz, 2003.

Boccaccio, Giovanni. *L'Elegia di madonna Fiammetta*. Edited by Franca Ageno. Paris: Tallone, 1954.

Calmeta, Vincenzo. *Vita del fecondo poeta vulgare Serafino Aquilano* in *Collettanee greche, latine e vulgari nella morte de l'ardente Seraphino Aquilano in uno corpo redutte*. Edited by Giovanni Filoteo Achillini. Bologna: C. Bazalesi, 1504.

Carretto, Galeotto del. *Poesie inedite di Galeotto del Carretto*. Edited by Alessandro Giuseppe Spinelli. Savona: Tipografia Bertolotto, 1888.

Castiglione, Baldesar. *Il libro del Cortigiano*. Edited by Giulio Preti. Turin: Einaudi, 1965.

——. *The Book of the Courtier*. Edited by Daniel Javitch and Charles Singleton, trans. New York: Norton, 2002.

Chassignet, Jean-Baptiste. *Le Mepris de la vie et la consolation de la mort*. Edited by Hans-Joachim Lope. Geneva: Droz, 1967.

Ciminelli, Serafino. *Opere dello elegantissimo Seraphino Aquilano nuovamente con diligentia impresse con molte cose aggiunte.* (1516). http://gallica.bnf.fr/ark:/12148/bpt6k704444/f2.image.

——. *Opera dello elegantissimo poeta Serafino Aquilano; quasi tutta di nuovo riformata, con molte cose aggionte. Nella quale si contengono tutte le infrascritte cose, cioe. Sonetti* CLXV, *Epistole* VII, *Disperate* III, *Barzellette* XIX, *Egloghe* III, *Capitoli* XX, *Strambotti* XXVII. Vinegia: Bartolomeo detto l'Imperador, et Francesco suo genero, 1544.

——. *Le Rime di Serafino de' Ciminelli dall' Aquila.* Edited by Mario Menghini. Vol. I. Bologna: Romagnoli-Dall'Acqua, 1896.

——. *Serafino Aquilano. Strambotti.* Edited by Antonio Rossi. Parma: Fondazione Pietro Bembo, 2002.

——. *Serafino Aquilano, Sonetti e altre rime.* Edited by Antonio Rossi. Rome: Bulzoni, 2005.

Dante Alighieri. *Le opere di Dante Alighieri.* Edited by Michele Barbi and Vincenzo Pernicione. Florence: Bemporad, 1921.

——. *The Divine Comedy: Hell, Purgatory, Paradise,* 3 vols, trans. With introductions, commentaries, and glossaries Dorothy Leigh Sayers and Barbara Reynolds. London: Penguin, 1949–62.

Deschamps, Eustache. *Oeuvres Complètes de Eustache Deschamps. Société des Anciens Textes Français.* 11 vols. Edited by Gaston Raynaud and Auguste Henri Edouard. Paris: Firmin-Didot, 1878–1903.

Desportes, Philippe. *Les Premières Œuvres.* Edited by François Rouget and Bruno Petey-Girard. Paris: Classiques Garnier, 2014.

——. *Les Amours d'Hippolyte.* Edited by Victor E. Graham. Geneva: Droz, 1960.

Du Bellay, Joachim. *La deffence et illustration de la langue françoyse.* Edited by Jean-Charles Monferran. Geneva: Droz, 2001.

——. *Œuvres Complètes,* vol. 2. Edited by Marie-Dominique Legrand, Michel Magnien, Daniel Ménager, and Olivier Millet. Paris: Champion, 2003.

——. *La Monomachie de David et de Goliath.* Edited by Ernesta Caldarini. Geneva: Droz, 1981.

Durand, Etienne. *Poésies complètes.* Edited by Hoyt Rogers and Ory Rosenstein, preface by Yves Bonnefoy. Geneva: Droz, 1990.

Gareth, Benedetto. *Le Rime di Benedetto Gareth detto il Cariteo secondo le due stampe originali.* Edited by Erasmo Pèrcopo. Naples: Tipografia dell'Accademia delle Scienze, 1892.

Giustiniani, Leonardo. *Poesie edite et inedite di Leonardo Giustiniani.* Edited by Berthold Wiese. Bologna: Romagnoli, 1883.

La Roque, Siméon-Guillaume. *Poésies. Amours de Phyllis et Diverses Amours* (1590). Edited by Gisèle Mathieu-Castellani. Paris: Nizet, 1983.

Magny, Olivier de, *Les Amours.* Edited by Françoise Charpentier, in *Œuvres poétiques.* Vol. I. Edited by François Rouget. Paris: Honoré Champion, 1999.

——. *Les Trois premiers livres des Odes de 1559.* Edited by Francois Rouget. Geneva: Droz, 1995.

Malherbe, François. *Les Œuvres*. Edited by M. L. Lalanne. Paris: Hachette, 1862–1869.

Montaigne, Michel de. *Essais*. 3 vols. Paris: Flammarion, 1979.

———. *Essais*. Edited by Villey-Saulnier. Paris: Presses Universitaires de France, 1988.

Morales, Francisco Merino. *Sonetos*. Edited by Donato Bramante. Castellón, Spain: Ellago, 2008.

Morani, Euralio. "Per la vita disperata di Eurialo d'Ascoli." In *Per vaghezza d'alloro. Olimpo da Sassoferrato, Eurialo d'Ascoli e altri studi*. Edited by Sandro Baldoncini. Roma: Bulzoni, 1981.

Morra, Isabella di, *Rime*. Edited by Maria Antonietta Grignani. Rome: Salerno Editrice, 2000.

———. *Canzoniere. A Bilingual Edition*. Edited and translated by Irene Musillo Mitchell. West Lafayette, IN: Purdue University Press, 1998.

Napolitano, Nocturno. *Opera Amorosa de Nocturno Napolitano ne la quale si contiene Strambotti. Sonetti. Capitoli. Epistole. Et una disperata. Libro primo*. Milan: Rocho e Fratello da Valle, 1519.

Ovid. *Metamorphoses*. New York: Penguin Books, 1978.

———. *Heroides and Amores*. Edited and translated by Grant Showerman and G. P. Goold. 2nd edition revised. Cambridge: Harvard University Press, 1986.

Peletier du Mans, Jacques. *Œuvres poétiques*. Edited by Léon Séché. Geneva: Slatkine Reprints, 1970.

Petrarca, Francesco. *Petrarch's Lyric Poems. The Rime sparse and Other Lyrics*. Edited and translated by Robert M. Durling. Cambridge: Harvard University Press, 1976.

———. *Le Cose Volgari di Messer Francesco Petrarcha. Impresso in Vinegia nelle case d'Aldo Romano, nel 1501, nel mese di luglio avuto da Pietro Bembo.*

Petrasanta, Giampietro da. MS It. 1543. Bibliothèque nationale de France.

Prato, Domenico da. In Antonio Lanza, *Lirici toscani del Quattrocento*, vol. 1. Rome: Bulzoni, 1973.

Ronsard, Pierre de. *Œuvres Complètes*, vol. XV. Edited by Paul Laumonier. Paris: Hachette, 1930.

Roselli, Rossello. *Il Canzoniere Riccardiano*. Edited by Giovanni Biancardi. Bologna: Commissione per i testi di lingua, 2005.

Saint-Amant, Antoine-Girard de. *Œuvres Poétiques de Saint-Amant*. Edited by Leon Vérane. Paris, Garnier, 1930.

Saint-Gelais, Mellin de. *Sonnets*. Edited by Luigia Zilli. Geneva: Droz, 1990.

Salvazo, Antonio. "Una disperata famosa," edited by Erasmo Pèrcopo, in *Raccolta di studi critici dedicati ad Alessandro d'Ancona*. Firenze: Barbèra, 1901. 701–718.

Sannazaro, Jacopo. *Arcadia and Piscatorial Eclogues*. Edited by Ralph Nash. Detroit: Wayne State University Press, 1966.

Sebillet, Thomas de. *Art Poétique francoys*. Edited by Félix Gaiffe. Paris: Droz, 1932.

Serdini, Simone. *Rime*. Edited by Emilio Pasquini. Bologna: Commissione per i testi di lingua, 1965.

Speroni, Sperone. *Dialoghi di Sperone Speroni*. Venice: Fra Lorenzini da Torino, 1550.

Tansillo, Luigi. *Rime*. Edited by Tobia R. Toscano, commentaries by Erika Milburn and Rossano Pestarino, Vol. 1. Rome: Bulzoni, 2011.

Tebaldeo, Antonio. *Opere de miser Antonio Tebaldeo da Ferrara. Sonetti, dialoghi, disperata, epistole, egloghe, capitoli, etc . . .*. Venice: A. de Bindoni, 1511.

——. *Rime*. Edited by Tania Basile and Jean-Jacques Marchand. 3 vols. Modena-Ferrara: Panini-Istituto di Studi Rinascimentali, 1989–92.

Tyard, Pontus de. *Les Erreurs amoureuses*. Edited by John A. McCelland. Geneva: Droz, 1967.

Vannozzo, Francesco di. *Rime di Francesco di Vannozzo tratte da un codice inedito del secolo XIV*. Padova: Tipografia del Seminario Editrice, 1824.

——. *Le Rime di Francesco di Vannozzo*. Edited by Antonio Medin. Bologna: Collezione di opere inedite o rare pubblicate dalla Commissione per i testi di lingua di Bologna, 1928.

Verville, François Béroalde de. *Les Souspirs amoureux*. Paris: Timothee Jouan, 1588.

Viau, Théophile de. *Œuvres poétiques, Première Partie*. Edited by Jeanne Streicher. Geneva: Droz, 1967.

Vives, Juan Luís. *The Education of a Christian Woman*. Edited and translated by Charles Fantazzi. Chicago: Chicago University Press, 2000.

Anthologies

Atanagi, Dionigi. *De le rime di diversi nobili poeti toscani, Raccolte da M. Dionigi Atanagi*, Libro Primo. Venice: Lodovico Avanzo, 1565.

Dolce, Lodovico, ed. *La Seconda parte delle Stanze di diversi autori, Novamente mandata in luce*. Vinegia: Gabriel Giolito de' Ferrari, 1563.

Domenichi, Lodovico, ed. *Rime diverse d'alcune nobilissime, et virtuosissime donne*. Lucca: Busdrago, 1559.

Fioretto di cose nove nobilissime et degne de diversi auctori noviter stampate cioè: Sonetti Capitoli Epistole Egloghe Disperate Strambotti Barzellette et una contra disperata. Venice: Giorgio de Rusconi, 1508.

Fioretto di cose nove nobilissime di diversi Autori noviter stampate; cioè sonetti, capitoli, epistole, egloghe, disperate, strambotti, barzellette, & una controdisperata. Venice: Nicolo detto il Zoppino, 1510.

Ms. It. 1543, Bibliothèque nationale, Site Richelieu.

Mathieu-Castellani, Gisèle. *Anthologie de la poésie amoureuse de l'âge baroque 1570–1640*. Paris: Le Livre de Poche, 1990.

Stanze di diversi illustri poeti, nuovamente raccolte da M. Lodovico Dolce. Venice: Gabriel Giolito de' Ferrari, 1553.

Stortoni, Laura Anna. *Women Poets of the Italian Renaissance. Courtly Ladies & Courtesans*. Edited and translated by Stortoni and Mary Prentice Lillie. New York: Italica Press, 1997.

Secondary Sources

Abulafia, David. "The South." In *Italy in the Age of the Renaissance*, edited by John M. Najemy, 208–25. Oxford: Oxford University Press, 2004.

Adler, Sara. "The Petrarchan Lament of Isabella di Morra." In *Donna: Women in Italian Culture*, edited by Ada Testaferri, 201–21. Ottawa: Dovehouse, 1989.

Alexander, Jeffrey C. *Trauma: A Social Theory*. Cambridge, UK: Polity Press, 2012.

Ancona, Alessandro d'. "Del secentismo nella poesia cortigiana del secolo XV." In *Pagine sparse di letteratura e di storia*, 63–181. Firenze: Sansoni, 1914.

Anderson, W. S. "The Heroides" in *Ovid*, edited by J. W. Binns, 49–83. London and Boston: Routledge, 1973.

Armstrong, Nancy and Leonard Tennenhouse, eds. *The Ideology of Conduct: Essays on Literature and the History of Sexuality*. London: Routledge, 1987.

Association des Amis d'Agrippa d'Aubigné. http://www.agrippadaubigne.org/association.htm

Augier, Denis. "Clovis Hesteau de Nuysement: Un certain désir d'immortalité," *Essays in French Literature* 38 (2001): 1–18.

Aukrust, Kjerstin. "'J'ouvre mon estomac': Agrippa d'Aubigné et le corps macabre." In *Corps sanglants, souffrants et macabres: Réprésentations de la violence faite aux corps dans les lettres en Europe, XVIᵉ–XVIIᵉ siècles*, edited by Charlotte Bouteille-Meister and Kjerstin Aukrust, 101–114. Paris: Presses Sorbonne Nouvelle, 2010.

Baïche, André. *La Naissance du Baroque français*. Toulouse: Le Mirail, 1971.

Baldacci, Luigi. *Lirici del Cinquecento*. Milan: Longanesi, 1975.

Balmas, Enea. "Note sulla fortuna dell'Ariosto in Francia nel Cinquecento." In *Saggi e studi sul Rinascimento francese*, 75–103. Padova: Liviana, 1982.

Balsamo, Jean, ed. *Ma Bibliothèuqe poétique: Sixième partie: Poètes italiens de la Renaissance dans la Bibliothèque de la Fondation Barbier-Mueller*. Geneva: Droz, 2007.

——. *Les Rencontres des muses: Italianisme et anti-italianisme dans les lettres françaises de la fin du XVIᵉ siècle*. Geneva: Slatkine, 1992.

——. "Les Italiens de la Cour et les Lettres sous le règne de Henri IV (1589–1610)." In *Les Lettres au temps de Henri IV. Volume des Actes du Colloque Agen-Nérac, 18–20 mai, 1990*, 77–95. Paris: J&D Editions, 1991.

——. "'Du Florentin les lamentables voix': Mythe pétrarquien et modèle pétrarquiste en France au XVIᵉ siècle." In *L'Italia letteraria e l'Europa*, Vol. 1, edited by Nino Borsellino and Bruno Germano, 109–126. Roma: Salerno Editrice, 2001.

——. "Traduire de l'italien: Ambitions sociales et contraintes éditoriales à la fin du XVIᵉ siècle." In *Traduire et Adapter à la Renaissance, Actes de la journée d'étude organisée par l'Ecole nationale des Chartes et le Centre de recherche sur l'Espagne des XVIᵉ et XVIIᵉ siècles (Paris, 11 avril 1996)*, edited by

Dominique de Courcelles, 89–98. Paris: Ecole des Chartes, 1998.

———. "Les Poètes français et les anthologies lyriques italiennes," *Italique Poésie italienne de la Renaissance* V (2002): 9–32.

———. "Sonnets italiens et impressions françaises (1570–1600)." In *Le Sonnet à la Renaissance des origines au XVIIe siècle, Actes des troisièmes journées rémoises 17–19 janvier 1986*, edited by Yvonne Bellenger, 253–364. Paris: Aux amateurs des livres, 1988.

Basile, Tania. *Per il testo critico delle rime del Tebaldeo*. Messina: Centro di studi Umanistici, 1983.

Beaumatin, Eric. "La violence verbale." In *L'Invective au Moyen Age France, Espagne, Italie: Actes du Colloque l'invective au Moyen Age. Paris, 4–6 février 1993*, 21–25. Paris: Presses de la Sorbonne Nouvelle, 1995.

Beckson, Karl and Arthur Ganz, eds. *Literary Terms. A Dictionary*. 1960. Reprint, New York: The Noonday Press, 1989.

Bellenger, Yvonne. "Desportes imitateur de Domenico Ragnina, poète ragusain," *Revue d'histoire littéraire de la France* 5 (1994): 47–68.

Bély, Lucien. *La Société des princes*. Paris: Fayard, 1999.

Bensimon, Marc. "La Porte étroite; Essai sur le maniérisme: Le Greco, Saint Jean de la Croix, Sponde, Chassignet, D'Aubigné, Montaigne." *The Journal of Medieval and Renaissance Studies* 10 (1990): 255–80.

Bentley, Jerry H. *Politics and Culture in Renaissance Naples*. Princeton: Princeton University Press, 1987.

Berchtold, Jacques and Marie-Madeleine Fragonard, eds. *La Mémoire des guerres de religion: La concurrence des genres historiques XVIe–XVIIIe siècles, Actes du Colloque International de Paris 15–16 novembre 2002*. Geneva: Droz, 2007.

Berriot-Salvadore, Evelyne. "Les Femmes et les pratiques de l'écriture de Christine de Pizan à M. de Gournay," *Réforme, Humanisme, Renaissance* 16 (1983): 52–69.

Bertoni, Giulio. "Comunicazioni e Appunti. Sasso Sassi allias Panfilo Sassi." In *Giornale Storico della Letteratura Italiana* XLVIII (1906): 272–74.

Bichard-Thomine, Marie-Claire. "L'Amour en exil. La métaphore amoureuse de l'exil dans quelques poètes de la Renaissance." In *L'Exil*, edited by Alain Niderst, 47–61. C.E.R.H.I.S. Paris: Klincksieck, 1996.

Blomme, Raoul. "'Le stelle universali e i ciel rotanti' di Maestro Antonio da Ferrara." In *L'ecumenismo della cultura. Atti dei Convegni Internazionali XII–XIII–XIV*, 11–20. Firenze: Olschki, 1981.

Bongi, Salvatore, ed. *Annali di Gabriel Giolito de' Ferrari da Trino di Monferrato*. 2 vols. Rome: Principali Librai, 1890.

Bontempelli, Massimo, ed. *Le più belle pagine di Pietro Aretino*. Milan: Treves, 1936.

Boucher, Jacqueline. *Société et Mentalité autour de Henri III*. Paris: Champion, 2007.

———. *La Cour de Henri III*. Paris: Ouest France, 1986.

Boudet, Jean-Patrice and Hélène Millet, eds. *Eustache Deschamps et son temps*. Paris: Publications de la Sorbonne, 1997.

Branca, Vittore. "Le raccolte di rime e le collezioni di classici." In *Notizie introduttive e sussidi bibliografici*. Milan: Marzorati, 1948.

Briggs, Robin. *Early Modern France 1560–1715*. 1977. Reprint, Oxford: Oxford Univerity Press, 1998.

Broomhall, Susan. *Women and the Book Trade in Sixteenth-Century France*. Aldershot and Burlington, VT: Ashgate, 2002.

Cady, Joseph. "Renaissance Awareness and Language of Heterosexuality: 'Love' and 'Feminine Love,'" in *Renaissance Discourses of Desire*, edited by Claude J. Summers and Ted-Larry Pebworth, 143–58. Columbia and London: University of Missouri Press, 1993.

Cameron, Alice. "Desportes and Ariosto: Additional Sources in the Orlando and the Liriche," *Modern Languages Notes* L (1935): 174–78.

Camos, Gorris Rosanna. "'Je veux chanter d'amour la tempeste et l'orage': Desportes et les Imitations de l'Arioste." In *Philippe Desportes (1546–1606): Un Poète presque parfait entre Renaissance et Classicisme*, 173–211. Paris: Klincksieck, 2000.

Carrai, Stefano. "Appunti sulla preistoria dell'elegia volgare." In *L'Elegia nella tradizione poetica italiana*, edited by Andrea Comboni and Alessandra Di Ricco, 1–15. Trento: Editrice Università degli Studi di Trento, 2003.

Caserta, Giovanni. *Isabella Morra e la società meridionale del Cinquecento*. Matera: Edizioni Meta, 1976.

Castor, Grahame. *Pléiade Poetics: A Study in Sixteenth-Century Thought and Terminology*. Cambridge: Cambridge University Press, 1964.

Cave, Terence. *Devotional Poetry in France, c. 1570–1613*. Cambridge: Cambridge University Press, 1969.

———. *The Cornucopian Text. Problems of Writing in the French Renaissance*. Oxford: Clarendon Press, 1979.

———. "The Mimesis of Reading in the Renaissance." In *Mimesis: From Mirror to Method, Augustine to Descartes*, edited by John D. Lyons and Stephen G. Nichols, 149–65. Hanover, NH: University Press of New England, 1972.

Céard, Jean. "Le Thème du 'monde à l'envers' dans l'œuvre d'Agrippa d'Aubigné." In *L'Image du monde renversé et ses représentations littéraires et para-littéraires de la fin du XVIe au milieu du XVIIe, Colloque International de Tours, 17–19 novembre 1977*, edited by Jean Lafond and Augustin Redondo, 117–27. Paris: J. Vrin, 1979.

Chambers, D. S. and F. Quiviger, eds. *Italian Academies of the Sixteenth Century*. London: The Warburg Institute, 1995.

Charon, Annie. "Regards sur le livre à la cour de Henri III." In *Il libro a corte*, edited by Amedeo Quondam, 389–99. Rome: Bulzoni, 1994.

Cian, Vittorio. *Le rime di Bartolomeo Cavassino notaio bellunese della prima metà del secolo*, vol. 1. Bologna: Romagnoli dall'Acqua, 1893.

Cioranesco, Alejandro. *L'Arioste en France des origines à la fin du XVIIIe siècle*. Paris: Les Presses modernes, 1938.

———. "Les Imitations de l'Arioste de Philippe Desportes." *Mélanges de l'Ecole Roumaine* XII (1934): 1–83.

Clark, John E. *Elégie: The Fortunes of a Classical Genre in Sixteenth-Century France.* The Hague-Paris: Mouton, 1975.

Cocco, Mia. *La tradizione cortese e il petrarchismo nella poesia di Clément Marot.* Florence: Olschki, 1978.

Colby, Elbridge. *The Echo-Device in Literature.* New York: The New York Public Library, 1920.

Colletet, Guillaume. *L'Art poétique I. Traité de l'épigramme et du sonnet.* Geneva: Droz, 1965.

Comboni, Andrea. "Rarità metriche nelle antologie di Felice Feliciano." In *Studi di filologia italiana. Bollettino dell'Accademia della Crusca*, 65–92. Vol. 52. Firenze: Sansoni, 1994.

Comboni, Andrea and Alessandra Di Ricco, eds. *L'elegia nella tradizione poetica italiana.* Trento: Editrice Università degli Studi di Scienze Filologiche e Storiche, 2003.

Conconi, Bruna. "Sulla ricezione di Pietro Aretino in Francia." *Rivista di letterature moderne e comparate* 59 (2006): 29–58.

Coniglio, Giovanni. *Il Regno di Napoli al tempo di Carlo V.* Napoli: Edizioni scientifiche italiane, 1951.

Cornish, Alison. "Translatio Galliae: Effects of Early Franco-Italian Literary Exchange." *The Romanic Review* 97, no. 3–4 (2006): 309–30.

Corsi, Giuseppe. *Rimatori del Trecento.* Torino: UTET, 1969.

Costa, Daniela. "Les Poètes de Henri III et Pétrarque." In *Les Poètes français de la Renaissance et Pétrarque*, edited by Jean Balsamo, 379–93. Geneva: Droz, 2005.

———. "Desportes et l'Académie du Palais." In *Philippe Desportes (1546–1606): Un Poète presque parfait entre Renaissance et Classicisme*, 163–72. Paris: Klincksieck, 2000.

Cox, Virginia. *Women's Writings in Italy 1400–1650.* Baltimore: The Johns Hopkins University Press, 2008.

Crescinbeni, Giovan Mario. *Dell'Istoria della volgar poesia scritta da Giovan Mario Crescinbeni.* Venice: Lorenzo Balegio, 1714. 2nd edition, 1731.

Croce, Benedetto. *Storia del Regno di Napoli. Milano*: Adelphi, 1992.

———. *Isabella di Morra e Diego Sandoval de Castro.* Bari: Latereza, 1929.

Crouzet, Denis. *La Nuit de la Saint-Barthélemy: Un rêve perdu de la Renaissance.* Paris: Fayard, 1994.

———. *Les Guerriers de Dieu: La violence aux temps des troubles de religion, vers 1525–vers 1610.* 2 vols. Paris: Champ Vallon, 1990.

———. "Le Règne de Henri III et la violence collective." In *Henri III et son temps Actes du colloque international du Centre de la Renaissance de Tours, octobre 1989*, edited by Robert Sauzet, 211–25. Paris: Librairie Philosophique J. Vrin, 1992.

Curtius, Ernst Robert. *European Literature and the Latin Middle Ages*. Translated by William R. Trask. New York: Pantheon Books, 1953.

Danzi, Massimo. "Sulla poesia di Antonio Tebaldeo." *Giornale storico della letteratura italiana* 171, no. 554 (1994): 258–82.

Davis, Natalie Zemon. *Society and Culture in Early Modern France*. Stanford: Stanford University Press, 1975.

Debenedetti, Emilio. "Notizie sulla vita e sugli scritti di E. M. da Ascoli." *Giornale storico della letteratura italiana* XXXIX (1902): 1–31.

Delany, Joseph. "Despair" in *The Catholic Encyclopedia*, vol. 4. New York: Robert Appleton Company, 1908.

DellaNeva, JoAnn. *Unlikely Exemplars: Reading and Imitating beyond the Italian Canon in French Renaissance Poetry*. Newark: University of Delaware Press, 2009.

——. "Reading Desportes through the Italians: Two Early Modern Readers Responses." *Italique Poésie italienne de la Renaissance* XI (2008): 31–52.

——. "An Exploding Canon; Petrarch and the Petrarchists in Renaissance France" *Annali d'italianistica* 22 (2004): 189–211.

——. "Reflecting Lesser Light: The Imitation of Minor Writers in the Renaissance." *Renaissance Quarterly* 12, no. 3 (1989): 449–79.

Diefendorf, Barbara. *Beneath the Cross: Catholics and the Huguenots in Sixteenth-Century Paris*. Oxford: Oxford University Press, 1991.

Dionisotti, Carlo. "Fortuna del Petrarca nel Quattrocento." *Italia medievale e umanistica* XVII (1974): 61–113.

Dornetti, Vittorio. *Aspetti e figure della poesia minore trecentista*. Padova: Piccin Nuova Libreria, 1984.

Dubois, Jean-Claude. *La Poésie du XVIᵉ siècle*. Paris: Bordas, 1989.

——. *Le Maniérisme*. Paris: Presses Universitaires de France, 1979.

——. *Le Baroque: Profondeurs de l'apparence*. Paris: Larousse, 1973.

——. *La Poésie Baroque*. Vol. 1 and 2. Paris: Nouveaux Classiques Larousse, 1969.

——. "Imitation Différentielle et poétique maniériste." *Revue de littérature comparée* 54 (1977): 142–51.

Durling, Robert and Ronald L. Martinez. *Time and the Crystal Studies in Dante's Rime Petrose*. Berkeley: University of California Press, 1990.

Duval, Edwin M. *Poesis and Poetic: Tradition in the Early Works of Saint-Amant; Four Essays in Contextual Reading*. York, SC: French Literature Publications Company, 1981.

Eco, Umberto. *The Role of the Reader: Explorations in the Semiotics of Texts*. Bloomington: Indiana University Press, 1984.

Eichel-Lojkinc, Patricia. *Les Seuils de la modernité*. Geneva: Droz, 2002.

Erlanger, Philippe. *Henri III*. Paris: Gallimard, 1948.

Eschrich, Gabriella Scarlatta. "Reading the Afterlife of Isabella di Morra's Poetry." In *Tulsa Studies in Women's Literature* 34, no. 2 (Fall 2015): 273–304.

——. "Philippe Desportes's Copy of Nocturno Napolitano's Opera Amorosa."

Bibliothèque d'Humanisme et Renaissance LXXIV, no. 3 (2012): 563–68.

———. "Reading Philippe Desportes in Les Rencontres des muses de France et d'Italie." *Renaissance Studies* 26, no. 3 (2012).

———. "Cariteo's 'Aragonia': The Language of Power at the Aragonese Court." *Forum Italicum* XXXVII, no. 2 (2003): 329–44.

———. "Adopting and Adapting: The Case of the Disperata." *Romance Notes* 43–3 (Fall 2003): 241–50.

———. "Le Printemps and the Poetics of Dissection." In *European Studies Journal* XVIII–XIX-1 (Fall 2002): 171–85.

———. "The Continuity of Baroque Poetic Vision: From the Italian Disperata to the French Neo-Petrarchans." *The Michigan Academician* XXXIII (Fall 2001): 261–271.

Fanlo, Jean-Raymond. "Topiques: l'œuvre inachevée." In *Poétiques D'Aubigné: Actes du Colloque de Genève, Mai 1996*, edited by Olivier Pot, 63–76. Geneva: Droz, 1999.

Fanti, Claudia. "L'elegia properziana nella lirica amorosa del Cariteo." *Italianistica* 14, no. 1 (1985): 23–44.

Farenga, Paola. "Di Costanzo, Angelo." In *Dizionario biografico degli Italiani*, 39. Rome: Istituto dell'Enciclopedia Italiana, 1991. 742–47.

Favre, Jules. *Olivier de Magny (1529?–1561): Etude bibliographique et littéraire*. Paris: Garnier, 1885.

Fenzi, Enrico. "Cariteo: il fascino del nome." *Il Nome nel testo VII. Rivista internazionale onomastica letteria* (2005): 49–76. riviste.edizioniets.com

———. "La lingua e lo stile del Cariteo dalla prima alla seconda edizione dell'Endimione." In *Studi di filologia e letteratura*, 1–83. Genoa: Università degli Studi di Genova. Istituto di letteratura italiana, 1970.

Ferguson, Gary. *Queer (Re)Readings in the French Renaissance: Homosexuality, Gender, Culture*. Aldershot, UK and Burlington, VT: Ashgate, 2008.

Ferrer, Véronique. "Le Printemps d'Agrippa d'Aubigné ou les épreuves du pétrarquisme." In *Les Poètes français de la Renaissance et Pétrarque*, edited by Jean Balsamo, 445–57. Geneva: Droz, 2004.

Finucci, Valeria. "Isabella di Morra." In *An Encyclopedia of Continental Women Writers*, vol. 2, edited by Katharina M. Wilson, 876–77. New York: Garland, 1991.

Flamini, Francesco. *La lirica toscana del Rinascimento anteriore ai tempi del Magnifico*. Pisa: Nistri, 1891.

———. "Le rime di Odetto de la Noue e l'Italianismo al tempo d'Enrico III." In *Studi di letteratura italiana e straniera*, 340–81. Livorno: Giusti, 1895.

Fontanier, Pierre. *Les Figures du discours*. Paris: Flammarion, 1977.

Forster, Leonard. *The Icy Fire: Five Studies in European Petrarchism*. Cambridge: Cambridge University Press, 1969.

Fredericksen, Erik. "Jacopo Sannazaro Piscatory Eclogues and the Question of Genre." *New Voices in Classical Reception Studies* 9 (2014): 19–29.

Frémy, Edouard. *L'Académie des derniers Valois*. Paris: Ernest Leroux, 1887.

Gabotto, Ferdinando. "Francesismo e antifrancesismo in due poeti del Quattrocento (Panfilo Sasso e Giorgio Alione)." *Rassegna Emiliana di storia, letteratura, ed arte* 1 (1888): 282–300.

Gentili, Gaia. "Il capitolo in terza rima di Niccolò da Correggio: non solo elegia." In *L'elegia nella tradizione poetica italiana*, 115–46. Trento: Editrice Università degli Studi di Scienze Filologiche e Storiche, 2003.

George Clubb, Louise and William G. Clubb. "Building a Lyric Canon: Gabriel Giolito and the Rival Anthologists, 1545–1590." *Italica* 68 (1991): 332–344.

Gibbs, Robin. *Early Modern France*. Oxford: Oxford University Press, 1998.

Ginsberg, Ellen. "Genre Theory in the French Renaissance." *French Literature Series* 4 (1977): 171–77.

Giordano, Michael J. *The Art of Meditation and the French Renaissance Love Lyric: The Poetics of Introspection in Maurice Scève's 'Délie, object de plus haulte vertu' (1544)*. Toronto: University of Toronto Press, 2010.

——. "Reverse Transmutations: Béroalde de Verville's Parody of Paracelsus in 'Le Moyen de parvenir': An Alchemical Language of Skepticism in the French Baroque." *Renaissance Quarterly* 56, no. 1 (2003): 88–137.

Gourier, Françoise. *Etude des Œuvres Poétiques de Saint-Amant*. Geneva: Droz, 1961.

Graham, Victor E. "Some Undiscovered Sources of Desportes." *French Studies* X (1956): 123–32.

Gray, Floyd. *Gender, Rhetoric, and Print Culture in French Renaissance Writing*. Ann Arbor: University of Michigan Press, 2006.

Greene, Thomas. *The Light in Troy: Imitation and Discovery in Renaissance Poetry*. New Haven, CT: Yale University Press, 1986.

Greengrass, Mark. *Governing Passions: Peace and Reform in the French Kingdom, 1576–1585*. Oxford: Oxford University Press, 2007.

Griffin, Robert. "'Solo e pensoso': The Context of Petrarchan Melancholy in French Renaissance Poetry." *Studi di letteratura francese* IV (1975): 50–84.

Griffiths, Richard. "Some Uses of Petrarchan Imagery in Sixteenth-Century France." *French Studies* XVIII, no. 4 (1964): 311–21.

Grignani, Maria Antonietta. "Per Isabella di Morra, Testi e documenti." *Rivista di letteratura italiana* 2, no. 3 (1994): 519–54.

Gros, Gerard and Marie-Madeleine Fragonard. *Les Formes poétiques du Moyen Âge à la Renaissance*. Paris: Nathan, 1995.

Guillot, Roland. "L'exil de l'amour ou l'amour au désert." In *L'Exil, Actes et Colloques No. 48*, 63–78. Paris: Klincksieck, 1996.

Hale, J. R., *Renaissance Europe, 1480–1520*. Oxford, UK: Blackwell, 2000.

Hall, Kathleen M. "Pontus de Tyard and His 'Disgrace.'" *L'Esprit créateur* V, no. 2 (Summer 1965): 102–109.

Harvey, Elizabeth D. *Ventriloquized Voices: Feminist Theory and English Renaissance Texts*. London: Routledge, 1992.

——. "Ventriloquizing Sappho: Ovid, Donne, and the Erotics of the Feminine Voice." *Criticism: A Quarterly for Literature and the Arts* 31, no. 2 (1989): 115–138.

Hempfer, Klaus W. "Per una definizione del Petrarchismo." In *Dynamique d'une expansion culturelle: Pétrarque en Europe XIVᵉ–XXᵉ siècles; Actes du XXVI congrès international du CEFI, Chambéry, 1–15 décembre 1995*, edited by Pierre Blanc, 23–52. Bibliothèque Franco Simone. Paris: Honoré Champion, 2001.

Hollinsgworth, Mary. *Patronage in Renaissance Italy*. Baltimore: Johns Hopkins University Press, 1994.

Hulubei, Alice. *L'Eglogue en France au XVIᵉ siècle*. Paris: Droz, 1938.

Hutin, Serge. *L'Alchimie*. Paris: Presses Universitaires de France, 2011.

Hutton, Edward. *Pietro Aretino: The Scourge of Princes*. Boston and New York: Houghton Mufflin, 1922.

Innamorati, Giuliano. *Pietro Aretino, Studi e note critiche*. Messina: G. D'Anna, 1957.

Jacobson, Howard. *Ovid's Heroides*. Princeton: Princeton University Press, 1974.

Jaffré, Jean. *Le vers et le poème*. Paris: Nathan, 1984.

Jameson, Frederic. "Magical Narratives: Romance as Genre." *New Literary History* 7, no. 1 (1975): 135–163.

Jasinski, Max. *Histoire du Sonnet en France*. Genève: Slatkine, 1970.

Jauss, H. R.. "Littérature médiévale et théorie des genres." *Littérature* 1 (1970): 79–101.

Javitch, Daniel. "Self-justifying Norms in the Genre Theories of Italian Renaissance Poets." *Philological Quarterly* 67, no. 2 (1988): 195–217.

Jeanneret, Michel. "Les Tragiques: mimesis et intertexte." In *Le Signe et le texte: Etudes sur l'écriture au XVIᵉ siècle en France*, edited by Lawrence D. Kritzman, 101–13. Lexington: French Forum, 1990.

Jost, François. "Le sonnet: sens d'une structure." In *Le Sonnet à la Renaissance des origines au XVIIᵉ siècle, Actes des troisièmes journées rémoises 17–19 janvier 1986*, edited by Yvonne Bellenger, 57–65. Paris: Aux amateurs des livres, 1988.

Jones, Ann Rosalind. "Surprising Fame: Renaissance Gender Ideologies and Women's Lyric." In *The Poetics of Gender*, edited by Nancy K. Miller, 74–95. New York: Columbia University Press, 1986.

——. "Nets and Bridles: Early Modern Conduct Books and Sixteenth-Century Women Lyrics." In *The Ideology of Conduct. Essays on Literature and the History of Sexuality*, edited by Nancy Armstrong and Leonard Tennenhouse, 39–72. New York and London: Methuen, 1987.

Jouanna, Arlette. *The St. Bartholomew's Day Massacre. The Mysteries of a Crime of State*. Translated by Joseph Bergin. Manchester, UK: Manchester University Press, 2013.

Jourde, Michel. "L'Imaginaire et l'histoire: sur la situation du sonnet en France vers 1550." In *Histoire et littérature au siècle de Montaigne. Mélanges offerts à Claude-Gilbert Dubois*, edited by Françoise Argot-Dutard, 313–25. Geneva: Droz, 2001.

Kastner, L.E. "Desportes et Angelo di Costanzo." *Revue d'histoire littéraire de la France* XV (1908): 133–45.

Keller, Luzius. "'Solo e pensoso,' 'Seul et pensif,' 'Solitaire et pensif': mélancolie pétrarquienne et mélancolie pétrarquiste." *Studi Francesi* LI (Jan-April 1973): 3–14.

Kennedy, William. *The Site of Petrarchism: Early Modern National Sentiment in Italy, France, and England*. Baltimore: The John Hopkins University Press, 2003.

——. "Petrarchan Textuality: Commentaries and Gender Revisions." In *Discourses of Authority in Medieval and Renaissance Literature*, edited by Kevin Brownlee and Walter Stephens, 151–68. Hanover, NH: University Press of New England, 1989.

Kirkham, Victoria and Armando Maggi, eds. *Petrarch: A Critical Guide to the Complete Works*. Chicago: The University of Chicago Press, 2009.

Knecht, Robert. *The French Renaissance Court*. New Haven and London: Yale University Press, 2008.

——. *The French Wars of Religion, 1562–1629*. Cambridge: Cambridge University Press, 2005.

——. *The French Civil Wars in Perspective*. New York: Longman, 2000.

——. "A New Parnassus." In *The French Renaissance Court 1483–1589*. New Haven: Yale University Press, 2008.

Kristéva, Julia. *Semiotikè: Recherches pour une sémanalyse*. Paris: Seuil, 1969.

——. *Revolution in Poetic Language*. Translated by Margaret Waller. New York: Columbia University Press, 1984.

Kolsky, Stephen D. "The Courtier as Critic: Vincenzo Calmeta's Vita del fecondo vulgare Serafino Aquiliano." *Italica* 67, no. 2 (1990): 161–72.

Lachèvre, Frédéric. *Bibliographie des recueils collectifs de poésies du XVIe siècle*. Paris: H. Champion, 1922.

Lamma, Ernesto. "Intorno ad alcune rime di Leonardo Giustiniani." *Giornale Storico di Letteratura Italiana* X (1887): 372–83.

Lanza, Antonio. *Lirici toscani del Quattrocento*, vol. I. Rome: Bulzoni, 1973.

——. *Polemiche e berte letterarie nella Firenze del primo Quattrocento*. Rome: Bulzoni, 1971.

Lavaud, Jacques. *Un Poète de cour au temps des derniers Valois: Philippe Desportes (1546–1606)*. Paris: Droz, 1936.

——. *Les Imitations de l'Arioste par Philippe Desportes, Suivies de poésies inédites ou non recueillies du même auteur*. Paris: Droz, 1936.

Lechi, Luigi. *Della tipografia bresciana nel secolo decimoquinto*. Brescia: Tipografia Venturini, 1854.

Leclercle, François. "Théoriciens français et italiens: une 'politique' des genres."

In *La Notion de genre à la Renaissance*, edited by Guy Demerson, 67–100. Geneva: Droz, 1984.

Le Roy Ladurie, Emmanuel. *L'Etat Royal, De Louis XI à Henri IV. 1460–1610.* Paris: Hachette, 1987.

Levi, Ezio. *Francesco di Vannozzo e la lirica nelle corti lombarde durante la seconda metà del secolo XIV.* Firenze: Tipografia Galletti e Coci, 1908.

Long, Kathleen Perry. *Hermaphrodites in Renaissance Europe.* Aldershot, UK: Ashgate, 2006.

———. ed. *Religious Differences in France: Past and Present.* Sixteenth Century Essays Studies 74. Kirksville: Truman State University Press, 2006.

———."The Representation of Violence in the Works of Théodore Agrippa d'Aubigné." In *Reposessions. Psychoanalysis and the Phantasms of Early-Modern Culture*, edited by Timothy Murray and Alan K. Smith, 142–67. Minneapolis: University of Minnesota Press, 1998.

———. "The Chemical Wedding in the Works of Clovis Hesteau de Nuysement." *Dalhousie French Studies* 56 (2001): 27–35.

———. "Salomon Trismosin and Clovis Hesteau de Nuysement: The Sexual Politics of Alchemy in Early Modern France." *L'Esprit Créateur* 35, no. 2 (1995): 9–21.

Longhi, Silvia. "Lettere a Ippolito e a Teseo. La voce femminile nell'elegia." In *Veronica Gambara e la poesia del suo tempo nell'Italia settentrionale. Atti del Convegno (Brescia-Correggio, 17–19 ottobre 1985)*, edited by Cesare Bozzetti, Pietro Ghibellini, and Ennio Sandal, 385–98. Florence: Olschki Editore, 1989.

———. "Una raccolta di Rime di Angelo di Costanzo." *Rinascimento* XV (1975): 231–90.

———. *Mantova e Urbino: Isabella d'Este e Elisabetta Gonzaga nelle relazioni familiari e nelle vicende politiche.* Turin: Roux & Co., 1893.

Luzio, Alessandro. *Pietro Aretino nei primi suoi anni a Venezia e la corte dei Gonzaga.* Turin: Loescher, 1888.

Luzio, Alessandro and Rodolfo Renier. *La coltura e le relazioni letterarie di Isabella d'Este Gonzaga.* Torino: Edizioni Sylvestre Bonnard, 2005.

Malinverni, Massimo. "L'edizione e il commento dei Sonetti e Capituli di Panfilo Sasso." In *Petrarca in Barocco. Cantieri Petrarchistici: due seminari romani*, edited by Amedeo Quondam, 361–89. Roma: Bulzoni 2004.

———. "Note per un bestiario lirico tra Quattro e Cinquecento." In *Italique: Poésie italienne de la Renaissance*, vol. 2, pp. 7–31. Geneva: Droz, 1999.

———. "La lirica volgare padana tra Boiardo e Ariosto: appunti su una tradizione rimossa." *Medioveo e umanesimo* 88–89 (1998): 695–721.

———. "Sulla tradizione del sonetto 'Hor te fa terra, corpo' di Panfilo Sasso." In *Studi di filologia italiana. Bulletino della Crusca* XLIX (1991): 123–65.

Manacorda, Giuseppe. "Galeotto del Carretto Poeta lirico e drammatico monferrino (14---1530)." In *Memorie della Reale Accademia delle scienze di*

Torino, Serie Seconda, Tomo XLIX. Turin: Carlo Clausen, 1900.

Manetti, Roberta. "Per una nuova edizione delle rime di Francesco di Vannozzo (ovvero: Perchè una nuova edizione delle rime di Francesco di Vannozzo)." In *La cultura volgare padovana nell'età del Petrarca, Atti del Convegno Monselice-Padova, 7–8 maggio 2004*, edited by F. Brugnolo and Z. L. Verlato, 403–41. Padova: Il poligrafo, 2006.

Marchand, Jean-Jacques. "Le disperate di Antonio Tebaldeo: dall'elegia al racconto dell'io." In *Feconde venner le carte. Studi in onore di Ottavio Besomi*, edited by Tatiana Crivelli, 160–71. Bellinzona: Edizioni Casagrande, 1997.

——. "I sonetti del Tebaldeo in morte del Serafino." In *Studi in onore di Pier Vincenzo Mengaldo per i suoi sessant'anni*, 423–34. Firenze: Edizioni del Galluzzo, 2007.

Marotti, Arthur F. "'Love is not Love': Elizabethan Sonnet Sequences and the Social Order." *ELH* 49 (1982): 396–428.

Martines, Lauro. *Strong Words*. Baltimore: Johns Hopkins University Press, 2001.

——. "Love and Hate in Renaissance Patronage: Italy." *The Italianist* 14 (1994): 5–31.

——. "Ritual Language in Renaissance Italy." In *Riti e rituali nelle società medievali*, edited by Jacques Cliffoleau, Lauro Martines, and Agostino Paravicini Bagliani, 59–76. Spoleto: Centro Italiano di Studi Medievali, 1994.

Marzot, Giulio. "Il tramite del Petrarchismo dal Rinascimento al barocco." *Studi Petrarcheschi* VI (1957): 123–75.

Mathieu-Castellani, Gisèle. *Agrippa d'Aubigné: Le corps de Jézabel*. Paris: Presses Universitaires de France, 1991.

——. *Éros Baroque: Anthologie de la poésie baroque 1570–1620*. Paris: Nizet, 1986.

——. *Mythes de l'Éros baroque*. Paris: Presses Universitaires de France, 1981.

——. *Les Thèmes amoureux dans la poésie française. 1570–1600*. Paris: Klincksieck, 1975.

——. "La Poétique de la fureur et l'esthétique des vers rapportés: l'exemple de Clovis Hesteau de Nuysement." *Australian Journal of French Studies* 39, no. 2 (2002): 167–86.

——. "Les Enfants de Pétrarque." In *Dynamique d'une expansion culturelle: Pétrarque en Europe, XIVe–XXe siècles, Actes du XXVIe congrès international du CEFI, Turin et Chambéry, 1995*, edited by Pierre Blanc, 623–42. Paris: Champion, 2001.

——. "Violences d'Aubigné." In *Poétiques d'Aubigné*, edited by Olivier Pot, 17–31. Geneva: Droz, 1999.

——. "Eros furieux: La rhétorique baroque des Soupirs amoureux." In *Studies on Béroalde de Verville*, edited by Michael J. Giordano, Biblio 17, 5–19. Paris, Seattle, Tübingen: Papers on Seventeenth Century Literature, 1992.

——. "La Notion de genre." In *La Notion de genre à la Renaissance*, edited by Guy Demerson, 17–34. Genève: Slatkine, 1984.

———. "Les Modes du discours lyrique au XVIᵉ siècle." In *La Notion de genre à la Renaissance*, edited by Guy Demerson, 129–48. Genève: Slatkine, 1984.

Mazzara, Richard A. "The Philosophical-Religious Evolution of Théophile de Viau." *The French Review* 41, no. 5 (1968): 618–28.

———. "Théophile de Viau, Saint-Amant, and the Spanish *Soledad*." *Kentucky Romance Quarterly* 14, no. 4 (1967): 393–404.

Mazzotta, Giuseppe. *The Worlds of Petrarch*. Durham: Duke University Press, 1993.

Maylender, Michele. *Storia delle Accademie d'Italia*. 5 vols. Bologna: Capelli, 1926–30.

Melançon, Robert. "La Fin du pétrarquisme en France." In *L'Automne de la Renaissance, 1580–1630*, edited by Jean Lafond and André Stegmann, 257–71. Paris: Librairie Philosophique J. Vrin, 1981.

Meozzi, Arturo. *Il petrachismo europeo: Secolo XVI*. Pisa: Vallerini, 1934.

Milan, Gabriella, ed. "Francesco di Vannozzo (Vannozii, Vannocci, de Vanotio, de Vannocchio)." *Dizionario Biografico degli Italiani* 50 (1998).

Milburn, Erika. *Luigi Tansillo and Lyric Poetry in Sixteenth-Century Naples*. Leeds, UK: Maney Publishing, 2003.

Miller, Nancy K. *Subject to Change: Reading Feminist Writing*. New York: Columbia University Press, 1988.

Moison, Clément. "Les Genres comme catégorie littéraire." In *L'Histoire littéraire aujourd'hui*, edited by Henri Béhar and Roger Fayolle, 67–80. Paris: Armand Colin, 1990.

Mourgues, Odette de. *Metaphysical, Baroque, and Précieux Poetry*. London: Oxford University Press, 1980.

Mulas, Alessandra. "Epistole e prosimetri inediti del Feliciano. Fonti delle Porretane." In *Italique Poésie itallienne de la Renaissance X*. Geneva: Droz, 2007. 60–84.

Murdock, Graeme, Penny Roberts, and Andrew Spicer, eds. *Ritual and Violence: Natalie Zemon Davis and Early Modern France*. Oxford: Oxford University Press, 2012.

Murphy, Stephen. "Diane et la disperata." In *Albineana 14, Le mythe de Diane en France au XVIᵉ siècle*, edited by Jean-Raymond Fanlo and Marie-Dominique Legrand, 119–29. Paris: Champion, 2002.

———. "Du Bartas, d'Aubigné et le triomphe militant." In *Dynamique d'une expansion culturelle. Pétrarque en Europe XIVᵉ–XXᵉ siècle. Actes du XVI congrès international du CEFI, Turin-Chambéry, 11–15 décembre, 1995. A la mémoire de Franco Simone*, edited by Pierre Blanc, 325–33. Paris; Champion, 2001.

Niccoli, Gabriele. "Romancing the Father: Writing as Weeping, Loss as Identity in Isabella di Morra's *Rime*." *Studi filologici di letteratura italiana*, edited by Danilo Aguzzi-Barbagli (1997): 159–72.

Nichols, Stephen G., *Eustache Deschamps. French Courtier-Poet. His Work and*

His World. Edited by Deborah M. Sinnreich-Levi. New York: AMS Press, Inc., 1998.

Nolhac, Pierre de. *Du Rôle de Pétrarque dans la Renaissance*. Paris: Durand, 1892.

Nuovo, Angela and Christian Coppens. *I Giolito e la stampa del XVI secolo*. Geneva: Droz, 2005.

Pallister, Janis. "Béroalde de Verville's *Stances de la mort* and *Soupirs amoureux*: Specimens of Baroque Poetry." In *Nottingham French Studies* 1 (1971): 57–70.

Parenti, Giovanni. *Benet Garret detto il Cariteo: Profilo di un poeta*. Firenze: Leo S. Olschki, 1993.

Pasquini, Giuseppe. "Saviozzo, Simone Serdini detto il." In *Dizionario critico della letteratura italiana*, 317–23. Torino: Unione tipografica torinese, 1973.

Pèrcopo, Erasmo. "Una disperata famosa." In *Raccolta di studi critici dedicati ad Alessandro d'Ancona*, 701–18. Firenze: Barbèra, 1901.

——. ed. *I Sonetti Faceti di Antonio Cammelli, in Studi di letteratura italiana*. Vol. 6. Naples: N. Jovene, 1908.

——. "Marc'Antonio Epicuro." In *Giornale Storico della Letteratura Italiana* XII (1888): 1–76.

Piéjus, Marie-Françoise. "Lecture et écriture selon des anthologies poétiques au XVIe siècle en Italie." In *L'Ecrivain face à son public en France et en Italie à la Renaissance*, edited by Charles Adelin Fiorato and J.-C. Margolin, 337–58. Paris: Librairie philosophique J. Vrin, 1989.

——. "La Première anthologie de poèmes féminins: l'écriture filtrée et orientée." In *Le Pouvoir et la plume: incitation, contrôle et repression dans l'Italie du XVIe siècle*, 193–213. Paris: CIRRI Sorbonne, 1982.

Piéri, Marius. *Pétrarque et Ronsard ou de l'influence de Pétrarque sur la Renaissance française*. New York: Burt Franklin, 1968.

Pigman, G. W. III. "Versions of Imitation in the Renaissance." *Renaissance Quarterly* 33 (1980): 1–32.

Pignatti, Franco. "Felice Feliciano." http://www.treccani.it/enciclopedia/felice-feliciano_%28Dizionario-Biografico%29/

Piscini, Angela. "Domenichi, Lodovico." In *Dizionario biografico degli Italiani*, vol. 40, pp. 595–600. Rome: Istituto dell'Enciclopedia Italiana, 1991.

Pitkin, Hanna Fenichel. *Fortune is a Woman: Gender and Politics in the Thought of Nicolò Machiavelli*. Chicago: Chicago University Press, 1999.

Plumb, J. H., *The Italian Renaissance*. 1961. Reprint, New York: Houghton Mifflin Company, 2001.

Poirier, Guy. "Interstices à l'imaginaire maniériste: les stances de Philippe Desportes." In *Philippe Desportes (1546–1606) Un poète presque parfait entre Renaissance et Classicisme*, edited by Jean Balsamo, 341–54. Paris: Klincksieck, 2000.

Pozzi, Giovanni and Giulia Giannella. "Scienza antiquaria e letteratura: Il Feliciano." In *Storia della cultura veneta dal primo Quattrocento al Concilio di*

Trento, edited by Girolamo Arnaldi and Manilo Patore Stocchi, vol. 3, pt. 1, pp. 459–77. Vicenza: Neri Pozza, 1980.

Puga, Maria Luisa Cerrón. "Materiales para la construcción del canon petrarquista: las antologías de Rime (libri I-IX)." In *Critica del testo*, 249–90. Roma: Viella, 1998.

Quadrio, Francesco Saverio. *Della storia, e della ragione d'ogni poesia*. Vol. 2. Milano: Francesco Agnelli, 1741.

Quillen, Carol Everhart. "Humanism and the Lure of Antiquity." In *Italy in the Age of the Renaissance 1300–1550*, edited by John M. Najemy. Oxford, UK: Oxford University Press, 2004.

Quondam, Amedeo. *Petrarchismo mediato. Per una critica della forma "antologia."* Rome: Bulzoni, 1974.

———. *La locuzione artificiosa: Teoria ed esperienza della lirica a Napoli nell'età del manierismo*. Roma: Bulzoni, 1973.

Racaut, Luc. *Hatred in Print. Catholic Propaganda and Protestant Identity during the French Wars of Religion*. Aldershot: Ashgate, 2002.

Rango, Luigi. "Prospettive di Letteratura Europea." In *Letteratura italiana, Le correnti*, edited by Carlo Marzorati, 1055–1186. Milano: Tripodi, 1956.

Ray, Meredith K. *Writing Gender in Women's Letter Collections of the Italian Renaissance*. Toronto: University of Toronto Press, 2009.

Raymond, Marcel. *Baroque et Renaissance poétique*. Paris : José Corti, 1955.

Reiss, Sheryl E. and David G. Wilkins, eds. *Beyond Isabella: Secular Women Patrons of Art in Renaissance Italy*. Kirksville, MO: Truman State University Press, 2001.

Renier, Rodolfo, ed. *I sonetti del Pistoia giusta l'apografo trivulziano*. Torino: Ermanno Loescher, 1888.

———. "Saggio di rime inedite di Galeotto del Carretto." In *Giornale storico della letteratura italiana* 6 (1885): 231–52.

Rhodes, Dennis. "Le antiche edizioni a stampa delle poesie di Simone Serdini." In *La Bibliofilia*, 253–66. Firenze: L.S. Olschki, 1998.

Ricciardi, Roberto. "Galeotto del Carretto." In *Dizionario Biografico degli Italiani*, http://www.treccani.it/enciclopedia/galeotto-del-carretto_(Dizionario-Biografico)/.

Richter, Bodo L. O. "Printers and Poets: Notes on Giolito and the Petrarchists." *The Library Chronicle* 19 (Spring 1953): 77–92.

Richter, Mario. *La Poesia lirica in Francia nel secolo XVI*. Milan: Istituto Editoriale Cisalpino, 1972.

Riffaterre, Michael. *Semiotics of Poetry*. Bloomington: Indiana University Press, 1984.

———. "Un faux problème: l'érosion intertextuelle." In *Le signe et le texte: Etudes sur l'écriture au XVIᵉ siècle en France*, edited by Lawrence D. Kritzman, 51–59. Lexington: French Forum Publishers, 1990.

Rigolot, François. *Poésie et Renaissance*. Paris: Editions du Seuil, 2002.

———. "Qu'est-ce qu'un sonnet?" In *Le Sonnet à la Renaissance des origines au XVIIe siècle, Actes des troisièmes journées rémoises 17–19 janvier 1986*, edited by Yvonne Bellenger, 3–18. Paris: Aux amateurs des livres, 1988.

———. "Quel genre d'amour pour Louise Labé?" *Poétique* 55 (1983): 303–17.

Rizza, Cecilia. "Persistance et transformation de l'influence italienne dans la poésie lyrique française de la première moitié du XVIIe siècle." *XVIIe Siècle*, no. 66–67 (1965): 22–42.

Rizzi, Nunzio. "'E donna son, contra le donne dico': il canzoniere di Isabella di Morra." *Carte Italiane* 1, no. 17 (2001): 17–30.

Robin, Diana. *Publishing Women: Salons, the Presses, and the Counter-Reformation in Sixteenth-Century Italy*. Chicago: The University of Chicago Press, 2007.

———. "Women on the Move: Trends in Anglophone Studies of Women in the Italian Renaissance." *I Tatti Studies in the Italian Renaissance* 16 (Fall 2013). Chicago: The University of Chicago Press, 2013.

———. "Morra, Isabella di (ca. 1520–1545)." In *Encyclopedia of Women in the Renaissance: Italy, France, and England*, edited by Anne R. Larsen, Diana Robin, and Carole Levin, 274–76. Santa Barbara, CA: ABC-CLIO, 2007.

Rosati, Giuseppe. "L'elegia al femminile: le *Heroides* di Ovidio (e altre heroides)." *Materiali e discussioni per l'analisi dei testi classici* 29 (1992): 71–94.

———. "Epistola elegiaca e lamento femminile." In *Lettere di eroine*, 5–51. Milan: Biblioteca Universitaria Rizzoli, 1989.

Rosenthal, Olivia. "Philippe Desportes. Esquisse d'une poétique des œuvres." In *Philippe Desportes (1546–1606) Un poète presque parfait entre Renaissance et Classicisme*, edited by Jean Balsamo, 355–374. Paris: Klincksieck, 2000.

Rossi, Antonio. *Serafino Aquilano e la poesia cortigiana*. Brescia: Morelliana, 1980.

Rossi, Carla. *Il Pistoia: spirito bizzarro del Quattrocento*. Alessandria: Edizioni dell'Orso, 2008.

———. "La 'Disperata' capitolo conclusivo dei Sonetti faceti del Pistoia." In *Letteratura italiana antica*, vol. 6, pp. 43–61. Rome: Moxedano, 2005.

Rossi, Vittorio. *Il Quattrocento*. 1933. Reprint, Padova: Oiccin Nuova Libraria, 1992.

———. "Il canzoniere edito di Andrea Michieli detto Squarzòla o Strazzòla." In *Giornale Storico di Letteratura Italiana* XXVI, Vol. 76–77 (1895): 1–91.

———. Book review of Cian, *Le rime di Bartolomeo Cavassico*, in *Giornale Storico della Letteratura Italiana* XXVI (1895): 214–22.

Rouget, François. *L'Apothéose d'Orphé. L'esthétique de l'ode en France au XVIe siècle, de Sébillet à Scaliger (1548–1561)*. Geneva: Droz, 1994.

———. "Academies, Circles, Salons, and the Emergence of the Pre-Modern 'Literary Public Sphere' in Sixteenth-Century France." In *Making Publics in Early Modern Europe: People, Things, Forms of Knowledge*, edited by Wilson, Bronwen, Yachnin, Margalit, Yael, 53–67. New York: Routledge, 2010.

———. "Philippe Desportes, médiateur du pétrarquisme français." In *Les Poètes français de la Renaissance et Pétrarque*, edited by Jean Balsamo, 331–51. Geneva: Droz, 2005.

——. "Desportes et les inflexions métriques de la voix lyrique." In *Philippe Desportes (1546–1606): Un poète presque parfait entre Renaissance et Classicisme*, edited by Jean Balsamo, 293–313. Paris : Klimcksieck, 2000.

——. "L'Éros et la démesure: la poétique des Odes et des Stances dans *Le Printemps* d'Agrippa d'Aubigné." *Albineana* 9 (1997): 9–28.

Rousset, Jean. *La Littérature de l'âge baroque en France: Circé et le Paon*. Paris: José Corti, 1954.

Russell, Rinaldina. "Intenzionalità artistica della disperata." In *Generi Poetici Medievali: Modelli e funzioni letterarie*, 166–96. Naples: SEN, 1982.

Salomon, Herman P. "Observations on the Definition, Evolution, and Separation of Genres in the Study of French Literature." *Yearbook of Comparative Criticism*, 209–28. University Park: Pennsylvania State University Press, 1968.

Salmon, J. H. M. *Society in Crisis: France in the Sixteenth Century*. London: Methuen, 1976.

Santagata, Marco. *La lirica aragonese. Studi sulla poesia napoletana del secondo Quattrocento*. Venice: Antenore, 1979.

Santagata, Marco, and Stefano Carrai. *La lirica di corte nell'Italia del Quattrocento*. Milan: FrancoAngeli, 1993.

Sapegno, Natalino. *Poeti minori del Trecento*. Milano: Riccardi, 1953.

Saslow, James M. *Ganymede in the Renaissance: Homosexuality in Art and Society*. New Haven and London: Yale University Press, 1986.

Saxby, Nelia. "Strutture narrative nella 'Storia di una fanciulla tradita' di Simone Serdini." In *Studi e problemi di critica testuale* 45 (1992): 103–112.

Scaglione, Aldo. "Cinquecento Mannerism and the Uses of Petrarch." In *Medieval and Renaissance Studies*, vol. 5, edited by O. B. Hardison Jr., 122–55. Chapel Hill: The University of North Carolina, 1969.

Scarlatta, Gabriella and Lidia Radi. *Representations of Heresy in Early Modern France*. CRRS, Essays and Studies 40, Toronto: University of Toronto, 2017.

Schiesari, Juliana. *The Gendering of Melancholia*. Ithaca: Cornell University Press, 1992.

——. "Petrarch's 'Ladies' and Sappho's 'Sirens': Fetishism and Mourning in Renaissance Women Poets." In *Grief and Gender: 700–1700*, edited by Jennifer C. Vaught, 95–103. New York: Palgrave, 2003.

——. "Isabella di Morra (c. 1520–1545)." In *Italian Women Writers: A Bio-Biographical Sourcebook*, edited by Rinaldina Russell, 279–85. Westport, CT: Greenwood Press, 1994.

Schmidt, Albert-Marie. *La Poésie scientifique en France au seizième siècle*. Paris: Albert Michel, 1938.

Schmitt, Jean-Claude. "Les images de l'invective." In *L'Invective au Moyen Age France, Espagne, Italie. Actes du Colloque l'invective au Moyen Age. Paris,*

4–6 février 1993, 11–20. Paris: Presses de la Sorbonne Nouvelle, 1995.

Sealy, R. J. *The Palace Academy of Henri III*. Geneva: Droz, Travaux d'Humanisme et Renaissance, 1981.

Shemek, Deanna. "The Collector's Cabinet. Lodovico Domenichi's Gallery of Women." In *Strong Voices, Weak History: Early Women Writers and Canons in England, France and Italy*, edited by Pamela Johnson Benson and Victoria Kirkham, 239–62. Ann Arbor: University of Michigan Press, 2005.

Smarr, Janet Levarie. "Substituting for Laura: Objects of Desire for Renaissance Women Poets." *Comparative Literature Studies* 28, no. 1 (2001): 1–30.

Spano Martinelli, Serena. "Note intorno a Felice Feliciano." *Rinascimento* 36 (1986): 221–38.

Stefanelli, Ruggero. "Il Petrarchismo di Isabella di Morra." In *Isabella di Morra e la Basilicata: Atti del Convegno di studi su Isabella di Morra*, edited by Mario Sansone, 55–73. Materia: Liantonio, 1981.

Tartaro, Achille. *Forme poetiche del Trecento*. Bari: Laterza, 1972.

Thierry, André. *Agrippa d'Aubigné: Auteur de l'Histoire Universelle*. Lille: Presses Universitaires de Lille, 1982.

Tiraboschi, Girolamo. "Sassi Panfilo Modenese." In *Biblioteca Modenese*, vol. 5. Modena: Società Tipografica, 1781; repr. in Bologna Forni Editore, 1978.

Tissoni Benvenuti, Antonia. *Il Quattrocento settentrionale*. Bari: Laterza, 1972.

———. "La tradizione della terza rima e l'Ariosto." In *Ludovico Ariosto: Lingua, stile e tradizione. Atti del Congresso organizzato dai comuni di Reggio Emilia e Ferrara, 12–16 ottobre 1974*, 303–14. Milano: Feltrinelli, 1976.

Toffanin, Giuseppe. *Storia Letteraria d'Italia. Il Cinquecento*. Milan: Francesco Vallardi, 1945.

Tomasi, Franco. "Alcuni aspetti delle antologie liriche del secondo Cinquecento." In *"I più vaghi e i più soavi fiori." Studi sulle antologie di lirica del Cinquecento*, edited by M. Bianco and E. Strada, 77–111. Alessandria: Edizioni dell'Orso, 2001.

Tortoreto, Alessandro. *Lirici cortigiani del Quattrocento*. Milano: Leonardo, 1942.

Toscano, Tobia. *Letterati Corti Accademie: La letteratura a Napoli nella prima metà del Cinquecento*. Naples: Loffredo, 2000.

———. *Diego Sandoval di Castro e Isabella di Morra Rime*. Rome: Salerno Editrice, 2007.

Trinkaus, Robert. *The Poet as Philosopher: Petrarch and the Formation of Renaissance Consciousness*. New Haven: Yale University Press, 1979.

Turba, Giuseppe. "Galeotto del Carretto, tra Casale e Mantova." *Rinascimento* 2, Vol. XI (1971): 95–169.

Ughetti, Dante. *François d'Amboise (1550–1619)*. Rome: Bulzoni, 1974.

Vaganay, Hugues. *Le Sonnet en Italie et en France au XVIᵉ siècle*. vol. I. New York: Burt Franklin, 1903.

———. "Le premier essai de traduction de *Roland Furieux* en vers français." *La Bibliofilia* X (1909): 281–93.

———. "Un modèle de Desportes non signalé encore: Pamphilo Sasso." *Revue d'Histoire littéraire de la France, Janvier-Mars*, 277–82. Paris: Colin, 1903.

Vecchi Galli, Paola. "Percorsi dell'elegia quattrocentesca in volgare." In *L'elegia nella tradizione poetica italiana*, edited by Andrea Comboni and Alessandra di Ricco, 37–79. Trento: Editrice Università degli Studi di Trento, 2003.

———. "La poesia cortigiana tra XV e XVI secolo." In *Rassegna di testi e di studi*, 95–141. Firenze: Leo S. Olschi Editore, 1982.

———. "Su una edizione poco nota di Serafino Aquilano." *Schifanoia* (1989): 87–90.

Verhulst, Sabine. "Fortuna, gioco e disperazione, in Antonio Beccari da Ferrara." *Revue belge de philologie et d'histoire* 59, no. 3 (1981): 585–96.

———. "Fonction sociale de la poésie du Quattrocento." In *Poétiques de la Renaissance. Le modèle italien, le monde franco-bourguignon et leur héritage en France au XVIe siècle*, edited by Perrine Galland-Hallyn and Fernand Hallyn, 354–56. Geneva: Droz, 2001.

Vianey, Joseph. *Le Pétrarquisme en France au XVIe siècle*. Montpellier: Coulet et Fils, 1909.

———. "Une Rencontre des muses de France et d'Italie demeurée inédite." In *Revue d'histoire littéraire de France* XIII (1906): 92–100.

———. "Marcello Philoxeno et Mellin de Sainct-Gelays." *Bulletin Italien* 4 (1904): 238–43.

———. "Un modèle de Desportes non signalé encore: Pamphilo Sasso." *Revue d'histoire littéraire de la France* 10, 1. Paris: Colin, 1903. 275–82.

———. "L'infuence italianne chez les précurseurs de la Pléiade." *Bulletin italien* III, no. 2 (1903): 85–117.

Volpi, Guglielmo. "La vita e le rime di Simone Serdini, detto il Saviozzo." *Giornale Storico della Letteratura Italiana* XV (1890): 1–78.

Wilkins, Ernest Hatch. *Studies in the Life and Works of Petrarch*. Cambridge: Medieval Academy of America, 1955.

Weber, Henri. *La Création poétique au XVIe Siècle en France. De Maurice Scève à Agrippa d'Aubigné*. Paris: Librairie A.-G. Nizet, 1994.

Yates, Frances A. *The French Academies of the Sixteenth Century*. London: Warburg Institute, 1947.

Zaccone, Aldo. "I luoghi morriani: sulle tracce d'Isabella." In *Isabella Morra e la poesia del Rinascimento europeo*, edited by Neria De Giovanni, 140–48. Alghero, Italy: Nemapress, 2001.

Zampieri, Adriana. "Il Notturno Napolitano." *La Bibliofilia* 78 (1976): 107–87.

Zilli, Luigia. "Mellin de Saint-Gelais et la Terza Rima" in *Passer les Monts: Français et Italie-L'Italie en France (1494–1525), X Colloque de la Société française d'études du Seizième Siècle*, edited by Jean Balsamo, 387–96. Paris: H. Champion, 1998.

Zumthor, Paul. "Perspectives Générales." In *La Notion de genre à la Renaissance*, edited by Guy Demerson. Geneva: Slatkine, 1988.

Index

Typeset in Garamond Premier Pro
Composed by Martine Maguire-Weltecke

Medieval Institute Publications
College of Arts and Sciences
Western Michigan University
1903 W. Michigan Avenue
Kalamazoo, MI 49008-5432
http://www.wmich.edu/medieval/mip

 WESTERN MICHIGAN UNIVERSITY